P9-DWS-774

CALGARY PUBLIC LIBRARY

AUG ⁻ 2012

An Illustrated History of

QUEBEC

Tradition & Modernity

Peter Gossage and J.I. Little

OXFORD
UNIVERSITY PRESS

OXFORD
UNIVERSITY PRESS

Oxford University Press is a department of the University of Oxford.
It furthers the University's objective of excellence in research, scholarship,
and education by publishing worldwide. Oxford is a registered trade mark of
Oxford University Press in the UK and in certain other countries.

Published in Canada by
Oxford University Press
8 Sampson Mews, Suite 204,
Don Mills, Ontario M3C 0H5 Canada

www.oupcanada.com

Copyright © Oxford University Press Canada 2012

The moral rights of the author have been asserted

Database right Oxford University Press (maker)

First Edition published in 2012

All rights reserved. No part of this publication may be reproduced, stored in
a retrieval system, or transmitted, in any form or by any means, without the
prior permission in writing of Oxford University Press, or as expressly permitted
by law, by licence, or under terms agreed with the appropriate reprographics
rights organization. Enquiries concerning reproduction outside the scope of the
above should be sent to the Permissions Department at the address above
or through the following url: www.oupcanada.com/permission/permission_request.php

Every effort has been made to determine and contact copyright holders.
In the case of any omissions, the publisher will be pleased to make
suitable acknowledgement in future editions.

Library and Archives Canada Cataloguing in Publication

Gossage, Peter, 1956–
An illustrated history of Quebec : tradition and modernity / Peter Gossage, John I. Little.

.

(Illustrated history of Canada)
Includes bibliographical references and index.
ISBN 978-0-19-900235-1

1. Québec (Province)--History. I. Little, John I. II. Title. III. Series:
Illustrated history of Canada

FC2911.G67 2012   971.4   C2011-908209-8

Cover image: Market Day, Jacques Cartier Square, Montreal, QC, 1913.
William Notman & Son. McCord Museum V5026

Printed and bound in the United States of America

1 2 3 4 — 15 14 13 12

CONTENTS

LIST OF ILLUSTRATIONS

COLOUR PLATES
Between pages 168–69

ACKNOWLEDGEMENTS

As authors of a general history of Quebec, our main intellectual debts are to the scholars who researched and wrote the hundreds of more specialized studies on which our narrative and our analysis rest. Some of these historians are friends, mentors, colleagues, and even former students, while some are perfect strangers to us, and still others are long dead. We thank them all sincerely for providing such a solid foundation of research into Quebec's past on which to build.

We spent many hours sifting through countless drawings, paintings, photographs, and other images in our effort to select just the right illustrations for this book. We have drawn in particular on the collections of Library and Archives Canada, the Bibliothèque et archives nationales du Québec, and the McCord Museum in Montreal. But all the people and institutions involved in the production and preservation of this rich visual record deserve our gratitude.

Oxford University Press has been a model publisher, and we thank them and their editorial staff for all the support they have provided since we first took on this project. Jennie Rubio merits a special mention for her enthusiasm, her efficiency, and her infectious belief in this manuscript in the months since it first landed on her desk. Katie Scott and Theresa Lemieux contributed many hours of dedicated, behind-the-scenes effort, and Beth McAuley did a superb job of copy editing, working with a tight deadline over the 2011–12 winter holidays. Although she is no longer an editor at OUP, we would also like to thank Laura Macleod who in a very real sense made this book happen when she approached us several years ago about writing the missing Quebec volume in The Illustrated History of Canada series. We are grateful to have been given the opportunity and hopeful that the result lives up to her expectations.

We had constructive comments on the penultimate draft of this book from two anonymous reviewers recruited by OUP. Their suggestions were astute and timely, as were those of Ronald Rudin, who generously read a sizeable chunk of the manuscript as it neared completion. We thank them all for their wisdom and their warnings, even as we assume full responsibility (as is the scholarly custom, and rightly so) for the end result and for any remaining errors of fact or interpretation.

This book would have featured a substantially poorer visual record of Quebec's past were it not for the financial contributions of Simon Fraser University and Concordia University. Both institutions contributed funds that covered the cost of reproducing key illustrations that otherwise would have wound up on the cutting-room floor. Concordia also paid the salaries of research assistants Sarah Doran, Abbey Mahon, Lisa Moore, and Jade Winsor, all of whom provided invaluable help as this project neared completion. They have our sincere thanks.

In closing, we would each like to add a few individual words of appreciation.

From Peter Gossage: I am grateful to several intellectual and academic communities that have welcomed and sustained me over the course of this project. I have been blessed with wonderful, supportive colleagues in history departments at both the Université de Sherbrooke and Concordia University. I thank them all collectively, as I would individually if space permitted. I also thank the members of the Canadian Studies Program at the University of California, Berkeley, especially Rita Ross and the late Tom Barnes, who provided a warm, collegial environment in which to draft several chapters during a particularly eventful sabbatical year. My colleagues in the Great Unsolved Mysteries in Canadian History project, especially John Lutz, Ruth Sandwell, and Merna Forster, are a constant source of intellectual companionship and support, which I warmly acknowledge. My greatest personal debts, of course, are to my family. I extend my deepest thanks to Annmarie Adams for her love, her grace, her good counsel, and for the example she sets every day as a person and as a scholar. And I thank our children, Charlie and Katie, who bring a special joy and a real sense of adventure and discovery into our lives. I dedicate my contributions to this book to them, with deep affection and in the hope that they may read it one day, both in order to figure out what Dad was up to all that time and, as young Quebecers, to learn something interesting and possibly useful about the place we call home.

From Jack Little: I began work on my section of this book after three very intense years as chair of a department that was undergoing fundamental renewal, and I'm very grateful to my former and current colleagues in the SFU History Department for the collegial environment that I've been privileged to work in throughout the past thirty-six years. I would also thank my Quebec history class for serving as a test audience when this book was still in draft form. My parental family ties to Quebec have now sadly been cut with the recent passing of the last three members of a generation with deep roots in one of the most beautiful areas of that province, but Andrea remains my rock and my strongest link to the vibrant west coast community where we live. My dedication is to our son and daughter, Mark and Brette, whose communities transcend many borders as they take wing in the exciting world of arts and entertainment.

P.G. and J.L.
Knowlton, QC, and Bowen Island, BC
March 2012

INTRODUCTION:
TRADITION AND MODERNITY

Polarities, oppositions, dualities, and dissonances: the long narrative of Quebec history is filled with many of these, beginning with the contact between First Nations and European newcomers. Nationalist accounts have long tended to focus on the province's persistent ethnic, cultural, and political conflicts: French vs. English, Catholic vs. Protestant, Quebec vs. Canada, and sometimes "founding peoples" vs. more recent immigrants. A recent generation of social historians—derided in some circles for taking the focus away from political and national debates[1]—remind us that oppositions between rich and poor, town and country, young and old, and especially between men and women have also shaped historical experience in Quebec. At their best, these discussions serve to deepen and enrich, rather than distract or detract from, the political narrative of identity formation within the French-speaking majority, a community that has identified itself at various times as *Canadien, Canadien-français,* and *Québécois.*[2]

For many, the basic polarities that have shaped Quebec's historical experience give rise to a question of identity, which can be expressed as follows: Should Quebecers fully embrace their distinctiveness as a people with a unique history, a deep sense of collective self, and the inherent right—perhaps even the duty—to seek greater autonomy for themselves and their descendants? Or are they better served by a narrative of participation, one that encourages them to situate their unquestioned distinctiveness within the eminently Canadian narrative of diversity, pluralism, cooperation, and consensus building across linguistic, ethnic, religious, and territorial divides?

We will certainly be addressing those central tensions in this new, concise account of Quebec's historical experience. But we have chosen to build that account around another fundamental polarity: the tension between *tradition* and *modernity.* We are interested, in other words, in the ongoing dialogue and the not infrequent confrontations between a collective Quebec identity grounded in the past and its traditions—some of them, of course, religious—and another, more forward-looking identity, one that is attentive to science and technology, to modern ideas from nineteenth-century liberalism to late twentieth-century globalization, and to the promise of what might be.

There are further polarities, of course, with which we must reckon in order to attend not only to the events of the past but also to the various and often contradictory ways in which historians have framed them. As the historian Ronald Rudin has pointed out, most Quebec historians who came of age during the 1970s were preoccupied with revising the persistent image of their province as an economic and cultural backwater. Their emphasis was on the entrepreneurialism and liberalism of the French-Canadian middle class, the market sensibility and independent-mindedness of the habitants, and finally, what came to be known as the essential *Américanité* (not to be confused with Americanization) of Quebec.[3] The pessimistic nationalism of the postwar era, with its focus on the British Conquest as a disaster for the development of a dynamic French-Canadian entrepreneurial class, was replaced by a more optimistic nationalism befitting the era of the Quiet Revolution. From this perspective, as the distinguished historical sociologist Gérard Bouchard argues, the crucial event in preventing Quebecers from fulfilling their destiny as an independent North American nation was not the Conquest but the defeat of the Lower-Canadian Rebellion of 1837.[4]

It was certainly after this defeat and the forced union with Upper Canada that French-Canadian nationalism became more defensive and the Catholic Church strengthened its hold in the province. As a result, we suggest, the tension between tradition and modernity that has characterized all industrializing countries in the nineteenth and twentieth centuries was particularly pronounced for French Canadians. Modernity can be a slippery and ambiguous term, but it is one which we—and many others—continue to find useful and compelling. Quebec historian Damien-Claude Bélanger has defined it as the erosion of traditional values and practices, the development of a strong faith in science and technology as leading to the illimitable progress of society, and the rise of mass culture and consumption.[5]

Modernity clearly represented a challenge to any cultural identity that was heavily based on religion; and certainly French Canadians in the nineteenth and early twentieth centuries were taught that *la langue* was guardian of *la foi*, rather than the other way around. In short, to embrace change was to risk assimilation, while to resist it was to invite economic and cultural stagnation.

Rather than viewing Quebec history as a relatively straightforward trajectory from tradition to modernity, or indulging in the value judgments that these two polarities may tend to imply, this book will examine how a distinct North American society survived and developed as a result of the continual interplay between these conflicting forces. Stated another way, what historian Jocelyn Létourneau refers to as *Québécité* has been formed "au carrefour des tensions incompressibles entre l'appel de la refondation et le souci de la tradition, entre le désir de la collaboration et la volonté d'autonomisation, entre l'attrait de l'altérité et le ressourcement dans l'identité."[6] There has emerged, in other words, a distinctive sense of the collective self in Quebec—a Quebec-ness—which is located at the crossroads of three ongoing and immutable tensions: between the call to renewal or reform on the one hand and an abiding respect for tradition on the other; between the will to collaborate on the one hand and the desire to assert more autonomy on the other; and between the appeal of alterity, or otherness, on the one hand and the nurturing potential of identity on the other.

Within this overall framework, we have adopted the generally chronological approach best suited to a relatively short book covering more than four centuries of history. Each of our chapters, however, is structured around a central theme, thereby providing some scope for analysis. Our aim is to be wide-ranging—with balanced attention to political, economic, social, and cultural history—but our focus is less on the great men and women of Quebec history than on historical forces, social classes, and ethnic groups. The illustrations—consisting largely of paintings, drawings, photographs, maps, and some political cartoons for the more recent periods—are much more than "window dressing," for they provide historical information that is not otherwise accessible, and they actively produce meaning through a variety of visual conventions, as will be discussed in our extensive interpretive captions.[7]

French-Canadian contributions to other parts of Canada have been examined in previous volumes of The Illustrated History of Canada series from Oxford University Press. So this history of Quebec is set within the current geographical and political limits of the province. Quebec, after all, is a relatively recent invention; its political identity was established in 1867 and its boundaries were not finally settled until 1927. Founded by French explorers in the seventeenth century, New France extended far beyond Quebec's current borders to embrace what are now the Maritime provinces, and the French sphere of influence then extended into the Ohio Valley and south to Louisiana. Most French settlers lived in the St. Lawrence Valley, in the colony then known as Canada. But their economy was heavily reliant on the fur trade of the continental interior, and the Catholic missions in Huronia and points beyond are a very important part of French regime history. During that era, the name "Quebec" referred only to the city on the St. Lawrence founded by Champlain in 1608. After the British Conquest, it was applied to the entire colony for a brief time; it was then changed to Lower Canada when the western boundary was fixed at the Ottawa River in 1791. The Act of Union dissolved that boundary in 1841, when Lower Canada formally became known as Canada East, finally becoming the Province of Quebec at the time of Confederation in 1867.

Conceived as a general introduction to the history of Quebec, this book focuses primarily on the French settlers in the St. Lawrence Valley and their descendants. It is the province's French heritage and its French-speaking majority, after all, that make it so distinctive in the North American context. But the polarities between majority and minorities, centre and periphery are important as well. So while we pay less attention than is merited to the indigenous inhabitants of the North in recent years, the earlier chapters in particular do examine the colonial interactions with First Nations people at a time when they played a particularly crucial economic and military role. Similarly, the need to make generalizations about Quebec as a whole can obscure the regionalized nature of a province that is widely varied in its topography and settlement history. To take an example we know well, the region known informally as the Eastern Townships, or Cantons de l'Est, was largely an English-speaking one until well into the nineteenth century, with the result that most general statements about Quebec society during that era simply do not apply to the substantial population that lived in the freehold territory north of the 45th parallel.[8] Still, as Quebec-born historians with deep family roots in the province, we pay more attention than others might to its substantial English-speaking communities, rural as well as urban.[9] There is also a considerable focus on Montreal, whose continental (now global) economic links and heterogeneous cultural makeup have long distinguished it from the rest of the province.[10] Indeed, the growing diversity of Quebec's population, especially in the postwar period, is an important theme running through the final chapters of the book, as we examine debates over the education of "allophone" immigrants (those whose first language was neither French nor English) and so-called reasonable accommodation measures for members of religious minorities.

History and heritage in Quebec can be hotly contested terrain, especially in light of the recent crisis over collective identities and destinies, which is discussed in Chapters 12 and 13. As Létourneau reminds us, this book was written during a "transitional, transitory" period, particularly where Quebec's universe of symbolic representations is concerned, "that is, a period of tension and ambiguity between its ancient founding myths, which have not disappeared and continue to structure its memory and collective identity, and the new myths, which have not fully emerged and have yet to find their legitimate place in the public space."[11] We will leave to others the considerable task of mapping the sometimes fractious and always impassioned twenty-first-century interplay among myth, memory, and identity in the province. We hope instead, and more modestly, to offer a fresh, serious, well-informed, and stimulating account of how the current transitional moment was fashioned, over time, from the fabric of Quebec's unique and uniquely interesting experience.

ONE

THE FUR TRADE COLONY

Recent archaeological excavations have unearthed evidence of Paleo-Indian encampments south of Lake Megantic near the Maine border as early as 12,000 years ago. The hypothesis is that nomadic hunters pursued caribou that far north during the warmer summer months.[1] But Quebec at that time truly was *l'hiver*, to echo Gilles Vigneault's famous phrase, for the continental ice sheet was only beginning to retreat far enough for the Champlain Sea to penetrate the lowlands between the Laurentian Mountains and the Appalachians. In fact, the ice did not recede sufficiently for the island of Montreal to appear until approximately 7,500 years ago. During the Archaic period of approximately 8000–1000 BCE, descendants of the Paleo-Indians occupied the Canadian Shield as well as the north shore of the St. Lawrence and the area known today as Labrador. Farther south, the meat diet of the Laurentian culture was supplemented by nuts and berries, and goods were traded from as far away as the Gulf of Mexico.

The Silvicultural era, beginning around 1000 BCE, brought two major innovations to southern Quebec—pottery and the cultivation of corn, beans, and squash by the Iroquois of the St. Lawrence Valley. Soil and climate conditions prevented the development of horticulture on the Canadian Shield and the Appalachians, to the north and south of the St. Lawrence, with the result that winter scarcity severely limited the growth of the second language group, the Algonquians. Further north several cultures successively swept eastward from Alaska, beginning with the Paleo-Eskimos who arrived in northern Quebec around 2000 BCE. By 1000 CE the people of the Thule culture had developed boats and sophisticated harpoon tackle, which enabled them to amass large quantities of food. They lived in winter villages comprised of partly underground houses of stone and sod with large whale bones for roof supports. Hunters of land mammals as well as cetaceans, the Thulians expanded as far south as the Gulf of St. Lawrence before being driven back to Labrador by the Montagnais and Mi'kmaqs; they died out around 1600 when the climate cooled, leaving only approximately 3,000 Inuits as inhabitants of what is today northern Quebec.[2]

Of the semi-nomadic Algonquian-speaking peoples at this time of initial European contact, there were some 3,000 Mi'kmaqs on the Gaspé Peninsula; 4,000 Montagnais on both sides of the St. Lawrence as far west as Quebec City; 1,000 Attikamegues in the St. Maurice basin (they would cease to become a distinct group by 1670); 10,000 Cree and 2,000 Naskapi farther north; and 1,500 Algonquins in the Ottawa watershed. The Mohicans expanded their territory from the upper Hudson River into the Yamaska and St. Francis Valleys south of the St. Lawrence, but they were forced to retreat by the Iroquois around 1660. In the following years, several thousand Abenaki refugees from New England came to occupy villages along the south shore near the mouths of the Chaudière, Becancour, and St. Francis Rivers.[3]

As hunting peoples, the Algonquians erected small portable lodges, or wigwams, inhabited by up to a dozen people, but most activities aside from sleeping took place outside except on the coldest days. During the winter they split into small bands and travelled into their respective hunting territories to pursue moose, caribou, deer, and bear. If the hunt was not successful, they faced starvation in the spring prior to the melting of the ice when they would become dependent on roots, maple sugar, and small game such as rabbits and porcupines. By the spring, the bands from the same river network would form larger groups, or tribes, along the lakes and rivers, or along the Atlantic coast, where they fished, gathered fruit and nuts, and hunted migratory birds and other small game.

The Algonquians also traded with neighbouring tribes and engaged in social activities, but the tribe was more a cultural unit than a political one. Members spoke the same dialect and followed the same customs, but the tribal unit had little practical meaning except during periods of crisis. The most important political unit was the village. The village leader was often the head of the senior lineage of the chiefly clan, but he might instead be chosen by the village council of elders. Chiefs and elders deliberated on what course a village should pursue, but, since no one was

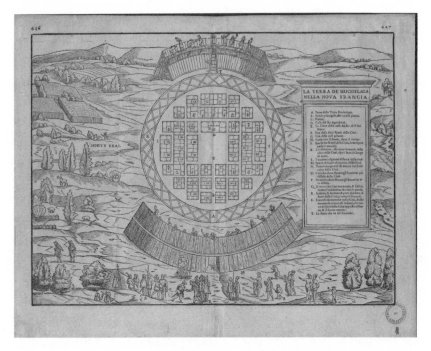

La terra de Hochelaga nella Nova Francia, 1565. The first printed map of settlement in North America, this woodblock print of the Laurentian Iroquoian village of Hochelaga, which may have been atop Mount Royal, was published by the Venetian geographer, Giovanni Battista Ramusio. It presents two perspectives, the central one being a vertical plan of an orderly Renaissance-style village with central piazza, while the perimeter is a bird's-eye view of the surrounding pastoral landscape. The bottom of the map shows Cartier being greeted with a European-style handshake. *Library and Archives Canada*

obliged to obey them, the French created the position of alliance chief in order to establish more coercive leaders as channels of their power. These chiefs represented their society to outsiders, but they did not claim the ability to command without the consent of their councils.[4]

Finally, there were 5,000 to 10,000 sedentary Iroquoian-speaking peoples in the St. Lawrence Valley. Centred on the villages of Stadacona, which became the site of Quebec, and Hochelaga, which became known as Montreal, they had developed a more complex social system than the Algonquians. Like their relatives, the Hurons of Georgian Bay and the Five Nations Iroquois south of the Great Lakes, the St. Lawrence Iroquois lived in groups of four or five related families within longhouses that were approximately thirty metres in length by nine metres in width, with walls covered by birch bark. These longhouses were erected within palisaded villages of approximately 1,500 people who belonged to a clan that claimed a common maternal ancestor. Several clans formed a nation within which social bonds were strengthened by the fact that no one could marry within his or her own clan. Several nations, in turn, formed a league or confederacy, although each nation could decide whether or not to join its partners in war. Unlike Algonquian descent, that of the Iroquoians passed through the female line, and when a man married he moved to his wife's longhouse. In addition, clan matrons chose the chiefs (who never made decisions without consulting the community) and played a central role in torture rituals.

Iroquoian agriculture did not involve ploughs, much less fertilizers or crop rotation. For this reason, the Iroquois moved their villages a few kilometres every ten to fifteen years, depending on when the soil or firewood supply was exhausted. While it was the men who cleared new fields and prepared new village sites, it was the women who made the decision to move because they grew the crops in addition to collecting the fuel and berries; preparing the meals; and making clothes, pottery, and baskets. Women also raised the children because the men were absent much of the year on fishing, hunting, or trading expeditions, as well as engaging in warfare. Warfare played an important cultural role among the Iroquois by easing the mourning process through the capture of warriors who were either integrated physically by being tortured to death and cannibalized or socially by being adopted to replace a recently killed warrior. Warfare and ritualistic torture also served as an outlet for tensions that arose within these densely settled societies as well as a way to reinforce male prestige after horticulture became the most important source of food and trade commodities.[5]

Because North American Natives did not forge metal, they found European knives and copper pots to be particularly useful, but there had been extensive continental trade networks long before the arrival of the Europeans. The Iroquoians produced surpluses of corn and tobacco, while the Algonquians traded smoked meat and animal pelts and the nations to the southeast provided the strings of wampum made from polished sea shells that served as currency as well as symbols of war and peace. The European market for beaver furs, which had not been an important First Nations exchange commodity prior to contact, intensified trade as well as transforming it to some extent. Northern Natives who had depended on Huron corn and tobacco now traded for French flour and biscuits, as well as tobacco from the West Indies and the St. Lawrence Valley, and the Hurons could now replace northern furs with European woollens. Even the precious strings of wampum came to be manufactured from French glass, with the result that they began to be replaced by beaver pelts as currency.[6] Traditional exchange networks were thereby disrupted by the arrival of the French, particularly after trading posts were built in the interior, known as the *pays d'en haut* (upcountry). Warfare also became more frequent, widespread, and lethal because competition for European commodities came to outweigh cultural motivations among the Iroquois. As the Iroquois forced the Algonquian nations farther north, they, in turn, battled with the Inuit who were also pressed farther east by the Mi'kmaq after they had exhausted the beaver in their own territory.[7]

Some historians also argue that Native women lost status after European contact because they played a secondary role in the fur trade,[8] but their role in the processing of furs was an essential one. In addition, even though Natives now had access to French sea biscuits, peas, prunes, and other low-bulk foods, horticulture may have become a more important source of food as the men were absent for longer periods of time, focusing their efforts on gathering furs rather than on hunting for game. The impact of the fur trade on indigenous societies was mitigated to a considerable extent by the practical limit to how many goods they could accumulate. From the Natives' perspective, material objects did not belong to a single person, although they could be vested with a person for a time. The object of trade was to satisfy needs, and the greater the need, the greater the claim on the supplier. But the fur trade did contribute to social inequality by conferring greater symbolic prestige on individuals and lineages that were more successful in acquiring beavers, and therefore more able to be generous with their gift-giving.[9]

European societies, with their highly stratified class system, operated on quite a different basis, particularly with the rise of capitalism in the fifteenth century. But it was Native customs that prevailed at the annual fur fairs in Montreal, Trois-Rivières, and Quebec where gift exchanges, feasts, games, speeches, and the smoking of peace pipes featured prominently. The Amerindians may have been impressed by European technology, but they valued their individual freedom too much to become peasant farmers or wage labourers or to embrace fully the Christian religion with its requirement of self-abnegation in this world in return for a reward in the next. Finally, they refused to recognize French sovereignty over their traditional territories, as we shall see.

European expansion to the New World was sparked by the appetite that had developed by the late fifteenth century for Eastern spices, silk, precious stones, and other luxury products. The influx of these commodities had led to a depletion of the gold reserves, exacerbated by hoarding, which in turn led to the drive to discover new deposits abroad along with a strong desire to find a route to Asia that would circumvent the Islamic enemy in the eastern Mediterranean. The growth of important new financial centres—such as the great Italian cities of Venice and Florence, or the French cities of Rouen, Lyon, and Bordeaux—had made it possible to fund voyages that had become less risky since the invention of instruments such as the pivoted rudder, the compass, the astrolabe (which measured latitude), and the ship's log (which measured distances). Indeed, explorers' ships were generally small even by the standards of the day, and the cargo was inexpensive. The large investments by the great merchants were made in the trading voyages that followed successful exploration.[10]

The Portuguese were the first to round Africa's Cape of Good Hope and to sail into the Indian Ocean, but this route was dangerous as well as being twice the distance of the overland route to Asia. Consequently, in 1492, Spain decided to send Christopher Columbus to determine if there was a shorter route across the Atlantic. When Columbus reached the Caribbean islands, he assumed at first that he had landed near the coast of Asia, naming the inhabitants "Indians." Within a year, however, the conflict between Spain and Portugal over the territories they had recently "discovered" led Pope Alexander VI to draw a line through the mid-Atlantic from the North Pole to the South Pole dividing all the territory not under the jurisdiction of Christian princes. With the Treaty of Tordesillas in 1494, the two countries agreed to move the line farther west, so that Newfoundland and Brazil, which lay east of the line, fell into Portugal's sphere, and any lands west of the line would belong to Spain.

The riches of South America soon made Spain the wealthiest country in Europe, but French investors had also established a foothold in that continent by 1504, extracting dyewoods from Brazilian forests for the famous cloth makers of Rouen and other Norman craftsmen.[11] The king of France was finally motivated to ignore the threat of excommunication by sending his own expeditions westward. In 1524 he commissioned the Italian, Giovanni da Verrazzano, to discover a shorter route to Asia than the one taken around the tip of South America by the Portuguese-sponsored Ferdinand Magellan a year earlier. Verrazzano proved that the American continent extended from Florida to Cape Breton Island, a territory that France claimed for itself even though the English and Portuguese had already reached Newfoundland and Cape Breton Island earlier in the century.

According to the principle of universal harmony, if God had created a passage between the two oceans in the south, He must also have done so in the north.[12] The explorer commissioned to find this passage in 1534 was Jacques Cartier, an experienced mariner who had transported fish from Newfoundland and dyewoods from Brazil. Sailing from his wealthy home port of Saint-Malo in Brittany, Cartier discovered that Cape Breton and Newfoundland were separated by a strait. After declaring that Labrador was the land that God gave Cain, Cartier planted a cross at Gaspé Bay, claiming the territory for France. When Donnacona, the chief of the Iroquois who were fishing there, objected to the presence of this cross, Cartier made him captive and eventually gained his permission to take his two sons to meet the king. Cartier returned with Taignoagny and Domagaya the following year to search for the rich "kingdom of the Saguenay" that they had described. This kingdom remained a myth, but the two Natives did serve as Cartier's guides as he sailed up the St. Lawrence River to their village of Stadacona, near today's Quebec City. Despite Donnacona's attempt to stop him, Cartier proceeded farther upriver to the larger village of Hochelaga, located on what became known as the island of Montreal and where he reported seeing fifty longhouses surrounded by vast corn fields.[13] After twenty-five of Cartier's men had died of scurvy at Stadacona the following winter, Donnacona saved the rest of the crew by giving them a brew generally presumed to have been made from the bark and leaves of white cedar.

Cartier repaid the chief's kindness the following spring by kidnapping him, his two sons, and three of his principal supporters, taking them back to France where they were paraded through the streets of several cities. They had all died by the time Cartier returned in 1541 with the mission of establishing a colony and converting the Natives to Christianity. The latter goal was, no doubt, announced for political purposes: the first two expeditions had been undertaken in secret in order not to attract the wrath of the pope, and Cartier's superior in the third expedition was a Protestant, Jean-François de la Rocque de Roberval. To bolster their position, the French argued that permanent European settlement was necessary for suzerainty to be established over newly claimed lands that were legally vacant because their Native inhabitants led migratory lives and had not organized themselves into nation-states.[14] In the face of Stadaconan hostility, Cartier sailed back to France the following spring with what he thought was a shipload of gold and diamonds, though they proved to be iron pyrites and quartz. Roberval arrived at Cap Rouge near the future port of Quebec shortly afterward, but his 200 settlers suffered through a terrible winter during which fifty died of scurvy (Cartier had neglected to inform them of the remedy), and he, too, pulled up stakes the following spring. Torn by religious wars from 1562 to 1598, France left the St. Lawrence Valley to the fishers and whalers until after the turn of the century.

Although much less glamorous than Spanish gold or silver, the most profitable commodity in the New World was cod because, with more than 150 fast days in the annual church calendar, fish was a regular feature of the European diet. The Grand Banks off Newfoundland offered a seemingly inexhaustible supply of cod, and French ships outnumbered those from England by three to one during the sixteenth century, returning with millions of pounds each year.[15] Much of this catch was simply salted down in the holds of small ships in what was known as the green fishery. But large crews from more northerly ports without easy access to sea salt dried their filleted fish in the sun before returning to Europe. In the Gulf of St. Lawrence they met Natives wishing to trade furs, initially engaging in a *commerce de pacotille* (trade in trinkets), the expression referring to the duty-free transport of merchandise by ships' officers and occasionally crew members in lieu of salary or as a means of supplementing their income.[16] Furs had the advantage of being a luxury item requiring no wage labour to produce, few ships to transport, and goods of low cost to exchange with the Natives. The most sought-after pelts were from the beaver because the tiny barbs in the under-fur caused felt to mat securely, producing a higher quality hat than one made from wool felt. After disappearing in the fifteenth century because of the exhaustion of European beaver stocks, wide-brimmed felt hats produced by Parisian hatters became very popular in Europe, with prices more than tripling between 1620 and the 1650s.[17]

For the same reason, the most sought after beaver pelts were the *castor gras* (or greasy beaver) that had been worn by the Natives until the guard hairs had fallen off and the skin had become soft and pliable. Because such furs could be obtained most easily up the St. Lawrence River, most of the French trade took place at Tadoussac, located on the St. Lawrence at the mouth of Saguenay River, which was visited by up to twenty vessels a year as early as the 1580s. A permanent French presence was necessary to ensure a steady supply of furs, but the expenses involved required that the merchants be granted a trade monopoly. The king was willing to oblige in return for the promotion of exploration and colonization, but all attempts to establish a permanent settlement during the 1590s ended in failure.[18]

The first continuous endeavour to establish a French colony in North America resulted from the grant of a ten-year trading monopoly from the 40th to the 46th parallel to the Protestant nobleman Pierre Dugua de Mons. In return, he was to pursue the exploration of a navigable water route to the western ocean. Searching for a milder climate than that of the St. Lawrence Valley, de Mons established a fort at the mouth of the St. Croix River in 1604, but moved to nearby Port Royal in the Annapolis Basin the following year, after half his men had died of scurvy. Here, the cartographer Samuel de Champlain and the lawyer Marc Lescarbot established the Order of Good Cheer, reasoning that good spirits, as well as fresh game and fish, were the best antidotes to disease. It was, however, the vegetables preserved from the colonists' gardens and the cranberries harvested during the exceptionally mild winter that actually caused the sharp decline in the death rate.[19]

In his explorations south to Cape Cod, Champlain failed to discover a major artery into the interior, though the aim was also to strengthen

French claims to the coast and find a site for the colony that would have direct access to the Atlantic.[20] The Port Royal colonists returned to France when de Mons's monopoly was interrupted in 1607, but the following year he decided to move his base to the St. Lawrence Valley. From this position, Champlain—who was placed in charge of the colony—could pursue inland exploration and the fur trade monopoly could more easily be protected against interlopers. A major diplomatic gathering with the Montagnais, Algonquins, and Malecites (of the Saint John Valley) in 1603 had granted the French permission to settle there in return for military assistance.[21] The best site for this purpose was where the St. Lawrence narrowed and where once had been the village of Stadacona, for the Laurentian Iroquois had now disappeared, presumably because of a combination of disease and warfare sparked by competition in the fur trade. This was where the settlement known as Quebec, the Algonquin word for narrows or strait, was established in 1608.

While contagious European diseases devastated Native populations in much of the Americas shortly after the early explorers arrived, recent research indicates that those in the northeastern part of North America did not experience demographic crises until some time after the first sustained contact. And, perhaps due to geographical and climactic factors, the devastation was not nearly as great for the Iroquoians and Algonquians as for the Aztecs and Incas.[22] As a result, historian Allan Greer notes, the French arrived, "not as conquering invaders, but as a new tribe negotiating a place for itself in the diplomatic webs of Native North America."[23] The Montagnais and their allies had agreed to the French settlement because it would offer year-round trade as well as protection against attacks by the Mohawks, the most easterly of the Iroquois Five Nations who lived to the south of Lake Ontario. While the concept of land ownership was foreign to them, each of the First Nations jealously guarded its river network, either preventing others from crossing its territory or exacting tribute. After refusing to allow other nations to trade directly with the French at Tadoussac, the Montagnais had been forced into a protective alliance with the Algonquins of the Ottawa Valley. Champlain had little choice but to join this alliance if he wished to convince the Montagnais to shun the free traders at Tadoussac as well as guide him up the Saguenay or St. Maurice Rivers to the northern

False portrait of Samuel de Champlain, Louis-César-Joseph Ducornet, 1854. The image commonly assumed to be Champlain is based on that of a corrupt superintendent of finance under Louis XIII and Louis XIV. Attributed to the early nineteenth-century French painter Ducornet, who was born without arms, the lithographed portrait of Champlain was registered with the legislature in Quebec City in 1854. While the obvious forgery was discovered in the early twentieth century, and has been denounced many times since, it continues to be reproduced as the image of Champlain. *Library and Archives Canada*

salt sea of which they had informed him.[24] Furthermore, his garrison at Quebec was vulnerable to attack by the Natives, as well as dependent on them for its supply of fresh meat, and the Mohawks were preventing other nations from bringing their high quality northern furs down the St. Lawrence. Consequently, Champlain used firearms to help his trading partners defeat Mohawk war parties at Lake Champlain in 1609 and at the mouth of the Richelieu in 1610, thus initiating a bitter rivalry that would persist until the end of the century.

In the short term, however, the Mohawks shifted their attention to the Mohicans of the upper Hudson River in order to acquire goods traded from the Dutch colony established at Albany in 1614. Because the French were now able to ascend the St. Lawrence each summer as far as Lachine to trade with the Algonquins in their own territory, the Montagnais role in the fur trade was diminished at a time when they had become dependent on European trade goods. Relations with the French deteriorated to the point that they would assist the English to seize Quebec in 1629.

In the meantime, the Iroquois of the Five Nations confederacy declared war on the Hurons of Georgian Bay because they had begun to trade with the Algonquins. The Hurons wished to deal directly with the French, but the Algonquins prevented Champlain from travelling up the Ottawa River until 1615. In that year, the Hurons invited the French

The oldest known navigation instrument, the astrolabe, was used to measure latitude by pointing the needle toward the sun or northern star and reading the angle of inclination on the grid ring. The instrument shown here, part of which dates to 1603, is the smallest of thirty-five astrolabes surviving from the early part of the seventeenth century, and the only one from France. It was discovered in 1867 with some other objects under a felled tree at Green Lake near Allumette Island. These objects, including two silver goblets that were sold to a peddler and melted down, suggest the contents of a lost or hidden cache. It came to be assumed, however, that Champlain had dropped the astrolabe as he ascended the Ottawa River in 1613, and it has become an emblematic object. Facsimiles were molded and offered to several museums as part of the centennial celebrations in 1967, and the original was acquired from the New York Historical Society for the new Canadian Museum of Civilization in 1989. *Canadian Museum of Civilization*

and the Algonquins to join a raid on the Oneidas, the Iroquois nation located west of the Mohawks. As a result, the Hurons only had to pay a toll thereafter when descending the Ottawa River, and they became the most important middlemen in the fur trade between the French and the nations to the northwest. Although they did relatively little trapping themselves, by the 1620s the Hurons were supplying from one-half to two-thirds of the furs traded to the French.[25] The Hurons traded mostly for metal arrowheads and cutting tools, leading to a flowering of their crafts as well as more elaborate ritualism and redistribution practices. The French, who initially depended more on the Hurons than vice versa, sent men to live with them in order to ensure that they did not form a trading alliance with the Dutch.

Meanwhile, the French state had become more centralized after the divisive wars of religion, and Louis XIII's leading minister, Cardinal Richelieu, was growing concerned that French settlement in North America was being outstripped by that of Spain, England, and Holland. The French trading monopolists, however, did not wish to cut into their profits by undertaking the expense of a large-scale agricultural settlement. They also feared that colonists would compete for furs. By 1627, when the English colony of Virginia alone had a population of approximately 2,000, and New Netherlands on the Hudson River had more than 200, there were only 72 settlers in Quebec, nearly all of whom were men. Given that there was still no plough to till the soil, Champlain feared that the small outpost would be struck by the famines periodically experienced by the Natives. The fur trade required little more than a warehouse, but his dream remained to have Quebec serve as a way station to the Orient, for he had promised the French king that customs revenue from ships sailing to and from China via the St. Lawrence "would surpass in value at least ten times all those levied in France, inasmuch as all the merchants in Christendom would pass through the passage."[26]

With the support of the Church, Richelieu in 1627 cancelled the existing monopoly, owned by a Huguenot family, and granted all French claims in North America as a seigneurie to the Company of One Hundred Associates, also known as the Company of New France. In return for the

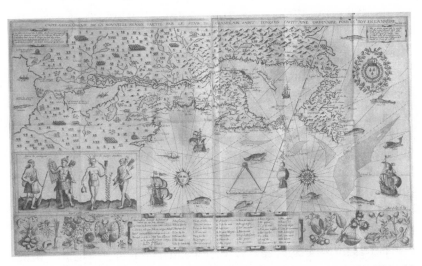

Carte géographique de la Nouvelle Franse, Samuel de Champlain, 1612. Produced by Champlain, this is the first "modern" map of the east coast of America, providing estimates of latitude, distance, and compass direction. It is also the first map to show accurately that the St. Lawrence River is connected to the Great Lakes. In addition to serving as an aid to navigation, it is a qualitative map, displaying a wide variety of fish, animals, nuts, berries, and other natural resources in an obvious attempt to attract funds and support for future expeditions and economic exploitation. Since Champlain could not draw the human figure well, he hired David Pelletier to depict two pairs of Natives. Not surprisingly, they resemble undressed Europeans, but the Montagnais are shown as a hunting people and the Almouchicois (the man is sporting an incongruous goatee) as sedentary. *Library and Archives Canada*

monopoly in perpetuity over all trade except fishing, which was limited to fifteen years, the company was required to establish 4,000 settlers within fifteen years. It was also to support them as labourers for at least three years before granting them land with sufficient improvements to ensure subsistence, and to supply each settlement with three priests. Protestants were to be excluded in order to avoid the religious divisions that continued to plague France.

The Company of One Hundred Associates had impressive financial backing, with a capital base of approximately 300,000 livres, for any noble or churchman could become a member without losing formal social status, but it immediately suffered major setbacks because of the war between France and England. The four ships with 400 people that were sent in 1628 at a cost of 250,000 livres fell into the hands of the English privateer David Kirke, and the following year the Kirke brothers laid siege to Quebec. Out of supplies and cut off from France, Champlain was forced to capitulate, and the Kirkes occupied the colony for the following three years. Having lost all of its investments, the Company of One Hundred Associates never fully recovered, nor did it do anything during the ensuing years to promote settlement. The resulting vacuum of authority, especially after Champlain's death in 1635, meant that for a time the Catholic Church became the principle force in the colony.

As the Catholic Counter-Reformation reached its peak of enthusiasm during the first half of the seventeenth century, there developed a current of thought that associated the conversion of the indigenous peoples of North America with the establishment of Christ's millennial kingdom. A convert from Protestantism, Champlain was caught up in this religious fervour,[27] though he was also aiming to strengthen the French alliance with the Natives for strategic reasons when he invited four priests to Quebec in 1615. Members of the Récollet order (a branch of the Franciscan Friars), these missionaries adopted the "civilizing" strategy of settling Natives among French farmers with the aim of eventually amalgamating them through intermarriage. The Récollets found little enthusiasm for assimilation into French society, however, and the seminary they opened in 1620 to train indigenous clergy soon closed its doors due to lack of students and funds.[28]

Because they lacked a large financial base, the mendicant Récollets turned in 1625 to the self-funded Society of Jesus, which was a non-monastic teaching and missionary order based in Rome. Members of the society, known as Jesuits, returned alone in 1632, after the interlude when the colony was controlled by the Kirkes. The Jesuits opened a college for Native boys and established a reserve (*réduction*) to encourage agriculture at Saint-Joseph de Sillery, about six kilometres west of Quebec. But most of the boys in the school soon died or ran away, and the men on the reserve were absent too frequently on war parties against the Iroquois to pay much attention to farming.[29] The Ursulines, who opened a convent for Native girls in 1639, had about as much success as the Jesuits.[30] Unlike the Ursulines, however, the Jesuits had the option of spending more time in the wilderness with the Natives, learning their languages, explaining Christianity in terms that conformed in some senses to Aboriginal spiritual beliefs, and serving as mediators with the colonial authorities as well as between tribes.

While Christianity focused on the supernatural and spiritual, Native religion manifested in mythical form a reciprocal relationship between humanity and nature. What mattered to the Algonquians was concrete experience, and their world was constituted by persons, human and otherwise, rather than by abstract concepts. The ability to hunt, practise medicine, and wage successful war depended on proper relations with other-than-human persons, such as the sun, moon, wind, thunder, plants, or minerals. Before a hunt, one attempted to establish contact with the animal being pursued by stimulating visions or dreams through prayers, fasts, sacrifices, sacred dances, feasts, or gifts.

The key to proper relations with all persons, whether human or non-human, was sharing and gift-giving, and certain taboos had to be observed. Thus, once an animal was killed, one had to show respect to its bones by not feeding them to the dogs. With the mounting crisis caused by the depletion of furs during the 1630s, the Montagnais began to conclude that the Jesuits had power on their side and sought baptism as a symbolically potent expression of solidarity with the French. But, for a time at least, they were able to incorporate the Christian God, or He-Who-Made-All, into a world organized by many plant, animal, and other personal powers. Jesus represented the person

"La pesche des sauvages" from *Codex canadensis*, Louis Nicolas, ca. 1700. This illustration of Natives fishing (with the bowman playing a flute to please the Spirit) is one of the 180 drawings from the *Codex canadensis*, a manuscript that describes the First Nations, plants, mammals, birds, and fish of Canada. It was produced by the independent-minded Jesuit missionary Louis Nicolas after he was dismissed from the order and returned to southern France where his last years were spent in obscurity. One of the great treasures of Canadian book culture, *Codex canadensis* became known to the wider public only in 1930 when a French bookstore published a facsimile. Nicolas's illustrations of Amerindians are distinctive for the attention he devotes to their tattoos, which serve to distance them from European and Christian influences. *Gilcrease Museum, Tulsa, OK*

of the sun, and their social relations with the non-human remained bound by mutual obligations.[31]

As well-educated rationalists, the Jesuits generally did not attribute Native spiritual beliefs and practices to the devil. They interpreted them, rather, as a misdirection of mental powers, resulting in incoherent ignorance. The Natives had reached the condition of wildness not by a gradual ascent from brute creation, as the theory of evolution would teach in the nineteenth century, but by a degeneration from civilization as populations spread out from the central hub of the Mediterranean and adopted a variety of idolatries and false religions. The Jesuits compared Native intelligence favourably with that of the French, and stressed the complexity of the Native vocabulary as evidence that it had a divine origin. They were supporters of St. Thomas Aquinas's view that grace was available to all people, a view that was challenged by those French Roman Catholics who adhered to Jansenism. The Jansenists, instead, promoted Augustine's more pessimistic theology that original sin had left human nature thoroughly corrupted, and they rejected the possibility that non-Christians could perform moral acts or have any innate knowledge of God.[32]

The Jesuits were convinced that Amerindians could be converted, especially where conditions were propitious, as among the sedentary agricultural Hurons on Georgian Bay. Christian metaphors of the harvest had more meaning to the Hurons than to the Natives engaged in a hunting economy, though the Jesuits did face the challenge of adapting the holy trinity to a matrilineal society in which the maternal uncle played a more important role than the father.[33] Furthermore, from the contrast depicted in the *Jesuit Relations* between virtuous Native simplicity and European moral failings, it was a short step to the myth of the noble savage corrupted by European society, a myth that the Baron de Lahontan turned against the Church with his invention of Adario in *Nouveaux voyages dans l'Amérique septentrionale*. This volume went through twenty-five editions and various translations between 1703 and 1758.[34]

Meanwhile, the Jesuits proposed in 1632 that French men settle in Huronia and marry Christian Huron women. They soon abandoned the idea, however, and promoted segregation instead because of the control the Huron wife's family would exercise in that matrilineal society.[35] In

1634 the Hurons reluctantly allowed the Reverend Jean de Brébeuf and two companions to establish the mission of Sainte-Marie on Georgian Bay as a condition of renewing the French alliance. The advantages offered in the fur trade did encourage some Hurons to convert to Catholicism, causing a social rift because Christians could not participate in important feasts and ceremonies. The smallpox and measles epidemics that wiped out 70 percent of the Huron population in 1639–40 understandably gave rise to considerable animosity against the missionaries at Sainte-Marie, especially as their practice of baptizing at the point of death, when there would be no chance of renouncing the new faith, came to be linked with the cause of death. The Jesuits were not murdered, however, because the Hurons had become dependent on French trade goods and they did not wish to alienate Champlain. Internally divided and seriously weakened in numbers, Huronia was destroyed a year after the Iroquois acquired a new supply of Dutch arms in 1648, and several Jesuits found the martyrdom they had been seeking when they came to the New World.[36]

Also facing the strong possibility of death at the hands of the Iroquois were the residents of Ville-Marie, established on the island of Montreal in 1642 under the leadership of the career soldier Paul de Chomedey de Maisonneuve. Deserted, as Quebec had been, by the Laurentian Iroquois, Montreal was acquired by a secret society of very influential laymen (known as *dévots*) to serve as a centre of Native Christianization. Although its forty colonists included dedicated women such as Jeanne Mance, who had raised money for a hospital, its religious nature was soon overshadowed by commerce because it depended on revenues from the fur trade to survive and it was ideally located near the mouth of the Ottawa River and its fur trade route.

As of 1645 there were still only 600 residents and a few hundred indentured labourers in Canada, the Iroquoian name for "village," "settlement," or "land" that the colony in the St. Lawrence Valley had now adopted. Fifteen local merchants of the colony had formed the Company of Inhabitants that year to acquire the fur trade monopoly from the deeply indebted Company of One Hundred Associates. They had agreed in turn to pay the costs of administering the colony as well as to bring over twenty settlers a year, a considerable reduction from the 200 to 300 per year specified in the 1627 contract. This reduction in numbers reflected the challenge posed by the Iroquois who, following their victory over the Algonquins and assumption of effective control over the Ottawa route in 1644, proceeded to ensure that the fur trade did not take an alternative northern route via the St. Maurice or Saguenay Rivers. This they accomplished by pushing the Attikamegues to Lac Saint-Jean during the early 1650s and driving out the Montagnais of the Saguenay in 1655.[37]

To keep the commerce alive, French fur traders—aided by maps drawn by the Jesuit missionaries—began to travel deep into the interior. The success of traders Pierre Esprit Radisson and Médard Chouart des Groseilliers, who became the first *coureurs de bois* ("runners of the woods") in 1653, inspired the French Crown to send agents such as the priests Jacques Marquette and François Dollier de Casson to discover new trade routes and establish missions in the Great Lakes area and beyond. As a result, posts were established at Michilimackinac, near the entrance to Lake Michigan, and at other western sites. Ojibway, Illinois, Ottawa, and members of other western First Nations travelled to the fur fair at Montreal every summer, where they confirmed their alliance with the French. This did not prevent the growing numbers of *coureurs de bois* from heading westward in an attempt to escape the control of the Montreal merchants and out-compete each other. They were never more than a few hundred men,[38] but they came to be seen as a drain on an economy that was short of labour. As virtually defenceless strangers in the wilderness, the *coureurs de bois* had to establish personal ties with the Natives, leading to intermarriages.[39] Horrified as the French elite was by this reverse acculturation, efforts to constrain it were undermined by local officials such as the governor, Louis Buade de Frontenac, and his associate, Robert Cavalier de La Salle, who promoted the expansion of the fur trade for their own financial gain. They established the post of Cataraqui, or Frontenac (present-day Kingston), at the outlet of Lake Ontario in 1673, and by 1680 there were approximately 500 men trading in the interior.

In the meantime, these activities had brought the wrath of the Iroquois down on the French settlers. Thirty-two had been killed and twenty-two captured between 1650 and 1653, forcing the French to adopt more effective defensive tactics by organizing militia units, erecting stockades, and practising Native-style guerrilla warfare. In 1660 Adam Dollard des Ormeaux and a small party were surprised by an invasion force of 300 warriors at Long Sault, northwest of Montreal. The resulting battle in which all the French were killed or captured and tortured to death did, nevertheless, save the colony by diverting the Iroquois long enough for the crops to be harvested. Dollard would remain a relatively unknown figure until the 1940s when nationalist historians such as Abbé Lionel Groulx found accounts of the battle and raised him to hero status.[40]

The persistent Iroquois attacks and fear of torture spread terror throughout the colony, but the death toll was much lower than that caused by epidemics and it did not prevent the colony's population from tripling in size during the 1650s. Despite the shortage of marriageable women, natural increase played an important role, for one-third of the 2,500 settlers in the St. Lawrence Valley at the end of the decade were Canadian-born. But Canada was still not agriculturally self-sufficient, given that one-third of the population lived in the three towns of Quebec, Montreal, and Trois-Rivières, and tradesmen outnumbered labourers and farmers by at least five to one.[41] The consumption of Native corn, beans, squash, and tobacco as well as the adoption of Native moccasins, snowshoes, toboggans, and canoes to survive in the wilderness were not the only cultural influences of this new frontier. The thinly dispersed settlement pattern and the struggle for survival in an often hostile environment, not to mention the appeal of the freedom from church and state that they observed among the Natives, instilled a certain lack of respect for authority among the French settlers in Canada. To take one example, despite the association of the practice with Native savagery, coureurs de bois and even military officers had their bodies tattooed as a signifier of adoption by Amerindian allies. The French did refrain, however, from marking their faces in deference to the Christian belief that humankind was created in the image of God.[42]

The young French colonies in the Caribbean and Africa eclipsed the fur-producing colony in North America by 1660, but Louis XIV and his finance minister, Jean-Baptiste Colbert, were about to centralize power in the hands of the monarchy and wrest control of the overseas colonies from the private companies. In 1663 the charter of the Company of One Hundred Associates was revoked (the Company of Inhabitants having failed in 1659), and New France was declared to be a royal colony, albeit one in which the *Compagnie des Indes occidentales* (West Indian Company) assumed the costs of administration in return for a monopoly on the export of beaver furs. Steps were taken to crush the Iroquois by sending a thousand soldiers from the Carignan-Salières Regiment to the colony in 1665, and, after two clumsy campaigns against the Mohawks, the Iroquois did sue for peace two years later. As a result, hostilities ended for two decades, a period during which the colony finally made rapid advances, as we shall see in the next chapter. The French were never able to impose their sovereignty over any of the First Nations, but this would have been of little comfort to those Native allies who had either been dispersed or destroyed.

TWO

THE SETTLEMENT COLONY

Approximately 27,000 people came to the St. Lawrence Valley during the French regime, more than half by accident or compulsion, and only a little over a third of whom became permanent settlers.[1] During the same period, the British colonies to the south were flooded with one million immigrants from a country with a quarter of France's population. Why the sharp contrast? There was certainly no lack of "push" factors in rural France. The peasants, who made up 90 percent of that country's population, bore a heavy tax burden, with one-fifth to one-half of their crops going to ground rents alone.[2] To make matters worse, roads were in such poor condition that no produce or merchandise, no matter how light, would stand the cost of transportation over a distance greater than twenty-five kilometres or so. As a result, crop failures commonly led to localized famines. Due to epidemics, hunger, and poor public hygiene, one French child in every two died before reaching adulthood. Despite these harsh conditions, however, few peasants emigrated, in part because they maintained a more secure hold over their land than did their counterparts in Britain where tenants had few rights due to freehold tenure. The inheritance system in much of France also gave all offspring a stake in the land, whereas in Britain some could be left to fend for themselves.

As for "pull" factors, land was obviously plentiful in Canada, but there were competing options, such as enlistment in the king's ballooning army or emigration to the south of Spain, which together attracted half a million people in the seventeenth and eighteenth centuries.[3] New France never overcame its image as an inhospitable wasteland where settlers froze in the winter and faced the year-round danger of wild beasts and attacks by hostile Natives. The French government might have made a greater effort to dispel this image, but it feared that France would be weakened militarily and economically by the loss of any part of its population.

While the English government shared a similar view, many of the English colonists in America were religious dissidents in search of freedom from persecution. France's Protestants, known as Huguenots, also emigrated in large numbers particularly after religious toleration ended with the revocation of the Edict of Nantes in 1685—but they were forbidden from settling in New France. One reason was that French colonization was promoted as a religious mission, and another was the desire to prevent the religious schisms that had plagued the mother country.

The majority who crossed the Atlantic from France to Canada in the early years were unmarried artisans from Paris and the western seaports. It would have taken a year's salary for most to pay for the voyage, but they were offered free passage in return for three years of work as indentured servants known as *engagés*. Because of the shortage of labour, the *engagés* were often promised not only food and wages but also a prepaid passage home should they decide not to stay upon expiry of the contract. After engaging in a trade for six years in the colony, one would be recognized as a master craftsman in France. The *engagés* performed much of the colony's heavy labour in the early years, unloading ships, constructing buildings, and clearing land, and they could not marry or conduct trade on their own account until their contracts had expired. Those who worked on the seigneuries were enticed to become settlers by the offer of part of the land that they were hired to clear, passage for their families, and some livestock. Despite these relatively generous terms, however, over two-thirds of the *engagés* sent by the Crown in the 1660s returned to France.[4]

Because ships carried less bulk on their return voyages to France, passenger fares were less expensive to return home,[5] but one of the main reasons for this sizable reverse migration was the gender imbalance. Into the early 1660s there were twelve unmarried French males aged sixteen to thirty for every eligible French female in the colony's same age group.[6] The government responded, beginning in 1663, by sending 770 *filles du roi* (king's daughters), almost half of whom were from a Paris orphanage, and most of whom married within three months of arrival. After 1670, the Canadian population expanded almost entirely by natural increase. As a result, by 1700 there were as many women as men in the colony. Many of the newcomers were now involuntary emigrants—petty criminals and wayward sons sent by their families to avoid embarrassment. But the most important source of French settlers in the eighteenth century was the colonial military garrison, for a number of discharges were granted each year to soldiers who undertook to marry and settle in the colony permanently. Historian Peter Moogk's estimate of immigrants who made a permanent home in Canada is as follows: 3,300 soldiers; 1,800 Acadian exiles after the expulsion of 1755; 1,500 women; 1,200 *engagés*; 650 British subjects—many of whom were captives from New England; 500 male clergy; 250 self-financed immigrants; and 200 transported prisoners.[7]

Immigration from France was effectively curtailed by the Conquest, with the result that today's six million French Canadians are descended from little more than 10,000 people, though there was also intermarriage with Irish and Scots Catholics who arrived in the late eighteenth and early nineteenth centuries. The population doubled every generation during the French regime, largely due to high fertility. The annual birth rate of fifty-five per thousand people was much greater than the thirty to forty per thousand in Europe. The average married Canadian woman gave birth every two years until menopause, but this was not unusual in pre-industrial peasant societies. What distinguished the Canadians was that they married at a younger age, especially prior to 1660 when the average bride was only fifteen years old. The marriage age had stabilized at twenty-two by 1700, when the average groom was twenty-seven years of age, but, in contrast to France, widows remarried quickly in Canada. Otherwise, the birth rate would have been considerably lower because in three out of four families one of the parents (most often the husband) died before the children reached adulthood. The Canadian infant mortality rate of one in four or five was slightly higher than that in France, but there were very low rates of suicide and murder, and no periods of famine when large numbers of people died from malnutrition, as in France.[8]

The French government did more in 1663 than send the first *filles du roi* to the colony, for that was the year that New France became a royal colony. As a result, it was given essentially the same governing framework as a French province, except that the centralization of authority was more complete because of the control exercised by the ministry of marine and the lack of a deeply rooted local nobility or independent church.[9] A good deal of influence lay in the hands of the ministry's chief clerks,

Quebec, 1722. The aristocratic city of the French was portrayed as two distinct entities, upper town and lower town. This illustration is from the same perspective as most of the others prior to the Conquest, for the city is invariably book-ended by the St. Charles River on the right and Cape Diamond on the left, and the focus is on the official and ecclesiastical buildings of the upper town. Conscious of the fact that these official images were produced for view in France, the Récollets erected a large tower on their hospice in the Place d'Armes (shown here as B), and Bishop Laval over-ruled his church wardens by insisting that the cathedral tower (shown here as E) be erected even before construction of the nave. *Library and Archives Canada*

or *grands commis*, who reviewed all reports from the colonies, as well as drafted orders after they had consulted the minister. Because the lines of communication were so tenuous, however, with letters reaching Canada only once a year, local officials tended to avoid implementing orders that they did not consider appropriate.[10]

As the king's viceroy, the governor was placed in charge of military and diplomatic relations. The governor's status as a member of the *noblesse d'épée* (nobility of the sword) did not prevent those who held this office from involvement in the lucrative fur trade through their control of the military posts in the interior. Second in status were the intendants, members of the class of experienced officials created by the monarchy that was known as the *noblesse de robe*. In charge of justice, finance, and administration, the intendant controlled all funds not specifically designated for the governor; indeed, he was responsible for any matters that did not fall explicitly within the purview of the governor or bishop, including public works, public health, agriculture, commerce, and the appointment of notaries and public servants.[11]

The governing system was not designed to be one of mutual checks and balances, as some historians have assumed, but there were inevitable clashes between the governor and intendant because of overlapping jurisdictions. For example, the governor was responsible for military policy but the intendant supplied and paid the troops. Traditional historiography has assumed that the intendant had more power than the governor because his position was of greater practical importance but, according to historian Louise Dechêne, the military nature of the colony ensured that the intendant was more subordinate to the governor than was the case in the French provinces.[12] Conflicts between the two officials nevertheless divided the wider community as different factions allied with either one or the other in their competition for patronage. Historian S.D. Standen has concluded that politics, defined as the play of interests, permeated all levels of the royal administration because it was denied an institutional arena of its own that would have implied opposition to the royal will.[13]

The sovereign council, whose role was to serve as a court of appeal and to register royal edicts, was the counterpart to a provincial *parlement* in France. Presided over by the intendant, and consisting of colonial officials from the lower nobility, the sovereign council initially had certain administrative responsibilities, such as the right to review the appointment of judges and oversee policing and fire protection, as well as to regulate trade with the Natives and fix import and export duties. By the 1670s, however, the intendant was drafting all important regulations, and the sovereign councillors were limited to serving as a court of appeal and registering royal edicts. There were originally five members in addition to the governor and intendant (the bishop did not attend after 1663), none of whom were lawyers because they were not allowed to practise in New France. The five grew to seven in 1675 and to twelve in 1703. Aside from an annual salary of 500 livres, officials earned income by charging for their services, but all served at the pleasure of the king rather than buying the title to their posts as in the venal system of the mother country.[14] This may have prevented the entrenchment of an oppressive office-holding elite in New France, as historian Jacques Mathieu suggests, but it also ensured that power was centralized in the mother country, which consistently favoured French appointees over Canadians.[15]

Finally, each of the three towns originally had general assemblies to deal with local affairs and elect a syndic who sat on the sovereign council. But the syndics were excluded from the council in 1657, and the position was eliminated in 1673.[16] Instead, the governor and intendant were represented at the parish level by the captain of militia, generally a habitant, who publicized government decrees and served a role similar to that of a local police agent.[17] The government, therefore, was essentially a relaxed absolutism. From 1717 onward, merchants were permitted to gather in order to discuss trade and elect a spokesman who could present their requests to the government, but the colonists had no right to participate in government except as royal appointees. During most of the French regime there were no popularly elected institutions aside from the *fabrique* (church vestry), and its role was confined to local church matters. Anyone could appeal to the intendant personally, and all court appeals to the sovereign council were free of charge, but any public assembly that had not previously received the permission of authorities was considered to be in the nature of a riot. The same applied to any delegation or petition; each person spoke for himself, and not for a group.[18]

Despite these restrictions, there is no evidence of political unrest or popular discontent with the government system. As in France, the state's infrastructural power was bolstered by offering rewards for service to influential subjects.[19] Furthermore, there was no deeply entrenched communal tradition; the nature of the economy and the constant warfare ensured that the colony lacked a disgruntled middle class to organize dissent; there was no printing press because France wanted to retain the book trade monopoly; and absolutism was tempered by paternalism. For example, local boards were appointed to suppress public begging by aiding the indigent and finding work for the able-bodied, and food retailers were forced to sell in a public market in order to keep prices competitive. There were only a dozen or so minor public protests during the French regime, some of them led by women demanding lower prices for food. These were tolerated (aside from small fines for the leaders) as a channel for collective expression with a minimum of violence.[20] Government was close at hand, for the districts of Montreal and Trois-Rivières had their own lieutenant-governors and subdelegates of the intendant, but colonial government was also too susceptible to internal rivalries and intrigue to be particularly efficient. Indeed, liberal historians have argued that the state played little role in the life of the average settler who lived on his own farm rather than in the rural village typical of France, who paid no government taxes, and who seldom saw a government official other than the captain of militia. As Dechêne has stressed, however, the colonial government increasingly controlled the distribution of grain, even in times of peace, and Canadian peasants were expected to risk their lives in military expeditions that often took them far from their crops for extended periods of time. They were also required to work on the towns' fortifications and to provide free lodgings for the regular troops. In short, they paid with their bodies rather than with their goods.[21]

"Vu des étalons" from *Codex canadensis*, Louis Nicolas, ca. 1700. The stallion illustrated here was one of two that arrived with twelve mares in the first royal shipment to the colony in 1665. Other small shipments followed, for a total of 82 horses by 1671, but Intendant Talon now felt there was a large enough number to supply colts to all who needed them because horses were not meant for the use of peasants. Those sent by the French government were rented out to leading colonists for three years, after which they became their private property. The number increased rapidly, reaching 1,872 in 1706, or approximately one horse per family, which raised concerns about the softening of the militia. Because most of the heavy farm work was done during the summer by oxen, horses were used primarily during the winter for going to church, socializing, and racing on the frozen rivers, as well as hauling grain to the seigneurial mills and produce to market. *Gilcrease Museum, Tulsa, OK*

As finance minister of France, Jean-Baptiste Colbert was determined to make the colonies contribute to the French economy. According to the mercantilist economic theory then in vogue, the wealth of countries depended upon acquiring and holding onto as much of the world's limited supply of specie or gold as possible. They could do this most effectively by restricting imports from competing nations. Colonies therefore played the very important role of providing raw materials unavailable at home, as well as serving as markets for the mother country's manufactures. But, given the weakness of France's navy, its colonies had to be able to survive enemy blockades, something they could not do if they were dependent upon the mother country for vital necessities. Aside from making agriculture the base of Canada's economy, therefore, some basic industries were encouraged. Jean Talon, appointed the colony's first intendant in 1665, was instructed to promote agriculture, fishing, logging, mining, and certain manufactures such as ship-building. He provided subsidies to assist these industries and established a brewery to consume excess grain.

As a result of government encouragement, more than 2,000 people arrived in Canada between 1663 and 1673, a decade when the colony's numbers doubled, but immigration slowed after that, and the population never became large enough to create a profitable local demand for industries.[22] Colbert's solution was to foster a triangular trade between Canada, the West Indies, and France. Canada would provide fish, grain, other foodstuffs; lumber; and barrel staves to the West Indies, and take sugar, molasses, and rum in exchange. Unfortunately, much of the ice-free season for Canada was hurricane season in the Caribbean, the cost of Canadian goods was higher than those of New England, and the small Canadian population could not absorb much West Indian produce. Consequently, the French West Indies continued to trade with the English colonies despite the official prohibition.

The construction of Louisbourg provided an entrepôt after 1720, but another handicap for Canadian economic development was the shortage and resulting high price of skilled labour due to easy access to land and high wages for working as voyageurs in the fur trade. The St. Maurice ironworks, established in 1739, and the naval shipyard at Quebec were the only significant industrial sites, and the cost to build a ship in Canada remained twice as high as in France. Finally, because the fur trade relied largely on Native labour and did not stimulate many subsidiary economic activities, there was little incentive to reinvest the profits in the local economy. It has been estimated that, as late as 1739, 70 percent of Canada's trade value was in furs, and only 18 percent in farm produce, 9 percent in fish and fishery products such as oil, and 2 percent in iron and wood products.[23]

If the fur trade did little to encourage economic investment in the colony, it did support the noble families because, in contrast to their counterparts in the mother country, they could engage in commerce without losing social status. Quebec's nationalist historians, anxious to prove that the French colony had a dynamic bourgeoisie, have argued that the result of this commercial activity was a watering down of the aristocratic ethos. Given that much of the 20 to 25 percent of fur trade profits that did not go to the mother country was spent on the importation of luxury items and the purchase of land, however, it seems more likely that this commerce encouraged bourgeois participants to ape the aristocracy in order to achieve noble status. In addition, because participation in the fur trade was limited by royal decree, those without social ties to the governing authorities were at a distinct disadvantage.

Furthermore, the colony was in a state of war more often than not, and the higher ranks of the *troupes de la marine* posted in Montreal and Quebec from 1683 onward were recruited from the Canadian population. It is not surprising, therefore, that the chief role model for the young men of the commercial and landed classes was that of military officer in the French forces.[24] As a feudal landholding system, seigneurial tenure also fostered an aristocratic ethos even though the fact that militia units were organized by parish rather than seigneurie prevented seigneurs from commanding their own vassals. Indeed, most Canadian seigneurs lived in town because they depended on income from the military or the state, and holding a seigneurie (or fief) did not necessarily make one a noble. Still, seigneuries were sought for prestige because nobility was tied to land and the seigneur occupied a rank above that of the majority of the people. In fact, a Canadian nobility of the sword owned two-thirds of the rural seigneuries by 1700.[25]

The seigneuries varied greatly in size, but all had frontage on the St. Lawrence River or its two major southern tributaries, the Chaudière and

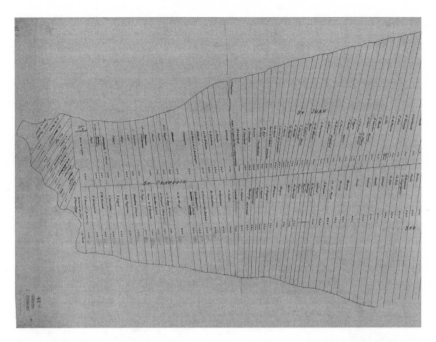

Plan de l'Isle d'Orléans (detail), Gédéon de Catalogne, 1709. A map of all the seigneuries and land grants in the Quebec district was produced by military engineer Gédéon de Catalogne in 1709 because of the inaccuracy of the seigneurs' records. As shown in this small section of the map, he included the names of the occupants, extent of their land, and their trades. The *censives* allotted to the habitants were long contiguous rectangles, perpendicular to the water's edge, thereby affording each *censitaire* access to the river for transportation. © *Bibliothèque et archives nationales du Québec*

the Richelieu, as did the narrow holdings (known as *rotures*) of the earlier settlers. As a result, the *chemin du Roi* between Quebec and Montreal would not be completed until 1737, and there would be no continuous south-shore road until after the Conquest.[26] There was nothing distinctively "seigneurial" about the long-lot settlement pattern—it simply provided the easiest communications route as well as access to fresh water and the opportunity to fish in the St. Lawrence, plus a source of firewood in the hillier land to the rear. On the negative side, the fact that the rural population was not concentrated in villages made homes difficult to defend.[27]

In contrast to the English system of freehold tenure, no one held outright ownership of land. Seigneurs owed obligations to people on the level below as well as to the King above. For his own use, the seigneur kept a portion of the land known as the domain, but the rest he was obliged to grant upon request from any settler for a modest annual rent that was fixed in perpetuity. Unlike British landlords, he had no power of eviction, and he had to resort to the courts in order to collect payments in arrears. There were obvious advantages to such a system of tenure as far as opening a new country was concerned, for land could not be hoarded by speculators and families did not need a large down payment before they could establish a farm, as with the freehold system.

The seigneur was also supposed to provide the services of a gristmill and a law court, although seigneurial courts became increasingly rare with time. In return, the seigneur's privileges included honours in religious ceremonies (for example, prayers for his family during religious services, and the right to take communion first as well as march at the head of parades); the collection of a nominal tax known as a *cens* by which the *censitaires* acknowledged their dependence; the collection of the above-mentioned *rente* agreed to by contract; a mutation fine (or sales tax) known as the *lods et ventes*, which was equal to one-twelfth the value of any land sold by a *censitaire*; the *droit de retrait* by which he could repossess a concession that had been sold by matching its sale price; the *banalité* or gristmill monopoly that provided one sack of grain for every fourteen that were ground at the mill; and the right to have each *censitaire* work three days on his land (the *corvée*). In short, the institutional framework of the seigneurial system was every bit as complete in Canada as it was in most of France where the system was dying out by the seventeenth and eighteenth centuries.[28] The chief mitigating factor was the abundance of land and shortage of settlers that forced the seigneurs to offer relatively generous terms to their *censitaires*. When population pressures began to increase by the end of the French regime, however, seigneurs in favoured locations conceded lots sparingly to selected *censitaires*, increased the *rentes* for new concessions, and imposed additional charges as well as restrictions over fishing, timber, and common pastures.[29]

The *censitaires* were popularly known as habitants to distinguish them from the feudal peasants of France. Like all peasants, however, they were small-scale agricultural producers who worked as a family, were economically self-sufficient to a degree, and managed their farms as they saw fit, while being forced to provide some of what they grew to support the privileged classes. Even though the abundance of land placed the *censitaires* in a relatively strong position as indicated by their geographic mobility throughout much of the French regime,[30] the weight of their seigneurial obligations should not be dismissed, especially given the lack of dependable markets for their produce. With little incentive to acquire more than the approximately forty hectares that the family could exploit, there was no equivalent in Canada to the small minority of wealthy peasants in France. Generally considered to be another obstacle to the development of a peasant elite was the colony's legal code, the Custom of Paris, which required the equal division of a deceased *censitaire's* property among all offspring. To prevent farms from becoming too small to support a family, however, they were generally passed on to a younger son when the aging parents were still living. In addition to supporting his parents, this son, in turn, had to compensate his siblings for their share of the *légitime*. This relatively equitable system of intergenerational transfer would also become characteristic of English Canada, where it simply reflected a sense of family obligation.[31]

Large acreages were not required because the focus was on grain rather than cattle production. With bread constituting between 60 and 85 percent of the habitant's diet by weight, two-thirds to three-quarters of the crop production throughout the French regime consisted of wheat, followed by oats and barley that were mostly fed to livestock. Favoured garden vegetables were peas, beans, onions, carrots, cabbages, and beets that could be stored for extended periods and be added to soups. After a generation, most families could hope to have two pairs of oxen, two or three cows, one or two calves, four of five pigs, and a dozen hens. By the eighteenth century, there would also be a few sheep for wool and one or two horses to take advantage of the frozen St. Lawrence during the winter and the road network that was developing as the settlement frontier moved onto back concessions (known as *côtes* or *rangs*). The authorities became so concerned about the number of horses that they attempted to limit them, arguing that they consumed fodder needed for more essential livestock and that the habitants were losing the ability to walk the long distances required for militia service.[32] Due to the small scale of agricultural production, Canada was spared much of the environmental impact that colonization had elsewhere in the New World. Because the original Iroquois inhabitants had abandoned the St. Lawrence valley by the time French settlers arrived, even the pigs that were allowed to forage in the woods did not have the disastrous consequences for Native survival that they did in New England, where they routinely damaged crops and food stores.[33]

The colonists' attachment to their traditional French diet meant that wild game made up a relatively small part of their food intake, though fish was essential because of the approximately 150 days a year of Church-prescribed abstinence or fasting. Eels and beaver tails, which the Church categorized as fish for dietary purposes, were popular because of their high fat content.[34] Farm families drew on the outside world only for such essential supplies as salt and hardware, as well as a few luxury products such as ribbons, pins, and wine, or even a stove, but they did rely on credit and their debts were recorded in monetary terms. The soldiers and fishermen of Louisbourg represented a good market for Canadian produce after the fortress was built in 1720, and it also served as a useful entrepôt for shipping wood, flour, peas, and horses to the West Indies, resulting in an era of unprecedented prosperity during the 1720s and 1730s. But there were disastrous crop failures in 1736 and 1737, as well as in the 1740s, and the habitants continued to rely partly on the fur trade, fishing, or logging to raise the money needed for rents and indispensable purchases.[35]

Earlier generations of historians invariably mentioned the career of Pierre Boucher, the missionary servant (donné) who ultimately became governor of Trois-Rivières, to support their argument that a rigid class system did not exist during the French regime. Social mobility was, nevertheless, quite limited. Sons of the elite could receive a good education at the Jesuits' College de Québec, which went beyond the standard classical curriculum to offer courses in hydrography and cartography as well as the sciences, but most of the schools were located in towns with the result that at least three-quarters of the population was illiterate.[36] Yet even this low ratio of literacy was higher than that of France,[37] and, because land was plentiful, there was also no equivalent to the large ratio of impoverished peasants on the other side of the Atlantic—the Canadian peasants' standard of living was roughly equivalent to the top 10 percent of their counterparts in the mother country. Exploitation of

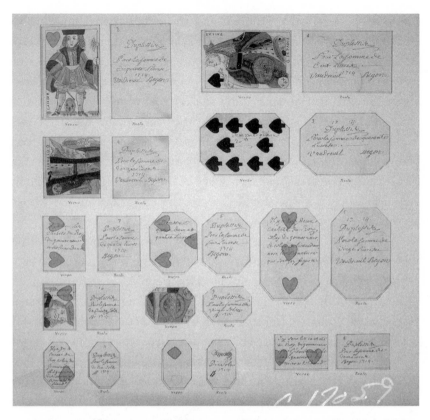

Design for twelve playing cards, 1714. Because no coins were struck in New France, and Canada's exports were more valuable than its imports, currency was generally in short supply. In 1685 Intendant Demeulle began to issue playing cards with various face values and affixed with his seal to pay the small sums owed to the government's suppliers, the colony's soldiers, and other state creditors. When a supply of specie arrived with the King's ship, these cards were reimbursed in coin. The government resorted to this tactic a number of times during the French Regime. Later cards without colours had their corners cut or were cut in smaller pieces according to a fixed table. But the value of the cards in circulation remained relatively insignificant compared to other forms of paper money, such as promissory notes signed by the intendant and letters of exchange or drafts between private citizens. *Library and Archives Canada*

this class would increase as the land filled up and markets developed, but seigneurs did not truly gain the upper hand until after the Conquest. Although this was more an Old World peasant society than an egalitarian or individualist one in the American sense, it was more heavily focused on the nuclear family than in France.[38] At the local level in the old country, the *communauté des habitants* met frequently to regulate the commons, serving as a significant force in resisting increased exactions from seigneur and state. In Canada, however, the role of the *communauté* was much reduced, and the annual parish meeting to elect churchwardens and vote on levies related to local church property provided the only regular opportunity to act as a corporate body. Nor did the militia contribute a good deal to the sense of community because members were distributed as individuals among various brigades under the command of professional officers when on military duty. Peasants resisted co-operation in mutually beneficial drainage projects, shirked statute labour on roads, and so on, but communities did gradually take root as neighbours assisted each other in time of need, congregated at holy Mass on Sundays, attended social gatherings during the winter season, and intermarried to form extended family networks.[39]

With more than 30 percent of its people living in towns up to the end of the seventeenth century, Canada was a more urban society than was France where 90 percent of the population were peasants.[40] Given, as well, that so many immigrants to the colony had an artisanal background, it may seem surprising that they did not become a powerful socio-economic group. But, while a wide variety of trades was practised in the three major towns, craftsmen's associations broke down in the face of official discouragement and unstable "frontier" conditions. Artisans simply became too independent-minded, and enjoyed too many economic opportunities, to become tied to guilds, particularly when the rank of master craftsman with the exclusive right to operate a workshop did not exist in the colony. The only trades licensed by the government were those that affected the health of the public, and they had to accept fixed price schedules as well as state supervision.[41]

As already noted, economic conditions did not favour the development of a dependent propertyless working class or proletariat in New France. Though many men arrived as *engagés*, their contracts had limited time periods, and most of them returned to the home country. There were few journeymen because this stage was not necessary to become an artisan, and apprentices had to be paid a salary after two years of a contract.[42] Fortunately for the economy, the French soldiers who were billeted in private homes did constitute an important pool of labour when not on active duty. In addition, domestic servants comprised 5 to 8 percent of the population in Quebec and Montreal. In the latter town, 40 percent of these servants were under sixteen years of age, most of them being

Chateau Ramesay, Montreal, Henry Richard S. Bunnett, 1866. Claude de Ramezay built the Château Ramezay on Notre-Dame Street in 1705, the year after he became the Governor of Montreal. Montreal's houses were still mostly of wood construction at this time, but the great fires of 1721 and 1734 caused the authorities to forbid its use in future, causing a flight to the outskirts on the part of poorer families. The Château Ramezay was used for official functions as well as to house a family that included sixteen children. At the time of this painting by Richard S. Bunnett, it was occupied by the Montreal branch of Laval University's Faculty of Medicine and Law. The Château Ramezay was converted into a museum in 1895, and in 1929 it became the first building in the province of Quebec to be declared a historical monument. *McCord Museum*

orphans or from large, poor families, and a slight majority being boys. Reflecting the paternalism of the *ancien régime* state, those who took an illegitimate or abandoned child as a servant received monetary compensation from the government.[43]

Slaves were another potential source of labour, for in southern colonies such as North Carolina they served not simply as plantation labour but also as sawyers, millwrights, and stevedores. In Cuba those not involved in constructing fortifications worked in shipyards or became metalworkers, among other skilled trades, as well as being encouraged to take up carting and petty commerce as contract labourers.[44] In 1716, Intendant Bégon called for more slaves for Canada, arguing that they could be used in agriculture, fishing, logging, ship building, and mining. But the vulnerability of the colony, which was more often than not at war, may have made colonists fear the possibility of slave insurrections similar to those that occurred quite regularly in the Caribbean colonies. Whatever the reason, the number of slaves never reached more than 5 percent of the Canadian population, and most of the 4,200 who lived in the colony during the French regime worked as domestics in Montreal. Over half were Natives, known as *panis*, a name that applied not only to the Pawnees but to other Plains tribes as well. The remaining slaves were of African origin, and the life expectancy of both groups was under twenty-five years of age.[45] The most famous of them, Angélique, has come to symbolize the African-American hunger for freedom because of her defiance in razing the house of her mistress (though she was executed on the basis of little evidence) in an apparent attempt to escape.[46]

Largely because of growing metropolitan concerns about racial purity, the initial support for intermarriage with First Nations women had transformed into hostility towards miscegenation by the last quarter of the seventeenth century.[47] The Native converts who were encouraged to settle in the St. Lawrence Valley were therefore also encouraged to remain separate and independent within their own villages. These included the Jesuit-established settlement of Christian Iroquois at Kahnawake near Montreal; the Sulpician community of Algonquins and Iroquois that finally was fixed at Kanesatake (Oka) near the Lake of Two Mountains in 1721; the mainly Huron village of Lorette near Quebec; and the Abenaki villages at the mouth of the Becancour and St. Francis Rivers not far from Trois-Rivières.[48] While hard to quantify because of the Natives' mobility, the St. Lawrence Valley mission population was in the thousands. Growth was limited by European diseases and military casualties, which in turn reduced birth rates, but this was offset to some extent by the adoption of prisoners as well as Canadian orphans and infants born out of wedlock.[49]

Significantly enough, the Native inhabitants of these communities were never integrated into the colonial workforce.[50] The Canadian

Catherine Tegahkouita Iroquoise, Jean Dominique Canu, ca. 1800. In 1980, Catherine (Kateri) Tekakwitha became the first Native American to be beatified. This illustration is based closely on the painting by the first promoter of that beatification, the Jesuit missionary Claude Chauchetière. Depicted as a saint-like nun, Tekakwitha has little to identify her with her Native origins. As part of the ongoing campaign for her canonization, however, and to suggest the contemporary relevance of the Catholic Church, she has now become the patroness of ecology and the environment. *Library and Archives Canada*

CATHERINE TEGAHKOUITA IROQUOISE,
Morte en odeur de Sainteté dans le Canada

Canu Sculp. rue S.t Jacques N.o 4.

Iroquois kept a few cows, pigs, and chickens, but they also continued to live in longhouses. And the women planted their traditional crops while the men were frequently absent on war parties or smuggling furs to New York. In some cases, however, the mission Natives took the Church's emphasis on the need for obedience quite literally, inflicting severe punishments on transgressors and thereby flouting their traditional value of solidarity.[51] The Christian doctrine that the spirit was in conflict with the flesh also inspired some converts to follow the penitential self-mortification practised by the missionaries, even to the point of death in the case of the twenty-four-year-old Catherine Tekakwitha in 1680.

But there were syncretic elements even to the saintly spirituality of this "Iroquois virgin," who was beatified in 2012. First, her baptismal acquisition of the same name as the ascetic Catherine of Siena was akin to the Iroquoian requickening rite in which a person received a name and assumed a metaphorical identification with the namesake. Second, although the penitential religious association she formed with her female friends had parallels with Catholic confraternities and even uncloistered religious communities, it also resembled Iroquoian women's societies. Finally, fasting and abstinence were accepted by both the Jesuits and the Iroquois as means of achieving spiritual power, and self-mortification may have been a substitute for ritual torture in the quest for that power. The Natives at Kahnawake appear to have viewed penance as a powerful healing and prophylactic ritual, particularly in the face of smallpox epidemics.[52]

Certainly, the Iroquois in the Montreal missions were not fully controlled by the priests, and, even though they were recognized as French subjects, they did not consider themselves bound by French law. This was particularly the case when alcohol was involved because Natives believed that responsibility lay with the spirit of the brandy itself. Because these Iroquois played an important role in the defence of the colony, the authorities had little choice but to punish the supplier of the brandy rather than the perpetrator of the crime and to turn a blind eye to the smuggling of furs to Albany.[53]

Intercultural exchanges were therefore not always in the direction favoured by the French authorities, and the wilderness itself continued to have an impact on the settler society, for a fifth to a quarter of Canadian males travelled west on fur trade journeys after 1680. Even though this was a transitory occupation for most, the image in France, where there was a visceral fear of disorder, was that all Canadian men were *coureurs de bois* and therefore lazy, independent, and debauched.[54] Still more important in encouraging independence among the common people, however, was the easy availability of land, as already noted. Like their male counterparts, Canadian women also exercised more independence and influence than they had in the old country, for younger women who were widowed in the colony soon remarried, and merchant-class women were recognized as female public traders in order to operate family businesses while their husbands were away from home trading furs or managing fisheries. Beneath the merchant-class women were those who supplied goods and services from within the fur trade posts, and farm women who played a crucial role in their family economy by engaging in the dairy work, taking part in the harvest, growing vegetables for the town market, and making cloth and clothing that went to the *pays d'en haut*.[55]

Under the Custom of Paris, husband and wife formed a two-person corporation known as the marital community. All contracts such as land purchases and mortgages required the signature of the wife, though hers was only a right of protest because managerial powers were vested in the husband. Even when a marriage contract removed from the husband's control the property brought to the marriage by the wife, she could not dispose of it or mortgage it without his permission.[56] When a husband died, however, his widow was entitled to half the inheritance, though she could also renounce the "community of goods" when debts outweighed the value of the assets. A small number of widows became influential entrepreneurs, but it was more common for them to operate small businesses such as taverns.[57]

A middle-aged matron might also play an important role outside the family by serving as a midwife, for surgeons were not present at most births in New France. The Church took an interest in this position because midwives were authorized to baptize newborn infants who were in danger of dying. Bishop Saint-Vallier's *Rituel du diocese de Québec* of 1703 recommended that they be elected by a meeting of other local women and that the election be approved by a priest. A decade later those who had been thus authorized were granted a salary of three to four livres per delivery.[58] The greatest source of female power and influence during the French regime was, nevertheless, the Church, for the simple reason that celibate religious women lived together in communities detached from the powers of the father and husband. The members of these communities were all Canadian-born by the eighteenth century, when they included 20 percent of the colony's adult noblewomen, while all members of the male religious orders apart from the Récollets, who served mainly as military chaplains, were born in France.[59]

Attractive as the religious life was to Canadian women, female religious orders could not escape the authority of the bishops. For example, Monseigneur Briand did not hesitate to criticize the sisters of Quebec's Hôpital Général for entertaining visitors, gossiping, and neglecting prayers as well as rules of silence. But the female orders did resist pressure from the male hierarchy to remain strictly cloistered. Although the Ursulines could not go beyond the boundaries of their wooden fence, large groups of Native girls and women came and went, listening to religious instruction and being fed. The Congregation of Our Lady, founded by Marguerite Bourgeoys of Montreal, even rejected dowries as well as solemn and perpetual vows so that the nuns could teach in parish schools. Members of the Ursuline Order and of the Hospital Sisters were more likely to come from the upper classes, and they played crucial social

Marguerite Bourgeoys, Pierre Le Ber, 1700. Marguerite Bourgeoys was the founder of the Congregation of Our Lady in Montreal, where she lived for forty-seven years. Though Bishop Saint-Vallier wanted to confine these nuns to the cloister, they remained secular, going in pairs into the countryside to teach children of both sexes. Because Marguerite Bourgeoys refused the vanity of a portrait in life, this one was painted after her death, nicely capturing the puritanical zeal of the colony's early nuns and clergy. It was hung in the convent chapel above the spot where she was buried. *Musée Marguerite-Bourgeoys*

roles in educating children as well as operating hospitals and charitable institutions. Indeed, these urban institutions were established at a much earlier date and were of a vastly superior quality than the small colonial population could ever have provided for itself.[60]

An increasingly important part of the religious orders' funding came from their landholdings, for one-quarter of all seigneurial land was in the Church's hands by the end of the French regime. These carefully managed seigneuries, including the island of Montreal, which had been owned by the Sulpicians since 1663, tended to be located near the three main towns. But the mystical Counter-Reformation Catholicism that characterized the first decades of colonization—when the missionary priests were involved in colonization, local administration, and probably even the fur trade—went into decline after Canada became a royal colony, and Intendant Talon was instructed to keep the clergy, especially the powerful Jesuits, subordinate to the state. As the national church of France, the Roman Catholic Church was presided over by the French king who was known as His Most Christian Majesty, and whose maxim was that "the church is in the state, not the state in the church." The king nominated the bishops and controlled the establishment of religious institutions and their recruitment, as well as supervising all educational, charitable, and other social institutions operated by the Church. In short, he defended the Gallican Church against encroachments by Rome. Furthermore, Protestantism was barely tolerated in France because it was considered not only as religious heresy but also as a political party favouring the theory that the king held his authority not by divine right but by popular consent. It was largely because the Huguenots were suspected of disloyalty that the settlement of New France continued to be restricted to Catholics.

The need for a local diocese was felt as early as the 1630s, especially because of jurisdictional quarrels among the religious orders in the colony, but it was blocked by tense relations between France and Rome. In 1659 the papacy created a vicariate apostolic rather than a bishopric in New France because it would be directly subordinate to Rome and not to an archdiocese in France. The first appointee was the austere and dedicated François de Laval who had been a student of the Jesuits and a member of secret *dévot* organizations. Laval waged a long and bitter struggle to impose a ban on trading brandy to the Amerindians, threatening excommunication against anyone so involved. Two governors were recalled because of his clash with them over this issue, but his power became much weaker with the establishment of the royal colony in 1663, and he did not sit on the sovereign council after that date.

Laval's successor, Bishop Saint-Vallier (1688–1729), was equally devout and orthodox, and his catechism and other publications planted in generations of Canadians the devotional norms of the Catholic Reformation. But Saint-Vallier spent five years in an English prison after his ship was captured en route to France, and the next two bishops seldom set foot in the colony, thereby reducing the prestige of religious authority. This was restored to some extent by Monseigneur Pontbriand, the last bishop of New France (1740–60), though his death on the eve of the Conquest left the Church in a very vulnerable position.

Because the government would accept only those religious communities that made a visible contribution to colonial welfare through schools, hospitals, charitable institutions, and parish duties, no contemplative orders were permitted to establish themselves in New France. The regular clergy lived in community and followed a rule (*règle*), while the secular clergy lived in the world and constituted the majority of the parish priests (*curés*). Not only did the secular clergy owe their obedience to the bishop but for many years they belonged to a chapter of the Quebec Seminary rather than being attached to parishes. There were only twenty fixed curial charges as late as 1720, and, even though a government-appointed commission defined the boundaries of eighty-two parishes the following year, most were to be served by missionaries or priests from the nearest parish. With the exception of two urban parishes, the *curés* were removable at the bishop's pleasure. By 1760, 51 of the 163 ecclesiastics living in Canada had been born in the colony, and they constituted the majority of the priests who had been assigned to the parishes.[61]

The parish, which provided the only framework for community life in New France, was democratically organized to administer its temporal affairs through elected wardens (*marguilliers*) known collectively as the *fabrique*. This council, whose membership was regularly renewed, held title to local church properties and was responsible for the building and

St Laurent Parish Church, Ile d'Orléans. This church was built in 1695 and destroyed in 1864. With walls of heavy fieldstone set in mortar, it conformed to Bishop Laval's Latin-cross plan, which represented a fusion of late medieval craft elements with academic trends in seventeenth-century French architecture. Characteristic of the six stone churches built on the ecclesiastical seigneuries of the Beaupré coast and the Ile d'Orléans under Laval's personal supervision were the high and steeply sloped roof, the oculus known in Quebec as an *oeil-de-bouc* over the round-headed door, the rounded windows, and the wooden tower superimposed on the roof just behind the front of the gable. Despite Laval's wishes, most parish churches were built of wood, though a small number were *en colombage*, with fieldstone rubble between the inside and outside walls. *Library and Archives Canada*

maintenance of church, cemetery, and presbytery. A congregational meeting had to set the level of assessment for new projects, but that assessment then became enforceable by civil power. Also legally enforceable was the tithe, the purpose of which was to support the *curé*. As its name suggests, it was supposed to be the equivalent of one-tenth of the harvest, but a royal edict in 1663 set it at one-thirteenth, and, to encourage rural settlement, it was halved four years later to one-twenty-sixth of the cereal crops only. It would remain at this level after the British Conquest.

The Church bolstered state authority by conferring divine legitimacy upon the social hierarchy in its religious processions, by bestowing honorific recognition through the reservation of the pews closest to the altar for senior government officials and seigneurs, and by preaching submission to the onerous militia duties.[62] In return, the state enforced Church taxes and set parish boundaries, as well as enacting legislation calling for the observance of Sunday rest, church attendance, respectful behaviour during divine service, and punishment by the courts for swearing (blasphemy) and eating meat during Lent. The priests complained of drunkenness, love of worldly pleasures, and vanity, but the people of this era lived in a world of supernatural forces that they attempted to influence in various ways, both orthodox and irregular. Formal accusations of witchcraft were relatively rare, but the belief that the actions and objects of the Church had a power that could serve profane ends was reflected in the *mariage à la gaumine,* namely, the declaration of marriage vows by a couple at the point during the communion service when the priest was blessing the host. Bishop Saint-Vallier threatened to excommunicate such couples, and the practice became rare, but his *Rituel* of 1703 reflected popular demands by including a blessing of fields to expel grasshoppers, caterpillars, and other insects.[63]

Even if spiritual and religious matters were not always among their uppermost preoccupations, almost without exception the people of New France wanted to live and die within the fold of the Church. Some belonged to religious confraternities that obliged them to attend Mass on a frequent basis, shun worldly pleasures such as dancing, and donate to the poor, among other duties. Furthermore, 95 percent of infants were baptized within three days of birth; illegitimacy rates were relatively low at 1.25 per thousand births between 1680 and 1729; nearly everyone took confession at Easter; many went on pilgrimages to shrines such as the chapel dedicated to Saint Anne in the parish of Beaupré; and most wills requested Church prayers to open the gates to heaven as soon as possible. In short, the colonists followed at least the minimum acceptable standards of their religious duties. But they were also independent and undisciplined, regarding the parish church and rectory as community property, resisting the curé's attempts to auction family pews when the owners died, leaving the church (if they were men) during the sermon, and even challenging the bishop's authority when he attempted to alter parish boundaries.[64]

THREE

THE MILITARY COLONY

More important than its economic role in the eyes of the French government was the geopolitical role played by New France because of its controlled access to the two major rivers of North America, the St. Lawrence and the Mississippi. Inspired by the example of ancient Rome, the French government dreamed of establishing a colony of soldier-citizens when it sent the Carignan-Salières regiment to New France to eliminate the Iroquois threat in 1665, and offered land to the officers and their subordinates who would settle there. The invasions into Iroquois territory did bring two decades of peace, but only about a third of the 1,310 soldiers remained behind when the regiment returned to France in 1668. Rather than settling in the seigneuries that had been granted their commanding officers as defensive outposts in the lower Richelieu Valley, most soldiers who did not return to France remained in the communities where they had been billeted. But the idea of the soldier-citizen survived in the form of instructions sent to the intendant in 1669 requiring every able-bodied man up to the age of sixty to serve in the militia.[1] Thus emerged the enduring image of the Canadian peasant as a skilled and eager combatant, one that Louise Dechêne has challenged while stressing the military importance of the Native *domiciliés* in the St. Lawrence Valley missions. These missions furnished as many as 500 warriors between 1687 and 1740.[2] Furthermore, the maintenance of a strong presence in the interior of the continent depended upon alliances with the First Nations, which in turn relied upon a well-regulated fur trade.

With approximately 500 men trading in the *pays d'en haut* by 1680, the competition for furs had intensified to the point that there were few profits for any of the traders or the merchants who financed them. As a result, the monopoly export company declared in 1681 that it would deal only with established traders, and the government authorized only those

who had been issued special permits known as *congés* to travel into the interior. The legitimate voyageurs thus came to be distinguished from the outlaw *coureurs de bois*. The trade was policed by military posts at strategic portages, and by the 1690s most of the independent voyageurs had become employees of the approximately twenty Montreal outfitters who had sufficient capital to maintain large stocks of trade goods and extend credit as the fur trade expanded westward.[3]

Their profits were threatened, however, by competition from the London-based Hudson's Bay Company, established in 1670, and by the diversion of furs by the Iroquois to New York, which was now also in English hands. In response, the French invaded the Iroquois country in 1684 and 1687, and Pierre Lemoyne d'Iberville took control of the English posts on Hudson's Bay between 1686 and 1690, and again between 1697 and 1713.[4] The Iroquois retaliated in 1689 when 1,500 warriors, with the aid of the English, attacked Lachine, destroying fifty-six farms and capturing or killing approximately 200 Canadians. Close to 600 more colonists would suffer the same fate prior to 1697.[5] During the 1690s, as well, the French ensured that the Abenakis remained firm allies by having professional soldiers and Canadian volunteers join them on winter raids against the northern frontier settlements of the British colonies. They spread terror by putting the settlements to fire, killing many of the inhabitants, and taking others captive to be marched north where they were tortured to death, ransomed, or adopted.[6]

Preventing peace from developing between the Iroquois and the French-allied nations had ensured that furs would not be diverted to the English, but this was no longer a major concern after the French established a post at Detroit in 1700, especially because the supply of

Canadians [sic] on Snowshoes Going to War on Snow, 1722. This somewhat fanciful illustration of a Canadian militiaman from Bacqueville de La Potherie's *Histoire de L'Amérique septentrionale* is the first to show the standard Canadian winter costume of a capot (blue being the favourite colour) tied at the waste with a belt. The militiaman is also wearing what appears to be a *tapabord*, a hat with a visor and wide flaps that could be lowered over the ears. These hats gradually gave way in popularity to the woollen toque. Militiamen not only wore their own clothes, they were also expected to use their own hunting rifles, which were of a lighter calibre than those carried by regular soldiers. Rather than being provided with tents, they had to sleep in the open at night. Note the tomahawk and the beads that are presumably meant to be wampum, the currency of the Amerindians. The French artist clearly had difficulty depicting two other Amerindian articles, moccasins and snowshoes. *Library and Archives Canada*

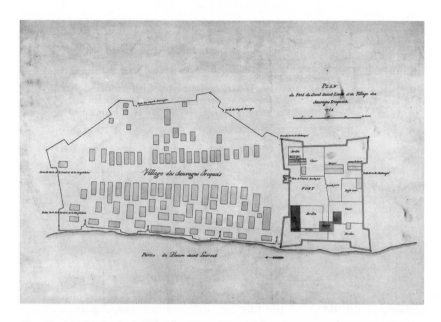

Plan of Fort Sault Saint-Louis and of the Village of the Iroquois Indians, 1754. The Christian Iroquois settlement, originally located on the Jesuit seigneurie of La Prairie opposite the island of Montreal, was moved three times to escape moral contamination (particularly the sale of alcohol) by French settlers before being established on the south shore above the rapids at Sault Saint-Louis or Kahnawaké in 1716. This illustration reveals that the settlement conformed to the traditional Iroquois pattern of village longhouses rather than the individual farmsteads of the French. The Natives were able to adhere to their own laws and customs as well as carry on a smuggling trade with New York because the French found them useful for military purposes, as the fortifications reveal, and they feared that they would defect to the Iroquois Confederacy or ally with the British. *Library and Archives Canada*

furs was four times the demand on the European market by that time.[7] Furthermore, in 1701 the exhausted Iroquois finally signed a peace treaty with the French and were joined by over a thousand representatives from thirty-eight Native nations that met in Montreal. What was known as the Great Peace would remain in effect throughout much of the remaining years of the French regime.[8]

Because of Louis XIV's designs on the Spanish possessions in North America, d'Iberville established the French colony of Louisiana at the mouth of the Mississippi River in 1699. The assumption was that it would provide ready access to the Spanish silver mines in New Mexico.[9] According to historian W.J. Eccles, French imperial policy henceforth dictated that New France would serve essentially as a military fortress. In fact, the military establishment was second only to the fur trade as the colony's economic mainstay, consuming five times as much government money as did its civil counterpart.[10] The need for a large standing army was, nevertheless, avoided by subsidizing strategic fur trade posts in the interior in order to maintain the extensive Native alliance.

Those allies proved to be indispensable when war with England broke out again in 1701 after the French king had placed his grandson on the Spanish throne, thereby threatening to upset the balance of power in Europe. When the Treaty of Utrecht was signed in 1713, French defeats in Europe forced them to relinquish Acadia (aside from Isle Royale and Isle Saint-Jean, today's Cape Breton Island and Prince Edward Island, respectively), Newfoundland, and their claim to Hudson's Bay territory. The treaty also acknowledged British suzerainty over the Iroquois, thereby opening trade in the *pays d'en haut* to the British.

Although English pincers were beginning to close around Canada, the colony flourished during the following thirty years. This was a period of peace during which France reinforced its position in North America, building the fortress of Louisbourg at the southern tip of Ile Royale to protect the fishery and the entry to the Gulf of St. Lawrence and financing the construction of thick earth and stone walls around the towns of Quebec and Montreal. The French also completed the chain of western forts that would hem in the English and cut off much trade to Hudson's Bay.

The renewal of the fur trade in 1715, after the surplus had rotted in French warehouses, paid for the garrisoning of western posts and emoluments of the officer corps who could either sublet their trading privileges to a merchant or become silent partners in trade.[11] But the New York fur traders enjoyed the advantage of English strouds (coarse woollen cloth), which was the most important manufactured product in the western fur trade, and there was a tenfold increase in the trade to Albany after 1720 when New York banned the smuggling of furs from Montreal. The founding of the English post at Oswego, south of Fort Frontenac, in 1727 threatened to detach France's Native allies, thereby forcing the French to expand into new areas and subsidize the trade in old ones.[12] The War of the Austrian Succession, which broke out in 1740, failed to resolve this western conflict, for the treaty signed in 1748 restored the status quo ante in North America. Thus continued the

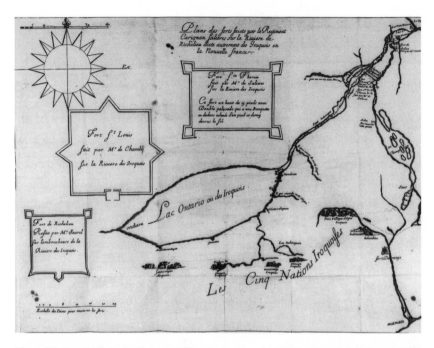

Plans of the Forts Made by the Carignan Salières Regiment on the Richilieu River, L.-P. Vallerand, 1666. The Carignan-Salières Regiment, consisting of twenty companies of fifty men each in addition to their superior officers, was sent to Canada in 1665 to quell the Iroquois. The Mohawks simply fled both times that the soldiers invaded their territory, but their crops were destroyed. The regiment also constructed the three forts shown here near the mouth of the Richelieu River, which was the traditional invasion route used by the Mohawks. When the regiment returned to France in 1668, 400 men remained behind, some of them settling in the new seigneuries on the lower Richelieu, thereby strengthening the colony's defences. This map also shows the Dutch settlements at and above Fort Orange, which would become known as Albany when taken over by the English. *Library and Archives Canada*

period of what Dechêne refers to as the sixteen years war, which ended with the Conquest in 1760.[13]

The population of Britain's Thirteen Colonies may have greatly outnumbered that of Canada, but the French believed they could hold onto their vast territory because of their military superiority after years of raids on the New England frontier, and because of their large network of Native allies. Furthermore, while the French maintained a small professional colonial force—the *troupes de la marine*—the English colonies had no common army, and they lacked a sense of joint purpose because the more southerly ones were not threatened by the French. The French did enjoy the advantage in the short run, for in 1754 they defeated

Fort Chambly, near Montreal, QC, 1863, William Notman. This photograph reflects the Picturesque tradition's fascination with ruined abbeys, castles, and riverside scenery. The introduction to volume 1 of Notman's *Photographic Selections,* where this photograph first appeared, refers to the fort as "the only relic of its kind in North America." The shot was taken twelve years after Fort Chambly (identified as Fort St. Louis in the previous illustration) had ceased to serve as a garrison. Located below the Richelieu rapids, its purpose was to block access to the navigable part of the river, but it was captured by the British in 1760 and the Americans in 1775, and again in 1812. It was restored as a historic site in 1921. *McCord Museum*

George Washington in the Ohio Valley, considered to be strategically crucial because it linked the colonies of Canada and Louisiana. And a year later, the French humiliated General Edward Braddock as he marched into the same valley with a much larger force. The Thirteen Colonies also did little for their own defence against renewed border raids, but the struggle became one for supremacy of the Western world when England officially declared war on France in 1756.

By the time of the Seven Years' War, France had four times Britain's population and ten times its army, but the navy was the crucial factor in a conflict involving overseas colonies, and that of France was less than half the size of Britain's. France also had the disadvantage of a weak European ally in Austria, while England was aligned with the more powerful Prussia and could therefore concentrate its efforts against the French in North America. While the French could spare only 7,000 regular troops for the colony, supplemented by 8,000 Canadian militiamen, Prime Minister William Pitt sent 20,000 regular troops to reinforce the 22,000 colonial troops and militia already in North America.[14] The French nevertheless managed to hold the upper hand until 1758 when a blockade by the

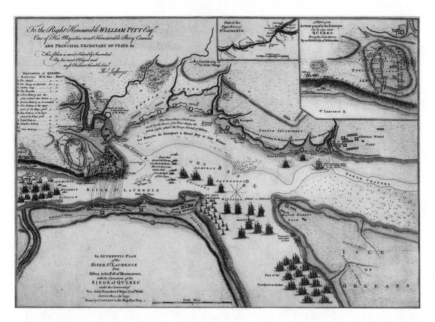

An Authentic Plan of the River St. Laurence from Sillery to the Fall of Montmorenci, with the Operations of the Siege of Quebec under the Command of Vice-Adm.'l Saunders & Major Gen.'l Wolfe, down to the 5 Sep,'r 1759. This map provides a detailed description of the military engagement that effectively ended French rule in much of North America. It depicts the bombardment of Quebec from the opposite shore, the feint made against the French encampment at Beauport while the British troops slipped upriver to Sillery, and the positions taken on the Plains of Abraham before the fatal battle. *Library and Archives Canada*

British navy, coupled with the growing shortage of food, began to take its toll.[15] As the French forces stopped their border raids to prepare for a larger scale of warfare under the command of General Louis-Joseph de Montcalm, Native allies—having been alienated by the haughty Montcalm and decimated by smallpox—concluded a separate peace with Great Britain. With the fall of Louisbourg in 1758, Canada was left vulnerable from the east as well as the west.

The following year, the English launched a three-pronged attack from the west on Fort Niagara (the last post remaining under French control), from the south via Lake Champlain on Montreal, and from the east on Quebec, known as the "Gibraltar of North America." Ignoring the conventions of eighteenth-century warfare, General James Wolfe's force of 40,000 men terrorized the countryside around Quebec, burning ships, destroying crops, and slaughtering livestock. But Montcalm refused to be drawn out of the fortress. Finally, on 13 September, facing the necessity of withdrawal before the river froze for the winter, Wolfe took the risk of sending 4,500 of his elite troops up the cliffs at Anse-au-Foulon. After they mustered on the field of farmer Abraham Martin, Montcalm sent his force of 4,000, which included a substantial number of poorly trained militia, to meet Wolfe instead of waiting for the French companies located to the rear of the British army at Cap Rouge. His second fatal mistake was to abandon the high ground overlooking the British lines. When the two sides were within close range, the French fired first, but they were shattered by the second volley of the British who had loaded their muskets with two balls each. While the battle was over within minutes, both generals lost their lives, Wolfe dying immediately on the battlefield and Montcalm expiring the next morning. Wolfe's body was shipped back to England for a hero's burial in Greenwich, but Montcalm's remained in the Ursulines' chapel until it was finally transferred in 2001 to the city's small Hôpital Générale cemetery where over a thousand members of his army and a number of Wolfe's men lay buried in unmarked graves.

The British control of Quebec was not challenged that fall even though two of the three French corps had not engaged in the battle, and many from the defeated third corps had joined the first two. Furthermore, most of the British soldiers contracted scurvy because it was still not understood that fermentation killed the vitamin C in spruce beer. With only 2,600 men of the original 7,300 fit for duty by April 1760, General James Murray decided to risk an open battle rather than attempt to guard Quebec against the advancing French.[16] This time the 2,264 Canadian militiamen were properly deployed, and the French were victorious. But it was the British who sent ships up the St. Lawrence when the ice broke up, and the Canadian militia laid down their arms when they were assured that they would not suffer reprisals for the bloody massacres they and their Native allies had inflicted upon the English colonial frontier.[17] England and Prussia maintained the upper hand throughout the remainder of the war, and, when the Treaty of Paris was signed in 1763, France placed its commercial interests first by choosing the Island of Guadeloupe over Canada. Surrendered were all its North American claims except for the two small islands of St. Pierre and Miquelon and fishing rights off the south coast of Newfoundland.

The Death of General Wolfe, Benjamin West, 1771. In Benjamin West's dramatic painting, Wolfe dies in imitation of Christ taken down from the cross (represented here by the British flag, which also suggests a shroud), making him a martyr in a cause that was both British and Christian. With his eyes rolled upward in the traditional expression of beatific ecstasy, Wolfe is being informed that a British officer is racing towards the group with the French colours. Despite the neo-classical composition, West portrayed the characters in contemporary dress rather than the togas that were then generally assumed to symbolize the universal significance of a historical event. Otherwise, the painting is historically inaccurate, for only four or five British soldiers were present at Wolfe's death, and only one of these men was included in the painting. As for the Native warrior poised in poetic contemplation, the suggestion of a First Nations alliance with the British is another historical inaccuracy because all of the Native participants were on the side of the French during this battle. But West was an American, and both the warrior and the American Ranger in buckskin who stands above him symbolize New World virtues and strength that might regenerate a decadent and enervated Europe. The painting was such a tour de force that the King commissioned a duplicate, and the sale of engraved copies made both the engraver and the publisher wealthy men. *Library and Archives Canada*

The war also determined the fate of France's First Nations allies, who had fought as equal partners rather than as subordinates.[18] The Hurons living in the vicinity of Quebec were allowed to remain on their lands and to hunt on the north shore from the Saguenay to the St. Maurice Rivers.[19] But the Abenakis on the south shore of the St. Lawrence were punished for joining the raiding parties against the New England settlements that had originally displaced them, and for fighting at the side of the French in the Ohio Valley and at Quebec. Several weeks after

Wolfe's victory, a company of American frontier rangers led by Major Robert Rogers made a surprise attack on the village of Odanak, near the mouth of the St. Francis, burning the church and all the houses to the ground. Rogers claimed to have killed 200 Abenakis, though French sources state that only thirty died, and Odanak subsequently recovered to become the main western Abenaki settlement, which it remains today.[20]

In addition to allowing American settlement to spread northward into the buffer zone occupied as hunting grounds by the western Abenakis and their allies, the Conquest threatened the notion of Native sovereignty. Historian Cornelius Jaenan argues that the French distinguished between nationhood understood locally and nationhood understood internationally. In other words, even though local Native bands could conclude agreements, enter into alliances, and wage wars, the French argued that they had not organized sovereign governments possessing coercive powers to maintain order in their communities by enacting and enforcing laws. Because the British assumption of the same international sovereignty over the First Nations was obviously of a greater threat to the First Nations, it, was contested in 1763 when Pontiac's Rebellion resulted in the destruction or occupation of all the posts west of Niagara except for Detroit. As a result, several months later, the Proclamation of 1763 reserved the western territory for its Native occupants, declaring that it could only be alienated with their permission.[21] The Natives were further protected by the Quebec Act of 1774, which extended the boundaries of the colony now known as Quebec into the Ohio Valley, thereby preventing the incursion of English-speaking colonists. Unfortunately for the First Nations, however, the territory became part of the United States as a result of the American War of Independence.

As for the Canadian colonists, they had suffered greatly from hunger and disease,[22] but the British victory at least brought relief from the sacrifices they had been forced to make during the preceding sixteen years of warfare, and in that era loyalty was still to the Crown rather than to the nation.[23] The king of England was certainly not the divinely ordained monarch the Catholic Church had taught the people to obey, but their bishop was now counselling them to accept rule by the Protestant George III. The Canadians were free to sail to France under

A View of the Cathedral, Jesuits College, and Recollect Friars Church, Taken from the Gate of the Governors House, Richard Short, 1761. One third of the houses in Quebec City were damaged by bombardment, and many had to be pulled down, though some of those shown here on Sainte-Anne Street still stand today. This engraving, based on the drawing by Richard Short in 1759, is one of several to focus on the colonial capital's church buildings, thereby catering to the anti-Catholic sentiment of the British during that era. The remains of the cathedral in the far right background evoke the ruins of antiquity that appealed strongly to middle-class travellers, as well as symbolizing the transition from an earlier era. *Library and Archives Canada*

the terms of capitulation, made generous by British vulnerability during the winter of 1759–60, but they were encouraged to remain by promises that they would retain their properties and enjoy the free exercise of their religion, "insofar as the laws of Great Britain would permit."

Unhappily for the Catholic clergy, British laws did not allow for state enforcement of Catholic tithes, and the three male religious orders were not allowed to recruit new members. The eight seigneuries that had made the Jesuits the largest landowners in the colony passed into the government's hands when the last member of the order died in 1800.[24] Of more immediate concern, Bishop Pontbriand died in 1760, leaving a vacuum of religious authority and no provision for the ordination of priests. Finally, in 1766, the British agreed to the consecration of Jean-Olivier Briand, although his title was not to be bishop but

A View of the Inside of the Recollect Friars Church, Richard Short, 1761. Aside from depicting the damage to Quebec's Récollet chapel caused by the British bombardment in 1759, this engraving provides a detailed view of an early eighteenth-century church interior. According to R.H. Hubbard (*The Development of Canadian Art*, 19), the chapel's slender spire, steep gable, baroque façade, scroll pediment, oval window, and broad stair (see previous illustration), "were all features used by French provincial architects who were unfettered by the classicism of Paris." When the new Anglican bishop arrived in 1793, he was horrified to find his flock holding services in a building still "loaded with all the pageantry and meretricious ornament of Popish superstition . . . crucifixes, images, pictures of saints, altars, tapers and burning lamps." The Church of England's cathedral, consecrated in 1804, still stands on the same spot. *Library and Archives Canada*

"superintendent of the Romish Church." Briand had been selected by the governor because he agreed to support the British authority in return for the guaranteed survival of his Church.

Because the British government expected a large influx into Quebec from the Thirteen Colonies once the war had ended in Europe, it had less reason to be conciliatory after the signing of the peace treaty. The Proclamation of 1763 therefore promised an elected legislative assembly even though Catholics would not be allowed by the oath of office to participate because it included a phrase recognizing the British sovereign as head of the Church. Magistrates and jurors would, for the same reason, have to be chosen from among the English-speaking merchants and retired officers, at least until the anticipated American influx materialized. In addition, the laws of England were to be introduced to the colony. But James Murray, who had been the military commander of Quebec City, was named civil governor of the colony, and he harboured an aristocratic antipathy towards the merchant class. He, therefore, refused to have a legislative assembly elected and resisted the application of English laws until merchant opposition led to his recall in 1766.

The new governor, Sir Guy Carleton, was also a military officer, and he subsequently became as sympathetic to the Canadians as Murray had been. In fact, unlike Murray, he concluded that Quebec would always be French, and so did not attempt to implement a policy of gradual assimilation. Carleton also hoped that a conciliatory approach would encourage the Canadians to help the British intimidate the restive colonies to the south, colonies that no longer needed British protection against their French enemy. His Quebec Act of 1774 made official the lenient policies that Murray and he had pursued. Catholicism was no longer to be an obstacle to holding office in the colony, even though it remained so in Britain. French civil law, including the provision for Catholic Church tithes, was reinstated. English criminal law, however, was retained on the grounds that it was more just and humane. Not only did it feature the jury system and public prosecutions, but judges could not use an executioner to apply torture in order to extract a confession in capital cases nor inflict extreme punishments such as the methodical breaking of bones on the wheel.[25] Finally, the Quebec Act declared that there would be no elected legislative assembly. The reasons were that Carleton had an exaggerated view of the conservative, monarchical sympathies of the Canadians, and he was influenced by the unruly behaviour of the colonial Assemblies to the south. In addition, London was not yet prepared to grant political power to a newly conquered people.

The English-speaking merchants of Quebec were furious with the Quebec Act because they had been deprived of English mercantile law and representative government. The colonies to the south were equally upset, for they resented the official recognition of the Catholic Church and the extension of Quebec's boundaries into the Ohio-Mississippi hinterland. As a result, the Quebec Act became one of the Intolerable Acts that led to the American War of Independence. Not surprisingly, then, when the Thirteen Colonies appealed to Quebec to join their revolt in 1775, they were rebuffed. But the habitants also resented the restoration of the tithe, and they refused to join the newly reinstated militia despite the pleas of their seigneurs and priests. They even supplied provisions to the American invaders who occupied Montreal and attacked Quebec in 1775, but only until the rebels' currency ran out. The basic attitude of the habitants was that they were now a conquered people, though obviously not a submissive one, and British wars did not concern them.

There would be no more fighting in Quebec after the withdrawal of the Americans from Montreal in the spring of 1776. Britain's loss of the Thirteen Colonies had been predicted by French negotiators when they surrendered Canada in 1763, and, in a sense, represented the last stage of the clash of European imperialisms in North America. The French Canadians may have stayed out of the conflict, but they were still affected by its outcome. During and after the hostilities, several thousand loyalists fled up Lake Champlain to that lake's Missisquoi Bay near the 45th parallel that marks the Canadian-American border, and further north to Fort William Henry (Sorel) at the mouth of the Richelieu River. After the war ended in 1783, however, they were directed to the upper St. Lawrence, beyond the seigneurial zone. Because these loyalists insisted on British institutions, the Constitutional Act of 1791 provided them with their own colony of Upper Canada that would be under English civil law. Upper and Lower Canada would henceforth each have an elected legislative assembly, but bills would have to be ratified by an appointed legislative council. And, even though under the British constitution money bills had to pass the lower house, the governor and his executive council would retain exclusive control of essential sources of revenue, particularly that from Crown lands, thus setting the stage for constitutional and political conflict.

In his monumental history of New France, Francis Parkman wrote that "a happier calamity never befell a people than the conquest of Canada by the British arms."[26] Parkman was referring to the fact that the British regime ushered in material growth and what he called "popular liberties." As a nineteenth-century New Englander, his views were shaped by anti-Catholicism and American liberalism, and by the assumption that the French regime was thoroughly feudal in nature, but what Donald Fyson has recently labelled the "jovialist" interpretation of the Conquest persisted in English Canada well into the twentieth century.[27] The priests who wrote most of the early histories of Quebec described the French regime as a golden age, but they also felt that the Conquest was providential because it saved French Canada from the impact of the French Revolution. Beginning in the 1920s, the influential Canon Lionel Groulx described the Conquest in more negative terms, but only with the secular nationalist historians of the post–Second World War era did what Fyson refers to as the "miserablist" interpretation emerge. Historians such as Michel Brunet and Guy Frégault now argued that Canadian society had once featured a dynamic bourgeoisie, one that exercised considerable political influence during the French regime. Forced to flee to France as a result of the Conquest, these merchants left a vacuum that resulted in the economic domination of the French Canadians by the English-speaking minority, and their social and cultural domination by the Catholic Church. The political implication of this social decapitation thesis was that French-speaking Quebecers would only recapture control over their own economy and become a "normal" secular society when their province separated from the rest of Canada.

From an economic perspective, critics of this thesis have argued that Canada lacked a dynamic bourgeoisie during the French regime because trade was largely controlled by companies based in France.[28] They also point out that the Canadian economy relied heavily on military expenditures during the era of imperialist expansion. Whether or not Eccles is right in suggesting that the military absorbed much of the Canadian talent pool, thereby hindering economic development,[29] the Canadian fur traders were certainly accustomed to a highly regulated system. Most of the pre-Conquest elites did not return to France, as assumed by proponents of the decapitation thesis, and French-Canadian merchants were able to take advantage of their close ties with the Natives to dominate the fur trade until the late 1770s. But even before the American War of Independence brought a flood of British fur-trading merchants from Albany to Montreal, British investment in the fur trade was growing more rapidly than that of the Canadians. The more competitive environment ultimately led to the marginalization of the French-speaking fur traders with the formation of the North West Company in 1783.[30] As we shall see in the following chapter, these merchants went on to become the economic elite of Montreal when they turned to the new staples of square timber and wheat in the early nineteenth century.

FOUR

POLITICAL CONFLICT AND REBELLION

The first half of the nineteenth century witnessed the rise of bourgeois democracy in all the British North American colonies, culminating in the granting of responsible government and the establishment of the foundations of the powerful modern state. But this was far from being a straightforward process, particularly in Lower Canada where it was complicated by conflicting national and class interests, resulting in political deadlock and rebellion before the way was cleared for fundamental constitutional and social reforms during the pivotal decade of the 1840s.

The North American colonies offered three basic benefits during the early nineteenth century as far as the British government was concerned. First, they contributed to British military supremacy by serving as a bulwark against American expansionism. Second, they benefited British trade by supplying timber and other raw materials, as well as serving as a market for manufactured goods. And, third, they offered an outlet within the Empire for Britain's surplus population after the end of the Napoleonic Wars. Up to the 1820s the British government assumed that most of the vital concerns of the colonies should be administered by a centralized governing system of British-born officials and merchants, but the demands for reform made the Colonial Office sensitive to the need for a more effective political role for the colonists. Given, however, that the British North American colonies relied on British capital for development, on British preferential tariffs for an external market, and on British taxes for defence and major public works, the question was how the mother country's interests should be represented in proportion to the amount of colonial expenditures that its investors and taxpayers provided. The answer from the Colonial Office was that each colony's executive council would have to remain responsible to the British government, and its legislative council would continue to be selected from the local socio-economic elite in order to ensure that colonial needs and desires would not eclipse those of the Empire. Consequently, those colonists who were best disposed to Britain were assumed to be the natural leaders, and the governors became reliant on the tight-knit group pejoratively known as the Family Compact in Upper Canada and the Chateau Clique in Lower Canada.

The crux of the political problem in Lower Canada was that the common interests of this elite and of the mother country tended to be in basic conflict with the needs and desires of much of the local population. The experience gained by Montreal merchants such as Simon McTavish, William McGillvray, and Joseph Frobisher in conducting the fur trade over great distances led to their exploitation of the new trade staples of wheat and square timber, beginning in the 1790s with the growth of British demand caused by the Napoleonic Wars. The value of timber exports from the port of Quebec, fueled by the French blockade of Baltic suppliers to Britain, jumped from £300,000 in 1790 to more than £1,200,000 in 1810.[1] The square timber industry provided jobs for Lower Canadians in the woods and on the docks and shipyards, as well as markets for farm produce, but the grain trade was a less straightforward matter. While timber could simply be floated down the Ottawa and St. Lawrence Rivers in rafts, the shipping of wheat and flour from the expanding Upper Canadian and American frontiers via Montreal relied on investment in canals that would sustain the competitive position of the Great Lakes– St. Lawrence system against that of the Hudson–Mohawk. This was particularly the case after the Erie Canal was completed in 1825. The English-speaking merchants of Montreal pushed for such investments, but canals west of Montreal would do nothing for most Lower Canadian producers who would have preferred to see public funds directed towards local improvements such as roads.

In fact, despite the growing British demand, very little wheat was exported from Lower Canada itself after the turn of the century. The reasons have long been the subject of vociferous debate. According to Fernand Ouellet, backward farming techniques, soil exhaustion, and the

Indian of Lorette and Habitant with Sleigh, attributed to George [sic] (1797–1847), ca. 1837. The Huron and the habitant, the former with a dead moose on a toboggan and the latter with a horse-drawn sled, appear to be engaged in some sort of barter. The habitant wears the traditional capot with hood, a toque on his head, and a ceinture fléchée around his waist, while the Native wears a blanket and hat that were very likely of European manufacture. Both wear moccasins. A visitor to the Huron community of Lorette in 1843 reported that the Natives produced "articles of leather worked with porcupine quills, and the hair of moose deer, richly coloured," as well as "birch and basket work of fanciful form and design." *Library and Archives Canada*

overcrowding of a population that doubled every twenty-six or twenty-seven years prevented the habitants from being able to produce a surplus of their traditional staple crop to meet the market demand.[2] The implication of Ouellet's thesis is that the habitants' deteriorating economic situation largely explains their receptivity to the anti-British rhetoric of nationalist politicians. In reaction, other Quebec historians have denied that there was an agricultural crisis in the early nineteenth century. They argue that farms were not subdivided as the population grew despite the civil law's provision for equal distribution of the inheritance among all offspring. And they claim that the decline in wheat exports reflected a rational decision in the face of fluctuating prices in England. Lower-Canadian farmers turned, instead, to the increased demand by the province's timber shanties for hay, oats, peas, and potatoes. The historical geographer Serge Courville also suggests that the growing cities and rapidly proliferating villages represented a significant market. There were approximately fifty villages in the seigneurial lowlands in 1815, and 200 in 1831.[3] While none

[Habitants], Cornelius Krieghoff, 1852. This domestic scene illustrates the importance of rural women's productive role during the pre-industrial era. By 1835 most families had one or two spinning wheels, but Krieghoff tended to exaggerate the habitants' resistance to change. By the time he produced this painting there had been a dramatic drop in domestic textile production as imported cloth had become an important part of the average person's wardrobe. Furthermore, the large sheet metal stove shown here had been largely replaced by the more efficient cast iron variety in the later eighteenth century. The homemade items visible in the painting include homespun clothing, straw hats, a rug, and several chairs. The latter would have been made by the husband/ father, though the painting indicates that his realm was the outdoors. *Library and Archives Canada*

of the internal trade can be directly quantified, and there are no census records to measure production prior to 1831, Ouellet's critics turned to post-mortem inventories and deeds of gift (drafted for the support of parents after they transferred the homestead to one of their offspring) to argue that rural living standards and productive capacities generally improved prior to 1835.[4]

The fact remains, however, that cities and towns were still small in this pre-industrial era, many villagers grew their own vegetables and raised a few livestock, and the shanty market was limited in comparison to the number of farms in the province. As a result, farms generally

Quebec. Lower Canada. View of the Market Place and Catholic Church Taken from the Barracks, Fabricque Street, Robert Auchmuty Sproule, 1830. Farmers sold their surplus produce at markets such as this one in the shadow of Quebec City's Catholic cathedral. Butchers used the outward-facing stalls of Market Hall, a corner of which is shown on the left. Though market was held every day, Saturday was busiest. The American journalist Nathaniel Parker Willis described the scene as follows in 1842: "The crowd of carters, with their wives and families, bringing in the productions of the surrounding country, their bawlings and vociferations in bad French and broken English, form a scene of noise and confusion, amid which appear a few Indian squaws, and gentlemen of the city and garrison going round to make purchases. Every kind of provision is abundant and cheap, except fish, which is less plentiful than might be expected from the situation." *Library and Archives Canada*

remained oriented towards family sustenance. This was true as well for the rest of British North America and the northeastern United States, but population pressure in Lower Canada meant that by 1831 one in four households was landless even in the most recently settled seigneuries. Furthermore, agricultural conditions took a significant turn for the worse after rust disease and insect infestation brought disastrous wheat crop failures during the mid-1830s.[5]

If the link between the decline of the wheat economy and the rise of nationalism in Lower Canada remains a matter of conjecture, a less contested factor is the resentment caused by Britain's policy of directing its excess population towards the North American colonies. Most of the 800,000 immigrants who disembarked from the overcrowded

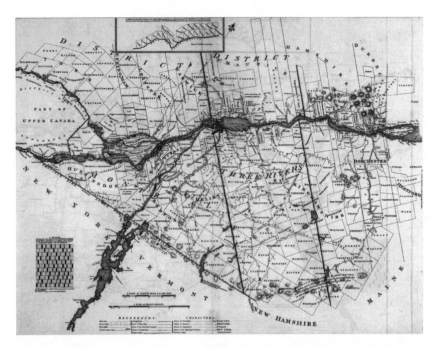

A New Topographical Map of the Province of Lower Canada, William Vondenvelden and Louis Charland, 1803. This western portion shown here of the map drafted by Vondenvelden and Charland includes the seigneuries adjacent to the St. Lawrence River and its two main southern tributaries, the Richelieu and the Chaudière, as well as the townships surveyed after 1792. Township land was granted in British freehold tenure, and most of the land near the Vermont border was claimed by post-Loyalist settlers. Lots were laid out in a grid pattern, as shown in the inset of the lower left corner, which also demonstrates how crown and clergy reserves were scattered throughout each township, thereby hindering settlement. The map also reveals how the boundaries of the judicial districts of Montreal, Trois-Rivières, and Quebec were simply extended into the freehold zones, cutting through individual townships. *Library and Archives Canada*

timber vessels at the port of Quebec between 1830 and 1855 moved on to Upper Canada and the United States, but they brought a series of epidemics beginning with the worst one in 1832. That year there were 2,723 cholera-related deaths in Quebec City, 2,547 in Montreal, and an unknown number in the rural parishes.[6] Furthermore, as many as 50,000 of these immigrants remained in Lower Canada, so that by mid-century one-quarter of the colony's population was English speaking. The Irish Catholics, in particular, became an important part of the urban workforce, lifting the English-speaking population to a slight majority in Montreal and a near majority in Quebec City. They also settled rural parishes such as Saint Columban in the lower Laurentians, and fought the French Canadians for control over the Ottawa Valley logging camps in what became known as the Shiners' War.[7]

Other British families joined the American settlers in the region north of the Vermont border. This hilly Appalachian plateau had been surveyed into townships after an instruction from London in 1791 stipulated that Crown land in Lower Canada would, henceforth, be granted in freehold tenure. The largely English-speaking population of what became known as the Eastern Townships would reach 37,000 by 1831.[8] The only other significant area of English-Protestant settlement was the Gaspé Peninsula where Loyalists had joined Acadian exiles to make up a population of approximately 5,000 settlers at the turn of the nineteenth century.[9] Small as the colony's rural English-speaking population was, the French Canadians feared that future immigration would leave no land for their own future generations, and that they would eventually be outnumbered and assimilated.

The spokesmen for French-Canadian grievances became the liberal professionals (doctors, lawyers, notaries) who were products of the Catholic seminaries and who found their professions overcrowded and their political ambitions frustrated by the dominance in government of the British office-holding elite and their merchant allies. French Canadians received no more than 20 to 25 percent of the public salaries, only about one-sixth of the pensions, and less than 1 percent of the contracts, though the fact that American-origin settlers were also denied their fare share of the patronage suggests that it was a colonialist issue more than an ethnic one.[10] The French-speaking liberal professionals therefore demanded more powers for the elected legislative assembly, which they dominated through their close ties with the habitants at the parish level. But British policy had become less conciliatory after the outbreak of the Napoleonic Wars when French agents were active in the colony. The British government could count on the support of the Catholic hierarchy, for the bishop of Quebec—mindful of the revolutionary attacks on the Church in France—ordained public thanksgiving when Nelson's ships defeated the French fleet in 1798. While distrust for modern France intensified with the influx of forty-three refugee French priests at a time when the number of clerics in Lower Canada was in decline,[11] the American and French Revolutions

His Excellency Sir James Henry Craig, Gerritt Schipper, ca. 1810–11. In his personal memoir, Pierre-Joseph Aubert de Gaspé described Governor Craig as "short and fat," with a "piercing, falcon-like glance [that] seemed to penetrate the innermost thoughts of those to whom he spoke in his harsh voice." After dissolving the legislature in 1810, the authoritarian Craig began his "reign of terror" by seizing the press of *Le Canadien,* which was the French-Canadian party's mouthpiece, and imprisoning its editors as well as some of its distributors. Craig's proposals to stiffen property qualifications for MLAs, create ridings in the Eastern Townships, and unite the two Canadas were rejected by London, which adopted a more conciliatory policy towards the French-Canadian majority on the eve of war with the United States. *Library and Archives Canada*

did contribute to the politicization of the masses. As agent of the American Continental Congress, Fleury Mesplet founded *La Gazette littéraire* to disseminate the radical ideas of Voltaire. Even though most of the population could not read, and Mesplet and his editor were soon sentenced to three years in the Quebec City dungeon, petitions circulated for the first time among the habitants who refused to join the British army in attacking the American patriots. They openly resisted the Militia Act in 1794, as well as the Road Act two years later when it imposed new *corvées.*

The legislative assembly provided the tool with which French Canadians could express this new political awareness. In 1808 Governor James Craig clashed with this body when it barred two members of the English faction from sitting, one on the grounds that he was Jewish and the other on the grounds that he was a judge. The chief principle in question, however, was that the governor's advisers should be drawn from the legislative assembly. Craig eventually dissolved the assembly, seized the printing press of its mouthpiece, *Le Canadien,* and jailed its three owners without trial. He then asked London to revoke the constitution of 1791 by eliminating the elected legislative assembly. It was also in this context that the government had stepped up its policy of anglicization in 1801 by creating the Royal Institution for the Advancement of Learning, under the authority of the Church of England, to manage the colony's school system. This institution was effectively boycotted by the French Canadians, however, with the result that illiteracy rates failed to change for many years.

Meanwhile, the growing threat of war with the United States meant that London grew more sensitive to French-Canadian grievances. Consequently, after Craig was recalled in 1811, he was followed by the conciliatory George Prévost. *Le Canadien* responded in kind by declaring its opposition to Napoleon. In 1813 the first French-Canadian regiment of regular soldiers, the Voltigeurs commanded by Lieutenant-Colonel Charles-Michel de Salaberry, repelled the American invasion at the Battle of Châteauguay. Consequently, some of the *Parti canadien* leaders were appointed to the executive and legislative councils. But London remained unwilling to increase the assembly's power, and the political situation deteriorated to the point that in 1822 a bill was introduced in Westminster to unite Upper and Lower Canada and to abolish French as an official language. The bill was dropped due to French-Canadian protests and Upper-Canadian opposition, but the central issue of dispute remained the civil list, which consisted of the salary scale for judges and other public officials. London was willing to accede to the assembly's demand that it control all the public revenue, but only in return for a "permanent" civil list, namely, one for the life of the sovereign. The reformers, who had adopted the more radical and more inclusive name of *Parti patriote* in 1826, continued to insist on an annual civil list, which was a major part of the colony's expenditures, as the only means of exercising some control over the executive and judicial powers.[12]

In 1831, however, a split developed in the ranks of the *Parti patriote* when John Neilson, the leading member from Quebec City, began to criticize the increasingly radical trajectory pursued under the leadership of the mercurial Montreal notary Louis-Joseph Papineau. Papineau's hand was strengthened by two events. First, there was the above-mentioned cholera epidemic spread by the thousands of Irish immigrants who landed at Quebec in 1832. Second, in 1834 the Colonial Office decided to respond to the rejection of its civil list offer by selling over 200,000 hectares of Crown land in the Eastern Townships to the newly

Louis-Joseph Papineau (1786–1871), Politician, attributed to T.C. Doane, ca. 1852. This daguerreotype of Papineau in his midsixties was taken after the *Patriote* leader had returned from self-imposed exile in Paris and had retired to his seigneurie of Petite-Nation on the Ottawa River. *Library and Archives Canada*

established British American Land Company of London. As a result, the Crown revenues controlled by the executive council were given a major boost, thereby weakening the power of the assembly. The company's purpose was also to inject British capital and settlers into the Eastern Townships, and thereby ensure the largely American-settled region's loyalty while weakening French-Canadian control of the assembly.

The voters of the Eastern Townships had initially supported the *Parti patriote* after finally being given seats in the legislative assembly in 1829.[13] They were not only expressing their gratitude for the road subsidies that were beginning to end their economic isolation but also their bitterness towards the monopolization of patronage positions by a small English-born elite. In addition, there was considerable resentment among the farmers in the region against the acquisition of most of the undeveloped land by the British American Land Company. But these farmers also supported the establishment of an effective land registry system, which would make land purchases and mortgages more secure,[14] a system that Papineau opposed on the grounds that it would promote the commodification of land and threaten the survival of the distinctively French-Canadian seigneurial system. With Tory newspaper editors stirring up fears about the rise of French-Canadian nationalism, only two of the deputies from the Eastern Townships voted with the assembly majority in 1834 when it passed the Ninety-Two Resolutions calling for a republican-style government. Thus, an elected legislative council would ensure that all legislative powers would be in the hands of the French-Canadian majority. After *Parti patriote* candidates won seventy-seven of the assembly's eighty-eight seats in the 1834 election, English-speaking militants in Montreal formed the vigilante group known as the British Rifle Corps, which was succeeded by the Doric Club. In return, the paramilitary *Fils de la liberté*, modelled on the American Sons of Liberty, acted as a security force for the *Patriotes*.

The Colonial Office responded to the deteriorating situation by appointing Lord Gosford to investigate and attempt to reach a settlement. As Governor General he handed over much of the public revenue to the assembly's control, and appointed well-known *Patriotes* as judges, thereby weakening Papineau's strength in the assembly to a majority of one. But when it became known that Gosford's instructions did not permit him to institute any constitutional reforms on his own authority, the assembly declared that it would no longer sit until the legislative council became elective. Britain was prevented from making any such widespread reforms by virtue of the fact that they would effectively mean colonial independence, and by opposition from the English-speaking minority, some of whom had organized themselves into constitutional associations demanding union with Upper Canada as well as Gosford's recall.

Gosford's report of 1836 supported more French-Canadian appointments to public office but rejected the assembly's constitutional demands. London then passed Lord Russell's Ten Resolutions, authorizing the governor to take funds that the assembly refused to grant. The *Patriotes* responded, in turn, by organizing mass meetings in the countryside that demanded republican institutions. The *charivari*, a traditional humiliation ritual that had hitherto targeted mismatched newlyweds such as an older wealthy man and a much younger woman, now gained a political character in the more disaffected communities. Threateningly disguised crowds making "rough music" visited the homes of captains of militia and justices of the peace after dark, forcing them into acknowledging the authority of the constitutional assemblies or resigning their commissions.[15] An armed uprising was not premeditated, but became inevitable as events began to mushroom beyond the control of the leaders. The public meetings now threatened rebellion, Montreal's armed clubs clashed in the streets, and in October 1837 the Lake of Two Mountains habitants decided to elect their own justices of the peace and militia officers to replace those dismissed by Gosford. A week later, against Papineau's wishes, a mass meeting at Saint-Charles in the Richelieu Valley called for a convention to replace the legislature, and spoke openly of resorting to arms.

The government decided to take the initiative before the winter freeze-up would make rebel movement easier. Warrants were issued for the arrest of Papineau and several others. Their escape to the Richelieu Valley brought armed resistance despite the bishop's threat that rebels would be excommunicated. Eight hundred *Patriotes* commanded by the Loyalist-descended Dr. Wolfred Nelson beat back the British troops at Saint-Denis on 23 November. Two days later, however, the British victory at Saint-Charles effectively ended the rebellion in the south-shore parishes. The following month resistance was crushed in the Two Mountains area to the north of Montreal when some 2,000 troops attacked the *Patriotes* barricaded inside the church at Saint-Eustache. Fifty-eight of the defenders were killed and the village was looted and burned to the ground, as was nearby Saint-Benoît shortly thereafter.[16]

The rapid quelling of the uprising was largely due to the overwhelming superiority of the British military, but the lack of preparation and commitment on the part of of the *Patriote* leaders was also an important factor. As a seigneur and a supporter of the privileged status of the Catholic Church for nationalist reasons (despite being a deist), Papineau feared the development of a truly popular and anti-feudal movement, such as the more radical leaders attempted to launch in the second wave of rebellion in 1838. Some of these more radical leaders were of Irish or American origin. Indeed, there had been pockets of support for the militant option among the English-speaking settlers of the Eastern Townships where a series of protest meetings were held in 1835 and 1836. But Papineau had damaged the cause by suggesting that Crown land, including that appropriated from the British American Land Company,

Back View of the Church of St. Eustache and Dispersion of the Insurgents, lithograph from a sketch by Lord Charles Beauclerk, 1840. The British officer, Lord Beauclerk, sketched a number of scenes in the Lower Canadian campaign of 1837. In this illustration of the last major battle of the rebellion, the British soldiers, who greatly outnumbered their poorly armed adversaries, are putting the *Patriotes* to flight after using artillery and fire to flush them out of the convent, church, rectory, and manor in the centre of the small village of St. Eustache, northwest of Montreal. Seventy *Patriotes* were killed, but only three British soldiers, and in the days that followed soldiers and volunteers terrorized the county of Deux-Montagnes, looting and burning two villages and torching the houses of rebel leaders in three others. *Library and Archives Canada*

would be converted to seigneurial tenure. As a result, there were only a few skirmishes in the region.

The Proclamation of Independence drafted by Wolfred Nelson's brother, Robert, in 1838 announced the abolition of the seigneurial system, the state expropriation of the clergy reserves and the lands of the British American Land Company, separation of church and state, universal suffrage, the secret ballot, and other reforms that would appeal to the popular majority, but the second stage of the rebellion, launched from Vermont and New York, was doomed to failure.[17] Despite the establishment in the United States of a large number of Hunters' Lodges dedicated to promoting rebellion in the Canadas,[18] the American federal and state governments were loath to antagonize Great Britain. The *Patriotes*' cross-border raids consequently served little purpose other than to bring down the wrath of the well-prepared British military, which put the countryside south of Montreal to the torch. Judicial leniency had been exercised after the first wave of rebellion, as Governor General Lord Durham pardoned all but eight of the leaders. This time, in contrast, twelve *Patriotes* were hanged and fifty-eight were banished to penal colonies in Australia.[19] In addition, Lower Canada's constitution was rescinded and an appointed special council governed for the following two years.

Needless to say, there is fundamental disagreement about the nature of the rebellions, the reasons for their defeat, and the subsequent political consequences. As we have seen, the anti-nationalist Fernand Ouellet argues that they essentially represented a frustrated, irrational reaction to straitened economic circumstances rather than an expression of intense vitality on the part of French-Canadian society. Ouellet's many nationalist critics argue, instead, that French-Canadian nationalism was the product of discrimination suffered by the French-Canadian community, and that the reform movement envisioned an alternative and more progressive socio-economic and political vision for Lower Canada. They also argue that the rebellion was part of a wave of national liberation movements, most of which were successful, during the first half of the nineteenth century. Finally, Allan Greer has stepped outside the debate, to some extent, by arguing that the political protest movement developed into a peasant revolt against the seigneurs and the Catholic Church as well as the colonial government.

Whatever the fundamental cause, the armed uprisings probably failed to become more widespread because of the opposition of the Catholic Church, but also because the most prominent *Patriote* leaders, such as Papineau, had essentially been bluffing the British authorities with their veiled threats of rebellion. Not only were they unprepared from a military perspective but also the colony was not yet sufficiently advanced economically to become independent. As for the consequences, the defeat of the rebellions and the subsequent union with Upper Canada effectively ended the dream of Lower Canada becoming an independent republic characterized by an egalitarian and agrarian society, though a victory would very likely have resulted in union with the United States. The subsequent regime removed all obstacles in the path of what historian Michel Ducharme refers to as modern liberty, with its emphasis on individual rights and private property. As we shall see in the next chapter, colonial self-rule would soon be granted, but a mixed British-style parliament with an appointed legislative council would continue to serve as a check on democracy, and a powerful executive branch would leave most elected deputies without a great deal of influence in government.

FIVE

THE LIBERAL STATE

In Lower Canada, as in the rest of British North America, the state remained limited in scope and effectiveness during the early nineteenth century, concentrating on the larger issues of revenue collection, justice, and war. Responsibility for social regulation was shifted onto leading members of local communities by appointing them to such unpaid offices as justice of the peace or constable. Recent studies have shown that the lack of centralized authority did not prevent the ancien-regime state that prevailed until the early nineteenth century from exercising considerable power over the popular classes at the local level, but it did tend to function according to a different logic than that of the modern, liberal, bureaucratic state that began to emerge in England during the 1830s.[1]

Lord Durham—a liberal once known as Radical Jack—was a committed proponent of increased popular representation in government as well as a greater role for the state. His task as the new Governor General of British North America in 1838 was not only to investigate the causes of the rebellions but also to make recommendations for reorganizing the administration of Lower and Upper Canada. Durham blamed the outbreak of rebellion in Lower Canada on the resistance of the French Canadians to economic and social progress. Consequently, he aimed to minimize their political influence and, ultimately, to assimilate what he felt was an essentially feudal peasant people ("with no history and no literature") into the modern progressive society of English-speaking North America.[2] To facilitate this goal, Durham's famous report, published in 1839, recommended the union of the two Canadas. This union would set the stage for Durham's second major recommendation, the liberalization of government, which would in turn solve the constitutional and political impasse that had marked the pre-rebellion era. A critic of the ruling oligarchy in both colonies, Durham recommended that in most internal matters the executive should govern in accordance with the wishes of the elected legislative assembly. He argued that this reform would strengthen, not weaken, the imperial tie because it would end colonial resentment of the mother country, which would, however, continue to control foreign relations, trade, public lands, and immigration. Crown lands were, in Durham's view, too important to be left in the hands of colonials who would be tempted to exploit them for financial gain rather than having the larger good of the Empire in mind, namely, the facilitation of emigration from Great Britain to the new province's undeveloped frontier.

Durham wrote his lengthy report after only six months' residence in Lower Canada. He resigned as Governor General when the British government failed to defend him against criticism that he had overstepped his authority in exiling eight French-Canadian rebels to Bermuda, which lay outside Durham's geographic sphere of authority. Durham's resignation did not prevent his recommendations from being accepted by the British government, but his failure to define precisely what he meant by responsible government soon led to a protracted debate concerning the composition and powers of the executive council.

Durham was replaced by a friend, the energetic and efficient Charles Poulett Thomson, whose chief tasks were to convince Upper Canada to accept union with Lower Canada and to implement many of the reforms recommended by Durham without conceding the full measure of responsible government. Because its constitution remained suspended and it was still ruled by the appointed special council, Lower Canada had no choice but to accept the union. As for the Upper Canadians, Thomson succeeded in allaying their fears of political domination by their more populous neighbour—Lower Canada had 650,000 people to Upper Canada's 450,000—by offering equal representation in the legislative assembly. This would prove to be a short-sighted decision as far as Upper Canada's interests were concerned, for, as Durham had been fully aware when he recommended representation by population, it would soon have a larger number of people than Lower Canada.

The other more tangible incentive offered Upper Canada in return for joining the union was that its burdensome debt of £1,200,000 would be charged to the province as a whole, even though Lower Canada owed only £95,000. The justification offered by Thomson was that canals built by Upper Canada to ship its wheat down the St. Lawrence benefited Lower Canada's commerce. This was only partly true because the great majority living outside Montreal and Quebec would not receive much of a share of those benefits. They would also be burdened with another incentive offered to promote the union, namely, a loan of £1.5 million guaranteed by the British government and aimed largely at completing the St. Lawrence canals. The Act of Union, passed in 1840, provided for a common legislative council whose members would be named for life, and a common legislative assembly of forty-two members from each section, now known officially as Canada West and Canada East, although the terms Upper and Lower Canada continued to be widely used. In keeping with the goal of assimilation, English would be the only official language of the legislature. But French civil law remained in force in Canada East, signalling that the union would not constitute a complete amalgamation, after all.

As for political reform, the newly minted Lord Sydenham (Thomson was rewarded with this title for implementing the union) conceded that the governor should rule in harmony with the wishes of the people insofar as possible. In practice this meant that, rather than effectively sitting for life as in the past, executive councillors would be chosen from the legislative assembly, and therefore have to face popular election. This reform would end the ruling oligarchy's hold on office, and thus represent a significant step towards "responsible government." But Sydenham claimed to stand for "harmony" over party rule, and his insistence on choosing his executive council from all political groups in the assembly meant that the Governor General would continue to play the leading role in government.

Despite his demand that the executive council consist solely of members of the political party with the majority in the legislative assembly, the Reform leader of Upper Canada, Robert Baldwin, agreed to enter the executive council with two other Reformers and four Tories. He reasoned that Sydenham's harmony principle would force him to listen to the majority in the assembly. Baldwin tried to convince one of the French-Canadian leaders, Louis-Hyppolite LaFontaine, to enter

Sir Louis Hyppolite Lafontaine, 1905 (photograph of a portrait). In later life, the dour and introverted Louis-Hyppolite LaFontaine, cultivated his resemblance to Napoleon. A lieutenant of Papineau's up until 1837, LaFontaine did not support the Rebellion, and in 1841 he took the crucial step of accepting the union of the two provinces by joining forces with Robert Baldwin of Canada West to push for Responsible Government. LaFontaine became increasingly conservative thereafter, forming a close alliance with the Catholic Church. Four years after he resigned from office in 1851, LaFontaine became the first French Canadian to be knighted by a British monarch. *Library and Archives Canada*

the ministry as well in order to ensure a majority for the Reformers and strengthen their demand for responsible government as Baldwin interpreted it. LaFontaine, who had been a lieutenant of Papineau's prior to the rebellion, initially refused to accept the post because he did not wish to indicate support for the Act of Union. With the election of 1841, however, he declared himself against the French-Canadian boycott of the executive council. Lower Canadians, he now felt, should join Upper Canadian Reformers in working towards a system of government that would offer colonial self-rule in all practical respects. When LaFontaine lost his bid for election in Montreal, Baldwin resigned one of the seats he had won in Canada West, enabling his French-Canadian ally to win the subsequent by-election in Toronto. But a more intransigent group from the pre-rebellion *Parti patriote* were not willing to take this risk, and its members continued to insist on the outright repeal of the Act of Union.

Baldwin's initial initiative was short-lived for, when his Upper Canadian Reform party won a majority in the 1841 election, he insisted that the four Conservative members of the executive council be replaced by French-Canadian Reformers. Upon Sydenham's refusal to take this advice, Baldwin and the other two Reformers resigned. But the party system was still in its infancy and Upper Canadians had an appetite for economic development. Sydenham therefore managed to retain legislative support from many Upper Canadian Reformers for initiatives that were funded largely by the £1.5 million British loan. Before Baldwin could gain control over his party in the assembly and undermine Sydenham's system of government, the governor died from injuries sustained in a fall from his horse.

Sir Charles Bagot, who succeeded Sydenham in 1842, found it increasingly difficult to govern without French-Canadian representation in the executive council. Initially, his liberal distribution of patronage appointments to influential French Canadians failed to convince anyone of prominence to join his administration. Eventually, he had little choice but to appoint LaFontaine as the Attorney General for Canada East, which meant agreeing to include Baldwin as his counterpart for Canada West. With five of six seats in the executive council now in the hands of the Reformers, Bagot admitted that "whether the doctrine of responsible government is openly acknowledged, or is only tacitly acquiesced in, it virtually exists."[3]

Upon Bagot's untimely death from a combination of maladies the following year, however, the Colonial Office appointed the former Governor General of India and Governor of Jamaica, Sir Charles Metcalfe, to take his place. Metcalfe was instructed to prevent any further undermining of the Crown's prerogative. An adherent of the old school of colonial rule, Metcalfe ignored the advice of his executive council in the distribution of patronage, which was crucial to the forging of political loyalties at the local level. As a result, all but one councillor resigned in November 1843. When the assembly supported the retiring councillors by refusing to proceed with business, Metcalfe prorogued it and governed by himself for the following ten months. At the same time, he attempted to undermine LaFontaine's political dominance in Canada East by pardoning many of the prisoners from the rebellion, facilitating the moving of the capital from Kingston to Montreal, and encouraging London to recognize the official status of the French language. As a result, the governor was able to convince a former *Patriote* leader, Denis-Benjamin Viger, to join his executive council. Viger's group continued to promote a separate status for Lower Canada, but argued that it would be better for the French Canadians to deal directly with a well-intentioned governor than to join Upper Canadians in a single party and thereby legitimize the union.

When Metcalfe called an election in August 1844 in order to avoid facing an unfriendly assembly, Viger was placed in the uncomfortable position of having to campaign with his former enemies, the English-speaking Tory merchants of Montreal. LaFontaine's party, on the other hand, benefited from the Catholic Church's fear of the radical nationalists who had succeeded the *Parti patriote*. While the Reformers swept the polls in Canada East, Metcalfe's personal campaign based on the loyalty cry in Canada West won him an overall majority of six in the assembly. He proceeded to try to split the Reform alliance by promising that members of the executive council would effectively be responsible for their own section of the province—another nail in the coffin of Durham's assimilation policy. As it was, a dual administrative system was emerging, with an Attorney General for each section, separate bureaucracies for the school system, and legislation commonly introduced that applied only to Canada East or Canada West. Metcalfe's offer was clearly very attractive to the French-Canadian nationalists, but the double-majority principle would mean that the governor would not necessarily have to follow the advice of his bisectional executive council. He might even play one half off against the other. LaFontaine, therefore, stuck to his alliance with Baldwin by remaining out of the administration. By the time Metcalfe died of cancer in 1845, he had ironically been forced into party rule because the Conservatives, with their small majority in the assembly, were in sole possession of the executive council.[4]

Meanwhile, economic forces favouring responsible government began to emerge by the mid-1840s. The necessity for inexpensive grain caused by the potato famine in Ireland and the Scottish Highlands led in 1846 to the repeal of the Corn Laws, the keystone of the British protective system. In addition to all import duties on grain being eliminated, tariffs on non-colonial timber were reduced. Politically, free trade meant that there was no longer any justification for opposing internal self-rule in the settlement colonies. The Colonial Office therefore chose Lord Elgin, Lord Durham's son-in-law, to succeed Metcalfe because he supported

Destruction of the Parliament House, Montreal, April 25th 1849. This print, based on a sketch made on the spot, illustrates the burning by a Tory mob in 1849 of the two-storey limestone structure in Montreal that served as the Province of Canada's Parliament building. From this point on, the parliamentary sessions would rotate between Toronto and Quebec City until Bytown (Ottawa) was chosen as the permanent capital in the 1850s. Destroyed with the building was the parliamentary archive and library of over 23,000 volumes. The site in Old Montreal, which became a parking lot, was excavated for archeological research in the summer of 2011. *Library and Archives Canada*

responsible government. When Elgin called an election in 1847, the Reform Party won an overwhelming victory in both sections of the province. Baldwin and LaFontaine were subsequently called upon to choose a new executive council, which meant that full party rule was instituted in 1848.

The test as to whether the governor would feel bound by the advice of his council came with the Rebellion Losses Bill in 1849. Elgin personally opposed it because it indemnified French Canadians who had been *Patriote* supporters for their property losses in 1837–38, but he nevertheless sanctioned the bill because it had passed both the legislative assembly and the legislative council. To express their outrage, a mob of English-speaking Tories pelted Elgin with stones and rotten eggs as he emerged from the legislative buildings in Montreal. That night they burned those same buildings to the ground, but this destructive act did not prevent the British parliament from ratifying the bill, thereby

Stanstead North Meeting House. Even before the municipal system was established in the 1840s, American-born settlers of the Eastern Townships gathered in buildings such as this one (erected in 1817) to discuss local issues, hear political speeches, and elect township officers such as road overseers and fence viewers. This building also would have hosted itinerant preachers from Vermont and a wide variety of social events. *Photograph by J.I. Little*

making responsible government official in Canada. While this was a major milestone on the road to Canadian independence and a more democratic system of government, it did not prove to be a victory for women because even those who held property in their own names (having never married or been widowed) lost the vote shortly thereafter.[5]

Despite the anger and frustration of the members of Montreal's merchant elite, many of whom signed a manifesto in 1849 to join the United States, responsible government did not signify the end of their dominant political role. Just as its economic fortunes would survive the end of preferential tariffs on the British market, so the capitalist class was generally able to exert indirect control over government by controlling the parties that put politicians into office. Party discipline would ensure that the executive branch continued to hold the key to power in government. It was no accident, therefore, that in the early 1850s the Baldwin-LaFontaine Reformers evolved into the Liberal-Conservative party, or that George-Étienne Cartier, LaFontaine's successor as co-leader, was also the solicitor for the Grand Trunk Railway. This company depended heavily on government largesse as it heralded a new stage of capitalist economic development in the Province of Canada.[6]

It would have been political suicide for a provincial government to levy direct taxes to meet the heavy demands imposed by public works projects such as railways and schools, but assessment by local councils offered an alternative solution. British authorities had associated town government with New England's independence movement, and therefore prevented its implementation in the post-revolutionary colonies, but Lord Durham felt strongly that it was a necessary complement to responsible government because it would train the average person to vote responsibly. He argued that by instituting an elected assembly with a broad franchise while denying local self-government the colonial authorities had put the figurative cart before the horse, leaving the people, whose world was then very localized, unable to see the tangible effect of their votes.

Prior to the introduction of the municipal system, centrally appointed justices of the peace or magistrates were given a good deal of administrative authority as groups of two or more meeting four times a year in the district court of quarter sessions. The justices even filled the legislative void resulting from the lack of elected town governments by enacting local legislation concerning police despite not having the official authority to do so. In the urban centres, where police offices with stipendiary magistrates and salaried staff were established during the 1810s, the justices of the peace were responsible for fortifications, interior and exterior communications, commercial and labour regulation, and the physical and moral state of the community. Because the legislative assembly had no say in these appointments, the English-speaking merchants found this form of government to be a more effective instrument for implementing their commercial projects than the provincial parliament where their authority was contested.[7] The citizens of Lower Canada's cities were finally allowed to elect municipal councillors in 1832–33, but in the rural parishes roads continued to be built and repaired by statute labour (*corvées*) supervised by local surveyors under the authority of the district roads inspector (*grand-voyer*). Inherited from the French regime, this system was particularly

ineffective in thinly populated or remote areas, and therefore hindered
the expansion of settlement beyond the increasingly overcrowded
seigneuries.[8]

Rather missing Durham's point about local self-governance as a means
of educating the masses politically, the ever-cautious Sydenham created
a district system in 1840 that was too centralized (with only twenty-
two districts in Canada East) and too undemocratic to win popular
acceptance. While ordinary councillors would be elected at the parish
or township level, the key positions—warden, clerk, and treasurer—
remained appointees of the provincial government. Invariably, these
officials were English-speaking, and the district seats were often in remote
English-speaking areas making access by most councillors difficult.
Furthermore, all council by-laws could be disallowed by the governor
within thirty days, and taxes were exclusively on landed property rather
than the movable goods that constituted much of the wealth of the village

The Toll Gate, Cornelius Krieghoff, 1861. This painting of a sleigh failing to stop at a toll gate
illustrates the defiant spirit of the habitants during the post-Rebellion era. During the early 1840s
they rejected the government's attempts to enforce legislation that required sleighs with higher
runners so that they would glide over the snow rather than pushing it ahead and packing it into
frozen bumps. Nor would toll gates have been necessary if the roads had been maintained by local
taxation, as required by the Municipal and Road Act of 1854. *National Gallery of Canada, Ottawa*

and town dwellers. Consequently, district councils managed to operate in the Eastern Townships where the people were desperate for the public improvements that would end their economic isolation, but they were simply boycotted as *machines à taxer* in the French-speaking parishes. The habitants also made it clear that they were not deferential to outside authority when, in 1840, they refused to obey regulations requiring them to abandon their traditional sleighs for ones with higher runners that would not produce bumps on the snowy roads.[9]

Steps taken towards decentralization and democratization during the 1840s generally failed, largely because the councils were not given sufficient powers to enforce local taxation.[10] Finally, the Municipal and Road Act of 1855 (like the Baldwin Act of 1849 in Canada West) established an effective system, combining county and township councils, and giving them the authority to initiate road projects for which they would then be legally accountable. The delay in passing this more coercive legislation was caused by the habitants' continued opposition to land taxes, as demonstrated by their forceful rejection of school reform (examined on pages 90–92). Generally attributed to the habitants' innate conservatism, this response probably had more to do with the fact that they already paid church tithes and seigneurial dues, and they were hard hit by an economic recession and crop failures during the 1840s.

In the Bois-Francs area (several townships bordering the south-shore seigneuries near Trois-Rivières), missionary priests appealed directly to the habitants' self-interest by circulating petitions demanding a reformed municipal system, one that would effectively tax absentee proprietors who were hindering population expansion from the old overcrowded parishes. These landowners, most of whom were English-speaking merchants or their descendants, would have to contribute towards local road construction or lose their properties, which would in turn encourage them to sell quickly at reasonable prices. Municipal reform was thereby made palatable to the rural population by linking it to French-Canadian nationalism and to the lure of affordable land as well as access to markets at a time when colonization was being promoted as the alternative to emigration to the United States. And municipal reform was also accepted by the capitalist class because expanded settlement served the interests of those who had invested in land as well as in railways such as the Grand

Trunk, which passed through the fertile Bois-Francs area. Furthermore, local councils were encouraged to invest in railway construction after the Municipal Loan Fund provided a provincial guarantee for their loans in 1857. As a result, most of Canada West's municipalities faced bankruptcy by the time of Confederation, though those in Canada East were more cautious.[11]

It was presumably no accident that the seigneurial system was abolished at almost the same time as the municipal reform bill of 1855 was passed. The habitants would obviously be more willing to pay local taxes once seigneurial exactions such as the 20 percent charged on all sales of landed property (*lods et ventes*) had been eliminated. They would, however, still be subject to a constituted rent equivalent to the *cens et rentes* they had previously been paying. They could pay this off in one instalment, but very few chose to do so, with the result that their subordinate status to the former seigneurs continued for many years. In fact, those former seigneurs who still had sizable tracts of ungranted land came out ahead with the new land tenure system because they were no longer legally required to grant any of that land for settlement purposes, though the new municipal taxes would encourage them to do so. More importantly, as far as capitalist investment was concerned, there would be an end to seigneurial monopolies over water-power sites and mills and to restrictions to the free transfer of landed property.

The third major reform initiative of the post-rebellion era, the reform of the school system, was considered to be essential at a time when the economy was industrializing and the general population was gaining more political power. The struggle for control between the Catholic Church and the state had undermined the education system in Lower Canada, where illiteracy was almost universal among the habitants. Schools began to proliferate after 1829, however, when government grants to locally elected *syndics* became available with very few strings attached. These schools served the needs of a population that required little formal education to function successfully on the land. But escalating costs and political conflict brought the grants to an end shortly before the rebellion broke out in 1837.

To manage the new system of schools in the post-rebellion era, the government appointed a superintendent of education charged with

The Old South School on Tibbits Hill, Brome Township. This school house, which still stands, was one of several in Brome and Missisquoi counties that were constructed of stone during the 1840s. The local families took advantage of the government subsidy to replace the square-timber structure that had been erected on the same site in 1827. Two sisters who were students on opening day in 1846 recalled that "the teacher was an Irishman who wore a paper hat, and had a long cane or whip with which he could reach the pupils from his desk." By this time, however, school reformers were frowning on such old-fashioned discipline, and women outnumbered men as teachers in part because they were considered to be more nurturing. *Brome County Historical Society*

apportioning monies from the province's public school fund to each district council according to school-age population. To receive this grant, an elected school council had to raise an equal amount of money from the inhabitants of its district. School councillors would also oversee the construction of school houses, hiring and firing of teachers, and regulation of the course of study. Legislation passed in 1846 decreed that voluntary contributions would no longer qualify for the matching government grant, and that the school councillors could be fined for failure to collect school taxes and compulsory fees. When a subsequent bill made this legislation still more coercive in 1849, the landed elite in the parishes south of Trois-Rivières spurred the habitants to resistance in what became known as the *guerre des éteignoirs* (candle-snuffers' war). Local school trustees were intimidated by *charivaris* (see Chapter 4), as well as the destruction of school buildings, and the burning of assessment roles. Only when the military intervened and leaders were prosecuted at mid-century was the agitation finally suppressed. The transition era therefore was marked by a political realignment in which the seigneurs and habitants, two groups that had been at odds prior to the rebellion, resisted the increased influence of the village notables who would control the municipal and school councils. Another feature of this realignment was the support of the clergy for school reform once the Church gained the influence over the system that it desired.[12] Even though the choice of textbooks and certification of teachers fell under the control of central state authorities, clerics would serve as school visitors with the right to choose books dealing with religious and moral issues, and they would also issue the certificates of morality required by prospective teachers. Furthermore, members of religious orders were exempted from the qualifying examination.[13] The Catholic Church would gain even more influence within the school system immediately after Confederation, but the legislation of the 1840s caused the literacy rate to rise quickly during the latter half of the nineteenth century, and it formed the basis of Quebec's education system that would last up until the 1960s.

Some historians view judicial, municipal, and school reforms as evidence of a "centralized and bureaucratized state."[14] In doing so, they fail to appreciate how much these institutions were decentralized during the 1840s due to public pressure, or the degree to which they reflected the limitations of centralized administrative capabilities in the nineteenth century. It should also be remembered that the municipal and school councillors represented local interests and desires rather than those of a government that offered relatively little in the way of funding. It is undoubtedly true that members of the rising middle class were quite aware that police forces and jails were inadequate tools to control the growing social unrest, such as the strikes and riots of the Irish canal workers, but the moral reform movement that fostered much of what is now known as the state formation process was essentially an optimistic impulse, not a fearful one.[15]

Still central to that optimism at mid-century was the belief that most social and moral evils could be eliminated by eradicating the consumption of alcohol. A parliamentary inquiry declared in 1849 that "one half of the crime annually committed, two-thirds of the cases of insanity, three-fourths of the pauperism are ascribable to intemperance."[16] Temperance societies associated with local Protestant churches sprang up in the Eastern Townships during the 1830s, and the Montreal Temperance

Society, with strong links to the Congregational Church, played a strong role in the 1840s, as did more secular organizations such as the Rechabites in the Eastern Townships.[17] While the Catholic Church was slower to embrace the temperance movement, the charismatic Reverend Charles Chiniquy's crusade, equating temperance with cultural survival, resulted in 400,000 French Canadians taking the pledge between 1848 and 1851. Due to its opposition to state regulation of morality, however, the Catholic Church would not support the transition in the 1850s from temperance to demands for state prohibition of the sale of alcohol. The role of the state would, in fact, remain limited to the licensing of outlets, and the sharp decline in liquor consumption would largely be due to social pressures at the local level.[18]

The public preference for voluntarism over state involvement in social matters was also demonstrated by the remarkable expansion of private charitable organizations. They reflected a new confidence in the capacity of civil society to manage the growing social problems, though they quickly became dependent on government subsidies. When it came to the delinquent and the insane, moreover, only the state had the power of constraint, and during the 1830s internment in penitentiaries or asylums was believed to offer the possibility of rehabilitation and reintegration into society.[19] While the mentally ill who were considered a danger to society had been confined in tiny hospital rooms or overcrowded jail cells, the Montreal Lunatic Asylum was opened by Governor Sydenham in 1839. Six years later it was replaced by a larger one in Beauport where patients could engage in morally "uplifting" agricultural labour.[20]

Because the penitentiary and the asylum appeared to hold such promise, there was a tendency to expand the range of what were considered to be criminal acts or insane behaviour. Internment was also viewed as a means of preventing contagion by dissolute members of society, so it was no accident that with the rapid increase in Irish immigration during the 1830s there was an explosion in the numbers sentenced for vagrancy and other crimes against public order, including a higher proportion of women than in the past. The establishment of urban police courts as well as police forces during the 1840s also contributed to the rapid escalation of arrests and imprisonments.[21] Local jails built in Lower Canada during the 1830s adopted the penitentiary model of individual cells, which were

Beauport Lunatic Asylum, Neighbourhood of Quebec, Robert C. Todd, 1849. The privately operated Beauport Asylum originated in an old manor house in 1845, but quickly became over-crowded. A new building was opened in 1850, a year after these architectural illustrations were produced. The founder, James Douglas, believed that rather than restraint his patients needed work, fresh air, religion, and amusement. They laboured at farming, broom-making, carpentry, and weaving, and the staff organized weekly balls, theatrical productions, magic lantern shows, and outdoor picnics. But space for charitable cases was limited, and only a very small percentage of Lower Canada's mentally ill people could benefit from treatment in this institution. Those who were considered dangerous continued to be confined in jails, and the Beauport Asylum, itself, eventually became little more than a prison, housing more than 5,000 permanent residents by the 1960s. *Library and Archives Canada*

viewed as facilitating systematic indoctrination without obstruction from other prisoners. Although the penitentiary was originally conceived for the incarceration of all condemned persons, disillusionment with its effectiveness as an agency of moral reform resulted in its being reserved after 1843 for those with a minimum sentence of two years. Consequently, there would be no systematic treatment for petty delinquents confined to the local jails, and the only penitentiary in the province of Canada (located in Kingston) simply became an instrument of repression for serious criminals.[22]

In short, the foundations of the modern interventionist state were in place as early as the 1840s, and there was little to distinguish Catholic Canada East from Protestant Canada West in this respect for they shared a government controlled by a rising liberal bourgeoisie. But differences would become more pronounced with time. The social reform movement had been driven to a considerable extent by a millennialist faith in moral progress, but the very diversity of Protestant churches made them amenable to state control of schools, hospitals, and social welfare. Quebec's Catholic Church was more inclined to view the expanding state as a threat to its traditional role in society; its determined opposition to the state prohibition of alcohol and to compulsory school attendance are two examples of this attitude. The Catholic Church also remained sceptical about the modern move towards liberalism and materialism, as we shall see in the following chapter, but it did co-operate with the state in launching the colonization movement that became linked to municipal reform, and it supported the establishment of a school system largely funded by local assessments and managed by elected commissioners. The Catholic Church was also skilful at co-opting reform initiatives such as the temperance movement to protect its hegemonic position in French-Canadian society. The fact that the LaFontaine Reformers had gained political dominance in part through alliance with the Church, and that the Liberal-Conservatives continued to court the clergy's political support, would ensure that the Church maintained a firm grip on social institutions well into the twentieth century.

SIX

THE NATIONALIST REACTION

The American and French Revolutions were both launched on the republican principle that the people have the right of sovereignty. The logical extension of this principle is that each national group ruled by a foreign power possesses this right, with the result that nationalism became the most important political force of the nineteenth century. In the eyes of Rome, however, both republicanism and nationalism were serious threats, the first because it challenged the hierarchical social order supported by the Church, and the second because Italian nationalists such as Mazzini and Cavour challenged the temporal authority of the papacy when they began to promote the creation of a nation out of the many Italian city-states. In reaction, Rome promoted ultramontanism, the doctrine that advocated papal supremacy over the entire Church, the Church's total independence from the state in spiritual matters, and the state's indirect dependence on the Church in questions of mixed jurisdiction. One example of the conservative trend in the Catholic Church was the introduction in 1864 of the Syllabus of Errors, which condemned Catholic liberalism and defined it as the attempt to accommodate the Church to modern political developments. Four years later came the assertion of papal infallibility in matters of faith and morals.

These European developments strongly influenced the Catholic Church in Quebec where its opposition to the rebellions had won it the permission to introduce new religious orders and expand the existing ones. The twelve new male communities established during the latter half of the nineteenth century all originated in France, while sixteen of the twenty-five new female communities were founded in Quebec. The ratio of priests to Catholics doubled between 1850 and 1890, by which time it had reached one priest for every 510 Catholics, and the membership

Bishop Ignace Bourget, Montreal QC, William Notman, 1862. After he became bishop of Montreal in 1840, Bourget led the ultramontane revival that saw the Catholic Church establish its deeply entrenched position within French-Canadian society. While ultramontanism favoured a colourful liturgy and ornate churches, Bourget has a distinctly ascetic appearance in this photograph. *McCord Museum*

in male religious orders grew from only 243 in 1850 to 1,984 in 1900. The number of nuns increased even more dramatically during the same fifty-year period, from 650 to 6,628, reaching the remarkable ratio of one nun for every 150 Catholics.[1] These religious communities provided social and educational institutions for the rapidly expanding cities where lay membership in religious confraternities also expanded rapidly. While only one-third of Montreal's parishioners conformed to the basic requirement of taking Easter communion in 1839, nearly everyone in the diocese of Montreal did so by the 1860s.[2] The general assumption that industrialization and urbanization quickly led to a decline in religious conformity and church influence—sometimes called the "secularization thesis"—therefore does not apply to Quebec.

Bishop Ignace Bourget of Montreal and the somewhat younger Bishop Louis-François Laflèche of Trois-Rivières were the province's leading champions of ultramontane principles. With the rise of the liberal state challenging the Church's social role, identification with Rome offered the international stature and prestige that would enhance the Church's image at home. Bourget zealously promoted the Romanization of the Catholic Church in Quebec by initiating liturgical reforms on the Roman model and by orchestrating a popular religious revival through the propagation of fervent Italian devotional practices. From radical political reform, people turned for hope to pilgrimages, processions, retreats, and confraternities, as well as devotions to the Blessed Virgin, the Blessed Sacrament, and the martyrs' relics imported in large numbers from Rome. During the pivotal decade of the 1840s, when four new female orders were created, Bourget was greatly assisted by the Jesuits and other religious orders recently attracted from Europe and by charismatic preachers such as the aristocratic French bishop, Monseigneur Charles de Forbin-Janson. At the end of the decade, as noted in the previous chapter, temperance crusader Abbé Charles Chiniquy also drew crowds never before seen in Lower Canada.[3]

As in Europe, the French-Canadian ultramontanes discouraged Catholics from supporting the Liberal Party, and they promoted Church control over education and social services on the grounds that these were inextricably linked to public morality. Unlike their European counterparts, however, Bourget and Laflèche were strong nationalists because they associated the survival and expansion of the Catholic faith in North America with the survival of French Canada itself. In short, French Canadians were told that they had a "providential mission" to preserve Catholicism in its purest form from the taint of Protestantism and the liberal Catholicism of the United States. These ideas were summed up in a pamphlet published by Bishop Laflèche in 1866, in which he declared: "A nation is constituted by unity of speech, unity of faith, uniformity of morals, customs, and institutions. The French Canadians possess all these, and constitute a true nation. Each nation has received from Providence a mission to fulfill. The mission of the French-Canadian people is to constitute a centre of Catholicism in the New World."[4] If the nation had a quasi-divine status, it followed that it was subordinate to the will of God, which was formulated by the Church. It also followed that the state was subordinate to the Church, which Laflèche's pamphlet did not distinguish clearly from the nation as a cultural entity:

> Authority derives from God. The best form of government is a moderate monarchy (the Church and the family are examples of it); the most imperfect is democracy. Liberalism commits the fundamental error of seeking to build society on other than religious

La [sic] *carême*, Cornelius Krieghoff, 1852. Krieghoff's genre paintings may create an impression of French-Canadian habitants as quaint, backward peasants, as his nationalist critics complain, but they also suggest that the rural population maintained an independent attitude towards church and state authority. In this scene, a stern parish priest finds a family (whose members appear more amused than chagrined), breaking the Lenten fast. *Library and Archives Canada*

principles. Electors not only exercise a right; they fulfill a duty for which they are responsible before God. The priest thus has a right to guide them. "It is an error condemned by reason, by history, and by Revelation to say that politics is a field in which religion has no right to enter, and in which the Church has no concern."[5]

Laflèche's ally, Bishop Bourget, had attempted to snuff out political radicalism by waging a holy war after mid-century against the Institut Canadien because its library included books that had been placed on the Papal Index. Membership in this independent educational society subsequently dwindled, and, after Rome finally condemned it in 1869, Bourget felt justified in denying the sacraments to its few remaining members. When he refused burial in consecrated ground to the printer Joseph Guibord, the case wound its way through the courts until the Judicial Committee of the Privy Council in London finally declared in 1875 that burial was a civil right. After Guibord's remains were turned

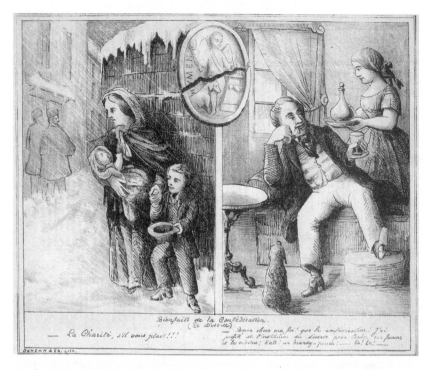

Bienfaits de la Confédération (Benefits of Confederation), Charles-Henri Moreau, 1865. This political caricature from the short-lived satirical newspaper *Le Perroquet* borrows on the imagery used by temperance advocates to express the editor's reservations about the prospect of Confederation, which he depicts as a divorce rather than a marriage. A well-dressed man is consorting with a woman identified by the English name of Kate while his wife and children are begging on a wintry day. The angelic figure overlooking the two scenes recalls the ex-votos of the French Regime, but the reference is not to salvation but rather to the loss of virginity or innocence. Hymen was the Greek god of marriage, which is clearly broken in this case, suggesting that Moreau had in mind the Catholic Church's concern that under the British North America Act a divorce could be granted by a private act of Parliament. *Library and Archives Canada*

away from the Côte-des-Neiges cemetery by an angry mob, he was buried under military guard and his grave filled with concrete and scrap iron to prevent its desecration. Bourget had the last word, however, when he simply deconsecrated the burial plot.

The *Rouges* had been effectively crushed as a political force, as their ineffectual opposition to the enactment of the British North America Act in 1867 had shown. In the critical post–Civil War climate, when the United States was threatening to take British North America in compensation for Britain's sale of frigates to the secessionist southern states, Cartier's Bleus were simply able to drown out the Rouge objection that the veto and emergency powers of the central government would seriously undermine the authority of the provincial governments. Certainly, the most attractive feature of the new constitutional arrangement to French Canadians was that it provided for a provincial government that had jurisdiction over social matters such as education and health.[6]

But the fact that provincial autonomy was insecure, and that French Canadians were a minority in a House of Commons based on representation by population, only intensified the nationalist sense of crisis caused by the increasing emigration from the overcrowded seigneuries to the cotton-factory towns of southern New England. From the Catholic Church's perspective, such emigration was a threat to the very souls of those who would face cultural assimilation south of the border. In an attempt to halt this exodus, the Church constructed the myth that French Canadians had a particular avocation to remain tied to the land, and the nationalist slogan became *Emparons-nous du sol* (Let us take possession of the soil). Colonization was the dominant theme of the early French-Canadian novels, which were known as *romans du terroir* (novels of the soil). Among the best known of these are Antoine Gérin-Lajoie's *Jean Rivard*, first published as a newspaper serial in 1862, and Louis Hémon's more literary *Maria Chapdelaine*, which appeared at the turn of the twentieth century.

The Catholic Church promoted colonization societies, but the government played the most important role in the expansion of the rural hinterland by building colonization roads and subsidizing the construction of railways. Thus, the completion in the early 1850s of the Grand Trunk Railway branch from Quebec City to the main Montreal-Portland line provided the Bois-Francs with ready access to outside markets for the first time. Colonization was also the official aim of railways constructed on the north shore of the St. Lawrence as well as from Sherbrooke to Quebec City and Lake Megantic during the 1870s.[7] Largely due to expansion onto land that was opened up by colonization roads and railways, the French-speaking population of the Eastern Townships increased from 23 percent in 1844 to 58 percent in 1871, when they numbered 97,000.[8]

The French Canadians also expanded onto traditional Native land north of the St. Lawrence. In the Saguenay region, where there were

First House in Louise Township, 1899. By the time this photograph was taken, the Catholic Church had been enlisting the state's support to promote French-Canadian colonization of the Eastern Townships for half a century, and mountainous Louise Township on the dividing line between the St. Lawrence and Atlantic watersheds was the last corner of the region to be settled. The Campagna family—shown here with five of twelve offspring, as well as the Bishop of Sherbrooke and two priests—had lived alone in the township for fourteen years. But their isolation was about to end as the bishop convinced the provincial government to build a colonization road along the eastern side of Lake Megantic shortly after the visit recorded in this photograph. *Bishop's University, Eastern Townships Resource Center, Eastern Townships Collection*

more than 4,000 settlers in the Saguenay Valley as early as 1850, only eight years after the Hudson's Bay Company lease had expired, the French-speaking population had reached 19,800 by 1871. The decline in hunting and trapping forced the Innu (formerly the Montagnais and Naskapi) to seek employment as loggers, canoeists, and guides for prospectors and recreational hunters.[9] As a result of the colonization movement, the number of farms in Quebec increased by 50 percent between 1851 and 1900, despite the increased production of labour-saving farm machinery in the post-Confederation period. But the demand for land created by the persistently high birth rate was still much greater, and Quebec's cities were not growing quickly enough to absorb all of the surplus rural population. The result was that the exodus to the United States had reached 200,000 by 1870, and 600,000 by the end of the century. Approximately 10 percent of Quebec's population had emigrated each decade between 1871 and 1901, a ratio that was equally high in the country as a whole but which caused greater consternation in a province where Curé Antoine Labelle, known as the province's "apostle of colonization," warned that it would be "the graveyard of the race."[10]

The colonization campaign succeeded in expanding the settlement frontier of the province. Unfortunately, however, its promoters took insufficient account of the ongoing economic hardships suffered by the families in the remote and barren areas they had been encouraged to settle. Colonization advocates certainly did not oppose the establishment of manufacturing industries, but they made little place for the colonists' long-term involvement in the only truly viable industry in the remote, thin-soiled Appalachian and Laurentian colonization zones—the lumber industry.

The American demand for lumber, which could be shipped to market by rail, led to the rapid growth of Quebec's sawmilling industry during the latter half of the nineteenth century. But the forest was seen throughout North America as a receding frontier, not suitable for the establishment of permanent communities. Anything that detracted from full-time farming, it was felt, would retard commercial agricultural production and, therefore, "progress." Consequently, Quebec colonists were allowed only small grants of land (a maximum of 81 hectares), while large lumber companies controlled the forest resource on immense tracts of Crown land. In the Mauricie, for example, fourteen merchant applicants received leases to 6,000 square miles of forest land in 1852, and two of them held more than half this territory. Even larger was the Price family's timber monopoly in the Saguenay-Lac-Saint-Jean area, where agricultural production languished due to the short growing season for grain and the inaccessibility of external markets for dairy products.[11] This system of managing the Crown lands was a sharp contrast to that of Norway and Finland where there were prohibitions against the control of timberland by lumber companies, and where northern colonists were encouraged to engage in a dual economy of subsistence agriculture and logging by being given very large land grants.[12]

In the meantime, with the *Rouges* threat essentially extinguished after the enactment of Confederation, the ultramontanes grew increasingly critical of George-Étienne Cartier and his party. Bishop Bourget's break with Cartier actually dated to the mid-1860s when the latter acted as solicitor for the Sulpician seigneurs of Montreal in their legal case against the Montreal bishop's division of the island parish with its 80,000 members. Bourget was incensed that Cartier would use the prestige of his public office to become involved in what he considered to be strictly an internal Church issue. Worse still, the anti-ultramontane Gallican arguments used by the Sulpicians' lawyers were published as the *Code des Curés* in 1870.

Bourget and his allies responded by taking the unprecedented step of helping a moderate liberal defeat Cartier in the 1872 by-election. The previous year the *Programme catholique* had declared that party loyalty should not prevail over religious interests in such matters as marriage, education, the establishment of parishes, and the registration of civil status. Given that laws pertaining to these matters currently "are defective in so far as they diminish the rights of the Church, limit its liberty, hamper its administration, or are open to hostile interpretation," Catholic deputies were required "to make the changes and modifications demanded by our Lords the Bishops of the Province." Catholic electors were instructed to vote only for those candidates who supported the Programme.[13]

This declaration threatened not only a split within the Conservative Party but also a Protestant backlash. As a result, Archbishop Elzéar-Alexandre Taschereau of Quebec, who was from an influential Liberal family, openly criticized it, thereby demonstrating that the Catholic hierarchy was divided into two camps. But the Church leaders did become temporarily united when some Liberals tried to have their seats recontested after the 1875 provincial election on the grounds that local clergy had employed "undue influence" in advising their parishioners not to vote for their party. Taschereau himself signed a joint pastoral letter warning against the dangers of Catholic liberalism and rejecting the claim that religion had nothing to do with politics. But, after the courts had supported the Liberals in two elections contested in 1876 for clerical interference, Taschereau declared that the two political parties were on the same footing as far as the Church was concerned. His stance was upheld by the papal envoy Bishop Conroy who declared that political liberalism was not to be confused with Catholic liberalism, and that only

Hon. George Etienne Cartier, Mr. Cuvillier and Three Priests, Montreal, QC, 1867 lliam Notman, 1867. The leading French-Canadian exponent of Confederation, George-Étienn rtier supported the Sulpicians in their struggle against Bishop Bourget for authority over th ish of Montreal. Cartier's stance contributed to his electoral defeat in 1872, shortly before his d .. Here he is shown with three priests and Maurice Cuvillier, who managed his financial affa as well as being the brother of the mistress who lived at Cartier's country estate. *McCord Muse*

the latter was condemned by Rome. Conroy also stated that the clergy were not to teach that it was a sin to vote for any particular candidate or party.[14] The Church's more tolerant approach to the Liberals was made easier in 1877 when the party's new leader Wilfrid Laurier publicly dissociated Canadian liberalism from what he criticized as revolutionary European liberalism.

The Conservative government in Ottawa also began to attract criticism from French-Canadian nationalists because of its failure to protect Catholic minorities outside Quebec. Arguing that it would create a precedent for federal intrusion in a provincial area of jurisdiction, Quebec's Conservative Members of Parliament failed to support New Brunswick's Catholics in 1871 when that province created a public education system that made no provision for separate Catholic schools. In the West, French had been recognized as an official language and the

Obsequies of Sir Geo. E. Cartier—The Funeral Service in the Parish Church of Notre Dame, 1873. Lavish public ceremonies such as religious processions, consecrations, and funerals of the religious and political elite served as a form of public theatre that reinforced values and hierarchies. After Cartier died in London, England, in 1873, his body was shipped across the Atlantic in a sealed coffin, and funeral masses were held in the Quebec City and Trois-Rivières cathedrals en route to Montreal where another service took place in the Notre-Dame Basilica. As illustrated by this print, published in *L'Opinion publique* in June 1873, the church was draped in purple crepe and 500 tapers burned atop a 4.3-metre bier with a three-storey, 12-metre tower topped by four funeral busts of Cartier. The 1,244 pews in the church's nave and galleries, which could accommodate 10,000 people, were all filled with mourners. Cartier had asked that the funeral mass be chanted by the Sulpician Superior, Abbé Bayle, but Bishop Bourget insisted that this be done by the ultramontane coadjutor, Bishop Fabre. *McCord Museum*

Catholic schools constitutionally enshrined when Manitoba became a province in 1870. Because of the execution of Ontario-born Thomas Scott by order of the provisional government, however, Métis leader Louis Riel had to flee the advancing army before the official transfer of authority took place. Riel would be tried and executed after leading a Métis rebellion at Batoche on the Saskatchewan River in 1885.

Prime Minister Sir John A. Macdonald's refusal to offer clemency despite Riel's unbalanced mental state, as well as a great deal of popular pressure from Quebec, intensified the defensive nationalism within that province. With the Conservative Party already divided between its ultramontane and moderate factions, provincial Liberal leader Honoré Mercier was able to establish an alliance with some of the more nationalist ultramontanes. Known as the *Parti nationale*, it swept the Conservatives out of office in 1887.

As premier, Mercier pressed for more provincial autonomy, hosting Canada's first interprovincial conference in 1887. He also precipitated a Protestant backlash outside Quebec by inviting the pope to arbitrate the distribution of government funds to various branches of the Catholic Church in compensation for property acquired by the province when the last Quebec Jesuit (before they returned in the 1840s) died earlier in the century. Macdonald's refusal to disallow this legislation caused the defection of one of his leading young lieutenants, D'Alton McCarthy, who formed the Equal Rights Association under the banner of equal rights for all denominations and special privileges for none. This movement helped, in turn, to ensure that Catholic schools lost their officially recognized status when the Manitoba Schools Act was passed in 1890. With French Canadians making up only 10 percent of Manitoba's population by that time, the provincial government also ignored the constitution by abolishing French as an official language.

The new schools act was challenged by Manitoba's Catholics, but the failure of the federal Conservative government to disallow it, and the long delay in drafting a remedial bill that would override it, led to the alienation of some of the key French-Canadian government supporters. As a result, Laurier's Liberals won the 1896 election with a sizable majority from Quebec despite the fact that the Catholic Church officially supported the Conservative government's remedial bill, which the Liberals opposed. Once in power, however, Laurier was careful to court the support of the Church. As early as 1897, he pressured the newly elected Liberal premier Félix-Gabriel Marchand into dropping his plan to re-establish the provincial ministry of education that had been abolished in 1875 due to Church pressure.[15]

While provincial rights trumped minority rights in 1896 as far as Quebecers were concerned, one of the leading Liberal spokesmen in the province, the fiery young Henri Bourassa, rebelled when Laurier succumbed to western pressure by failing to reinstate the dual system of schools in Saskatchewan and Alberta when they became Canadian provinces in 1905. Meanwhile, Bourassa, an ultramontane Catholic despite his Liberal political affiliation, had already taken a strong stand against the strengthening of imperial ties during an era when British industrial and military supremacy was being challenged, by Germany in particular. The imperial unity movement struck a strong chord in English Canada where it was fuelled by intense interest in overseas missionary activities, theories of racial superiority, and the desire to belong to a powerful international federation that would give Canadians the same sense of pride as their American neighbours.[16]

The isolationism of French-speaking Quebecers should not be exaggerated, for their press closely followed the international struggles of the Catholic Church.[17] During the late 1860s, for example, Bishop Bourget had recruited a contingent of 400 Papal Zouaves from as many parishes as possible, taking care to select only those from reputable families and with good moral character. The papacy was more in need of money than men in its armed struggle against the Italian nationalists, and the Canadian volunteers did not engage in combat, but mammoth demonstrations in Montreal and extensive newspaper coverage ensured that for most French Canadians a strong personal link had been forged with Rome.[18]

The British imperialists followed a similar strategy on a much broader scale by requesting that the dominions contribute to the war effort in South Africa in 1899. In this case, however, the French Canadians were less than eager to take up arms against another small minority group within the Empire. War coverage by the press in France also made them more aware than English Canadians of the scorched-earth tactics

Alfred Laroque, Papal Zouave, Montreal, QC, 1868, William Notman. Over 500 Canadians, mostly from Quebec, enrolled in seven contingents of the papal army between 1868 and 1870. The aim of the Zouaves was to defend Rome against the Italian troops fighting for Italian unification. Most of those from Quebec were recruited by Bishop Bourget's organizational committee for their moral qualities rather than their fighting abilities because the main goal was to combat the liberal ideas formally condemned by the pope. Care was taken to ensure that as many parishes as possible provided volunteers and financial support. *McCord Museum*

employed against the Afrikaaner guerillas, as well as the conditions in the refugee camps where nearly 20,000 women and children died of disease.[19] Laurier succumbed, nevertheless, to imperialist pressure from English Canada by authorizing the raising and equipping of 1,000 "volunteers" without summoning Parliament. Once in South Africa, these troops (8,400 were eventually sent) were to be commanded and paid for by the British army. While Laurier claimed that authorization for the small sum provided by his government would not create a precedent for the future, Bourassa disagreed, arguing eloquently that it would be used to justify compelling Canada to participate in future imperial wars. Bourassa's resignation as a Liberal Member of Parliament, and his re-election by acclamation as an independent (he would run again as a Liberal in 1900) won him a good deal of attention and support in Quebec.

The South African War, which ended in 1902, left a deep scar between English and French Canada. Governor General Lord Minto noted when he wrote to his brother that in Britain "you do not call a man disloyal if he disapproves of the war. Here, if he is lukewarm, and is a French Canadian, he must be a rebel!"[20] In 1903 Bourassa

Sir Wilfred and the Extremists—Where Laurier Stands, Fergus Kyle, 1911. Cartoonist James Fergus Kyle comments here on Laurier's positions in advance of the 1911 federal election. Laurier's naval policy and his proposed trade agreement with the United States are presented here as balanced, calm, and reasonable, in contrast to two emotional and antagonistic extremes: Borden's flag-waving imperialism and Bourassa's angry French-Canadian nationalism. *Library and Archives Canada*

became the leading figure in the newly formed anti-imperialist *Ligue nationaliste* with 10,000 members, rumoured to be the foundation for a new political party to challenge Laurier in Quebec. The threat did not materialize immediately, for Quebec opinion ensured that Laurier would resist pressures exerted to strengthen imperial ties during the years immediately following the South African War. But those pressures intensified in 1909 with Britain's growing concern over the rapid growth of the German navy. In response to the Colonial Office's request that the dominions contribute to the Royal Navy, Laurier offered the compromise solution of a Canadian navy of five cruisers and six destroyers. But the Naval Services Bill appeased neither the English-Canadian imperialists, who called it a "tin pot navy," nor the French-Canadian nationalists who pointed out that Canada was automatically at war when Britain was at war, and, in the case of an emergency, the Cabinet could place the navy under British command without seeking Parliamentary approval.

With the 1911 federal election, Robert Borden's Conservatives campaigned on pro-imperialist policies in the fifteen English-speaking constituencies of Quebec. In the fifty French-speaking ridings, however, they put their machine and considerable financial resources at the disposal of Bourassa, who had founded the influential daily *Le Devoir* a year earlier. During the campaign, the *Autonomistes*, as they called themselves, denounced the naval policy of Borden as well as that of Laurier. Bourassa hoped to elect a bloc of independents large enough to hold the balance of power in the House of Commons, and thus prevent any naval aid to Britain. He did succeed in reducing the Liberal majority in Quebec from forty-three to eleven seats, but his strategy backfired when the Liberals were routed in Ontario. Consequently, Borden's new Conservative government could afford to govern without the support of the sixteen *Autonomistes*. His one French-Canadian nationalist Cabinet member resigned when the government decided in 1912 to make a $35-million contribution to the Royal Navy for the construction of three dreadnoughts. When the First World War broke out two years later, the country was already in a dangerously divided state.

SEVEN

AN INDUSTRIAL REVOLUTION

The early nineteenth century saw significant economic changes in Lower Canada. Steamboats began plying the St. Lawrence in 1809, merchant capitalists grew rich from the import–export trade, the Bank of Montreal was founded in 1817, and the colony's first railway project, the Champlain and St. Lawrence, linked Laprairie to Saint-Jean in 1836. But the Industrial Revolution had yet to make significant inroads in Lower Canada at the time of the Rebellions. Quebec City had its busy shipyards, certainly, and the Trois-Rivières area, its historic iron foundries. Sawmills, tanneries, and other rural industries were sprouting here and there, stimulated by the growth of internal markets for necessities like lumber and leather.[1] But this was small fare compared to the manufacturing revolution that swept the British Isles in the 1780s and crested on New England's shores by the 1820s.

Some Quebec historians have bemoaned the province's industrial "lag" (*retard*) compared to neighbouring New England, and later Ontario.[2] But others see the glass as half full rather than half empty. The province, they point out, did experience a significant transition to modern, industrial-capitalist production in the later nineteenth century. Between 1851 and 1896, the value of production in manufacturing industries grew by a factor of seventy-five, from about $2 million to over $154 million. Water, wind, and muscle gave way to steam engines and, later, electricity. And modern, mechanized factories replaced traditional craft shops and small mills as the dominant way of organizing the manufacture of an increasingly wide variety of goods.[3]

Several events mark the 1840s as a key decade in this transition. Extended to the entire province in 1854, the dismantling of the seigneurial regime began in 1840 when *censitaires* in the three seigneuries held by the Sulpician Order, including the island of Montreal, were allowed to commute their holdings to freehold tenure. A year later, in 1841, Lower Canada's new Registry Act achieved a similar end; land targeted for commercial, industrial, residential, or other development could now circulate more freely and at lower risk to investors since all transactions had to be recorded in county registry offices.[4] At the same time, Lower Canada's network of transportation and communications was expanded, taking on elements of nineteenth-century modernity. The later 1840s saw the development of Lower Canada's first major railway line, the St. Lawrence and Atlantic Railway, which connected Montreal with Portland, Maine, and which provided a winter port for Montreal and market access for the landlocked Eastern Townships. It was soon swallowed up by the megaproject of the prosperous 1850s, the Grand Trunk Railway, which was a boon for Montreal merchants and the key to the future development of small towns located along its path, such as Richmond, Saint-Hyacinthe, and Sherbrooke.

Samuel Morse's telegraph was to communications what the steam locomotive was to transportation: a remarkable new technology that was faster and more reliable than anything that had come before. As the railway network expanded, so too did a web of telegraph lines, usually along the same rights of way, allowing for the instantaneous transmission of information about prices, markets, politics, the weather, and a thousand other topics. Founded in 1847, the Montreal Telegraph Company was one of the first in British North America and the most important in the early years, providing instantaneous communication between Montreal and cities such as Detroit, Ottawa, and Portland.[5]

The 1840s also saw significant industrial development along the banks of the Lachine Canal. Built in the 1820s, the canal served the interests of Montreal merchants by allowing river traffic to bypass the Lachine rapids off the southern tip of the island. Between 1843 and 1848, the waterway was widened and new, high-capacity locks were installed as part of a major program of canal construction and refurbishment in the St. Lawrence–Great Lakes system. The expansion also provided a wealth of hydraulic energy and encouraged local artisans and merchants to make the leap into industrial pursuits. Indeed, the cluster of manufacturing industries that emerged along the canal in the 1840s, driven by water power and by the labour of the Irish and French-Canadian residents

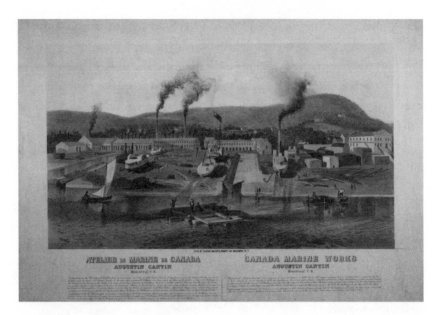

Canada Marine Works, Augustin Cantin, Montreal C.E., ca. 1865. Beginning in the 1840s, improvements to the Lachine Canal allowed the surrounding area to develop into British North America's first industrial neighbourhood. The Canada Marine Works, established by Augustin Cantin in 1846, was among the first of the large workshops and factories that came to characterize the district. This promotional print dates from the 1860s and depicts Cantin's six-hectare shipyard, including a dry dock, a sawmill, a sailmaker's loft, and a boiler shop. By this time, as the four industrial smokestacks indicate, stationary steam engines were in use, supplementing the hydraulic power that was generated by the canal's locks and channelled into specially constructed industrial basins. *Library and Archives Canada*

of St. Ann's Ward, is rightly thought of as British North America's first industrial neighbourhood.[6] At the end of the 1840s, the area boasted the colony's most significant concentration of manufacturing activities, including flour mills, shipyards, sugar refineries, and shops producing nails, furniture, doors and windows, saws, axes, and hammers. In 1856, these mills, foundries, and factories already employed some 1,200 workers; fifteen years later, in 1871, there were forty-four industrial establishments in the area and the number of workers had more than doubled.[7]

So, by the time of Confederation, Quebec's industrial capacity was already quite impressive. In 1871, the value of manufacturing output across the province had reached $77 million, rising dramatically from the modest mid-century figure of $600,000.[8] Much of the activity was concentrated in Montreal, which was well served by its prosperous business class, its water-power resources, its labour supply, and its strategic position in the transportation network. But mills and manufactories of all sorts had been popping up all over, especially in market towns like Sherbrooke and Saint-Hyacinthe, which had both railway connections and significant sources of water power.

Throughout this period, the leading manufacturing sector was food and food products, including flour milling (led by the Montreal mills of Ira Gould and the Ogilvie brothers), sugar refining, and dairy production. At the time of Confederation, Montreal's two main sugar refineries, Redpath and Sons and the St. Lawrence Sugar Refining Company, were processing about 36 million pounds per year; in 1882, their combined labour force was estimated at 500 workers.[9] Leather-based industries were also important. The value of the boots, shoes, harnesses, saddles, and other leather products produced in the province was rising rapidly.[10] The shoemaking industry, in particular, was totally transformed by mechanization, capital investment, and waged labour, as production stepped out of the traditional craft shop and into the modern factory.[11] Montreal's boot and shoe factories produced fully three-quarters of the shoes bought in Canada.[12] But mechanized production made significant strides in other parts of the province as well: in Quebec City, for example, where some 2,000 workers toiled in boot and shoe factories by 1872,[13] and in Saint-Hyacinthe, where the industrialist and inventor Louis Côté, in collaboration with the leather merchant Victor Côté, established the town's first real factory in 1865.[14]

At the same time, Quebec sawmills benefited from the rising American demand for boards, shingles, and every manner of construction material. Entrepreneurs established significant sawmilling operations at points along Quebec rivers that had sufficient hydraulic potential to support them, many of which were located far from Montreal in the new colonization zones (see Chapter 6). Particularly impressive were the installations near the junction of the Ottawa and Gatineau Rivers in the Outaouais region of western Quebec. This was an area where in the 1870s, more Crown land was devoted to forestry than in all other regions combined,[15] and where lumber barons such as Ezra Butler Eddy had, by 1872, established ten major sawmills capable of producing close to

Workers pose in front of the Adams Shoe Company in Quebec City, photograph by Philippe Gingras, 1894. The transition from traditional craft to modern factory production in the province's boot-and-shoe industry was essentially complete by this time. Leather products manufacturing was among the leading industrial sectors in the province and one in which Quebec City had a significant share. © *Bibliothèque et archives nationales du Québec*

300,000 board feet of lumber each year, with highly mechanized sawing equipment and the labour of over 4,000 employees.[16] In addition to the province's sawmills, most Quebec towns in the 1870s also had workshops and factories engaged in the transformation of wooden logs and boards into everything from furniture, doors, and window frames to carriages, barrels, and axe or scythe handles.[17]

Quebec at the time of Confederation, then, had a diversified and significantly industrialized manufacturing sector. Capitalist labour relations combined with new technologies had begun to transform production in virtually every sector. These included those so-called light industries: labour-intensive activities such as shoemaking and clothing production for which the province came to be known. The garment industry, for example, had grown exponentially in the 1860s and was the fourth leading manufacturing sector in 1871 with output valued at almost $6 million.[18] More and more garments were mass produced— often by French-Canadian or Irish women working at home for piece rates—and offered for sale on domestic and external markets, not least

Grand Trunk Railway engine erecting shops, Point St. Charles, 1859. Railways stimulated industrial development in countless ways. Steam locomotives, for instance, had to be built and maintained, as they were in the Grand Trunk Railway's engine shop in Point St. Charles, pictured here in 1859. Foundries, engine works, and other heavy industries clustered in manufacturing and railway towns, especially Montreal. *Library and Archives Canada*

to fill military demand south of the border during the Civil War.[19] But the story of Quebec's early industrial development was also about heavier, more capital-intensive businesses such as the foundries and machine shops, which—with annual production worth about $3 million— were the fifth leading sector in 1871, not to mention the manufacture of locomotives and railway cars. Taken together with the shipbuilding industry, locomotive and railway car manufacturing added another $3 million to the province's overall industrial output.[20]

In the decades between Confederation and 1900, the industrial-capitalist transition accelerated, conquering one manufacturing sector after another. The process was never even, however, either in its chronology or in its geography. Given the absence of a social safety net or government bailouts and recovery packages, the boom-and-bust pattern associated with modern business cycles was an even starker reality then than it is today. The most severe international economic crisis of the era occurred in the 1870s, with profound consequences for Quebec's economy. Hundreds of entrepreneurs declared themselves insolvent; in 1875 alone, 678 businesses filed for bankruptcy, defaulting on total debts valued at almost $14 million. As the depression deepened, credit became tighter and tighter, creating further difficulties for merchants and other entrepreneurs. At least two Quebec banks failed and others reduced their capital or dipped into emergency reserves. Without labour legislation or collective agreements, workers were presented with wage reductions, which in certain trades might run as high as 60 percent. No wonder that many chose the path of collective resistance, sometimes through spontaneous strikes and even riots, such as those that rocked the streets of Quebec City in the summers of 1878 and 1879.[21]

Federal politics in the 1870s focused to a large extent on extricating the new Dominion from this economic quagmire. The solution offered by John A. Macdonald's Tories, known as the National Policy, was a high tariff wall designed to protect domestic producers against American imports. This worked to the advantage of Quebec manufacturers especially after 1885, when they could reach expanding markets in the west thanks to the new Canadian Pacific Railway. Eventually, the lean years of the 1870s gave way to the more prosperous 1880s, meaning new manufacturing growth and an acceleration of the modern industrial practices already noted, such as mechanization and the recourse to relatively unskilled (and therefore "cheap") labour. By 1891, the extent of manufacturing production in the province was fully double what it had been in 1871, with significant growth coming from many sectors, including clothing, textiles, tobacco, iron and steel, transportation equipment, and interestingly in an increasingly urban society where literacy and education were on the rise, printing and publication.

One of the key vectors, and a lasting symbol, of Quebec's industrial development in these years was its textiles industry. Domestic textile production in the province already had a long history; think of the *Canadienne* peasant women who spun yarn from wool or flax and wove their *étoffe du pays* on household looms. Certainly carding and fulling mills existed all over the province at the turn of the nineteenth century. But the commercial manufacture of cloth in integrated textile mills dates from 1825, when a Massachusetts draper named Joseph Atwood and his local partners launched Quebec's first woollen textiles factory in Magog with such success that they were able to triple the size of their operation a year later. Many other merchants, millers, and entrepreneurs followed Atwood down the path of mechanized textile manufacture in the ensuing decades. Most of these early mills focused on woollen textiles and on local or regional markets, with the Eastern Townships remaining a stronghold. At mid-century, mills were in operation all over the region, not just in Magog and Sherbrooke but also in smaller places with good hydraulic resources such as Way's Mills, Waterville, and Stanbridge. The Townships' predominance in the woollens industry was confirmed and reinforced in 1866 when Andrew Paton built his enormous woollen textiles factory at Sherbrooke's most advantageous industrial site, near the junction of the Magog and St. Francis Rivers. Using American and British machinery and wool imported from Australia or South Africa, the Paton mill sold its tweeds and flannels all over the country and saw its workforce increase from 150 at Confederation to almost 1,000 men, women, and children at the turn of the twentieth century.[22]

But the most dramatic growth in the textiles industry came from another quarter: cotton. Prior to the 1870s, the manufacture of cotton cloth was seldom attempted in Quebec; sources of the raw material were distant and competition from Great Britain and the United States was too imposing. Although John Lomas had established a cotton textiles mill in Sherbrooke as early as 1845, the true beginnings of the industry date to the establishment of the Dominion Cotton Mills near Montreal in 1873 and of the Montreal Cotton Company in Valleyfield a year later. Soon afterwards, the 1879 National Policy tariff served the interests of these manufacturers admirably by sharply increasing the duties on imported cotton fabrics. The result was considerable investment and growth in the Quebec cotton industry, to the point where textiles came to represent one of the province's leading sectors with output valued at over $12 million in 1901.[23] A key chapter in this story was written in Valleyfield, some sixty-five kilometres southwest of Montreal. It was there in 1877 that the Montreal Cotton Company began production in its new factory located on the banks of the Beauharnois Canal, driven by the ingeniously diverted hydraulic power of the St. Lawrence. Workers at Valleyfield experienced the same low wages, long hours, harsh work discipline, dangerous

Valleyfield, Quebec, Montreal Cotton Mills. The textile factory in Valleyfield opened for business in 1877. Between 1882 and 1905, it was expanded no fewer than five times to become the largest factory of its kind in Canada with some 5,000 looms and a labour force composed of up to 2,500 men, women, and children, most of them French Canadian. © *Bibliothèque et archives nationales du Québec*

conditions, and grinding monotony as textile workers all over the world. No wonder, then, that despite Montreal Cotton's attempts at welfare capitalism—including company housing, recreational equipment, and a milk dispensary—there were at least eleven strikes, some of them violent, in the Valleyfield mill between the 1880s and 1908.[24]

Indeed, industrial capitalism had spawned labour activism in Quebec since the early decades of the nineteenth century, even though labour unions were officially illegal—defined by British law as criminal conspiracies—until 1872. The first documented labour union in the province was an association of carpenters formed in Montreal in 1818 to offer social services such as burials and widows' pensions to craftsmen and their families. Similar groups emerged in the 1820s and 1830s to represent a wide range of trades, including typographers, ship carpenters, and tailors. Typically, such a "workingmen's association" would also have enjoined its members to accept only a certain level of remuneration from employers, although this could not be admitted openly.[25] The earliest labour conflicts in Quebec history were among

Loading Ship with Square Timber through the Bow Port, Quebec City, QC, 1872, William Notman.
Longshoremen like these were among the workers who organized mutual aid societies in the mid-
nineteenth century. The Quebec Ship Labourers Benevolent Society was incorporated in 1857, its
membership consisting mainly of Irish stevedores. *McCord Museum*

the most violent, partly because workers had yet to win the right of free
association for the purposes of collective bargaining. Illegal by definition,
strikes could occur spontaneously and tended to be quashed violently by
the state and its agents. The construction workers' strikes at the Lachine
and Beauharnois Canal sites are a tragic case in point. Most of the canal
workers were Irish immigrants and they were forced to work fourteen-
hour days and to take their wages in the form of credit at the company
store. During a spontaneous work stoppage in June 1843, soldiers called
in to restore peace and to protect the entrepreneurs' property fired on a

*Les émeutes de Québec—Les Ca-
nadiens-français attaqués dans la
rue Champlain. L'Opinion publique,
4 September 1879.* The economic
crisis of the 1870s sparked labour
unrest and social conflict. This
September 1879 confrontation,
on Champlain Street in Quebec
City, pitted well-organized groups
of Irish and French-Canadian
ship labourers against each other.
© *Bibliothèque et archives nationales
du Québec*

crowd of strikers, killing ten and injuring fifty. In all, there were over 130
strikes in the province between 1815 and 1880.[26]

By 1860, American-based unions had begun to organize workers
along craft lines on both sides of the border. International craft unions
were established by cigar makers, typographers, shoemakers, and many
other trades in this period. Montreal's iron moulders, for example,
many of them of British origin, organized a union in 1859 and, in
1861, affiliated themselves with the Iron Molders' Union of America as
Section 21.[27] Prior to the 1880s, Quebec workers rarely organized along
anything other than craft lines. There were only two brief exceptions. In
the spring and summer of 1867, Montreal journalist and city councillor
Médéric Lanctôt organized La Grande Association, which assembled
workers in twenty-six different trades to defend their collective interests
as labourers.[28] And, in 1872, the Ligue ouvrière de Montréal carried the
banner of the Nine-Hour Movement on behalf of the city's workers in a
range of trades and industries. Indeed, it was an 1872 strike by Toronto

Saint-Jean-Baptiste parade on Saint-Paul Street in Quebec City, photograph by Philippe Gingras, June 1892. Parades gave expression to working class and other solidarities in the nineteenth century. The banner on the side of the horse-drawn float ("Société des ouvriers travaillant le bois") indicates an association of woodworkers. Gingras also took numerous photographs of Labour Day parades in the same city. © *Bibliothèque et archives nationales du Québec*

typographers for the nine-hour day—the standard in most industries was from ten to twelve hours in this period—that forced the federal government to revise the labour laws in such a way as to guarantee labour unions the right of free association for the purposes of collective bargaining. Still, most unions were craft-based and there was nothing in the province that could be described as a coordinated labour movement, one that might incorporate both skilled and unskilled workers and bridge the distance between the various trades and industries.

With a new legal context and a booming industrial economy protected by the new federal import tariffs, however, labour unions flourished in the 1880s. The number of recognized labour unions in the province more than quadrupled in the course of the decade, reaching ninety-one in 1890.[29] Many of these were local chapters of American international craft unions, which in 1886 organized into a powerful coalition, the American Federation of Labour. Labour federations were launched north of the border as well. Established in 1883, the Trades and Labour Congress of Canada sought to federate labour unions of all kinds, with a view towards representing the working class in discussions leading to new industrial legislation at the federal level. Delegates representing Quebec unions began to participate in 1886. The same year saw a new, more lasting effort at "horizontal" organization in Montreal. The Conseil central des métiers du travail de Montréal pledged to lobby governments and defend working-class interests in the areas of education, justice, labour legislation, public health, and political rights.[30] (Many working men would not have been allowed to vote in this period because property qualifications were still attached to the electoral franchise.)

These labour federations, clearly, did more than negotiate with employers for better pay, safer workplaces, and shorter work days— although they certainly did plenty of that. They also sought to influence governments to act in the interests of working people and to effect changes to the basic structure of industrial society. More than any other, one working-class organization, the Knights of Labor—known as Les Chevaliers du Travail to most Quebecers—stood for this expansion of the objectives and demands of the labour movement beyond the shop floor and into the social-political arena. Organized in Philadelphia in 1869, the Knights were unique among the American labour organizations that migrated to Quebec because they appealed to all categories of workers, irrespective of trade, ethnicity, race, gender, or skill level. They were distinguished by their utopian social and economic program, which included the abolition of waged labour, sweeping reforms to the legal and educational systems, and mandatory arbitration rather than strikes as a means of settling labour disputes. There was also an air of ritual and mystery surrounding the group, which began as a fraternal society under the name The Noble and Holy Order of the Knights of Labor.

The Knights were surely the fastest growing labour organization in the province in the early 1880s. The first assembly was organized by a group of Montreal telegraphers in 1882; five years later, there were some forty-five assemblies in Quebec, including twenty-nine in Montreal.[31] They were also the first working-class organization in the province to be formally condemned by the Catholic Church. For, in 1885, the archbishop of Quebec, Monseigneur Elzéar-Alexandre Taschereau, forbade his clergy from hearing the confessions of parishioners who refused to cut their ties with the Order. From Taschereau's perspective, the Knights

Monseigneur Elzéar-Alexandre Taschereau (1820–1898), Archbishop of
Quebec. Taschereau served as archbishop from 1870 to 1894. More moderate than some of his ultramontane
contemporaries, Taschereau was nonetheless wary of working-class organizations, especially those with secret rituals and foreign, non-Catholic leadership. Accordingly, he condemned the
Knights of Labor as a subversive organization in 1885, a decision that was
initially supported then reversed by the
Pope. Taschereau is pictured here in a
portrait made by photographer Jules-
Ernest Livernois in 1886, surely on the
occasion of his elevation to the rank of
Cardinal; he was the first Canadian-
born bishop to be so honoured. *Library
and Archives Canada*

were a subversive organization that, by requiring of its members both
secrecy and obedience to an unidentified (and no doubt non-Catholic)
leadership, gave off a whiff of Freemasonry. He also saw labour unions
more generally as sowing the seeds of disorder, especially by challenging
a traditional, hierarchical view of society by which a servant owed
deference and obedience to his master.[32]

The archbishop's condemnation in 1885 did not put an end to the
history of the Knights of Labor in Quebec. Initially supported by Pope
Leo XIII, the ban provoked vigorous opposition from Catholic bishops
in the United States who saw little harm in the Knights and convinced
the pontiff to reverse his decision a year later. The strength of the Knights
did decline dramatically in the 1890s, but not due to clerical opposition.
Rather, the renewed strength of international unionism weakened the
Order by drawing skilled workers away from the broader, more inclusive
Knights and back into craft-based unions concerned mainly with shop-
floor issues in specific industries. By 1903, there were only three Knights
of Labor Assemblies left in Quebec. That these in fact were the only

such assemblies remaining in all of Canada is perhaps a testament to the special and persistent appeal of the Order's ideals and rituals to French Canadians and to the failure of episcopal orders to elicit anything in the nature of blind obedience within the flock.

Working-class organizations promoting reforms in Quebec's industrial workplaces were well established, then, by the 1880s. As factory production expanded, moreover, so too did a sense that such reforms were badly needed. Frequent strikes drew public attention to long hours, low wages, child labour, industrial accidents, and abuses of power by foremen and managers. Provincial and federal authorities therefore took their first, halting steps towards regulating the industrial workplace. Inspired by an 1883 Ontario law, the Quebec legislature passed its first Factory Act in 1885, imposing a maximum work week (72.5 hours for men, 60 for women and children) and a minimum age (12 years for boys, 14 for girls) in the province's factories. The legislation also dealt with workplace safety and hygiene, but it was full of loopholes, nearly impossible to enforce, and in any case extremely lax in its provisions. There was no restriction whatsoever, for example, against employing a 12-year-old boy for six 10-hour days of hard, manual labour each week.[33]

Meanwhile, the federal government undertook a comprehensive inquiry into the state of industrial relations in the Dominion. Established in 1886, the Royal Commission on the Relations of Labour and Capital held public audiences in industrial towns all over the country. Its two reports recommended, among other things, the nine-hour day, a minimum age of fourteen years for both boys and girls employed in factory work, a compensation program for injuries suffered in the workplace, and mandatory arbitration in the event of industrial disputes. None of these proposals had any real legislative impact in the short term, however. Some were in areas of provincial jurisdiction, and most flew in the face of the economic liberalism that inspired the governments of the day, filled the pages of the commercial press (including French-language publications like Le Moniteur de Commerce), and treated any degree of government interference in industrial relations as an assault on individual liberties and the rights of private property.[34]

By 1891, as we have seen, most of the province's manufacturing sector had moved out of the traditional craft shop and into the modern factory. Flour, refined sugar, shoes, window frames, matches, cigars, woollen and cotton cloth, clothing, steam engines, and steel rails were all mass-produced in huge industrial buildings, each crowded with steam-powered machinery and tended by hundreds of wage-earning men, women, boys, and girls. Manufacturing industries were concentrated in the growing cities and, as we shall see in the next chapter, the rush of people into those cities, especially Montreal, forced all Quebecers to engage with the challenges and opportunities of modern, urban life. But the economic changes of the later nineteenth century were also felt in the vast rural regions of the province, where a majority of the population continued to live.

Beginning at mid-century, in fact, the growing export market and railway construction in the province stimulated greater commercialization and specialization of agricultural production. Farmers on the fertile land of the Montreal plain met growing competition from grain producers in Upper Canada and the American Midwest by consolidating their holdings and slowly mechanizing to eliminate the cost of seasonal labour.[35] But the future for Quebec agriculture as a whole lay with the dairy production (butter and cheese) for which the province's farmers enjoyed the crucial advantage of closer access to the growing British and eastern urban markets at a time when there was no mechanical refrigeration. The Eastern Townships had a head start since it had been a livestock-producing region from the beginning. The province's first cheese factories opened in Missisquoi County during the 1860s and Quebec production multiplied from slightly less than eight million pounds in 1881 to over eighty million pounds in 1901, when it eclipsed butter production for the first time. But cheese production declined thereafter because of New Zealand's competition on the British market.[36]

The quality of Quebec's dairy products remained inferior to those of Ontario due to the slow consolidation of rural factories, which in turn was probably largely due to the poor condition of rural roads. Oats, hay, and horses for the American market remained important agricultural commodities as well, but, in much of rural Quebec, the first priority remained production for the family's own consumption. Lack of capital and large families slowed farm mechanization, which largely explains why, at the end of the century the average Ontario farm was two and a half times more productive than that of Quebec. Nowhere was this more evident than in the colonization zones. According to Gérard Bouchard's co-integration model, based on exhaustive research on the Saguenay region, the increased production for the extra-regional market that came with the dairy industry in the 1880s did not result in a conversion to agrarian capitalism. Rather, the money generated by the sale of butter and cheese, combined with the labour of the young both on and off the farm, reinforced the existing social order by enabling families to sustain a high birth rate and expand the settlement zone until the Second World War, when the system finally ended.[37]

In the meantime, between the 1890s and the 1920s, Quebec entered a new phase of its economic development, often referred to as the "Second Industrial Revolution." Fresh waves of economic prosperity, the application of new industrial technologies to the extraction of natural resources, the reorganization of capital into larger and larger units, and the growing importance of the United States, both as a market for semi-finished products and as a source of capital investments, combined to alter the character and scale of the province's industrial base. In particular, this new phase of manufacturing growth emphasized new productive sectors like newsprint and aluminum and incorporated new energy sources like diesel power and especially hydroelectricity.

Indeed, the fulcrum and the lasting symbol of the Second Industrial Revolution in Quebec was the emergence of hydroelectric energy. Electrical power had been produced in thermal generators in the province as early as the 1880s. But the first large-scale hydroelectric project was begun at Shawinigan, on the St. Maurice River, in 1898. The idea of harnessing the energy of a river to produce electricity was imported from the United States, as was much of the equipment and capital used to build Shawinigan and the other early power dams. Quebec had vast natural potential in this area, with its hundreds of rivers, many of them fast moving, especially those located on the rugged Laurentian shield. The exploitation of these resources required capital investments on a far larger scale than ever before seen in the province. Corporate giants like Shawinigan Water and Power, private companies financed in large part by American and English-Canadian investment, came to dominate the production and transmission of electrical energy, the demand for which expanded exponentially after the turn of the century. With major investments in dam-building in the St. Maurice River Valley and elsewhere, the energy supply increased apace, from just 83,000 horse power in 1901 to over two million in 1930.[38] In these early decades of the new century, moreover, hydroelectric power came to be associated with modernity, for producers and consumers alike. In the 1890s, electrical energy was used mainly for street lighting and for operating tramway lines, with manufacturers only just beginning to explore its potential. By 1920, however, electricity was being used across the province in a vast array of industrial applications and, increasingly, as a source of domestic energy. As historian Claude Bellavance reminds us, this was a modern consumer trend that began in urban areas, which "would soon be transported beyond the theatre of the big city to reach an ever growing number of smaller localities," and which was fast becoming "the symbol par excellence of progress" in the province.[39]

As with hydroelectricity, most of the other growth industries in turn-of-the-century Quebec were based on the application of modern technologies to the extraction and processing of natural resources, particularly for the export market. Like the sawmills of the previous generation, these new, highly capitalized plants were most often located in rural areas close to the resources, rather than in Montreal or Quebec City. A good example is the pulp and paper industry. Small paper mills had been in existence since the opening years of the nineteenth century; the earliest one, in Saint-André d'Argenteuil, dates from 1804. By 1851, the province had perhaps a half-dozen of these establishments, which used traditional materials such as rags and straw in the manufacture of paper. The new idea of using resinous wood pulp was introduced in the 1860s: propitious timing from the perspective of sawmill operators, because it allowed them to harvest smaller trees with inferior wood, at a time when there was a growing shortage of pine and other species suitable for lumber production. Modern pulp and paper production in Quebec dates from 1877, when Montrealer John Foreman began operations at Grand-Mère, upstream from Shawinigan on the St. Maurice River. By 1892, the Laurentide Pulp Company was producing some 45 tonnes of wood pulp daily, a figure that would climb to 120 tonnes by 1900, not to mention 40 tonnes of manila paper and 30 tonnes of cardboard. With the

INTERNATIONAL PAPER COMPANY'S PLANT, THREE RIVERS, P.Q.

The International Paper Company plant in Trois-Rivières, with working-class housing in the foreground, early twentieth-century postcard. Pulp and paper production totally transformed the forestry sector in the late nineteenth century and was one of the driving forces behind Quebec's Second Industrial Revolution early in the twentieth. It was a short commute for employees of this paper mill. One is struck by the contrast between their simple wooden houses, some with the steeply pitched roofs common in rural Quebec, and the gigantic modern factory in the background. © Bibliothèque et archives nationales du Québec

development of several other mills, especially in the St. Maurice Valley and in the Saguenay-Lac-Saint-Jean region, Quebec pulp and paper producers increased their annual capacity to over $6 million by 1901.[40]

Initially, Quebec producers focused on the production of wood pulp for export to paper factories in the United States, where the market for newsprint—stimulated by the growth of daily newspapers and especially their advertising content—was expanding quickly. Quebec-based entrepreneurs, however, soon moved into newsprint production, realizing the efficiencies that were to be found in the integrated production of continuous rolls of newsprint in huge mills located close to the coniferous forests that provided their raw material. In order to encourage the production of paper in Quebec mills, the provincial legislature followed an Ontario example by moving in 1910 to prohibit the export of pulp logs cut on Crown lands. American papermakers were thus leveraged into setting up or expanding Quebec newsprint operations in order to continue serving the vast United States market.

With all of these stimuli, the province's pulp and paper industry grew rapidly, with the annual value of production growing almost tenfold between 1910 and 1929.[41]

There were no significant coal reserves in Quebec, so the soot-faced pit workers of contemporary Wales or Pennsylvania had no equivalent in the province. Prior to the 1880s, commercial mining of any kind was extremely limited in scope. Much of it was done in the Eastern Townships, where access to American markets was excellent and where, in the absence of seigneurial restrictions, landowners were free to exploit the copper and other mineral resources (other than gold and silver) that lay beneath their property. Beginning in the 1850s, copper mining emerged as a significant regional industry, particularly in the Massawippi Valley. Stimulated by American demand during the Civil War, copper mines in Hatley and Ascot Townships thrived during the heyday of the early 1860s. Copper mining was a volatile sector in the ensuing decades and highly sensitive to international demand conditions, so many ventures lasted only a few years. Those that endured did so on the basis of New York or Boston capital and sometimes, as was the case for the Capleton mine near Lennoxville, by combining mining with secondary activities such as the manufacture of chemicals, fertilizers, and explosives.[42]

At the turn of the twentieth century, the Quebec mining industry expanded, following the patterns associated with the Second Industrial Revolution. The Eastern Townships, once again, was the focus of the first wave of this expansion. When asbestos was discovered in Thetford Township in the 1870s, the stage was set for the emergence of another highly capitalized, resource-based industry. Asbestos mining began with the opening of the Johnson mine in Thetford in 1878 and grew rapidly in the 1880s, to the point where Quebec soon emerged as one of the world's leading producers of the heat-resistant fibre. Production was concentrated in five centres: Asbestos, Coleraine, Black Lake, Thetford Mines, and East Broughton. By 1911, this part of the Townships region was extracting 100,000 tonnes of asbestos, valued at $3.5 million, each year.[43] Competition among independent producers had begun to give way to corporate concentration and to American capital, a trend that culminated in 1925 with the merger of eleven companies into the Asbestos Corporation. Asbestos mining was an extractive industry located in a rural area that involved rather little transformation of the natural resource, other than separating the fibre from the rock.[44] It was driven by international demand, funded by American capital, organized into larger and larger corporate entities, and relied on a male labour force. As such, it was typical of the new industries that transformed Quebec's industrial landscape at this time. The same could be said of two new "heavy" industries that emerged in the 1920s: the aluminium smelters that combined imported bauxite with the substantial hydroelectric potential of the Saguenay River, and the significant gold, silver, zinc, and copper mining operations that transformed the newly colonized Abitibi-Témiscamingue region in northwestern Quebec.

As Quebec's industrial base took on new dimensions and new characteristics in the opening decades of the twentieth century, so too did its labour movement. International craft unions remained strong in the province, with about 6,000 members in 1902.[45] But they were not without rivals, chief among which were the Catholic unions that began to appear around this time. One of the earliest, fittingly, was established in a capital-intensive resource industry situated hundreds of kilometres away from Montreal. In 1907, when Father Eugène Lapointe organized French-Canadian workers in the Dubuc group of pulp factories into the Fédération ouvrière de Chicoutimi, he helped set into motion a movement that gained momentum in the years following the First World War. The Catholic clergy's establishment of its own network of labour unions, twenty years after Monseigneur Taschereau's denunciation of the Knights of Labor, may seem a great paradox, but the logic of the initiative was crystal clear from a Catholic and nationalist standpoint. Although sympathetic to the plight of the working poor, the Catholic clergy feared international unions because they were religiously neutral and therefore open to socialist and anticlerical ideas and because they represented a foreign influence on French-Canadian workers. Rather than denouncing all labour unions, the Church's response now was to establish denominational unions that would be strictly supervised by a chaplain, in which the membership would be exclusively Catholic, and in which the centres of decision-making would remain within Quebec. The idea was promoted actively and successfully in the years leading up to 1921, when the Catholic labour movement was consolidated with

La foule attendant à la porte de la filature hier matin, que l'on decide de leur donner leur paie attendue depuis quelques semaines. La Patrie, 21 August 1907, front page. Some 2,200 men and women participated in the August 1907 strike at the Montreal Cotton Company's Valleyfield mill. Labour conflicts there were frequent; at least eleven strikes occurred between 1880 and 1908. The caption in *La Patrie* reads as follows: "The crowd waiting outside the offices of the textile mill, yesterday morning, for the decision to give them their wages, for which they have been waiting for several weeks." © *Bibliothèque et archives nationales du Québec*

the formation of its own federation, the Confédération des travailleurs catholiques du Canada (CTCC). Estimates for the following year suggest that there were some 120 Catholic unions in the province at this time, representing up to one-quarter of all unionized workers, with the greatest numbers located outside Montreal and in the new, resource-based industries characteristic of the Second Industrial Revolution.[46]

The tensions between tradition and modernity are nowhere more apparent than in the study of industrial capitalism and its consequences.

The depth and scope of the changes associated with Quebec's industrial revolution were immense and were already apparent to many by middle of the nineteenth century. By the 1920s, social relations were vastly more complex than they had been at the dawn of the industrial age. Agriculture and rural life remained key references in most efforts to define the majority's French-Canadian identity and culture. But for all its rural and agricultural traditions, the province was an increasingly urban and industrial place: a reality we shall continue to explore in the next chapter. It was also fertile ground for the new cultural, ideological, and political currents that are examined in Chapter 9.

EIGHT

CITIES AND TOWNS

As a built environment and as a system of social relations, the city of Montreal is a lasting testament to the industrial capitalism of the nineteenth century. Indeed, the first thing to know about Quebec's urban network is the extent to which it was dominated by a single city. Montreal was already established by the late 1840s as British North America's most important commercial city, as an emerging railway hub and maritime port, and briefly as the political capital of the United Canadas. But the city's development in the second half of the century was nothing short of spectacular. Its population tripled between 1831 and 1861—from 30,000 to 90,000—and then tripled again in each of the ensuing forty-year periods, reaching 267,000 by 1901, and 903,000 by 1941. As the city grew, it came to encompass an ever greater proportion of the province's overall population. In 1871, one in every eleven Quebecers lived in the metropolis; by 1901, that proportion had risen to one in six, and it would continue to rise through the twentieth century, so that by 1941 over one-quarter of the province's 3.3 million people lived in Montreal.[1]

Two successive waves of migration fuelled this growth, the first of which was transatlantic in scope while the second was internal to the province. The tide of emigration from the British Isles in the decades following the end of the Napoleonic Wars in 1815 brought new waves of English, Scots, and especially Irish newcomers to British North America. Montreal was a prime destination for many of those immigrants, including Scots merchants eager to try their hand at the import-export trade and impoverished Irish labourers fleeing rural poverty who were forced to accept whatever work they could find. Indeed, transatlantic migration to Montreal after 1815 was sufficient to place the city's British-origin population in a majority position in the three decades prior to Confederation. The tide began to turn in the 1860s, however,

Custom House Square, Montreal, QC, 1830, watercolour by John Henry Walker, copied 1896. Montreal and Quebec City were colonial towns of roughly equal size in the 1820s and 1830s. Montreal's harbour facilities, as the painting shows, were not well developed at this time. Steam technology had been applied to river navigation—several paddle wheelers are seen here plying the St. Lawrence—but there was no railway until 1836, and steam-powered factories did not appear until much later in the century. *McCord Museum*

as the effects of the next wave of migrants—comprised of thousands of French-Canadian families from the St. Lawrence Valley looking for wages and a better life in the city—began to be felt. By 1871, French-speaking Montrealers were once again in the majority, and by 1901 they were well established as the city's largest ethnic or linguistic community, with 61 percent of the urban population.

As Montreal's population expanded, so did its territory. In 1867, the city's borders were still defined by a 1792 law that had established them as a polygon parallel to the stone fortifications surrounding the pre-Conquest city (defining the area we now call "Old Montreal") but at a distance of about two kilometres in each direction from that perimeter. Twenty years after Confederation, this historic territory, once covered with farms, orchards, and woods, was filled in and fully urbanized. So the city began to grow by accretions. By 1893, it had annexed neighbouring communities such as Saint-Gabriel to the west, Saint-Jean Baptiste and Côte-Saint-Louis to the north, and Hochelaga to the east; in addition, it claimed the land occupied by Mount Royal Park, which had been developed for the city in the 1870s by the renowned American landscape architect Frederick Law Olmstead. By 1911, only about half of the city's population lived within its 1792 boundaries, with the other half (almost one-quarter of a million people) residing in former "suburbs" like Saint-Henri, Côte-des-Neiges, and Longue-Pointe, all of which were annexed to the city in the first decade of the twentieth century.

The city expanded upwards as well. Imposing new buildings such as the neoclassical Bank of Montreal (1848) and the new city hall, constructed in the early 1870s in the Second Empire style, asserted the power of the city's financial elite and its elected officials, respectively. In the 1880s, new monuments joined a skyline long dominated by the twin towers of Notre-Dame Basilica. St. James Cathedral (now Mary, Queen of the World) on Dorchester Street, for example, was commissioned by Monseigneur Bourget and built between 1875 and 1885 as a scaled-down replica of St. Peter's Basilica in Rome. The religious power of ultramontane Catholicism could find no better symbol than its Italianate, neo-baroque architecture, audaciously sited near the centres of English-Protestant financial power. The 1880s also saw the arrival in the city of Chicago-style steel-frame skyscrapers, beginning with the eight-storey New York Life Insurance building, completed in 1887 on Place d'Armes.[2] The same building principle that allowed modern office towers to rise to these unprecedented heights—a steel framework sheathed with non-load-bearing curtain walls of brick or stone—was applied in industrial architecture to supply the enormous interior spaces required by the factories of the day.

Montreal's expansion was a function of its growing commercial and industrial importance. Built between 1854 and 1859, the new Victoria Bridge provided a modern alternative to ferries and ice bridges across the St. Lawrence River and consolidated the city's central position in the railway network. The "tubular" iron span was heralded as a marvel of modern engineering, and inaugurated with great ceremony by Albert, Prince of Wales, in August 1860. By the 1880s, Montreal was a crucial hub for the Grand Trunk and Canadian Pacific railway systems, dominating east–west commercial traffic within the expanding Dominion. It was also a major international port, handling almost 40 percent of all

Victoria Bridge, Grand Trunk Railway, photograph by Alexander Henderson, 1878. The Victoria Bridge was the first permanent span across the St. Lawrence River. Built for the Grand Trunk Railway, it was completed in 1859 and inaugurated by the Prince of Wales in 1860. The bridge represented a huge engineering challenge, especially given the harsh climate and the sheer force of the ice in the river. At the time, it was the longest span ever built: 2,787 metres. Construction took five years, cost $6.6 million, and employed some 3,040 men and boys during the peak year (1858). Ultimately, the bridge stimulated Montreal's commercial and industrial development by consolidating the city's position in the North American railway network. *Library and Archives Canada*

Canadian imports along with one-third of all exports in the late 1880s. As historians Jean Hamelin and Yves Roby point out, "The twenty or so consulates and vice-consulates established in the city at the end of the nineteenth century proclaimed Montreal's uncontested supremacy in Canadian international trade."[3] The city, moreover, was at the heart of the new industrial economy described in the last chapter. By 1910, Montreal and its suburbs accounted for $195 million worth of manufacturing production: more than half of the provincial total and almost one-fifth of the industrial output for all of Canada.[4]

With urban growth came the contrasts and inequalities associated with all industrial cities. Neigbourhoods and streets took on specific functions—residential, commercial, or industrial—and distinct social and cultural profiles. Wealthy English-speaking Montrealers fled the

City of Montreal, A.W. Morris & Bro., 1888. This bird's-eye view of Montreal shows the industrial area surrounding the Lachine Canal in the lower left foreground. By this time, Montreal was as much a city of chimneys and smoke stacks—as this artist was keen to emphasize—as it was, more famously, of church towers and steeples. *McCord Museum*

city's core and built mansions on the slopes of Mount Royal, giving rise to opulent residential districts like the "Square Mile" in St. Antoine ward and, beyond the municipal boundary, Westmount. At the same time, working-class neighbourhoods grew up in proximity to the mills and factories, especially those of St. Ann's ward in the southwest and St. Marie ward in the east. Inevitably, class-based inequalities came to be conflated in the popular imagination with the ethnic and linguistic differences they approximated. In fact, English speakers were not uniformly rich and they did not all live in nice, big houses located west of St. Lawrence Boulevard—still a fascinating liminal space and the city's key cultural boundary—just as French Canadians were not all crowded into poorly built wooden tenements in working-class areas to the east. But there was enough truth in those stereotypes to encourage both a Victorian sense of superiority and entitlement within the anglophone elites and the deeper feelings of social and political injustice that would fuel French-Canadian and later Québécois nationalism for generations to come.

Fireplace, Lord Strathcona's house, Montreal, Quebec, 1916. In Montreal a century ago, the contrast between the domestic spaces of the rich and the poor could not have been starker. Donald Smith was a Scottish-born entrepreneur who began his Canadian career as a clerk for the Hudson's Bay Company and who ultimately accumulated a vast fortune with interests in commerce, banking, railways, and manufacturing. He was a leading figure at the Bank of Montreal and the Canadian Pacific Railway. He became one of the city's most prominent philanthropists, making especially generous contributions in support of hospitals, medical training, and women's education. Smith was knighted in 1886 for his work on the CPR and entered the British peerage in 1897 as Lord Strathcona. A richly decorated interior space from his opulent residence on Dorchester Street (now René-Lévesque Boulevard) is depicted in this Notman photograph, taken in 1916, two years after Strathcona's death. *McCord Museum*

While Montreal was at the heart of Quebec's network of cities and towns, industrial capitalism spawned urban development in other parts of the province as well. Quebec City had been comparable in size and importance to Montreal in the early decades of the nineteenth century. But in the 1840s, when the river channel was dredged upstream to permit the passage of large seafaring vessels, Quebec's strategic position at the head of maritime navigation was lost. And its key industries— wooden shipbuilding and the trade in squared timber—reflected the traditional "wood and wind" technologies of the eighteenth century rather than the "steam and steel" of the modern era. Certainly, Quebec

City benefited from the constitutional arrangements of 1867, taking on new government and administrative functions as the provincial capital. But it suffered from the departure of the British garrison in 1871 and from its peripheral position in the continental railway network. Over the next thirty years, as Montreal's population grew by 160,000, Quebec City added only 9,000 inhabitants to reach a population of just under 70,000 (roughly one-quarter the size of the metropolis) by 1901. Yet it easily remained the province's second city, with a population five times that of third-place Hull.

In addition to its status as the provincial capital, Quebec was home to important religious and educational institutions, including Laval University, which was the only French-language university on the continent from its inception in 1852 up until 1919, when its Montreal satellite (launched in 1876) acquired an independent charter as the Université de Montréal. Quebec City also had an active manufacturing sector, including a boot-and-shoe industry that featured approximately thirty factories employing close to 4,000 workers at the turn of the twentieth century.[5] Its entrepreneurial class, unable to compete with the Montrealers on the continental stage, focused instead on projects that solidified the city's influence over a growing regional hinterland. Many of these were railway projects such as the Quebec Central, which linked Lévis (on the south shore opposite Quebec) with Sherbrooke in the 1880s, and the Quebec and Lake St. John, which, when completed in 1893, linked Quebec City with the Saguenay region, disrupting traditional Aboriginal (Innu) hunting and trapping territories in the process.[6] Improved railway connections also helped Quebec establish its reputation as a travel destination for Americans and English Canadians drawn to its history, architecture, and culture. With its proximity and its "European charm," tourists viewed Quebec as an entirely unique city within North America: an impression that civic leaders and private entrepreneurs were eager to foster—the impressive Chateau Frontenac, completed in 1893, is a case in point—and which gave rise to a tourist industry that continued to thrive throughout the twentieth century.[7]

Below Quebec City in the urban hierarchy were a handful of towns such as Trois-Rivières, Sherbrooke, and Valleyfield that had been reshaped by the social and economic forces of the times—industrial capitalism, railway development, and internal migration—but none of which had more than 14,000 inhabitants at the turn of the twentieth century. Across the Ottawa River from the federal capital, Hull's growth was the direct result of industrial development in the forest products sector, most of which was initiated by a single entrepreneur. By 1902, E.B. Eddy's various enterprises provided 2,000 jobs to local men, women, and children engaged in the transformation of the region's forests into everything from wooden matches—a particularly dangerous industry that employed many women and girls—to newsprint.[8] Saint-Hyacinthe, for its part, was already a market town with 3,000 inhabitants in 1851— the railway had arrived in the late 1840s—and its population tripled in the ensuing fifty years. Its new institutional position as the seat of a judicial district and a Catholic diocese generated some limited growth in the 1850s and 1860s. But in the 1870s, local authorities began actively to promote industrial development by offering cash bonuses and long-term tax exemptions to prospective manufacturers. These policies and the factories they attracted, by creating jobs in local industry, offered alternatives to French-Canadian families who might otherwise be drawn to the manufacturing Meccas of New England and Montreal. As a result, the town's population grew more quickly after 1871 than before, reaching 5,000 in 1881 and surpassing 9,000 by 1901.[9] The two largest manufacturing industries in Saint-Hyacinthe were boot-and-shoe and knitted-goods production, although there were also foundries, a woollens mill, tanneries, a corset factory, and one of the province's leading musical instrument builders, the Casavant organ company.

The expansion of Quebec's cities, both large and small, created a need for urban infrastructures and services. Private entrepreneurs and local authorities jostled to develop the massive new systems that were needed to provide city dwellers with water, warmth, light, communication, and local transportation. Whether such services should be developed as profit-making enterprises or as public utilities was one of the great debates of the day.[10] Throughout the province, the approach of municipal authorities was often to use franchising arrangements in which private developers were contracted to provide specific services to the public. They could take profits on the services they provided but were required to meet certain conditions stipulated by the municipality in the contract. This kind of system encouraged monopolistic business practices, not to mention political patronage and cronyism.

Modernizing and sanitizing water supplies was one of the great urban challenges of the period. Montreal established a municipal water supply in 1845 and a new waterworks was installed in 1856, to be expanded and improved over the ensuing decades. While the city had a publicly owned and operated waterworks, most neighbouring communities franchised the service to a series of private utilities, which eventually amalgamated to form the Montreal Water and Power Company. As the urban territory expanded through annexations, this situation led to a two-tiered water utility, with a public service in the original territory and a private utility (with rates to match) in the newly annexed suburbs.[11]

This mix of public and private initiatives ensured the provision of water in sufficient quantity to the burgeoning city. Water quality was another matter entirely, however, and one with serious consequences for public health. The source of Montreal's drinking water, the St. Lawrence River, was also the destination for its industrial effluents and the daily sewage produced by hundreds of thousands of human bodies. A water supply contaminated with bacteria was, without doubt, part of the reason why infant mortality in the city was so high, averaging 25–30 percent within the French-Canadian population, with significant peaks in the hot summer months. It took a major public health reform campaign to correct this situation in the early decades of the twentieth century.[12] Important parts of the solution were the chlorination of the city's water supply, initiated in 1910, and the completion in 1918 of a water treatment facility.[13]

Smaller cities also had to grapple with these issues. Industrialist and mayor Louis Côté, for example, championed the creation of a waterworks in Saint-Hyacinthe. But the fact that he was at the same time president of a private utility, the Compagnie de l'Aqueduc de Saint-Hyacinthe, became a subject of controversy in the 1880s. In the spring of 1884, local critics began to complain that the intake pipe in the Yamaska River had been placed directly adjacent to sewage pipes. Public health was compromised—infant mortality levels in Saint-Hyacinthe were every bit as dramatic as in Montreal—and Côté, under intense criticism, was

Hull after the 1900 fire, from Geological Survey of Canada Photographs. Four in every ten residents of Hull lost their homes in the devastating fire of 1900. The bricks in the foreground of this photograph are most likely the remains of a factory, since most residences in this community were made of wood. *Library and Archives Canada*

forced to submit his resignation as mayor, although it was rejected by a majority on council that included other partners in the waterworks.[14]

Quebec's towns and cities needed water for fire protection as well. Fire was a constant worry and a perennial scourge in cities and suburbs where many structures were built entirely of wood and where most of the rest were of brick or stone over wooden beams; during the winter, wood-burning stoves heated iron pipes and chimneys in most private dwellings and places of business. Just about every town and city in the province has as a chapter of its local history a dramatic conflagration—and often two or three. A massive fire in July of 1852 razed major sections of Montreal's St. Lawrence and St. Marie wards; it destroyed 1,200 houses, left 10,000 people homeless, and prompted the city to ban the construction of wooden houses throughout its territory.[15] In September 1876, one-third of the buildings in Saint-Hyacinthe, including 600 houses, the central market, and the Côté shoe factory, were burned to the ground.[16] But Hull holds the sad record, perhaps not surprisingly for a town devoted to and made of wood, for it suffered no fewer than eight such disasters between 1880 and 1933. Many of these left indelible scars, none more so than the great fire of 1900, which put 42 percent of the local population into the streets.[17] Initiating and updating fire-protection services was absolutely crucial under these circumstances. Montreal established its municipal fire service in 1863 with twenty-nine regular firefighters and three companies of volunteers. The size of the force and the sophistication of its methods—including the steam-powered pumps first used in 1871—increased as the century progressed. Other municipalities had no choice but to follow suit.

At the same time, urban communities developed their infrastructures for the delivery of energy in the form of natural gas and, later, electricity. In Montreal, gas for lighting streets, homes, and businesses was provided by a private monopoly, the Montreal Gas Light Company, founded in 1836. By the 1870s, the company had gained a dubious reputation among customers for its high rates and poor service, while delivering nice fat dividends to shareholders. Competition from electricity and from an upstart gas company in the 1880s, however, led to pressures for reduced rates and for a restructuring of the gas utility. By 1895, when the utility's contract with the city had to be renegotiated, Montreal Gas and its new president, the financier Herbert Holt, had managed to absorb the rival company and to stake out a niche within the energy market. With the increasing use of electric light, the gas utility had been forced to focus instead on domestic heating and cooking. But a rapidly expanding customer base meant that Holt was nonetheless able to satisfy the demand for lower rates without seriously affecting profits.[18]

Public transportation was the other item of modern infrastructure that Quebec's cities developed in the nineteenth century. Montreal's privately owned horse-drawn tramway line was inaugurated in November 1861. The Montreal Street Railway, with its terminus in east-end Hochelaga, began small but soon grew in scale and efficiency. From 1.5 million passengers in 1864, the annual ridership rose to 11.6 million by 1892 and then, dramatically, to 107 million by 1914.[19] In 1892, the Montreal

Tramway Crossing under Construction, St. Catherine Street and St. Lawrence Boulevard, Montreal, QC, 1893, William Notman & Son. By the time of the First World War, modern electric streetcar systems were in place in not just in Montreal and Quebec City, but in smaller centres like Hull, Trois-Rivières, and Sherbrooke as well. *McCord Museum*

streetcar system began its conversion from horsepower to electricity and, at the same time, entered a phase of expansion, both within and beyond the city. By 1904, the number of electric streetcars had reached 300, and the network had spread beyond the city into suburbs like Maisonneuve to the east, Saint-Louis to the north, and Westmount to the west.[20] At the same time, larger towns all over Quebec embraced the new technology by installing their own electric streetcar systems. Quebec City's horse-drawn streetcars were converted to electricity in the 1890s and Hull, Trois-Rivières, and Sherbrooke all had modern electric tramway lines in place by 1915.[21]

As Quebec's cities expanded, urban poverty and public health emerged as the most pressing social issues of the day. In 1897, the industrialist turned alderman and social activist Herbert B. Ames published *The City Below the Hill*, a scathing indictment of living conditions in the working-class Saint-Henri district of Montreal.

Poverty in Montreal, 1914. Many working-class families were forced to endure miserable living conditions like those illustrated in this photograph of a Montreal courtyard in 1914. Reformers like Herbert Brown Ames struggled to improve the urban environment in the face of social and public-health problems associated with poverty, inadequate housing, and poor sanitation. Ames campaigned in particular for modern sewerage systems and the elimination of the outdoor pit toilets that predominated in neighbourhoods like this, polluting the ground water and contributing to high levels of infant mortality. © *Bibliothèque et archives nationales du Québec*

Inspired by contemporary American social-science methods, Ames differed from those (and there were many) who ascribed poverty to personal moral failings such as laziness and intemperance, finding fault instead with an industrial system that did not provide willing workers with any protection against low wages or unemployment.[22] The study focused on the grinding poverty endured by the labouring population and brought into the light of day such urban scourges as overcrowded tenement housing, inadequate sewage systems, contaminated water supplies, and the shockingly high infant mortality rates that were linked to these and other urban problems.

No longer tied to agriculture or the land, Quebec's labouring population in the age of industrialization was in constant motion, as families and individuals moved from place to place in search of adequate, steady wages. French-Canadian workers continued to migrate in their thousands from the countryside into industrializing towns and cities, including those located south of the border in New England. At the same time, working-class families moved frequently *within* cities like Montreal, constantly adjusting their expenditure on rental housing to family size, revenues, and the availability of appropriate flats, apartments, and houses. The local tradition of an annual moving day, in which thousands of rental units changed hands on the same day—the first of May, which gave way to the first of July in the 1970s—was well established by the 1860s.[23]

Geographic mobility, over longer and shorter distances, was just one strategy that working-class Quebecers used to cope with the rigours of industrial capitalism and urban life. Working-class families drew on the cooperative principle of kinship solidarity that stood at the heart of rural society. This often depended, for example, on the waged work of as many members as possible, including school-aged children. Shocking to liberal commentators, child labour was rooted in a number of factors, including the industrialists' failure to pay a "family wage" to male household heads, the weakness of the factory legislation first adopted in the 1880s, and the absence of compulsory schooling legislation until the 1940s. At the same time, married women were conspicuous by their absence from the formal labour market. Their unpaid work as household managers, childcare providers, laundresses, and cooks kept them more than busy enough. Indeed, working-class women were at the heart of the coping strategies that allowed their families to persevere in the face of poverty and unemployment. They did so in a variety of ways: by carefully stretching scarce wages as shrewd shoppers, by tending to urban kitchen gardens, chicken coops, and even pigsties (until they were abolished in the mid-1860s for public health reasons), and by taking in boarders, washing, sewing, or even piecework from local factories.[24] They were still doing so in the 1930s when the Great Depression brought the fragility of working-class family economies into the foreground, as we shall see in Chapter 10, with fresh calls for state-sponsored programs to offset the worst effects of industrial capitalism.[25]

Despite these efforts, some were unable to avoid the slide from sustainable poverty into destitution and pauperism. In the absence of a state-run social welfare system, a two-pronged, denominational, private system of charitable aid for the neediest families and individuals was constructed in the province. Spread across the territory, the network of Catholic social service institutions, most of them run by women's religious orders, expanded exponentially. As the urban population expanded, so too did the number and scale of Catholic orphanages, hospices, crèches, and asylums—all catering, unlike the *hôpital général* or almshouse of an earlier period, to specific categories of destitute, abandoned, or infirm Quebecers. Orders such as the Misericordia Sisters (Soeurs de la Miséricorde, founded in 1848) and the Sisters of Providence (Soeurs de la Providence, founded in 1843) specialized in health and social services, providing institutional care in austere surroundings, with an emphasis on moral and religious improvement. Founded in 1737 by Saint Marguerite d'Youville (she was canonized in 1999), the Soeurs de la Charité, or Grey Nuns, played a major role in this area. From their imposing 1870s Mother House on Dorchester Boulevard (now René-Lévesque Boulevard) in Montreal and with satellite convents reaching across the province and beyond, the Grey Nuns built and managed a web of institutions catering to orphans, Irish immigrants, unwed mothers, the sick, the mentally ill, the elderly, and many other categories of people in need.[26] One of the most pitiful victims and a powerful symbol of poverty in the Victorian era was the foundling, and the Grey Nuns had been caring for abandoned infants in their Crèche d'Youville since the 1750s. By the late 1860s, hundreds of helpless babies from all over the province were abandoned each year to the care of the Grey Nuns. Deprived of maternal care in their most fragile hours and subjected to bottled milk and other risky feeding methods, most did not survive their first year of life under institutional care.[27]

Meanwhile, the English-Protestant minority developed its own system of social services that was concentrated in Montreal, with a presence in centres like Quebec City and especially Sherbrooke. The Protestant system was based on the principles of voluntarism, philanthropy, and social reform and grounded on a partnership between middle-class women and a socially active clergy. It was also grounded on some key distinctions within contemporary philanthropy, those between the "deserving" and the "non-deserving" poor and among various categories of indigent people, categories based largely on age, gender, and condition. The Montreal Ladies' Benevolent Society, for example, was founded in 1832 and remained a key social service agency in the city for many subsequent decades.[28] The Protestant House of Industry and Refuge was established in 1863 as a general almshouse providing a winter refuge and sustenance for all categories of destitute and homeless people. It later grew into a more specialized institution, focusing on the elderly and the infirm and leaving the care of poor and abandoned children to specifically Protestant orphanages, reform schools, and foundling homes. Another important Protestant initiative was the Old Brewery Mission, a soup kitchen established by the city's Methodist churches in 1890. Two years later, the St. Antoine street mission was offering bed, bath, and a meal to the indigent for ten cents a night. By the turn of the century it was providing tens of thousands of overnight stays and meals per year to the city's homeless and hungry, a service it continues to provide up to the present day.[29]

Victorian cities, large and small, were distinctly unhealthy places, especially for the poor. Infant mortality was one of the major public health issues of the day and it was closely associated with the kind of desperate, overcrowded living conditions that Ames exposed in *The City below the Hill*. In Montreal in 1895, one-quarter of French-Canadian Catholic children died before their first birthdays; so did one-fifth of other Catholic infants (most of them Irish) and about one-sixth of Protestants.[30] Sanitary reformers shocked their readers by comparing Montreal to underdeveloped cities overseas—especially Calcutta in India—for its abysmal record on child survival.[31] Ames and others ascribed the clear differential between Catholics and Protestants to the significant discrepancies in wealth, housing quality, and sanitary amenities between the two communities, pointing specifically to the absence of flush toilets in many working-class flats and apartments; Ames earned the moniker "Water Closet Ames" for his determined campaign to eliminate the dangerous pit privy.[32] Recent research, however, shows that social and cultural factors, such as a wider recourse to bottle feeding among French Canadians, must also be considered alongside the economic and environmental ones.[33]

Like infant mortality, tuberculosis was associated with urban poverty, both in fact and in the popular imagination. TB, or consumption, was poorly understood by medical science until the discovery by German physician Robert Koch of its cause, the tubercle bacillus (*Mycobacterium tuberculosis*) in 1882.[34] Known in French as *la peste blanche* (the white plague), tuberculosis was the leading cause of mortality among young adults, accounting for about 3,000 deaths in the province each year in the first decade of the twentieth century. As a whole, Quebec recorded over 120 deaths from TB per thousand inhabitants in 1921, compared to just fewer than 90 for Canada as a whole.[35] French Canadians appear to have been more likely than others to catch the deadly respiratory form of the disease. This was especially true if they were living in the crowded, poorly ventilated rental housing that characterized many working-class neighbourhoods, particularly in Montreal, which suffered more from the ravages of tuberculosis than any other North American city.[36]

Urban Quebec also suffered disproportionately from the mortality crises of the nineteenth and early twentieth centuries. Epidemic diseases were among the great dangers of the industrial city and could in a matter of months leave hundreds or thousands of dead in their wake. In the 1830s and 1840s, outbreaks of cholera and typhus (sometimes called ship fever) were associated with Irish immigration and led to early public health measures such as the establishment of a quarantine station at Grosse-Île, in the St. Lawrence River just downstream from Quebec City. The events surrounding the smallpox epidemic of 1885 were particularly dramatic, the deadly viral disease having been carried to Montreal from Chicago by a railway conductor in March of that year. The conductor survived but a young Acadian woman who had handled his bedding in the Hôtel-Dieu laundry caught the disease and died on 1 April. She was the first of some 3,000 people lost to smallpox in Montreal between April and November of 1885. The epidemic caused no small measure of panic and confusion, particularly after the city council decreed quarantine measures for the sick and mandatory vaccination for the rest of the population. English-speaking doctors and journalists pressured Mayor Honoré Beaugrand to enforce these public health measures, which were radical for their time. But smallpox vaccines, although available for decades, were feared and mistrusted, particularly within the French-speaking, labouring population. Resistance to forced vaccination, therefore, assumed an ethnic dimension and provoked violent confrontations, particularly on the evening of 28 September when an anti-vaccination rally at City Hall escalated into a full-scale riot. Sentiment against mandatory inoculation

St. George (Mayor Hingston) and the Dragon (Small Pox), 1876, Henri Julien. William Hales Hingston was a McGill-trained physician who served as mayor of Montreal from 1875 to 1877. He was an advocate of health and sanitation reform and is depicted here by the noted caricaturist Henri Julien as St. George, locked in combat with the dragon of smallpox. Although he was unable to slay this particular monster—the smallpox epidemic of 1885 was among the worst on record—Hingston's accomplishments and reputation earned him a knighthood in 1895 and an appointment to the Senate in 1896. *McCord Museum*

was fuelled by the francophone press, which interpreted the campaign as yet another attempt by English Canadians to impose their will on the province's French-speaking majority.[37] Thirty-odd years later in 1918 and 1919, in the wake of the First World War, the worldwide outbreak of Spanish Influenza caused some 13,000 deaths in the province and demonstrated that, even with cholera and typhus under control, as they then were, epidemic disease could still be a major concern in the twentieth-century city.[38]

The 1885 smallpox epidemic was a wake-up call for public health officials in Quebec. The following year, the provincial government required municipalities to institute mandatory smallpox vaccination programs and to set up local departments of public health. This was part of a campaign to reform the province's sanitary services, which was underway by the 1880s and which would pick up steam in the early twentieth century. Two of the major thrusts of that campaign were in the problem areas discussed above: tuberculosis and infant mortality. Founded in 1902, Montreal's Anti-Tuberculosis League made major strides in the fight against the disease in the ensuing years, not least of which were the Montreal

Tuberculosis Exhibition, which attracted 50,000 participants to the city in 1908, and the establishment in October of the following year of the Royal Edward Institute (later the Montreal Chest Institute), the province's first tuberculosis dispensary and outpatient clinic.[39]

The parallel battle against infant mortality was part of an international campaign waged by medical hygienists for more "scientific" child-rearing practices. It saw clean-milk dispensaries, known as Gouttes de Lait, established all over the province in the first two decades of the twentieth century.[40] Two pediatric hospitals founded in this period, the Children's Memorial Hospital (1902) and the Hôpital Sainte-Justine (1907), also furthered the cause of children's health in the city. Other strategies included pre-natal consultations, visiting nurses, and well-baby clinics, some of which were run by a new Catholic agency known as l'Assistance Maternelle. As historian Denyse Baillargeon has shown, many mothers resented or ignored the medical experts and their interference. But along with rising standards of living and falling fertility, the meddling doctors probably played a role in stemming the tide of infant deaths in the twentieth century, as provincial rates fell steadily and dramatically, from 18 percent during the First World War to about 3 percent in the late 1950s.[41]

All of these new initiatives were built on an institutional foundation that, as in the social service area, was divided into Catholic and Protestant sectors. For French-speaking Catholics, health care services were provided in hospitals such as the Hôtels-Dieux, which had been established during the French regime in the province's largest towns. These hospitals were operated mainly as charitable institutions, catering to the poor and infirm and staffed by nuns who specialized in nursing care. New institutions patterned on these venerable ones were erected all over the province; Saint-Hyacinthe's, for example, dates from 1866 and was established by the Grey Nuns, who were active in both social services and health care. Although institutions like the Sherbrooke Protestant Hospital were important regionally, the province's English-Protestant health care system was focused on Montreal, home to major institutions such as the Montreal General Hospital and McGill University's Faculty of Medicine, both founded in 1821.[42] The city's reputation as a centre for medical care, research, and teaching grew later in the century, aided by the presence of pioneer clinician Sir William Osler at McGill from 1870 to 1885 and by major projects such as the new, state-of-the-art Royal Victoria Hospital that was completed in 1894 on the south side of Mount Royal. Despite some limited state involvement in the form of public health laws, health care remained a private matter and, like charitable activities, tended to break down along the religious lines that so closely reproduced the linguistic ones. No amount of scientific progress, or so it seemed, could overcome this basic cultural duality, especially in the metropolis, where the English-Protestant minority was larger and more influential than it was in the regions.

Quebec's industrializing towns and cities, furthermore, were bustling with ideas, culture, associational life, and the symbols and rituals of tradition, modernity, and cultural dualism. Science, technology, and the cult of material progress were as influential here as in other Western societies. But religion was at the core of the value and belief systems, both for Catholic and for Protestant Quebecers, and would remain there for some time yet. As we have already seen (Chapter 6), the decades following the failed rebellions witnessed a kind of religious revival within Quebec Catholicism. During this period, ultramontane ideas and the increasingly theatrical public rites of devotion and worship swept the province. Although more diverse in their theology and less attached to hierarchy and ritual, Protestant Quebecers were just as committed to their beliefs and institutions and to Christian moral teachings as were Catholics. Whether in the majestic stone towers of Notre-Dame Cathedral or in the more modest spires that rose above towns and villages all over the province, Quebec's increasingly urban landscape reflected this basic nineteenth-century reality, as Mark Twain famously noted when he visited Montreal in 1881: "This is the first time I was ever in a city where you couldn't throw a brick without breaking a church window."[43] Any notion that fervent religious belief and practice were traditional, rural phenomena that broke down on contact with cities and modern life— the idea known among specialists as the "secularization thesis"—fails to stand up in the case of Quebec, where the period that saw the greatest wave of industrial and urban development also witnessed a flowering of religious culture.

Differences of language, religion, and national origin were profound and they were central to the province's distinct experience and to its

Sun Life Building at night, Montreal. At the turn of the twentieth century, Montreal's downtown—its central business and financial district—was located along Saint-Jacques Street, near Place d'Armes and the Notre-Dame Cathedral, in the oldest part of the city. In 1912, however, the Sun Life Assurance Company (established 1871) announced plans to locate its new, twenty-four-storey headquarters on Metcalfe Street facing Dominion (now Dorchester) Square: a prestigious site but not one associated with corporate power. Designed by Toronto architects Darling and Peterson and built in three phases between 1913 and 1931, the Sun Life building was touted as the tallest in the British Empire; it was certainly the tallest in Montreal for many decades, until it was dwarfed by the modernist skyscrapers of the 1960s. Sun Life's migration was the first step in the emergence of a new downtown business district in Montreal, located further up the mountain along Dorchester Street (now René-Lévesque Boulevard). © *Bibliothèque et archives nationales du Québec*

emerging urban culture, particularly in Montreal, Quebec City, and Sherbrooke. The province's confessional approach to worship, social services, and health care was replicated in a wide range of sectors, including education. Literacy levels remained lower than in other parts of North America throughout the nineteenth century; and the Catholic majority had consistently and significantly lower rates than the Protestant minority. As we've already seen in Chapter 6, the tax-based school system introduced in the 1840s was resisted by groups of rural French Canadians, culminating in the 1848–49 episode known as the *guerre des éteignoirs* (the candle-snuffers' war). But in the space of a generation or two, these and other reforms significantly reduced the literacy lag with respect to other places and narrowed the cultural divide within the province. By the late 1880s, for example, over 80 percent of the men and women who took their marriage vows in Saint-Hyacinthe were literate enough to sign the parish register, up from barely 50 percent just thirty years earlier.[44]

Rising literacy rates among Catholic francophones were a response to the new urban environment and to employment in industry and commerce. Even more directly, they were the product of a growing network of publicly funded primary schools that, in this period of religious "revival," also grew increasingly Catholic in character. In 1853, barely one in ten teachers in Quebec's Catholic schools was a priest, a nun, or a brother. By 1887, that proportion had risen to almost half as French-teaching orders such as the Christian Brothers and the Marist Brothers established a foothold in the province, as new orders such as the Sisters of the Holy Names of Jesus and Mary were founded, and as long-standing ones like the Congrégation de Notre-Dame and the Ursulines expanded their educational mandate.[45]

Opportunities for Catholic secondary and post-secondary education also increased in the period, particularly for boys from prosperous families. In the private, fee-paying *collèges classiques*, the adolescent sons of the province's lawyers, doctors, notaries, and merchants received a classical education in the Jesuit tradition, with emphasis on Latin, Greek, philosophy, languages, literature, history, mathematics, and religion. Nineteen such colleges catered to young French-Canadian males at the dawn of the twentieth century, as did Laval University, its Montreal satellite campus, and the school of applied sciences founded in 1873 as the École Polytechnique de Montréal.[46] Efforts to diversify the kinds of education available to young men and, in particular, to train young French Canadians for careers in the world of commerce and industry led to the establishment in 1907 of the École des Hautes Études Commerciales.

Secondary and post-secondary education for girls and young women was a different matter entirely. Women could train to be teachers in the province's Normal Schools or they could choose to enter a convent and combine the religious life with a career in teaching, nursing, or social work. Other educational establishments geared for young women, such the *écoles ménagères*, were designed instead to prepare young women for careers as wives and mothers. One such school was founded by the

Ursuline sisters in the Saguenay region in 1882 to teach rural girls the domestic skills they would need as homemakers, including gardening, tending to farm animals, cooking, laundry, and bookkeeping.[47] Since the path to university education for young francophones at this time was via the all-male *collèges classiques*, young women were effectively excluded from post-secondary education until 1908, when the Congrégation de Notre-Dame opened the first girls' college in the province, although it was not recognized as such until 1926 when it became the Collège Marguerite-Bourgeoys.[48]

Despite improvements in Catholic education and the corresponding rise in French-Canadian literacy rates, Quebec's English-Protestant minority continued to enjoy an educational advantage rooted in at least three factors: social class, religious culture, and political influence. Socially and economically, anglophones were more likely to belong to the wealthier merchant and professional classes, groups whose members could best afford to educate their children and did so as a matter of course. Culturally, Protestant worship involved personal contact with the Bible through reading, whereas Catholics had traditionally been expected to leave interpretation of scripture to the clergy. Politically, with the Catholic Church and its influence on the rise, prominent English Protestants fought for legislation that would establish and maintain under their control a distinct network of good-quality denominational schools. Most significant in this respect was section 93 of the British North America Act of 1867, which granted the provinces jurisdiction over education and which, at the insistence of Quebec Protestants such as Alexander Tilloch Galt, enshrined in the constitution specific protections for the acquired educational rights of religious minorities. These protections served Quebec's Protestant population well, as did a provincial funding formula for primary education that as of 1869 divided school taxes between Catholic and Protestant school commissions on the basis of the taxpayer's religion. Since the school tax was assessed on landed property and since the value of Protestants' real-estate holdings was disproportionate to their numbers, their schools were funded at levels well above the rate for Catholic schools: $1.80 per child compared to 84 cents on the Catholic side, according to one contemporary estimate.[49] English Protestants enjoyed still greater advantages with respect to

Funeral procession of the late Hon. Thomas D'Arcy McGee. D'Arcy McGee was a prominent member of the city's Irish community and a minister in Sir John A. Macdonald's first federal cabinet. Following his assassination in Ottawa, his body was returned to Montreal and buried at St. Patrick's Church on 13 April 1868. The public rituals of mourning were elaborate and well attended, as this photograph of McGee's funeral procession through the streets of Montreal attests. *Library and Archives Canada*

post-secondary education. McGill University—with its seven faculties, its annual enrolment of 1,600 new students, its vast Sherbrooke-Street campus, its record of achievement in medicine and science, and its millions of dollars in endowments from prominent local families like the Redpaths and the Macdonalds—was easily the best and most prestigious university in the province on the eve of the First World War.[50]

The twentieth century saw the rise of new cultural and leisure activities in Quebec's cities and towns, as in urban places all over North America. Gender and social class were key components in the pattern of associational life that emerged. While working-class men, for instance, could be found partaking in the masculine camaraderie of the tavern or the playing field, bourgeois women enjoyed reading and music and took active part, in this age of social and moral reform, in philanthropic activities designed to "uplift" the less fortunate. More specific to Quebec was the fact that so many of these leisure and associational activities tended to divide along ethnic, religious, and linguistic lines.

Organized sports provide one example of this. As in other outposts of the Empire, the British-Protestant minorities in Montreal, Quebec City, and Sherbrooke participated in the Victorian culture of masculinity, which equated physical fitness with moral and spiritual virtue. By the 1850s, they had already begun organizing sporting associations such as the Montreal Snowshoe Club (1840) and the Montreal Lacrosse Club (1856), which would merge with the Montreal Bicycle Club in 1881 to form the Montreal Amateur Athletic Association.[51] One of the MAAA's affiliates was the Montreal Hockey Club, which won Lord Stanley's Challenge Cup when it was first offered in 1893 and then three times again in the ensuing decade. The young players on this team were members of the city's prosperous British-Protestant elite and, as long as hockey and other sporting clubs retained their amateur status, they would continue to organize along ethnic and religious lines. Irish Catholics in the city had their own club, the Shamrocks, which won the Stanley Cup in 1899 and 1900. A French-Canadian boy might learn the new sport of hockey as part of his classical education, assuming his family could afford one. By 1900, the Jesuits' Collège Ste-Marie, in particular, was a veritable breeding ground for francophone hockey players, with its own intramural league and players such as the Millaire brothers, Édouard and Albert, who went on to star with Montreal's first French-Canadian teams, the Nationals (1895) and the Montagnards (1898). Neither of these amateur teams ever won the Stanley Cup,

Engraving of Quebec winter carnival, from *Le Monde illustré*, 1 February 1896. This image of the winter carnival in Quebec depicts one of the highlights of the event: the storming of the ice castle amidst a spectacular display of fireworks. The Catholic tradition of feasting in the week of Mardi Gras, prior to the Lenten fast, is an old one. But the idea for a major winter festival in Quebec City dates to 1893, when it was proposed by Frank Carrel, editor of the *Quebec Daily Telegraph*, as a way to promote tourism and stimulate the slumping local economy. Similar winter festivals were held frequently in the first half of the twentieth century, although not in periods of war or economic crisis. The modern *Carnaval d'hiver de Quebec*, along with its snowy mascot *Bonhomme Carnaval*, dates from the 1950s; it has been held on an annual basis, without interruption, since 1955. © *Bibliothèque et archives nationales du Québec*

however, because they were never admitted to what hockey historian Michael McKinley calls "the English leagues," that is to say, the Amateur Hockey Association and the Canadian Amateur Hockey League, which controlled the prize.[52]

In the 1910s, as hockey, football and other spectator sports became clearly defined as commercial endeavours featuring professional players, the religious and linguistic identities of the club teams began to fade. The Club de hockey canadien (founded 1909) was a professional team featuring francophone players and was supported by the French-Canadian public, but its promoters, J. Ambrose O'Brien and George W. Kendall (Kennedy), were of Irish origin. By the 1920s, now owned and coached by a French Canadian, Léo Dandurand, the Canadiens were playing in an impressive new arena—the Montreal Forum, opened in 1923—and winning championships with a culturally mixed squad featuring great players such as Georges Vézina from Chicoutimi, Aurèle Joliat from Ottawa, and Howie Morenz from Stratford, Ontario.[53]

Physical and moral fitness were linked in other important ways, including via one of the great social-reform crusades of the era, the temperance movement. Prohibition was the watchword of the Dominion Alliance for the Total Suppression of the Liquor Traffic, founded in Montreal in 1875 as a federation of English and Protestant temperance associations.[54] Temperance work within the Catholic-francophone majority took place at the parish level, especially in urban, working-class parishes. Montreal's Saint-Pierre-Apôtre parish, for example, formed its Temperance Society in 1877 with a core group of 139 parishioners; the mainly working-class membership expanded over the ensuing decades, drawing from within and beyond the parish boundaries.[55] As we saw in Chapter 5, however, Catholic temperance advocates never moved to the more radical position in favour of state-enforced prohibition that had characterized the Protestant movement since the 1850s. The results of the September 1898 Dominion plebiscite on prohibition are eloquent on that score and on the cultural divide it reflects. Fewer than one in five voters in Quebec declared themselves favourable to a federal law prohibiting the manufacture and sale of alcoholic beverages, compared to more than half (51 percent) across Canada and over 80 percent in the Maritime provinces. In only eight Quebec counties did prohibition receive a majority of votes, all of them in areas with significant Protestant populations, particularly the Eastern Townships.

Industrial capitalism and urban development, then, reshaped Quebec society and culture in the decades around the turn of the twentieth century. Quebec's economic, social, and political structures were modernizing in ways that were comparable to other Western societies. Yet its ethnic, religious, and linguistic mix was unique in North America and added new dimensions to the class, racial, and gender tensions that other places experienced as they were transformed by industrial capitalism and urban life. As the rural parish and the family farm gave way to the faster pace of cities and factories, Quebec certainly modernized between 1840 and 1920. But the province also remained distinctive and extraordinary, not least because of its still recent history of colonial conflict and the unique patterns of institutional development and identity politics that developed as a result.

NINE

NATIONALISTS AND LIBERALS

It would be the 1970s before the modern nationalist movement gained enough structure and support to take power in Quebec City and put sovereignty-association before the people in a pair of referendums. But nationalism of a more traditional strain was a driving force in Quebec politics and society well before that. Louis Riel, in death, had given French-Canadian nationalists new energy and a new agenda. Macdonald's Tories might well be lauded in English Canada as the party of the "National Dream." But in Quebec—the erstwhile bailiwick of George-Étienne Cartier and his big *Bleu* machine—the hanging of Louis Riel in 1885 (see Chapter 6) had spurred some, like Jules-Paul Tardivel, to renounce the federal system and prompted many others to abandon the treacherous Tories and throw their support behind Liberal politicians like Honoré Mercier and Wilfrid Laurier.

At the same time, capitalism, industry, and urban life had come to provide the backdrop for much of the social and political discussion in Quebec. "Small-l" liberalism was always an important component of that conversation. French-Canadian business leaders believed in individual freedom, in material progress, in the benefits of thrift and sobriety, and in technical and commercial education.[1] But the province's population still featured a rural, agrarian majority, most of which was francophone, Catholic, and conservative in outlook. As urban neighbourhoods like the east-end Montreal parish of Saint-Pierre-Apôtre filled up with recent migrants from the countryside, their adaptation to city life certainly did not include a quick conversion to secular, pluralist values or a rejection of traditional institutions, such as the Catholic parish itself.[2]

So as the twentieth century dawned, some French Canadians embraced the liberal, materialist values of the Industrial Age. But others resisted modernity and promoted a collective identity and a community

Caughnawaga Lacrosse Team, Montreal, QC, 1876, Notman and Sandham. Members of a lacrosse team from the Kahnawake Mohawk reserve near Montreal posed for this 1876 Notman studio photograph. Quebecers of French and British origin appropriated certain aspects of First Nations culture—including lacrosse, snowshoes, canoes, and toboggans—and adapted them to their own purposes. But neither French-Canadian nationalists nor English-Canadian imperialists recognized Aboriginal people as equals or as partners in a culturally diverse and inclusive nation. Their economic, health, and educational disadvantages and their physical isolation in dwindling reserves makes this point even more eloquently than the romance and nostalgia surrounding traditional pursuits and customs, like lacrosse and the feathered headdress worn here by team captain Sawatis Aiontonnis, also known as Big John Canadian. *McCord Museum*

of interests rooted in traditional values: the French language, the Roman Catholic faith, the land, rural life, family, and kin. The period from the 1890s to the 1920s, therefore, saw an intriguing juxtaposition of the traditional and the modern in Quebec society and politics. Liberal leaders such as Lomer Gouin (premier, 1905–20) and Louis-Alexandre Taschereau (premier, 1920–36) dominated provincial politics by sticking to a consistent program of economic liberalism and limited social and educational reform.[3] At the same time, conservative nationalists focused on the dangers to French-Canadian survival represented by industrial capitalism, urban life, English-speaking Protestants, and most federal politicians. Indeed, as the twentieth century advanced, the nationalist movement—identified by many as "clerical nationalism" because of its close links to the Catholic Church—grew in scope and influence, laying much of the groundwork for the secular independence movement of more recent memory.

French-Canadian nationalists in the years before 1920 were especially concerned with two sets of issues: the extent to which Canada should be bound by British-imperial commitments overseas and the position of the French-speaking Catholic minority within the Canadian federation. They were also the first to point out that there was a price to be paid for a Second Industrial Revolution that was driven by foreign capital and that focused on extractive resource industries (see Chapter 7). Quebec's leading politicians placed a higher priority on revenues from the sale of timber, water, and mineral rights than on economic autonomy or "national" self-reliance. The jobs created by the massive American and English-Canadian investments in hydroelectricity, pulp and paper production, and asbestos mining could be held up as proof that the laissez-faire approach to economic development was working. What was missing was a role for French Canadians—besides that of construction worker or factory hand—in the new development strategies and a decent share in the material benefits created by modern industries. Or so went the nationalist critique of Quebec's economy, a critique that gained ever greater purchase in the province as the century progressed, as we shall see.

Britain's imperial entanglements and threats to the minority rights of French Canadians crystallized nationalist sentiment in a way that American access to energy, mineral, and timber resources could not . . . at least not yet. Indeed, French-Canadian nationalism was redefined and reinvigorated in this period by the issue of Canada's status within the Empire. Against the Canadian imperialists who identified so strongly with British military and diplomatic causes overseas, Henri Bourassa gave voice to a more independent view of Canada, one that saw the Dominion's interests as separate from Britain's. From this perspective, the need to commit troops to a bloody war in distant South Africa or to launch an ostensibly independent naval force that could be placed under British command at a moment's notice was anything but obvious (see Chapter 6). Founded by Bourassa in 1910, the independent nationalist

"The Angel of Peace," 1908. The Champlain Tercentenary events of July 1908 in Quebec City were financed and orchestrated by Ottawa as a celebration of the British imperial connection at a time when nationalist sentiment was rising among French Canadians. With the Prince of Wales in attendance, the festivities consecrated the Plains of Abraham as a national historic site and celebrated a heroic version of the French colonial past through a series of elaborate pageants. Governor General Earl Grey was the chief promoter of the Tercentenary celebration. His vision included plans for a gigantic "Angel of Peace," which would stand high above the historic battlefield as a symbol of peace and co-operation among the diverse peoples living under enlightened British rule. Often compared to New York's Statue of Liberty, the massive winged figure was never built. *Montreal Standard: Tercentenary Souvenir Number, Commemoration 1908, 25 July 1908, n.p.*

newspaper *Le Devoir* would provide a respected forum for these and similar views for generations to come. By the time of Laurier's electoral defeat in 1911, the approximate contours of the fault line that divided the Dominion on the issue of its imperial connection were apparent to anyone who was paying attention. The full depth of that fissure, however, would not be revealed for a few years yet.

In the meantime, the issue of minority rights for French-speaking Catholic communities elsewhere in Canada had emerged again. In the later nineteenth century, eastern Ontario had begun to attract a modest but steady flow of French Canadians looking for alternatives to the mill towns of New England. By 1900, a significant Franco-Ontarian population was already in place. By 1910, press reports were claiming that the province's francophone population had reached 10 percent.[4] In the eastern districts, the proportions were much higher; in Prescott County, for example, fully 70 percent of the population was French speaking in 1901.[5] As these communities took root and grew, bilingual schools developed without any formal standing, most often within the network of separate, publicly funded Catholic schools guaranteed by the BNA Act in 1867.

In 1912, however, Bishop Michael Fallon of London complained that in the bilingual schools of his diocese, teachers were poorly trained and children were acquiring an insufficient grounding in English. Fallon was an Irish Catholic bishop with a history of linguistic conflict in the Ottawa Valley. His comments sparked controversy and led to a commission of inquiry, which upheld much of his critique and prompted the provincial government to adopt Regulation 17, imposing strict limits on the use of French in Ontario's public schools.[6] Franco-Ontarians organized in defence of what they took to be their constitutional right to education in French. But the highest court in the British Empire saw things differently. For in 1916, the Judicial Committee of the Privy Council held that the Ontario government had full jurisdiction to legislate the language of instruction in its schools, while expressing misgivings about the regulation from an enforcement standpoint. Caught once again between the rock of minority rights and the hard place of provincial autonomy, Quebecers could do little more than voice their displeasure with Ontario and their solidarity with its French-Canadian community. The federal

Liberal member for Kamouraska, Ernest Lapointe, went so far as to table a motion of support for French-language education in Ontario. But with Laurier's party in opposition and many western Liberals already sympathetic to a wartime Conservative government preoccupied with matters of loyalty, the motion was soundly defeated in the House of Commons.

French Canadians everywhere reacted vehemently to Ontario's Regulation 17 because they believed that access to French-language education, especially at the primary level, was their main bulwark against assimilation into the dominant English language and culture and therefore the key to cultural survival outside Quebec. Protecting the French-Canadian community within the province's borders—which were extended northward in 1912 to conclude the Ungava territory bordering James Bay—was a numbers game of a different nature. Although emigration was a constant worry for nationalists, the large Catholic families of rural Quebec provided a measure of demographic strength and remained a source of patriotic pride as the new century began. Even Honoré Mercier's natalist law—which, between 1890 and 1905, rewarded families with 12 or more living children with 100 *arpents* of free land—was part of a discourse of celebration that hailed high fertility as a keystone of Catholic virtue and the guarantor of national survival.[7]

By the second decade of the century, however, some nationalists had come to doubt whether French-Catholic Quebec could rely on its prolific rural mothers and its church-run schools to ensure demographic and cultural survival in the future. Modern industrial and urban development was eroding the economic underpinnings of the traditional French-Canadian family. Some women were having fewer children; and the crippling infant and child mortality levels associated with urban life helped to raise the spectre of smaller families and slower demographic growth.[8] When the results of the 1901 and 1911 censuses were published, alarm bells went off and Ottawa's census takers were accused of systematically underenumerating French Canadians, an issue which had been raised loudly in the wake of the 1891 census as well.[9] "[I]f it is true that French-Canadian families are exceptionally prolific," wrote one editorialist in 1910, "how is it that the census does not disclose this fact, which is nonetheless common knowledge? . . . It is difficult to

Les Filles du Roi, Eleanor Fortescue-Brickdale, early twentieth century. This colourful and highly imaginative painting is a good example of the romanticization of New France's history, for the Pre-Raphaelite artist Eleanor Fortescue-Brickdale appears to have taken the term *King's daughters* literally. Talon and Laval appear on the left and the would-be suitors in the background. The semi-naked dark-skinned sailor at the bottom of the steps symbolizes the dangers (sexual and otherwise) that their stern-looking female chaperone had carried them through. *Library and Archives Canada*

A View of Château-Richer, Cape Torment, and Lower End of the Isle of Orleans near Quebec, Thomas Davies, 1787. The talented military artist Thomas Davies (1737–1812) served in North America during the Seven Years' War and the American Revolution, and commanded the Royal Artillery in Quebec City from 1786 to 1790. This scene would have been much the same prior to the Conquest. The diversity of the habitants' economic activities is suggested by the proximity of the hills and forest, the eel traps that stretch beyond the floodplain into the St. Lawrence, the kitchen garden in front of the white-washed stone farm house, and the livestock in the shadow of the barn. The painting also provides a good sense of the density of the settlement pattern on the riverfront ranges (known as *côtes*), though it should be noted that scarcely 10 percent of rural houses were of stone even in the eighteenth century. *National Gallery of Canada, Ottawa*

Cholera Plague, Quebec, Joseph Légaré, ca. 1832. The 51,700 British and Irish immigrants who sailed up the St. Lawrence in 1832, many of them suffering from cholera, overwhelmed the quarantine station at Grosse-Île. The result was that 2,723 people died from the disease in Quebec City (one-eighth of the population), 2,547 in Montreal, and an undetermined number in the countryside. Légaré's painting, which is basically a nighttime version of Sproule's *View of the Market Place* (see page 68), depicts recently arrived immigrants with their baggage, people stricken by the disease, and bodies being carried off for burial. Cannons were fired in the belief that this would clear the air, barrels of tar and other "anti-contagious" materials were burned between 6:00 and 10:00 p.m., and people held lighted tapers of smoking tar between their teeth. *National Gallery of Canada, Ottawa*

The Timber and Shipbuilding Yards of Allan Gilmour and Company at Wolfe's Cove, Quebec, Viewed from the South, Robert C. Todd, 1840. Napoleon's 1806 embargo against the shipping of Baltic timber to Britain was a boon for the forest industry of Lower Canada. During the winter huge white pines were felled and hewed into square timber, and in the spring they were bound together as rafts that river men guided down the Ottawa and St. Lawrence Rivers. Once the rafts reached the coves of Quebec City, they were dismantled and loaded into ships bound for the sawmills of Liverpool. Three hundred sixty-two ships were cleared through the colonial capital's port in 1812, 796 in 1825, and 1,213 in 1834. Many of those ships were built in Quebec, for the four shipyards operating there in 1799 had become twenty-seven by 1854. The largest, shown here, was owned by Allan Gilmour at Wolfe's Cove. *National Gallery of Canada, Ottawa*

Longue-Pointe, Québec, William Napier, 1860. This painting illustrates two versions of the traditional French-Canadian sleigh known as a carriole, as well as the habitant practice of hitching one horse in front of the other whenever two horses were used. Given that the lead horse was not between shafts, control required considerable skill on the part of the driver. The setting sun, the frozen St. Lawrence, and the prominent position of the austere parish church overlooking the thin line of drivers probably returning home from mass is balanced by the fact that the occupants of the two carrioles in the foreground (note the low runners) have stopped for a chat. *Library and Archives Canada*

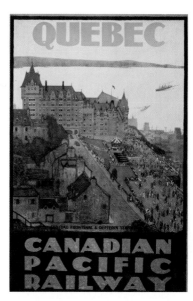

Quebec: Chateau Frontenac and Dufferin Terrace, Canadian Pacific Railway. Quebec City was already an important tourist destination in the opening decades of the twentieth century. This CPR travel poster, in which the Chateau Frontenac Hotel (completed 1893) features prominently, dates from 1922. *Library of Congress*

Hockey legend Maurice "Rocket" Richard signing autographs. This painting represents a throng of young boys in their Canadiens sweaters surrounding their hero at a Montreal banquet organized by *Les Loisirs de L'Immaculée Conception.* The Rocket was a prolific goal scorer, a perennial Stanley Cup champion, and an iconic figure for Quebecers in the 1950s. This image appeared on the cover of *Maclean's* magazine in March 1959, suggesting the extent of Richard's fame and popularity in the rest of Canada. *Maclean's*

French president Charles de Gaulle speaking at Montreal City Hall during his visit to Expo '67, 24 July 1967. Quebec nationalists were galvanized by the deep and carefully enunciated *"Vive le Québec Libre!"* proclaimed by de Gaulle from this balcony. But the unexpected declaration of support for a "free" Quebec was a serious breach of diplomatic protocol that left Canadian officials reeling. De Gaulle spent the following day visiting the World's Fair but flew back to Paris that evening, cutting short a visit that was to have included a stop in Ottawa and a meeting with Prime Minister Pearson. *Archives de la Ville de Montréal*

Naskapi quilt block, James and Minnie Uniam, 1998–2005. The Naskapi of Labrador, possibly the last Native group in North America to make sustained contact with Europeans, are descended from nomadic caribou hunters of the barren subarctic Ungava region of Quebec. The caribou, which remained important for food, shelter, and tools, is the central feature of this quilt block, designed by James Uniam and embroidered by his mother, Minnie Uniam, on hand-tanned and smoked caribou hide. Also important, but to a lesser degree, are fish and geese. The double curve motif is distinctive to the Naskapi, possibly representing the means by which the hunter unites with his brother caribou. Since 1956 the Naskapi have been settled in Kawawachikamach, near Schefferville. *Quilt of Belonging*

Henri Bourassa and his wife, Joséphine Papineau, with their children, 1915. As a politician, journalist, and nationalist leader, Henri Bourassa (1868–1952) was well known for his strident defense of French-Canadian interests and of Canadian autonomy on the world stage. He was also a devout Catholic who celebrated the traditional patriarchal family, valued rural life and agriculture over cities and industry, and took conservative positions on social and moral issues such as divorce, birth control, and women's rights. Nearing fifty years of age, Bourassa is pictured here with his wife and six of the eight children she bore before her untimely death in 1919. *Library and Archives Canada*

conceive that our families of six, eight, or ten children—to say nothing of those of twelve or more—do not raise us further above the average."[10]

Behind this rhetoric stood a fundamental fear: that legendary French-Canadian birth rates—to some extent the key to *la survivance* since the Conquest—would falter and decline under the combined influence of urban life, industrial work, liberal and individualist values, Protestantism, and the English language. By the war years, when nationalist sensitivities were at their peak, statistics had begun to reveal the slow, inexorable decline in French-Canadian fertility, which set the stage for the more dramatic collapse of birth rates associated with the Quiet Revolution.[11] Indeed, fear of demographic decline moved some nationalist commentators to shift from celebrating French Canada's prolific mothers to a more strident discourse of exhortation, sometimes couched, in keeping with the times, in military terms. The most influential of these was the Jesuit Louis Lalande who, in 1918, coined the term "Revenge of the Cradle" to describe French-Canadian birth rates and their role in maintaining a certain religious and linguistic balance within Canada. Lalande was aware of the ironies embedded in his metaphor, which associated aggression and conflict with the innocence of infants in their beds. Still, the expression gained currency and was used throughout the twentieth century as a way of describing the French-Canadian fertility surplus over English Canada that persisted until the 1960s.[12]

Debates over schools and birth rates helped shape a defensive strain of nationalism that was conceived in Quebec during the First World War and that gained considerable purchase in the 1920s. But these were mere rumblings compared to the crisis over compulsory military service that shook the province and the Dominion in 1917 and 1918. Quebecers had been uneasy with Laurier's compromise positions on the South African War and the naval issue, and their nationalist votes had helped defeat him in the federal election of 1911. But they had yet to experience the unalloyed imperialism of a Conservative federal government with massive support in English Canada and with no need of French-Canadian support to govern. Once Germany's invasion of Belgium had led to a British declaration of war in August 1914, it became clear that they would have that opportunity. For Borden's government, there was no question as to whether or not Canada should contribute soldiers and resources; Canada was a British Dominion and, when Britain was at war, so were all the daughters of the Empire. The question, rather, was about the extent of Canadian participation and, for nationalists in Quebec, about what would happen if the federal government, now dominated by English-Canadian Conservatives, began to make excessive demands.

In the fall of 1914, no such demands were forthcoming. Recruitment levels were high as the unemployed signed up in droves for the Canadian Expeditionary Force and as recently arrived British immigrants rushed to the defence of the Empire. As the war progressed, however, the Borden government repeatedly raised its target for the size of the Canadian force, which reached 500,000 soldiers in January 1916: a tall order indeed for a country with a total population of about 8 million.[13] This was to have been an all-volunteer force; in December of 1914, Borden had announced to a Halifax audience that "there has not been, there will not be, compulsion or conscription."[14] But casualties were high and, as the long, bloody war of attrition dragged on, the effort to maintain a force of half a million volunteers began to seem more and more unrealistic.

It was becoming increasingly clear, meanwhile, that recruitment levels in Quebec and especially among French Canadians were substantially lower than in English Canada. And, despite the entry of American forces into battle in April 1917, the military situation was becoming critical and the need for reinforcements at the front all the more urgent. So on 11 June 1917, Borden introduced a Military Service Bill that would impose mandatory service on some 100,000 men between the ages of twenty and forty-five. His ultimate justification for the broken promise was framed as a pledge to stay the course and to "keep the faith" with embattled soldiers in the European trenches: "If we do not pass this measure, if we do not provide reinforcements, if we do not keep our plighted faith, with what countenance shall we meet them on their return?"[15]

The greater difficulty of recruiting French Canadians for overseas service ought to have surprised no one. Unlike many English Canadians, they did not have close personal or family ties to the European countries most directly involved. Furthermore, the Canadian militia was a deeply British institution with English as its working language and in which French Canadians had little opportunity for advancement into the officer corps. Most francophone recruits were scattered through the general military population, and attempts to form distinct French-Canadian fighting units were strongly resisted. Direct appeals to potential francophone recruits might have yielded more military success stories, such as that of the 22nd (French-Canadian) Infantry Battalion, CEF. This precursor of the storied Royal 22nd Regiment (the "Van Doos") went to France with the Second Canadian Division in 1915 and fought with distinction throughout the war, earning two Victoria Crosses and suffering almost 4,000 casualties.[16]

Support for conscription in English Canada was widespread, although some labour and farmers' groups did not share the general enthusiasm for the measure. Opposition was virtually unanimous among French Canadians, however. In *Le Devoir*, Henri Bourassa published editorials that both shaped and reflected the intensity of feeling on the matter in Quebec. Why should French-Canadian blood be spilled in defence

Canadiens: C'est le moment d'agir ("Canadians: Be Men! Don't Stay Behind. Enlist in Our French-Canadian Regiments!"). This military recruitment poster appealed directly to French Canadians during the First World War. These "Huns" seem to be marching on a snowy Quebec village, leaving a trail of atrocities in their wake. *Library and Archives Canada*

of British liberties when the rights and liberties of his own people (on French-language education in particular) could so easily be dismissed? With so many Canadian casualties already suffered at the Somme, at Passchendaele, and in the iconic victory at Vimy Ridge, where over 3,500 Canadians had been killed and 7,000 wounded, had not the senior Dominion already done more than its share in the cause of imperial defence? By breaking his promise not to use conscription to raise reinforcements, was not Borden simply caving in to imperial pressure and thereby showing his disdain for Bourassa's cherished principle of Canadian autonomy? And, even if a majority of Canadians were in favour of conscription, did the fact that an even stronger majority of French-speakers opposed it make no difference at all?

Fought on a single issue, the December 1917 federal election was certainly among the most divisive in Canadian history. With the explosive conscription question separating the two sides, the campaign degenerated into a pageant of insults, intimidation, and sometimes violence. Portrayals of francophones as disloyal and cowardly had become commonplace in the English-Canadian press. Few Unionists (Borden's Conservatives plus pro-conscription Liberals who had split with Laurier on the issue) dared venture into Quebec for fear of angry crowds. Albert Sévigny, a federal minister and one of the few francophones who supported Borden's conscription law, had to face gunshots, flying stones, and smashed windows when he attempted to make a campaign speech in the province.[17]

The results at the polls reflected the hostile, polarized climate in which the campaign was conducted. Laurier's Liberals swept francophone Quebec and elected MPs in all but three of the province's sixty-five ridings while Conservative or Liberal-Unionist candidates won all but twenty seats outside the province, with many of those coming from French-speaking areas of the Maritimes and Ontario. Never before had the federal Parliament been so starkly and ominously split along linguistic lines; and never before had French Canadians been so clearly and effectively isolated. Small wonder, perhaps, that in the wake of the December election, the Liberal MLA for Lotbinière, Joseph-Napoléon Francoeur, stood in the Quebec City chamber to move that the provincial legislature would be "disposed to accept the breaking of the Confederation Pact of 1867 if, in the other provinces, it is believed that she [the Province of Quebec] is an obstacle to the union, progress and development of Canada."[18] The provocative motion never came to a vote. But the point was made and, not insignificantly, it was made in the Quebec legislature, the only remaining forum in which most French Canadians felt they had any real power.

Ultimately, conscription yielded some 80,000 new recruits, about one-quarter of whom were from Quebec, and very few of whom saw action in Europe before the end of the war in November 1918. Meanwhile, the home front had come to resemble a battlefield, sometimes quite literally. Surely the worst moments came over the Easter weekend in 1918 when violent anti-conscription riots erupted in Quebec City. When Dominion Police officers arrested a man who could not produce his draft-exemption papers on the evening of 28 March, a crowd of 2,000 demonstrators sacked their local headquarters in the working-class St. Roch district. The protests continued for the next five nights, with crowds setting fire to a recruitment centre and squaring off with rocks, bricks, and chunks of ice against hundreds of militia men, most of them called in from Ontario and western Canada. On the foggy evening of Monday, 1 April, the riots spun out of control. Gunshots were fired at the troops "from side streets, snow banks, and other places of concealment."[19] In response, the soldiers opened fire on the crowd with rifles and machine guns, killing at least four and injuring dozens. "Blood Flows in Quebec City—Five Peaceful Citizens Killed," screamed the headline of Henri Bourassa's *Le Devoir* the next day. Whether the victims were bystanders, rioters, snipers, or even draft dodgers was of little consequence compared to the symbolic importance of Ottawa dispatching its soldiers to *la vieille capitale* to gun down Quebecers for refusing to comply with a coercive law foisted upon them by English Canada.[20]

The First World War, certainly, was a watershed in the history of nationalism in both Canada and Quebec. In the wake of the armistice, Canadians reinvented the excruciating war years as a kind of national coming of age. Having made huge sacrifices and key contributions to the war effort, Canada demanded recognition as a full partner in the community of nations. The war had been a rite of passage in Quebec as well, but of another kind and for different reasons. Bloodied by

Lionel Groulx (1878–1967) in his study. Groulx was a Catholic priest, a historian, and the most influential French-Canadian nationalist of his generation. *Université de Montréal archives*

major defeats on Ontario's schools and conscription, French-speaking nationalists turned inward, focusing less on their community's troubled relations with the Dominion and the Empire and more on the serious issues they faced on their own turf, defined increasingly as the Province of Quebec. The nationalism that emerged in the 1920s also advocated specifically Catholic responses to such modern challenges as industrial work, urban life, individualism, commercial culture, and family break-down. Frequently referred to as clerical nationalism, this new current found expression throughout Quebec in the various activities of the Catholic Action movement. And it found leadership in one of the interesting and controversial figures in the history of Quebec, the priest-historian Lionel Groulx.

Born in Vaudreuil in 1878, Groulx grew up there in a large farming family and was educated at the seminary at Sainte-Thérèse in the lower Laurentians, where he found his vocation for the priesthood and was ordained. In 1900, he returned to southwestern Quebec to teach history and literature at the *collège classique* in Valleyfield. Save for three years of study in Europe, he remained there until 1915 when he was appointed to the newly created chair in Canadian history at Laval University's Montreal campus, which became the Université de Montréal five years later (see Chapter 8). As a historian, Groulx developed and popularized the thesis that the British Conquest was a catastrophe for the French-Canadian people and that the great theme of Quebec history for the ensuing 250 years had been *la survivance*—the struggle for survival of a conquered people against formidable odds and in the face of sustained pressure for assimilation into the dominant British culture.[21] Groulx's political engagement was firmly rooted in this reading of history. An energetic thinker, writer, and teacher, he was a founding member of the Ligue des droits du français, which became the Ligue d'Action française in 1921, with Groulx by now its leader and the editor of its journal, *L'Action française*.[22] From that pulpit and others, he encouraged his countrymen to resist liberal, Protestant, and American ideas and values and to build social relations around everything ancient, traditional, and distinctive in French-Canadian society and culture. Indeed, Groulx set the tone for other clerical nationalists by defining the distinct identity of his people in terms of three elements: family, faith, and the land.

Like conservative Catholics elsewhere, Lionel Groulx believed that the traditional, patriarchal family was the fundamental unit of society and its main source of continuity and order. This collectivist conception of family and kin relations romanticized large, rural families like the one in which Groulx had grown up. It also served to perpetuate gender inequities, to reinforce paternal authority over children, and to buttress the position of the family and the Church, rather than the state, as the ultimate arbiters in matters such as education and social welfare.

Equally important to Groulx's conception of the French-Canadian nation were its shared Roman Catholic faith and traditions. Catholic values and identity were seen to extend beyond matters of theology and into virtually all areas of public and private life, from formal politics, to the halls of commerce and industry, to the intimacy of the marital bed. It followed that the Catholic clergy should play a major social and political role, retaining a high degree of control over education, health, and social services, sponsoring all manner of exclusively Catholic clubs and associations, and providing French Canadians with a conservative brand of intellectual and spiritual leadership.

The third dimension of this clerical-nationalist ideology was an anti-modernist belief in the evils of the city and the moral superiority of a rural, agricultural way of life. Modern-day Quebecers would do well to emulate their ancestors, those diligent, devout, and dutiful settlers who had flourished under difficult circumstances in the St. Lawrence Valley three centuries earlier. The way forward for French Canada was not so much by adjusting its values to the exigencies of city life as by living up to a strong agrarian ideal, firmly rooted in the family farm and its core values of hard work, mutual respect and co-operation, gender and generational hierarchy, material self-sufficiency, and a healthy disdain for luxury.[23]

Groulx used his position as editor of *L'Action française* to circulate this conservative nationalist vision.[24] His appeal to traditional forms of French-Canadian solidarity struck a chord in the 1920s, as a wide range of groups and associations emerged to promote specifically "national" (i.e., Catholic and French-Canadian) solutions to a broad range of economic and social issues. By 1921, for example, the denominational labour unions first formed in the opening years of the century (see Chapter 7) were numerous enough to warrant the establishment of a Catholic labour federation, the Confédération des travailleurs catholiques du Canada (CTCC). Quebec's farmers also organized in this period, forming the Union catholique des cultivateurs de la Province de Québec in 1924. At the same time, the Caisses populaires movement was gaining strength; there were 178 Catholic credit unions in place with $11 million in assets by 1929.[25] The idea of its founder Alphonse Desjardins was that parish-based credit unions could mobilize French-Canadian savings while providing an alternative to the large chartered banks, controlled mainly by wealthy anglophones in Montreal or Toronto. Desjardins had died in 1920, but the movement he started was actively promoted by the Catholic clergy and fit well with the defensive and increasingly territorial nationalism of the time.

Associations devoted to specific areas of Catholic social action also emerged or gained new currency and support in the 1920s. The broadest concern was urban poverty and all of its corollaries, from inadequate housing and sanitation and the health problems they fostered (see

Chapter 8) to the intemperance, moral weakness, and violence that—at least according to the popular press—could be seen as both its cause and its most unfortunate consequence. The solution from the clerical nationalist perspective was education, not in the form of free, compulsory public schooling—anathema to the Church—but rather popular, social education focused on moral values such as temperance, self-restraint, and respect for others. Founded by the Jesuits in 1911, the École sociale populaire was at the heart of this project, publishing a widely circulated series of pamphlets and, in 1920, launching the Semaines sociales du Canada: an annual public conference aimed at educating working-class French Canadians with speeches and public lectures by prominent clergymen, Catholic intellectuals and educators, and other opinion leaders.

The fourth Semaine sociale was held in Montreal in August 1923 and focused on one of the issues of greatest concern to clerical nationalists, the family. The event featured public lectures by Lionel Groulx, Louis Lalande, Henri Bourassa, labour leader Clovis Bernier (president of the Conseil central des Syndicats catholiques de Montréal), and Bourassa's cousin Henriette Dessaulles, author of a popular advice column in *Le Devoir*, which she signed with the pseudonym Fadette. Bourassa's talk, about the dangers facing French-Canadian families in the 1920s, gives a sense of the proceedings. The many perils he enumerated included individualism, communism, statism (as regards education, social services, income tax, and conscription), industrial capitalism, democracy, and feminism. He also warned against urbanization, proclaiming that the best thing for a sprawling Montreal would be if 200,000 of its inhabitants would simply leave. And he railed against the rising tide of criminality and the yellow journalism it inspired: "Our elders," he intoned, "can recall a time when murder was a shocking thing of which we did not speak except in horror. Do you believe that murder and other crimes can inspire that same, salutary horror when your favourite newspapers relate their most minute details in full-page spreads, to be devoured by your children?"[26]

Participants in activities such as these were part of the Catholic social action movement inspired by Pope Leo XIII's 1891 encyclical Rerum Novarum, which provided the underpinnings for the Church's social doctrine for the ensuing decades. The encyclical called on Catholics to reject class struggle and to form a network of lay associations in which activists would work together to alleviate suffering and promote clerically sanctioned solutions to the problems of the day. The Catholic labour unions, farmers' associations, credit unions, and temperance societies that flourished in this period must all be seen in this context. By the later years of the 1920s, moreover, the uncertain situation of young French Canadians torn between the traditions of their parents' generation and the exigencies of the modern world had come to provide the main focus for the Catholic Action movement. Founded in 1927 in Montreal, the Jeunesse ouvrière catholique (JOC) was the first in a long series of association that, as we shall see (Chapter 10), would mobilize young French Canadians around issues of concern to young Catholics for decades to come.[27]

Clerical leadership, retrenchment around the solidarities of family, faith, and farm, and a focus on the economic and social issues of the day were the priorities of the clerical nationalists of the 1920s. Their nationalism was territorial in that it focused on *la patrie*, or the homeland, defined increasingly as the St. Lawrence Valley and its contiguous regions, in other words the Province of Quebec. But clerical nationalists were also deeply conservative politically and, although frustrated by their status in Canada as a national, linguistic and, in the parlance of the day, "racial" minority, they did not actively promote Quebec independence or any other radical change to the constitutional order. They did, however, think about the idea and occasionally hint that it might be a good one. In his novel *L'Appel de la race* (1922), for example, Lionel Groulx famously used a mixed marriage doomed to failure as a metaphor for Confederation. Also in 1922, Groulx published a year's worth of articles on the idea of independence in *L'Action française*. Many contributors concluded that, given French Canada's wartime humiliations, such an outcome was desirable and, perhaps, inevitable. But the question soon faded into the background and Groulx would deny the inference that he had converted to the cause of a sovereign Quebec up until his death in 1967.[28]

The most prominent nationalist of the time, then, flirted only briefly with the idea of a separate Quebec. His was an exclusive form of ethnic nationalism that focused on the shared attributes and traditions of the

French-Canadian "race," while not necessarily endorsing a "two-state solution" for the divided Dominion. His conservative ethnic nationalism was also tinged with intolerance of other communities, particularly non-Christians such as the Jews who had begun migrating to Montreal and other urban centres in significant numbers at the turn of the century.[29] Groulx is a controversial figure in Quebec history for this reason, reviled by some as an anti-Semite but widely recognized nonetheless as "the most important Quebec intellectual of his generation."[30]

Like nationalism, liberalism was already a complex ideological brew in late nineteenth-century Quebec, variously associated with the *Rouges* and their opposition to Cartier and Confederation, with the Institut canadien and its struggles against Monseigneur Bourget, and sometimes with the overt anti-clericalism of a Louis-Antoine Dessaulles. But in the new century, fresh material and ideological challenges would arise. How to manage economic development, whether in the resource-rich periphery or in Montreal and the other manufacturing centres? What to do about urbanization and the vast array of social problems it generated? What would be the place of French Canadians in Canada, and of Canada on the North American continent and within the British Empire? And, as ever, where to draw the line between spiritual and temporal power in a province that had a strong Catholic majority, but which was embedded, for better or worse, within a largely Protestant British Dominion? As the issues became more and more complex, so too did the range of liberal responses and, therefore, the shades of liberalism on the political and ideological canvas of Quebec.

Radical liberals in the tradition of the *Rouges* and the Institut canadien were certainly part of this tableau. Although they were few in number and their ideas too controversial to influence government policies, they remained a presence within the provincial Liberal Party and a force in the world of journalism and letters. Among the best known was Télesphore Damien (T.D.) Bouchard, who began his public life as a journalist before entering politics, serving concurrently as mayor and as the Liberal MLA for Saint-Hyacinthe for the better part of three decades, until his appointment to the Senate in 1944. Over the course of his long career, Bouchard developed a reputation as a firebrand, taking progressive and controversial positions on a wide range of issues. A local hero in Saint-

Hyacinthe, he is perhaps best remembered provincially as a champion in the cause of free, compulsory, state-run schools. Bouchard spoke in the legislative assembly in favour of such a reform and campaigned for it in his newspaper *Le Clairon*, most notably in 1918 when school commissioners in Drummondville and Saint-Jérôme sought a provincial mandate to institute compulsory school attendance for children in urban areas aged between seven and fourteen. Such a measure was not instituted in Quebec until 1943, despite the fact that the Vatican endorsed the principle of compulsory education in 1931.[31] Unlike his more powerful colleagues in the provincial Liberal caucus, Bouchard and others were unwilling to sacrifice the modern "statist" principle of compulsory public education to the vested interests of the Council of Public Instruction and of the Catholic clerics who controlled it.[32]

Equally uncompromising in the face of clerical edicts was Godefroy Langlois, a journalist, politician, and Freemason from Sainte-Scholastique in the lower Laurentians. Like Bouchard, Langlois combined journalism with provincial politics, and made some of his most significant public statements in the cause of educational reform, arguing that "[the] masses must be enlightened . . . ; they must know of the progress being made and they must have the tools to compete."[33] Langlois was much more anti-clerical in his views than the more moderate Liberals who controlled the federal and provincial parties. As a young journalist in the 1890s, he denounced Church tithes, fiscal immunity for religious corporations, clerical interference in politics, and the curriculum of the classical colleges. Along with the liberal poet Louis Fréchette, he also helped to expose a series of scandals involving unscrupulous or criminal members of the clergy.[34] Langlois's ideas moved still further to the left in the 1910s, during a surprising, and surprisingly effective, mandate as the Liberal MLA for Montreal-Saint-Louis, which ended abruptly in 1914 with his appointment as Quebec's agent general in Brussels.[35] In 1910, he had founded the radical newspaper *Le Pays*, its title an homage to the *Rouge* organ of an earlier generation. In 1913, the publication fell victim to clerical censorship and was placed on the Papal Index by Montreal Archbishop Monseigneur Paul Bruchési. Langlois's European exile a year later was a further indication of the marginal status of progressive ideas within Quebec liberalism at this juncture.

T.D. Bouchard and Godefroy Langlois were the heirs of the radical *Rouge* tradition. Harder to categorize were those social liberals, both French and English speaking, who, under the influence of the American progressive movement, sought to improve and modernize early twentieth-century Quebec in a variety of ways. Sanitary and housing reformers like Herbert Brown Ames (see Chapter 8) can certainly be seen in this light. So, too, can first-wave feminists like Marie Lacoste Gérin-Lajoie, one of the many middle-class women who began to demand a greater role for women in society. They did so by campaigning for the revision of antiquated laws that denied married women civil and property rights; for a broader range of educational and employment opportunities for women, including access to universities and the professions; and, ultimately, for the right to exist as full-fledged citizens and to exercise the suffrage in democratic elections. Gérin-Lajoie was the co-founder in 1907, along with Caroline Béïque, of the Fédération nationale Saint-Jean-Baptiste, Quebec's first specifically francophone and Catholic feminist organization. The FNSJB was modelled on Canada's National Council of Women, acting as a central, coordinating body for women's groups and associations of all kinds. Its establishment, in fact, represents a schism within the Quebec women's movement, since French and English, Catholic and Protestant women had previously worked together within the NCW and especially its Montreal branch.

Gérin-Lajoie was particularly active in the campaign for legal changes and, without any formal training in the law, wrote several treatises on the inherent sexism of Quebec's 1866 Civil Code. The process of legal reform began during the First World War, at which time a married woman in Quebec was virtually without legal identity and subject to her husband's authority in almost every respect. She was unable to enter into legal contracts or judicial proceedings on her own behalf; she was legally obliged to obey her husband in exchange for his protection; she had no right to exercise a profession other than her husband's; and she could not use her husband's adultery as grounds for a legal separation unless he kept his mistress in their common residence. Gérin-Lajoie's work contributed to the passage in 1915 of the Pérodeau Act, which brought improvements to a widow's inheritance rights in the case where her husband had died intestate. She continued to seek broader legal reforms

Marie Lacoste Gérin-Lajoie (1867–1945). Gérin-Lajoie was among the leading French-Canadian feminists of her generation. She was co-founder, with Caroline Béïque, of the Fédération nationale Saint-Jean Baptiste and a self-taught expert on the legal subordination of women under Quebec's Civil Code. Like other Catholic feminists, she was mindful of clerical opposition to political equality for women. But by the 1920s, with the federal franchise now in hand, she had joined the long campaign to reform the provincial law that continued until 1940 to deny women the right to vote or stand for office in Quebec City. © *Bibliothèque et archives nationales du Québec*

and, in 1929, helped pressure Louis-Alexandre Taschereau's provincial government into appointing a commission of inquiry to examine the Civil Code and its ramifications for twentieth-century women. But the all-male panel, headed by the conservative Catholic judge Charles-Édouard Dorion, recommended only minor changes to the laws of the province, ensuring that most of the gender inequities would remain in place until the 1960s.[36]

Also on the agenda for Quebec's feminists in this period was women's participation in the political process. Within the FNSJB, however, the push for voting rights was fettered by a complex set of issues, which is all too easily dismissed as "clerical resistance." Many French-Canadian feminists were devout Catholics and their ideological universe was inhabited by both the modern ideas of British, French, and American suffragettes, and by traditional conceptions of family, God, and the nation. Clerical opposition to women's suffrage was real, tenacious, and largely based on the notion that civil society was a collection of families, each best represented in the public sphere by its natural leader, the male household head. It is telling, then, that the first women's suffrage group in the province was an English-language group, the Montreal Suffrage Association, founded by McGill biologist Carrie Derrick in 1912. Thanks to the concerted efforts of similar associations across Canada, women won the campaign for the federal suffrage in 1918 and for provincial voting rights in every other province, plus Newfoundland, by 1925. Resistance remained strong in Quebec, however, and the provincial vote was not achieved until 1940. But by the 1920s, more and more French-Canadian women, led by Gérin-Lajoie and her contemporaries Thérèse Casgrain and Idola Saint-Jean, were flouting the social conservatives, campaigning actively for electoral reform, and organizing into new associations like the Comité provincial pour le suffrage feminin (1921) and the Ligue des droits de la femme (1929).

Although they sought significant reforms, Catholic, "maternal" feminists like Gérin-Lajoie did not go so far as to demand full equality for women or to challenge the separate-spheres ideology that privileged men in the public realm and assigned women to a private world of procreation, childcare, and domestic work. Egalitarians like Eva Circé-Côté pushed the feminist critique a little further. Circé-Côté was a prolific journalist, a strong believer in educational reform, particularly for young women, and a vocal critic of Catholic social doctrine. She frequently wrote under a male pseudonym and published widely in the popular, liberal, and even socialist press, including Langlois's Le Pays and Le Monde ouvrier. To Circé-Côté, it was a matter of course that women were fully fledged "persons" deserving of equality before the law, a useful education, and full political rights. She used her acerbic pen to ridicule those who might believe otherwise and had no scruples about offending the clergy or anyone else. But she also went further, boldly challenging the gender hierarchy and division of labour within the family, as in 1919 when in Le Monde ouvrier she articulated, with her usual wit, the radical idea that housewives should go out on strike for better compensation and working conditions.[37]

The dominant strain of liberalism in early twentieth-century Quebec, however, was something quite different. It was the economic liberalism that held material progress, private property, and individual liberty as its core values. It embraced the laissez-faire philosophy of the industrial capitalists, the entrepreneurs, the managers, and the professionals: men who could claim to have made their way in the modern world through thrift, hard work, and sound investments. That, at least, was the recipe for success they proposed to the masses: individual self-betterment through practical education, moral rectitude, and honest labour. Individuals were thus cast as the main architects of their own successes and failures in life. Governments had no place interfering in the labour market or tinkering with the distribution of wealth, such things being best left to Adam Smith's "invisible hand": the capitalist market. And religious authorities should stick to Sunday devotions and other spiritual matters, leaving the rest of the week and the temporal world to the entrepreneurs and to those in government who would heed their advice.

These were, of course, among the most widely circulated and influential ideas in the Western world at this time. In a Quebec setting, they are most readily associated with the English-speaking elites whose control over the economy is so often noted and sometimes attributed to these liberal values. This was a mode of thinking that contrasted starkly with the collectivist, traditionalist, anti-modernist values of the clerical nationalists. To associate it exclusively with privileged anglophone business leaders, however, would be a mistake. Thanks to a number of detailed studies, we now know just how pervasive the liberalism of material progress was within the French-speaking bourgeoisie as well.[38] Fernande Roy's analysis of French-language business periodicals, for example, reveals a world full of individual success stories in which private property and individual freedom were championed as the keys to material, intellectual, and social progress. As in other liberal publications, a modernized system of education was a recurring theme in the francophone business press. Here, however, the focus was not on universal primary education (as with the radicals) but rather on the promotion of an educational system better suited to training the kind of workforce required by a modern industrial economy. Technical, vocational, and commercial education were keys to personal success in the modern world and more important to the rising generation of French Canadians than the classical curriculum offered by conservative priests in the province's Catholic collèges. The opening of the École des Hautes Études Commerciales in 1907 (Chapter 8) reflects this influence. So, too, do the establishment that same year of technical schools in Montreal and Quebec City and the expansion of the provincial network to the point where, in 1926, a Corporation des Écoles Techniques was needed to coordinate their activities.[39]

Although not necessarily anti-clerical, then, economic liberals were prepared to criticize the clerically sanctioned approach to higher education, with its emphasis on religion, letters, and the humanities and its corresponding inattention to commerce, science, and technology. The liberalism of material progress also favoured the kind of capital investment, whether domestic or foreign, that generated economic development both in Quebec's cities and its resource-rich hinterland. As well, it saw the resulting industrial and urban development as the key to stopping the "haemorrhage" of emigration; decried labour unions, strikes, and the principle of collective bargaining as so many impediments to operation of a free labour market; and embraced a form of French-Canadian nationalism in which "individualism takes priority over community values." After all, they believed, "[t]o be enclosed in the province of Quebec, refusing to open up to the world, would be to turn one's back on progress and to encourage the economic inferiority of French Canadians."[40]

This ideology of material progress was the dominant chord within Quebec liberalism in the early decades of the twentieth century. Indeed, it may have been in some respects a more pervasive and influential current than the defensive nationalism for which this period of Quebec history is better known. Certainly, the history of electoral politics in this period, especially at the provincial level, would tend to support this view. For a period of four decades, from 1897 through 1936, a succession of four Liberal premiers governed the province, all of them wedded to the ideology of economic progress. The provincial Conservatives were tainted by the sins of their federal counterparts, from Riel's execution in 1885 to conscription in 1917, and were unable to find a truly effective leader. They were also challenged by their own diversity and especially by the presence in their midst of both British Canadian imperialists and French-Canadian nationalists. Against such weak opposition, the Liberal Party under Félix-Gabriel Marchand (premier 1897–1900), Simon-Napoléon Parent (1900–1905), Lomer Gouin (1905–20), and Louis-Alexandre Taschereau (1920–36) was able to hold power for forty years. In fact, the party won an astonishing series of ten general elections in succession, always attracting between 55 and 70 percent of the popular vote, and usually holding at least three-quarters of the seats in the

Portrait of Louis-Alexandre Tasch-ereau (1867–1952) by Rodolphe Carrière. Taschereau was Liberal premier of Quebec from 1920 to 1936. *Library and Archives Canada*

legislative assembly.[41] In two of these election years, 1904 and 1919, voters could go to sleep on the evening *before* the election secure in the knowledge that the Liberals had won. This was because their candidates went unopposed and were therefore acclaimed in a sufficient number of ridings to constitute a legislative majority.[42]

The lopsided character of provincial politics underlines the weakness of the Conservative Party, which in the early 1920s under its leader Arthur Sauvé had to dissociate itself from the federal Tories in order to get any electoral traction whatsoever. The situation was virtually reversed for the Liberals who, as of 1896, were the party of Prime Minister Wilfrid Laurier: a formidable and eloquent leader whose prestige, popularity, and political success translated into patronage and votes for those with Liberal connections at any level. As one of the most distinguished Quebecers of his generation, Laurier's own brand of liberalism (and of Liberalism) bears at least some attention. A former *Rouge* and an opponent of Confederation, Laurier was a talented McGill-trained lawyer who rose to the leadership of the federal Liberal Party and, in 1896, to the office of prime minister; he was the first French Canadian to hold that post. His meteoric rise to power began with a historic 1877 speech in which he articulated his own liberal principles: "I am one of those who believe that in all human affairs there are abuses to reform, new horizons to discover and new forces to develop," he pronounced. The best example of such a program of reform, discovery, and development could be found in Great Britain, where William Gladstone's Liberal Party had "carried out a series of reforms which have made the English the freest of peoples, the most prosperous and the happiest in Europe." Laurier's liberalism was thus grounded in his firm belief in British parliamentary institutions. He saw the policy of the Liberal Party as being "to protect [our] institutions, to defend and spread them, and, under the sway of those institutions, to develop the country's latent resources."[43]

Beginning in 1896, Laurier's Liberals won a series of four consecutive federal elections, buoyed in large part by massive majorities in Quebec, with the home-grown Liberal leader now compounding the misfortunes of a Tory party led by imperialists and stigmatized in the province as Riel's executioners. Once in power, Laurier established a new tradition in federal politics whereby the Liberals would come to stand for linguistic dualism and to promote clever but often flawed political compromises designed to achieve harmony between Canada's two "founding peoples." (The examples would include the prohibition plebiscite of 1898, the Naval Bill of 1910, and Laurier's call from the opposition benches for a national referendum on conscription in 1917.) Laurier's liberalism was broader, more British in its inspiration, and less exclusively materialist than that of business leaders who organized francophone Chambres de commerce in Montreal and other cities during his time in Ottawa. But it was no less optimistic for all that.

If Liberals dominated the legislative assembly for four full decades beginning in 1897, however, it was only in part because of weak opposition and the broad coattails of a prestigious federal leader. Their impressive string of electoral victories also reflected the popular appeal of a program that the historians Linteau, Durocher, and Robert have summarized neatly as follows: "economic growth through the development of natural resources and support for foreign capital; hesitant social policies; limited educational reforms aimed at more effectively gearing the system to the needs of the economy."[44] The electorate's continuing faith in this program, despite the deeply seated misgivings of conservative nationalists and others, might be seen as strong evidence for the strength of liberal ideology in this period of Quebec history. It must be said, however, that many devout, conservative Catholics would also have voted Liberal, secure in the knowledge that leaders like Gouin and Taschereau would not challenge the Church's dominance over social institutions or its patriarchal view of the family and gender relations, to name just those two areas.

The economic liberalism of material progress translated into what is usually, and fairly, described as a "pro-business" approach to government. As we have seen (Chapter 7), the Second Industrial Revolution, featuring rapid growth in resource-based industries like hydroelectricity, pulp-and-paper, and aluminum manufacturing, was in full swing. The main concern of Liberal governments under Marchand and Parent, and especially Gouin and Taschereau, was to create a legislative context that would favour investment and development in these new industries. This meant keeping wages and taxes low, labour activism in check, budgets balanced, and government regulation at a minimum.[45] Gouin, for example, favoured rapid, resource-based industrialization and, as historian Bernard Vigod points out, he fully realized the implications of this policy: "[Gouin believed] that French Canada's future was primarily industrial rather than agricultural; that at least in the short term, ownership of resource-based industries would rest primarily in the hands of non-French-Canadian entrepreneurs; [and] that the long-range hope for indigenous control lay ... in a more vocationally oriented concept of education and a generally more materialistic and progressive attitude within French-Canadian society."[46]

Economic nationalists like Errol Bouchette might well complain, as he did in *L'Indépendance économique du Canada français* (1906), that the result was a pattern of development in which economic rents and advantages flowed disproportionately southward, into the pockets of American capitalists, leaving French Canadians with only such earnings as could be had from low-paying jobs in the labour force. What was needed in this view was a provincial government that would take a tougher regulatory position, even if it meant alienating the business community in general and American investors in particular. Bouchette argued that timber and water-power rights should be leased to investors for a fixed term, rather than sold outright, and he did so in language that anticipated more recent discussions of renewable resources.[47] This critique did ultimately convince Gouin's government to switch to long-term leases for water and power rights. This was despite the fact that the sale of such rights had been a very lucrative revenue stream in previous years, helping to underwrite an ambitious infrastructure program focused on road building; the twentieth century was the age of the automobile, and Quebec, like every other jurisdiction, needed highways. The nationalists also spurred Gouin's Liberal government in 1910 to regulate the pulp and paper industry, thereby stimulating newsprint production in the province (see Chapter 7). But more tellingly, it chose to leave hydroelectric development in the hands of huge, private corporations, or trusts, rather than follow the example of Ontario, which in 1906 established the Hydro-Electric Power Commission of Ontario as a public utility. Quebec's Liberal governments, then, strove to keep economic regulation to a minimum and thereby to demonstrate to American investors that the province, with its vast, resource-rich territory and a large labour force willing to work cheaply, was open for business.

Moderate educational and social legislation was also on the Liberal agenda, particularly during the postwar Taschereau years. As we have seen, T.D. Bouchard's endorsement of compulsory schooling did not sway the leadership of his party. But the government's commitment to technical, vocational, and commercial education was real enough and resulted in important innovations. Mainstream education was run by denominational school boards and overseen by two distinct committees, respectively Catholic and Protestant, under the authority of the Council of Public Instruction. Short of abolishing these structures and taking direct control of primary education—a reform that would have to await the 1960s—the government could make no fundamental changes in this area. But it did what it could within those limits, aggressively implementing a new curriculum adopted by the Catholic committee in 1922, increasing the authority of school inspectors, notably in the area of teachers' salaries and qualifications, and increasing financial assistance to schools and school boards willing to make new investments in facilities and staff. Taschereau's government also invested in Normal Schools for teacher training and in 1926 appointed a Commission of Inquiry, headed

École des hautes études commerciales, Montreal, Quebec, ca. 1910. The HEC, as it is widely known, opened in 1907 and was housed in this stone structure on Viger Street. Economic liberals believed that commercial education was one of the keys to progress and prosperity. And the establishment of a French-Canadian business school, affiliated with Laval University's Montreal branch (later Université de Montréal), was part of that project. The impressive heritage building, oddly identified on this postcard as the "School of Higher Studies," now houses the Montreal Archives Centre, a branch of the Bibliothèque et archives nationales du Québec. *McCord Museum*

by former premier Gouin, into the delivery of French-language Catholic education in Montreal.[48]

Similarly in the area of social legislation, the Liberal path to progress was via moderate reforms that sought to deal with specific issues without antagonizing either the Catholic Church or the business and investment communities. Easily the most significant of these was the Public Charities Act, passed in 1921, which set up a new funding structure for poor relief in the province. "Indigents" of all descriptions—including the elderly infirm, the physically or mentally disabled, and orphaned or abandoned children—would continue to be cared for in private institutions run, at least on the Catholic side, by religious congregations. But the cost of their care would now be shared equally among three partners: the provincial government, the municipality, and the institution itself.[49] This was Quebec's first, cautious step into the twentieth-century world of state-run social assistance programs. But it was bold enough to draw the ire of Henri Bourassa, who described it as "so serious an invasion of the church's jurisdiction . . . that it destroyed the existing equilibrium between civil and religious authority."[50] Few would have gone that far. But the Catholic hierarchy did see the new legislation as an instance of state interference in its affairs and, after a committee of bishops had studied it in detail, began pressuring Taschereau to have it withdrawn or rewritten. The premier was willing to negotiate the details but stood firm on the general principles, not least out of sensitivity to outside accusations that his modern, progressive Quebec might still be a "priest-ridden society."[51] Noteworthy social legislation under Taschereau also included the 1921 law that gave a provincial Crown corporation, the Quebec Liquor Commission, a monopoly over the sale and distribution of alcoholic beverages; the 1922 measure creating a Provincial Bureau of Health, which made significant advances in the troublesome area of infant mortality (see Chapter 8); and the 1924 Adoption Act, which for the first time made it possible to formally adopt a child in the province, thus creating a family-based alternative to institutional care for orphans and abandoned children.

Legalizing adoption was a pragmatic measure meant to put needy children—and the province's many crèches and orphanages were full of them—together with families who could give them a home, a name, and a future. It was also a quintessentially *liberal* measure, both in its optimism and in its grounding in the expert, scientific advice of the day, especially that of social workers and psychologists. Children did better in families than in institutional settings, they reasoned, and the state should do everything in its power to foster that approach to childrearing. The 1924 Adoption Act was strenuously resisted by clerical nationalists who opposed any kind of state initiative that might undermine the traditional definition of the family, one composed of a biological father and mother plus their numerous offspring and in which the legal principle of *la puissance paternelle* (paternal authority) cemented both the gender hierarchy and filial respect and obedience. Indeed, it had to be rewritten in 1925 in such a way as to specify that only children without a pre-existing filial bond—those born out of wedlock or whose legitimate parents had both died—were eligible for adoption.[52] A modern measure that nonetheless incorporated traditional elements, the 1920s adoption

La moisson, Orphelinat d'Huberdeau, P. Q.

Harvest at the orphanage, Huberdeau, Quebec, ca. 1910. Located some 35 kilometres south of Mont-Tremblant in the Laurentians, this orphanage was established in the 1880s and run by a French religious order, Les Pères de Montfort, until the 1920s. Children raised in orphanages like this one could not be legally adopted until 1924. *McCord Museum*

legislation thus encapsulated many of the social and political tensions of the decade.

This was, after all, the decade during which Quebec, along with the rest of North America, entered the age of the flapper, the Model T, the Charleston, radio broadcasting, and New Orleans jazz; *les années folles* (the crazy years) is the French equivalent of "The Roaring Twenties." French-Canadian culture, especially in the cities, was not nearly so dominated by traditional Catholic values as to be immune from these influences. Social conservatives fought back with a vengeance, denouncing consumerism and virtually every form of commercial entertainment in diatribes that can sound humorous to the twenty-first century ear, pitched as they were against such dangerous delights as billiard rooms, non-denominational clubs, novels, newspaper coverage of criminal trials, and the foxtrot. Their angst and their anti-liberal, anti-modern sentiment were real enough, however, and they focused as often as not on the threat that such innovations posed to the family, a central dimension of Groulx's definition of the French-Canadian identity. The wartime plea for a "Revenge of the Cradle" is easily understood in this context, the particular moral danger here being the heresy of contraception. Another area of concern and consternation was family violence. When, in 1920, a ten-year-old girl named Aurore Gagnon was found beaten to death by her father and stepmother in a rural village in Lotbinière county, a massive wave of outrage and disgust swept the province.[53] What had happened to social relations in the province if a little girl's family could no longer be trusted to care for and nurture her? The French-Canadian family and the moral and practical challenges it faced in the modern era were the stuff of advice columns in the popular daily press—including Henriette Dessaulles as "Fadette" in *Le Devoir*—and, as we have seen, were discussed and debated at length by Catholic clerics and intellectuals during the 1923 Semaine sociale.

Children, the family, and the challenges of modernity were brought into sharp focus by one of the worst tragedies of the period: the Laurier Palace fire. The St. Catherine Street cinema was popular for its Sunday matinees, attended by hundreds each week. At about 1:45 in the afternoon on 9 January 1927, fire broke out during a screening of a Stanley Laurel comedy entitled *Get 'em Young*, which was attended by some 250 people, most of them children from the neighbourhood. Firefighters were on the scene quickly and worked frantically to free a large group of children trapped in a stairway. But when the smoke cleared, seventy-eight children aged five to eighteen had been asphyxiated or trampled to death in the panic to flee the theatre's crowded balcony. In the wake of the tragedy, municipal fire authorities issued tighter regulations that forced the closing of several theatres. The owners of the cinema faced charges of criminal negligence, and socially conservative Catholics called for the closing of all cinemas on Sundays and the exclusion of children at all times. Respect for the Sabbath, after all, was one of the battle cries of the Catholic Action movement and a Ligue du Dimanche had been organized by the École sociale populaire as recently as 1923. Some militant Catholics, writes historian Paul Laverdure, even suggested that the fire "was a punishment from God for the theatres' Sunday desecration."[54]

The Laurier Palace Theatre on St. Catherine Street East in the wake of the devastating fire of 9 January 1927. Dozens of children were trampled or asphyxiated when they became trapped in a stairway leading down from the balcony, where the fire had started. Others broke through the second-storey windows and escaped via the marquee. *Cinémathèque québécoise*

As for the Taschereau government, it appointed a commission of inquiry, with terms of reference that went well beyond the issue of criminal negligence and into the fuzzier realm of public morality, especially as regards children. The commissioners focused on the corrupting influence of the cinema in general and of Sunday screenings for children in particular. They puzzled over the growing popularity of commercial films: why did people keep attending and even sending their children, often unaccompanied, to the pictures when the community's spiritual leaders were so clear and adamant on the moral dangers they represented? They concluded, writes Laverdure, "that immorality, free love, adultery, divorce, thefts, murders, suicides, and, more importantly, the depiction of people flouting legal and religious authority attracted paying customers."[55]

With these conclusions in hand, the Taschereau government went ahead with legislation that banned children under the age of sixteen from all motion-picture theatres but that did not go so far as to close down all cinemas on Sundays, as conservative critics had demanded. As in other situations, a Liberal government faced with staunch clerical opposition chose a moderate course, designed to assist Quebec society in its sometimes painful adaptation to the realities of modern urban life. The state could no more abolish the cinema, even for one day per week, than it could reverse the course of industrial and urban development. The discussion would shift in 1929 as the Great Depression began moving the focus away from the moral dangers of modern life (although this thread never really disappeared) and towards the problem of basic human survival.

TEN

A GREAT DARKNESS?

It is with the looming figure of Maurice Duplessis that the widely circulated idea of *la grande noirceur* (the great darkness) is most closely associated. But if a gloom fell over Quebec in the mid-twentieth century, it was probably in 1929, when the stock markets crashed, rather than 1936, when Duplessis was first elected premier. There is no underestimating the sombre cast of the early 1930s, when falling commodity prices, bankruptcies, and unprecedented unemployment levels hit Quebec as hard as any North American jurisdiction, and perhaps harder than most. Agriculture, forestry, and the new export-driven resource industries were particularly sensitive to the free-fall in international demand. But the ripple effects hit every sector of the economy. Between 1929 and 1933, the number of manufacturing jobs in the province fell by 25 percent, the value of production in that sector by 45 percent, and total wages by 40 percent.[1] Thousands were thrown out of work and, in the absence of a social safety net, forced to cope as best they could with the hardship of unemployment.

For many, dealing with joblessness was nothing new. Working-class women in particular were well used to taking in washing or mending, housing boarders, tending vegetable gardens, and relying on kin and parish networks to pull their families through hard times.[2] As jobless rates climbed to 25 percent or 30 percent, families coped by making do with poorer food, wearing patched or borrowed clothes, enduring cold winter nights without sufficient fuel, and drawing on family and community networks of sharing and solidarity.[3] But with so many struggling for survival, these coping mechanisms could only go so far. The Public Charities Act of 1921, moreover, had not been designed to provide income supports to tens of thousands of unemployed household heads but rather to finance institutional care for orphaned and abandoned children, the elderly, the infirm, and other categories of "deserving poor."

The sheer scale of the crisis had transformed poverty and unemployment from an individual moral issue into a collective social one. But the Liberal government in Quebec City was slow to come to that realization. True, it provided millions of dollars in funding for relief efforts administered and delivered by the municipalities, in collaboration with private charitable agencies such as the St. Vincent de Paul Society. But it continued to resist proposals that would have provided direct cash contributions to the budgets of needy families. Taschereau had refused, for example, to sign on to the federal old-age pension program in 1927. In the wake of the stock-market crash, he did appoint a Royal Commission on Social Insurance, headed by the renowned economist Édouard Montpetit. But the commission's recommendations for greater state intervention in areas such as unemployment, old-age security, and workers' compensation essentially fell on deaf ears.[4] In Taschereau's mind, the Quebec public was still wedded to the principles of economic liberalism and not yet ready for a modern, comprehensive, provincially funded and administered social welfare system.

Through the early years of the Depression, the state instead responded to poverty and unemployment using the approach known as "indirect relief." Municipalities conceived of vast public-works projects and hired teams of unemployed workers to build or upgrade roads, bridges, parks, and the like, giving priority to married men with dependent wives and children. Such initiatives were consistent with economic liberalism, but they left many jobless people in the lurch (women, for example) and were expensive for the towns and cities, which had to bear fully half the cost. By 1936, at least seventy-five municipalities had been driven into bankruptcy as a result, and many more were teetering on the brink.[5]

In 1932, with unemployment levels still rising, a system of direct relief was finally instituted, funded in equal parts by the federal, provincial, and municipal governments. For the first time, able-bodied men received income support payments directly from the government. But payments were parsimonious at best and there were plenty of strings attached. At first, the funds could only be used to pay for essentials such as food and fuel. And they took the form of vouchers and coupons, so that those using them had to reveal themselves publicly to merchants and others as being on the dole. Even so, tens of thousands of families in

City workers digging up sidewalk on Park Avenue. Social assistance for unemployed men during the Great Depression often took the form of low-paid manual labour in public-works projects organized by municipal governments. In Montreal, a number of urban landmarks—including the iconic Atwater Market—owe their origins to these initiatives. In this 1933 photograph from the City of Montreal archives, a group of workers is burying electric wires under the sidewalks along Park Avenue. *Archives de la Ville de Montréal*

urban Quebec applied for and received direct relief. Rural families had their cash incomes cut drastically as commodity prices fell during the Depression. But the fact that they usually owned their own homes and produced their own food and fuel generally kept them off the relief rolls, while encouraging a resurgence of the colonization and "back-to-the-land" movements.[6]

Politically, the economic crisis was grist for the mill of radical options and third parties on the right and the left.[7] English-speaking academics like McGill's Frank Scott and Leonard Marsh were prominent in the League for Social Reconstruction, a group of socialist intellectuals with close ties to the Co-operative Commonwealth Federation, the pan-Canadian social democratic party founded in Calgary in 1932. Socialist ideas, however, never took hold among working-class francophone Quebecers the way they did on the Prairies. Quebec's labour movement, moreover, was weakened by its many internal divisions. Catholic unions under the banner of the Confédération des travailleurs catholiques du

Canada vied for membership with international trade and industrial unions affiliated with the American Federation of Labor or, as of 1938, the Congress of Industrial Organizations. International unions were more permeable to socialist ideas, such as those promoted between 1929 and 1935 by the Communist-affiliated Workers Unity League. But with the glutted labour market of the time, no workers' organization was able to make serious inroads, so that fewer than one in ten Quebec workers in 1931 belonged to any kind of union.[8]

At the other end of the political spectrum, fascism and other right-wing ideologies—often couched in the familiar rhetoric of tradition, authority, Christianity, and homeland—were attractive to some French Canadians, especially those with clerical nationalist leanings. The generation of youth that grew to maturity in the 1930s, especially those with a good *collège classique* education, were searching for explanations and for a path through the economic cataclysm that would keep their cultural identity intact. The paradigm that historian Susan Mann has called the three C's—corporatism, colonization, and the co-operative movement— was central to this search.[9] Corporatism, in particular, was promoted by Catholic intellectuals as an economic and social system that could provide an alternative to both the injustices of unfettered capitalism and the evils of socialism, of which Stalin's Soviet Union provided the most frightening example. The corporatist idea was to transcend class conflict and restructure society as a community of professional bodies in which owners, managers, and workers in each economic sector might recognize their shared interests and work together towards common goals. Along with this optimistic vision, unfortunately, came some of the less noble ideas common to right-wing nationalisms all over the west. The xenophobic and anti-Semitic leanings of Jeune Canada (1932) and some of the other French-Canadian youth movements of the time, for example, are unmistakable. But militarist, overtly racist, Nazi-inspired groups such as Adrien Arcand's Parti national social chrétien (1934) remained strictly on the fringes and without any real influence on the political direction of the province.

During the 1930s, elected governments all over the Western world were called to task for their inability to manage the crisis. Quebec was no different. The Liberals, who had dominated the legislative assembly since the late 1890s, were finally turned out in 1936, with their program of economic development, balanced budgets, and minimal social intervention in tatters. Individual self-sufficiency was still at the heart of Taschereau's liberalism and this was not likely to change as he entered his seventies.[10] But the need for economic and political reform was pressing. The laissez-faire capitalism of the turn of the century had certainly created jobs and generated revenue streams, allowing the government to build modern infrastructure, especially a network of roads and highways for the new automobile age. But the wage reductions, layoffs, and plant closings of the 1930s proved to many that the system subordinated workers' welfare to corporate and shareholder interests. The huge private corporations that controlled the hydroelectric utility and other key industries continued charging high rates and taking significant profits, while so many working-class families struggled to pay for rent, heat, and groceries. The fact that most workers and ratepayers were francophone Catholics and most corporate bosses and shareholders were English-speaking Protestants was not lost on the nationalists, leading many to criticize the provincial government for not doing enough to protect and promote the interests of French Canadians. Meanwhile, the Liberal government was developing a serious image problem. The wealthy, well-connected premier made no apology for the fact that he sat on the boards of directors of large financial corporations such as Royal Trust and Sun Life Assurance or that he counted the top executives of powerful hydroelectric trusts, including Shawinigan Water and Power, among his personal friends (and poker partners).[11] Such cozy alliances fuelled criticism of the premier as "*un trustard*" who put the interests of his big-business buddies before that of the Quebec people, criticism that gained intensity as the crisis deepened, along with antitrust sentiment and the associated calls for a public hydroelectric utility.

The Liberals, moreover, had become used to something like absolute power in provincial politics, and they had developed some bad habits, especially as regards political ethics. A full list of shady dealings would certainly include their refusal to redraw a lopsided electoral map that benefited them by ensuring that fast-growing urban areas remained under-represented; the reckless and arrogant Dillon Act by which the government intervened to prevent the Conservatives from bringing court

Charles Fontaine, Montagnais de Bersimis, et sa femme fumant sa pipe, photograph by Paul Provencher, ca. 1937. In the interwar years, Quebec was an increasingly urban place, but one in which rural dwellers, especially First Nations people, continued to engage in traditional subsistence activities such as hunting, trapping, and fishing. This Montagnais (Innu) couple from Bersimis with their fishing nets in the background was photographed by Paul Provencher, probably in 1937. In the 1950s, their community on the Betsiamites River, some 400 kilometres Northeast of Quebec City, was chosen as the site of the first generating station developed by the new public hydro-electric utility, Hydro-Québec. © *Bibliothèque et archives nationales du Québec*

action for alleged irregularities during the 1931 election; an ingrained system of patronage appointments, which had come to feature a high degree of nepotism (according to one account, forty-five of the premier's own relatives enjoyed positions in the provincial civil service); and some even more serious abuses involving the misappropriation of public funds that came to light in 1936 and which would, in fact, precipitate Taschereau's resignation.[12]

The Depression spurred intellectuals and activists of all ideological stripes to carve out positions on its causes, on the proper response of government, and on the means of averting such economic cataclysms in the future. This was especially true of the nationalists, who drew strength and conviction from the failings of the Liberal government and its policies. Political corruption, foreign and anglophone control of the province's resources and industries, and the economic weakness of French Canadians, brought into stark focus by unemployment and bread lines—all of these themes found frequent expression in influential nationalist publications like Bourassa's *Le Devoir* and *L'Action nationale*, a new journal launched in 1933 by Esdras Minville to succeed Groulx's *Action canadienne-française*.

The Catholic Church took a leading role in this discussion. In his 1931 encyclical Quadragesimo Anno, Pope Pius XI updated the Catholic social doctrine formulated forty years earlier in Rerum Novarum. Sparked by the new encyclical, Quebec's Catholic hierarchy entrusted the Jesuit order and its École Sociale Populaire with the formulation of a position. The result was the *Programme de restauration sociale (PRS)*, published in the fall of 1933, which outlined a comprehensive series of reforms, organized under four headings: rural reconstruction, the labour question, trusts and finance, and political reforms.[13] The program contained some modern ideas about the role of the state, especially as regards the regulation of industry and the provision of income supports for the needy. But it was also deeply imbued with a nostalgic vocabulary in which the key concepts were renaissance, restoration, and redress; with a persistent agrarian ideal that blamed all society's ills on industry and urban life; and especially with the principles of corporatism, which the authors (a committee of prominent Catholic laymen) and their Jesuit sponsors promoted as the best antidote to class conflict.

Both progressive and conservative nationalists found much to support in the PRS, which served to focus much of the opposition to the Taschereau government and its policies. The beginning of the end for the Liberals came in 1934 when a dissident group emerged within the ruling party itself. Led by the former premier's son, Paul Gouin, the Action Libérale Nationale (ALN) began to promote the PRS agenda, hoping at first to convince the governing Liberals to change course. But Gouin and his young allies soon broke with the government and set themselves up as a new, progressive option in Quebec politics. Meanwhile, the provincial Conservatives had voted the young lawyer and Trois-Rivières

MLA Maurice Duplessis as their new leader in October 1933. Duplessis was a shrewd politician and a skilled parliamentarian. At the risk of alienating his party's English-speaking business constituency, he took the provincial Tories in a more nationalist direction, hounding Taschereau for corruption and complicity with the trusts, and endorsing many of the reforms outlined in the PRS.

On 8 November, less than three weeks before the 1935 election, Gouin and Duplessis announced an electoral coalition to be known as the Union Nationale Duplessis-Gouin. The leaders agreed to campaign on the ALN's ambitious program of reforms and to present "a united front against the common enemy of the people, of the province of Quebec: the Taschereau regime."[14] The coalition promised agrarian reform in the form of low-interest agricultural credit, accelerated rural electrification, farmers' marketing co-operatives, and a vast colonization program. It would revise working conditions with a new minimum wage law, legislation on the hours of work and industrial hygiene, and a new labour code. It would engage in "slum clearance" and provide income supports to the poor through health insurance, supplements for needy mothers, and old-age pensions. Gouin and Duplessis also promised to release the Quebec people from the burden of monopolistic business practices, particularly those of the electricity trusts. This process would begin with the establishment of a state-owned hydroelectric utility to develop new sources of power and would include the creation of a commission to examine the possibility of nationalizing the private power companies. In addition, they would reform the province's political institutions, barring cabinet ministers from sitting on corporate boards or holding shares in companies with government contracts, placing limits on campaign contributions, and replacing Quebec's upper house, the legislative council, with a new economic council, organized along corporatist lines.[15]

This was a popular platform among Quebec electors who, after decades of one-party rule and years of economic crisis, were looking for new ideas and new faces. In the end, the Union Nationale coalition lost the 1935 election. But it won a stunning forty-two seats in the legislature, almost four times the Conservative tally in 1931, and reduced the Liberal majority from 79 to 6. As leader of the opposition, Maurice

Duplessis moved quickly to consolidate his gains. In the spring of 1936, he used his position as chair of the Public Accounts Committee to make sensational revelations about the extent of patronage, nepotism, and corruption within the provincial government. Gravely damaged by the scandal, Taschereau resigned on 11 June, naming as his successor the minister of agriculture, Joseph Adélard Godbout. In the ensuing election campaign, Duplessis rode the popularity of the former ALN candidates and his own new reputation as an anti-corruption crusader to a massive victory at the polls. On 17 August, Union Nationale (UN) candidates won 57 percent of the popular vote and 76 of the 90 seats in the legislative assembly, dealing the final blow not just to a severely compromised Taschereau/Godbout government but to four decades of Liberal power in Quebec City.

The new premier was poised to emerge as one of the most powerful figures in the province's history, with a political machine to rival anything the Taschereau Liberals had assembled, a profound conservatism that acted as a brake on social and economic reform, and an authoritarian leadership style that earned him the nickname *Le Chef.*

Monsieur Maurice Duplessis, chef de l'Union Nationale, vainqueur d'hier et premier ministre de demain. La Patrie, 18 August 1936. News of the 1936 election results, which gave Maurice Duplessis a large majority and his first term as premier, was splashed all over the front page of the Montreal newspaper *La Patrie* the day after the 17 August vote. In translation, the caption reads as follows: "Mr. Maurice Duplessis, leader of the Union Nationale, yesterday's winner and tomorrow's premier." © *Bibliothèque et archives nationales du Québec*

By the time he took power in 1936, Duplessis had reinvented the UN as a formal political party, absorbed most of the former ALN members into its ranks, and asserted his own leadership by outflanking his former coalition partner Paul Gouin. But his first term in office, from 1936 to 1939, was deeply disappointing to anyone who had expected him to deliver on the platform of sweeping change first outlined in 1935. Few of the reforms proposed in the PRS found their way into legislation in the late 1930s. Most galling to his progressive allies was Duplessis's refusal to alienate the business community by expropriating the hydroelectric trusts; indeed, those within the *unioniste* caucus who clung to that position soon found themselves on the margins. His social-assistance legislation was limited to modest income-support measures for needy mothers and the blind. Although he did establish a commission on wages, which led to new "Fair Wage" legislation, Duplessis introduced no new labour code. Instead, he gained a reputation as a staunch opponent of organized labour, taking rigid positions against workers' tactics in the Dominion Textile strike of August 1937 and outlawing the closed union shop the following year.[16] Only the agrarian-reform chapter of the PRS seemed to influence public policy in the late 1930s, inspiring a successful farm-credit scheme, rural electrification and road-building programmes, and the creation of agricultural schools. Vote-rich rural districts had helped propel Duplessis into the premier's chair in 1936, and he had not forgotten.[17]

The first Duplessis government is also noteworthy for its intransigence in dealing with dissent. The premier set the tone just weeks into his mandate in September 1936 by firing the entire Montreal squad of the Quebec Provincial Police.[18] More famously, he took strong measures to muzzle those on the left who would advocate political violence or revolution. In March 1937, with the Spanish Civil War underway and Catholic authorities denouncing Communism from every available pulpit, the Quebec government banned the publication and distribution of materials deemed to be Communist or Bolshevik in content or inspiration. Known as the Padlock Act, the legislation empowered the Attorney General (a position held by Duplessis himself) and police forces to seal for one year, by means of padlocks, any premises used for the dissemination of such ideas.[19] It thus provided authorities with an

Communistic Literature, photograph by Conrad Poirier, 22 January 1938. Under Maurice Duplessis's infamous Padlock Act, premises used for the dissemination of Communist ideas could be closed (by means of padlocks) for a year and literature promoting those ideas could be confiscated. This Conrad Poirier photograph, taken in January 1938 at the Montreal City Hall, shows three men examining stacks of newspapers and magazines so confiscated, including copies of *Clarté*, the *Revue de Moscou*, and *Soviet Russia Today*. © *Bibliothèque et archives nationales du Québec*

extraordinary instrument of repression, which was used against not only revolutionary socialists but also the province's unionized workers. For many, especially on the left, it revealed Duplessis in his true colours, as an authoritarian, arch-conservative leader who valued order, tradition, and stability over civil liberties and human rights.[20]

Usually a shrewd tactician, Duplessis was defeated at the polls in 1939 due to a rare miscalculation. With war clouds breaking in Europe, Canadian participation in the Second World War was confirmed by Mackenzie King's Liberal government in Ottawa on 10 September. In the circumstances, the divisive issue of compulsory military service was bound to resurface. Duplessis called a snap election, hoping to win a fresh mandate by rallying widespread anti-conscription sentiment behind UN candidates. But Liberal leader Adélard Godbout was in a position to remind voters of King's explicit promise never to introduce conscription for overseas service.[21] Quebec's representatives in the federal cabinet, led by Minister of Justice Ernest Lapointe, vowed to resign should voters re-elect Duplessis. What influence, they warned, would Quebec retain over Canadian military policy in that scenario? Besides, the electorate was disappointed with Duplessis's record on economic and social reform, disconcerted by his authoritarian style, and unconvinced by his campaign for provincial autonomy, framed in slogans such as *Coopération Oui— Assimilation Jamais* (Cooperation Yes—Assimilation Never). So in the general election of 25 October 1939, they handed *Le Chef* a crushing defeat, electing seventy Godbout Liberals to only fifteen UN candidates, including Duplessis who retained his Trois-Rivières seat and so survived to fight another day.

Adélard Godbout's arrival in the premier's office coincided not only with the outbreak of a new war in Europe but also with the beginning of a new phase in the history of federal–provincial relations, characterized by a ramping up of Ottawa's push into domains reserved in 1867 for provincial action. Not surprisingly, nationalists have interpreted this as *l'ingérence du fédéral* (federal interference) and Godbout as a failed guardian of Quebec's legislative turf. He acquiesced in 1940 to a constitutional amendment transferring jurisdiction for unemployment insurance from the provinces to Ottawa. He accepted the wartime "Tax Rental" agreements by which the provinces ceded their main instruments of direct taxation (personal and corporate income tax and succession duties) to the federal government in exchange for lump-sum payments. He raised no great objection when, in 1944, the federal government introduced its universal family allowance plan, a form of social assistance. As we shall see shortly, he also hewed against the nationalist grain in not standing firmly against conscription in the run-up to the 1942 plebiscite organized by his Liberal colleagues in Ottawa.[22]

Yet, in a province where so many interpret the 1930s, 1940s, and 1950s as an era of profound darkness, the proponents of liberal modernity could point, at least, to a few rays of sunlight that managed to pierce the gloom during the Godbout years. Women's civil and political rights, for example, took an important step forward early in 1940 when the Godbout government passed legislation allowing women to hold public office and to vote in provincial elections. Activists like Idola Saint-Jean and Thérèse

Casgrain had been campaigning for electoral reform since the 1920s, only to have a dozen legislative bills voted down on first reading. Women's suffrage was framed by its conservative opponents as inconsistent with traditional French-Canadian and Catholic conceptions of family, society, and the state. Cardinal Jean-Marie Rodrigue Villeneuve, the archbishop of Quebec, expressed this position in March 1940, claiming that such a reform would constitute a blow to family "unity and hierarchy," that it would expose women to the sordid world of electoral "passions and adventures," that most of the province's women did not seek or desire the right to vote, and that the promised gains for society in terms of economic, social, and hygiene reform could just as easily be achieved by women's organizations on the margins of formal politics.[23] Faced with these traditional arguments, the Godbout government instead took a modern liberal position, promoting legislation which on 25 April 1940 gave Quebec women the same voting rights as in every other jurisdiction in Canada and the United States.[24]

Just as striking was a raft of social and economic initiatives undertaken late in Godbout's term, including a commission to study the idea of public health insurance (established 23 June 1943), a new child protection law (Bill 39, passed 3 June 1944 but never implemented), and a modernized industrial-relations law requiring collective bargaining and union recognition in workplaces where 60 percent of workers had been organized.[25] There were substantial improvements to the province's educational system, especially at the primary and post-secondary levels. In 1943, Godbout defied tradition and the Catholic hierarchy once again by introducing compulsory school attendance for all children aged six to fourteen and abolishing tuition and textbook fees for elementary school children.[26] The same year saw the completion of the new Université de Montréal campus on the northern slopes of Mount Royal, featuring Ernest Cormier's bold Art Deco tower that stands as a monument to French-Canadian modernity, both in higher education and architecture.[27] Godbout also took action against the hated electricity trusts, creating the Quebec Hydroelectric Commission, or Hydro-Québec, with power to expropriate the assets of private electricity corporations, beginning with the Montreal Light, Heat and Power Company in April 1944. This was all in addition to the federal social welfare initiatives, especially unemployment

"Chore man" Andres Budge of Maniwaki, Quebec, carrying water in buckets by means of a yoke across his shoulders at M. Kearney's logging camp in the Outaouais region on a winter day in 1943. As wartime demand stoked modern industrial production in the 1940s, logging was one of many economic activities, especially in rural areas, which continued to be carried out along more or less traditional lines. *Library and Archives Canada*

insurance and family allowances, which nationalists found so galling.[28] In supporting these initiatives, the Liberals both adhered to a party line established in Ottawa and acted in what they understood to be the best interest of Quebecers. They also laid some important groundwork for the rapid modernization of the 1960s, particularly in the key areas of social welfare, education, and energy policy.

But the Godbout government's achievements in the 1940s have faded in public memory, overshadowed by the war and by a second conscription crisis, similar in kind to that of 1917–18 but more skilfully managed in Ottawa and leaving somewhat fewer scars in Quebec.[29] With Mackenzie King's pledge in place, a strong Quebec contingent in the federal Cabinet, and Canadian forces not yet actively engaged overseas, debates over mandatory military service were easily held in check prior to the spring of 1940. But the tide turned after the Nazis defeated the Anglo-French alliance in Belgium, forced the massive troop evacuation from Dunkirk, and pressed France into capitulation on 16 June. This was no longer a "phoney war" and calls for maximum mobilization of Canadian resources began to be heard, especially in Ontario. Responding to such sentiments, King's government on 21 June 1940 passed the National Resources Mobilization Act, which authorized conscription for the defence of Canadian territory. For nationalists like Kamouraska MLA René Chaloult, who denounced the measure in the provincial legislature, this was the thin edge of the wedge. Conscription for homeland defence was now a *fait accompli*; could conscription for overseas service be far behind? Others replied with actions rather than speeches. Men as yet unmarried as of 15 July 1940 were first in line for registration, and so there was a noticeable rush to the altar in the first two weeks of the month. Still, the summer of 1940 saw the registration of over 800,000 men, over one-quarter of them in Quebec. The process was surprisingly orderly, except in Montreal where Mayor Camilien Houde denounced the draft and encouraged young men to defy the federal law and refuse to register. He was arrested for his troubles and forced to spend the war years in a federal internment camp.[30]

By the winter of 1941–42, calls for an unrestricted draft had grown louder and more insistent in English Canada. For some, like former Tory prime minister Arthur Meighen, now ensconced in the Senate, it was a matter of loyalty and fairness. Meighen believed that conscription was "the only way that Quebec could be forced to do its share,"[31] and this was the position adopted by the federal Conservative Party when he resumed the leadership in November 1941. Meanwhile, the death of Ernest Lapointe on 26 November silenced the strongest anti-conscription voice in the federal Cabinet. And Japanese attacks on Pearl Harbor and Hong Kong complicated the home-defence situation by opening the Pacific theatre and thus creating new vulnerabilities, real and imagined, in British Columbia.

Weighing English-Canadian calls for total mobilization against a Quebec population mindful of 1917 and keenly aware of his promise to fight the war with a volunteer force, King announced a new position in January 1942. His government would hold a national plebiscite, not on whether to send an army of conscripts to Europe but on whether to release Ottawa from its prior commitment *not* to do so. Quebecers reacted with discomfort and deep suspicion. In the months leading up to the 27 April vote, many participated in a spirited and forceful campaign for a "No" vote, with Catholic youth groups, francophone business leaders, organized labour, and nationalist associations all united under the banner of the Ligue pour la défense du Canada and the leadership of *L'Action nationale* editor André Laurendeau. The results divided the Dominion as clearly as those of the 1917 election. Quebec stood squarely in the "No" camp, with 73 percent of all voters and perhaps 85 percent of French Canadians voting against the proposal. But across Canada, 64 percent had voted in favour of King's position, with the "Yes" votes in Ontario alone sufficient to offset the impact of Quebec's resounding "No" on the Dominion-wide result.[32]

King's next steps were careful ones, as through a political minefield. Ottawa would not institute "conscription for conscription's sake" and would not send conscripts overseas except in the event of clear military necessity. But it did amend the registration law of 1940 so as to remove any restrictions on where trained conscripts might serve, prompting a fresh wave of angry reaction in Quebec, the resignation of the most prominent federal minister from the province, P.J.A. Cardin, and a motion of protest supported by all but seven members of the legislative assembly in Quebec City. When passed into law on 7 July, Bill 80 was opposed by six CCFers and forty-eight French-Canadian MPs, some of whom would follow Maxime Raymond, who left the Liberal Party to found a new liberal-nationalist political party, the Bloc populaire canadien, in October 1942.

It was not until the fall of 1944, with the Normandy invasion well advanced and victory in Europe mere months away, that King came to believe that conscription for overseas service was a military necessity. And so the federal Parliament authorized the expedition of up to 16,000 trained conscripts into the European theatre, provoking further expressions of shock and outrage from Quebecers—not least, of course, from Bloc populaire leader Maxime Raymond—and the resignation of another Cabinet minister, Charles (Chubby) Power of Quebec City. Nor was it a simple matter, once the orders were given, to convince the conscripts to report for overseas duty. Episodes of absenteeism, desertion, and even mutiny—mainly kept out of the public eye by strict press censorship—included a three-hour street fight in Drummondville that pitted a government raiding party against conscripts and their civilian supporters. By all accounts, however, those who reported served well; there were in total 12,908 recruits, of whom 2,463 were posted to northwest Europe (69 were killed, 232 were wounded, and 13 were taken prisoner).[33]

The real impact of the conscription debate was political rather than military. Its consequences were profound and lasting, although somewhat less so than in 1917–18. King had carefully avoided Borden's worst mistakes; there had been no divisive wartime election and no "union" government to isolate French Canadians politically. So with Quebecers like Compton-born minister of justice Louis St. Laurent in powerful positions, the federal Liberals managed to remain popular in the province, winning 50 percent of the popular vote and all but twelve Quebec seats in the 1945 election, for example.[34] The Tories, it must be said, were not an option: their strong support for the draft had been laced with accusations of French-Canadian disloyalty and cowardice. The socialist leanings of the Co-operative Commonwealth Federation, moreover, rendered it doubly suspect in a province where the growing anti-Communist tendencies of the Cold War period were reinforced by the continued strength and influence of the Catholic Church. And although Raymond's Bloc populaire fielded federal candidates in 1945 and won two seats, it never gained the nationalist voice in Ottawa that another Bloc, Québécois this time, would achieve half a century later (see Chapter 12).

In Quebec City, Godbout's provincial Liberals would not fare so well. They were hard pressed to defend the broken promises and centralizing initiatives of their federal allies and, in the August 1944 election, faced anti-conscriptionist adversaries to their left and their right. The progressive, intellectual nationalism once embodied by Paul Gouin and the ALN had been quickened by the conscription debate and by recent federal encroachments on provincial legislative and fiscal powers. Building on momentum established during the plebiscite campaign, the Bloc populaire canadien had its greatest success in this election, attracting 15 percent of the popular vote and electing four MLAs, including provincial leader André Laurendeau, with a platform built around provincial autonomy, Catholic social doctrine, social welfare reforms, and a nationalized hydroelectric industry. But outrage at all manner of federal encroachments, especially conscription, was also a staple in the more conservative diet of the Union Nationale. As leader of the opposition, Duplessis had warned of federal betrayals on conscription, trumpeted his "No" vote in the plebiscite, and rebuilt both his personal profile and his party's autonomist reputation. With the skewed electoral map still in its favour, the Union Nationale won a slim majority—forty-eight of the ninety seats in the legislative assembly—on the basis of a popular vote of only 38 percent. Split between Laurendeau and Duplessis, the nationalist, anti-conscription vote was nonetheless sufficient to send the Liberals to the opposition benches, where they would remain until 1960.

Quebec's modern industrial base, in the meantime, was consolidated and expanded during the wartime mobilization. Indeed, the war effort brought full employment and accelerated economic development focused on munitions, aviation, and other strategic industries. Compulsory school attendance, women's suffrage, and family allowances, moreover, were not the only significant social developments of the war years. To offset labour shortages in strategic industries and to free men for military service, Ottawa invited women to participate as never before in the paid labour force and, in particular, to work as welders, streetcar drivers, and in other trades traditionally reserved for men. Young single women answered the call in unprecedented numbers. So, too, did wives and mothers, prompting the federal government to create a short-lived network of publicly funded daycares and launching one of the most significant new social trends of the postwar period: married women's work outside the home.[35]

Wartime fears of social dislocation were fanned by these trends and by newspaper and radio accounts of rising criminality, corruption, family violence, prostitution, venereal disease, and the like. They encouraged the

Worker Margot Bourassa at the Cherrier munitions plant near Montreal, 1944. Women's work in the munitions industry and in other non-traditional sectors was a feature of war-time mobilization in Quebec, as elsewhere in North America. Munitions worker Margot Bourassa was photographed in July 1944 carefully shellacking the body of a fuse in the Cherrier plant, in St-Paul-l'Ermite (Repentigny) near the eastern tip of the island of Montreal. Operated by Defense Industries Limited, the Cherrier plant was a huge industrial complex built in 1941 at a cost of nearly $20 million, consisting of some 345 buildings, and covering 546 hectares. The women and men employed there were engaged in dangerous work: the assembly and charging of artillery shells, mines, bombs, grenades, torpedoes, and a wide range of specialized explosives and detonators. See Geneviève Létourneau-Guillon, "'Mains féminines et monstres de fer': La santé et la sécurité des ouvrières montréalaises durant la Deuxième Guerre Mondiale," MA thesis, History, Université du Québec à Montréal, 2008, 42–43. *Library and Archives Canada*

growth of lay Catholic groups committed to *l'action sociale* (social action) and bent on arming the province's youth against these and other modern scourges.[36] Among these groups were specialized student, worker, and farm associations, as well as others associated with a Catholic *mouvement familial* that had emerged to promote conservative family values in an era when many saw the province as increasingly permeable to a dangerous Hollywood model of individualism, secularism, sexual freedom, and moral relativism.[37] In the 1950s, with postwar prosperity, the rise of automobile culture and the North American suburb, and the concomitant celebration of the nuclear family, women were encouraged to return "from the firing line to the frying pan." Many did but others, having enjoyed the experience of productive work outside the home, chose to remain in the labour force. Wartime frugality had given way to the postwar consumer culture celebrated in advertising, at the movies, and via an exciting new medium, television, that effectively blended the two. As incomes rose during the postwar boom, the trappings of that culture—a *bungalow*[38] in the suburbs, an automobile, an electric washing machine, and so on— became accessible to more Quebec families than ever before.

The autocratic, arch-conservative Duplessis government, on the other hand, did little to advance the cause of Quebec's modernity in the postwar period. Duplessis had returned to power as an opponent of that most invasive of federal initiatives, conscription, and remained there as a champion of provincial autonomy and of a unique Quebec identity that owed more to tradition than to modernity. An enduring symbol of that identity was introduced on 21 January 1948 when the legislature adopted as Quebec's official flag the *fleurdelysé*: a central white cross defining four blue quadrants, each with a white *fleurs de lys* at its centre.[39] The distinctive flag proclaimed the French and Catholic character of the province and announced to the world that Quebec had its own priorities, values, interests, and identity. The new symbol also helped to rally progressive and conservative nationalists behind the idea of provincial autonomy, thereby boosting the Union Nationale's popularity. Later that year, Duplessis won a new term in convincing fashion, consolidating the nationalist vote, sweeping back into power with eighty-two seats, and reducing the Liberal opposition to eight MLAs. He would win the 1952 and 1956 elections almost as handily, capturing more than 50 percent of the popular vote each time and retaining the premier's office until his sudden death in September 1959.

Duplessis's quest for autonomy, however, was not just about symbols. It was framed primarily, rather, as a defence of the province's legislative turf against an expansive federal government, now led by Louis St. Laurent. In most of English Canada, the idea of a strong central government, galvanized by its wartime achievements and ready to face the challenge of postwar reconstruction, played well. Not so in Quebec, where federal initiatives in areas of provincial jurisdiction raised alarm bells. The issue of direction taxation is a case in point. In 1947, every province except Quebec and Ontario signed agreements to perpetuate the wartime arrangements whereby Ottawa collected all direct taxes and provided compensatory grants to the provinces. George Drew's Ontario government held out for five years but eventually signed such an agreement in 1952, leaving Duplessis alone in his defence of fiscal autonomy.

The position was both principled and costly. How could Quebec hope to exercise its authority over local matters, as foreseen in 1867, if all the key revenue streams were controlled by Ottawa? According to one estimate, Quebec lost some $136 million in federal compensatory grants by standing firm on this point between 1947 and 1955.[40] Once Ontario had given in, Duplessis appointed a royal commission, chaired by Justice Thomas Tremblay, to look into postwar constitutional issues, with specific reference to the thorny question of fiscal powers. Early in its mandate (1953), the commissioners encouraged the province to take an affirmative approach, so the government announced its plan to defy Ottawa and impose its own 15 percent tax on personal income. The ensuing negotiations were vigorous but, in the end, the provincial income tax was adopted at the lower rate of 10 percent, with Ottawa consenting to a corresponding reduction in the amount of federal tax paid by Quebecers. In its voluminous 1956 report, the Tremblay Commission also revealed a surprising and unprecedented degree of identification with the Quebec state and its institutions, and provided the basis for a critique of Canadian federalism that would inspire progressive nationalists in the decades to come.[41]

Meanwhile, Ottawa used its fiscal powers to fund a postwar development scheme featuring shared-cost, federal-provincial social programs such as universal old-age pensions (1951) and hospitalization insurance (1958); similarly structured infrastructure projects such as the Trans-Canada Highway (1949); and conditional grants that attached federal strings to Ottawa's funding of provincially controlled fields such as higher education. Quebec's leaders could hardly oppose financial security for the aged, improved medical care, good roads, or better universities. All the same, Duplessis was unlikely to surrender jurisdiction the way Godbout had done on unemployment insurance. Instead, new federal initiatives were treated on a case-by-case basis.

The big federal road-building project, for example, got underway in 1950 without much jurisdictional wrangling. Quebec cried foul, however, when a new constitutional amendment was proposed that same year to allow passage of the federal Old Age Security Act. Duplessis eventually agreed, but only on the condition that the measure include an opting-out clause allowing any province to institute its own equivalent program; Quebec alone would do so, but not until 1964. In 1951, the St. Laurent government decided to adopt a recommendation of the recent Royal Commission on the Arts, Letters, and Sciences by offering federal funding to universities across Canada. Duplessis's resistance to this incursion into the field of education—vastly more sensitive than highways—hardened to the point where in 1953 he instructed university administrators to refuse the badly needed funds outright. Duplessis maintained this controversial stance until the end of his regime, drawing no small measure of criticism from those who saw him as a twentieth-century *éteignoir* (or candle snuffer) more concerned with protecting traditional interests than with promoting a modern, adequately funded system of post-secondary education.

Duplessis's government also took credit for a wave of infrastructure development, especially road and school building and rural electrification, bringing broader portions of the population into regular contact with modern consumer culture, its automobiles, electrical appliances, and the like. This was part of the reason for his persistent popularity in rural areas, along with his reputation as a strong leader capable of standing up to Ottawa. But these modest legacies pale in public memory compared to other events, specifically those that illustrate the arch-conservative, authoritarian approach to governance that also characterized the Duplessis years and that have led many to view *Le Chef* as a demagogue and his regime as a latter-day Dark Ages.

Duplessis has sometimes been described as an economic liberal; he was certainly keen on free enterprise and material progress, eager to

Central Station from St. Geneviève and La Gauchetière Street, Montreal, Quebec, Canada. This photograph, from the Canadian National Railway's collection, was surely intended to frame the recently completed Central Station as a new, modern landmark in downtown Montreal. The composition seems to do more than this, however, by physically juxtaposing three sources of power in the province and the city at mid-century: first, the federal government, its infrastructure and its spending power (Central Station was built by the Canadian National Railway, a federal Crown corporation); second, Montreal's well-heeled British Protestant business and financial community (the Sun Life Building was the tallest in the city at this time); and third, the Catholic Church, represented here by St. James Cathedral and Basilica, which was built during the episcopate of Mgr. Ignace Bourget as a scaled-down replica of St. Peter's in Rome and which was re-dedicated as Mary, Queen of the World Cathedral and Basilica in 1955. *Canada Science and Technology Museum*

attract American investment, and, like Taschereau, unconvinced of the merits of an interventionist state.[42] But his approach to government also drew on the conservative, nationalist principles enunciated a generation earlier by Bourassa, Groulx, and others. This defensive, traditionalist nationalism was still supported by influential groups within and beyond the Catholic Church, including the Société Saint-Jean-Baptiste, and communicated in publications such as *L'Action catholique* and the Jesuit monthly, *Relations*. It was sceptical of all manner of social and political reforms, which could undermine traditional sources of authority and social cohesion. French-Canadian leaders should not be blinded by the glare of postwar, North American modernity. Instead, they should work together to preserve traditional values like Catholic moral education, paternal authority within the family, and the inherent superiority of rural life.

By the late 1940s, however, influential groups of intellectuals, artists, journalists, and others had grown impatient with the government's resistance to change, its intolerance of ideological diversity, and its alliance with vested interests, whether in the boardrooms or the episcopal palaces. Traditionalist nationalism, they argued, was hopelessly out of step with the new realities of an increasingly urban, industrial, forward-looking Quebec, bent on sharing fully in the postwar prosperity and on taking its place as a modern North American society. Two events in the late 1940s were especially important in focusing public attention on this critique.

First, in August of 1948, a group of Montreal artists called the Automatistes and led by painter Paul-Émile Borduas published a social and political manifesto they called *Refus global*. The text called for an end to conformity and subservience in all things, from art to religion, and for the beginning of a new era of self-expression and creativity. French Canadians had lived for generations under the thumb of an authoritarian, puritanical, and obscurantist Catholic Church. Borduas famously referred to his national community as *un petit peuple*: "a small people huddling under the shelter of the clergy . . . ; excluded from the universal progress of thought with all its pitfalls and perils, and raised, when it became impossible to keep us in complete ignorance, on well-meaning but uncontrolled and grossly distorted accounts of the great historical facts."[43] As such, French Canadians had a particular duty to reject all vestiges of traditionalist oppression, from academic dogmatism in painting to conservative notions of sexual morality. The manifesto created a stir in the press, cost Borduas his teaching job at Montreal's École du Meuble, and was widely read as a denunciation not just of the clergy's influence but also, more broadly, of the conservative, Catholic, authoritarian nationalism that underpinned the Duplessis regime.

The next year, 1949, the mutual hostility between the Duplessis government and organized labour was brought into sharp focus when 5,000 unionized workers staged a four-month strike against Canadian Johns-Manville and other asbestos mining operations in the Eastern Townships. The miners were affiliated with the Congrès des travailleurs

Miners on their lunch break at the Asbestos Corporation's installations in Thetford Mines, photograph by J.B. Scott for the National Film Board of Canada, July 1944. These asbestos workers are enjoying their lunch, as well as what appears to be mickeys of rum or some other alcoholic beverage, during the Second World War when the fire-proof insulating material was in particularly high demand. Asbestosis would first become an issue, albeit a minor one, five years later during a strike by 5,000 mine workers from the town of Asbestos as well as Thetford Mines and surrounding area. The strike would be made famous by a collection of essays edited by Pierre Elliott Trudeau whose introduction to the volume concludes as follows: "In 1949, the memorable asbestos strike occurred because the industrial workers of Quebec were suffocating in a society burdened with inadequate ideologies and oppressive institutions; because the national importance of the working class was out of all proportion to its low prestige; because its economic gains as a class were accompanied by a loss of social status (the peasants became proletarians only through sacrificing their social standing as parishioners, voters, patriots, etc.); because our moral and political philosophy of labour did not take enough notice of the fact that we had become an industrialized people." See Pierre Elliott Trudeau, "Quebec at the Time of the Strike," in Pierre Elliott Trudeau, ed., *The Asbestos Strike* (Toronto: James Lorimer, 1974), 66. *Library and Archives Canada*

catholiques du Canada, and the CTCC's secretary-general, Jean Marchand, was an influential leader. Demands included the elimination of the asbestos dust permeating their workplaces (later proven to be carcinogenic), a 15 percent hourly wage increase, automatic deduction of union dues from paycheques, and union involvement in decisions around hirings, firings, and transfers.[44] Wary of the pro-business bias they had observed on arbitration panels, union leaders proved unwilling to submit to such a process, as required by provincial law. So workers at the Jeffrey Mine in Asbestos, Quebec, went out on strike at midnight on 13 February, to be followed shortly afterward by those at Thetford Mines.

Duplessis was no friend of organized labour and his cozy relations with foreign investors in the resource industries were well known. For him, the illegality of the work stoppage was the crux of the matter; for his critics, it was a mere pretext for swift, decisive action. The government immediately stripped the union of its accreditation and sent squads of provincial police to protect company property. Six weeks into the strike, with negotiations at a standstill and several violent incidents on record, police were given a new assignment: to protect the strike breakers who had been sent in by Johns-Manville to replace unionized miners. Far from quelling the disturbances, this tactic enraged the community and sparked the most violent confrontations of all. Early in the morning of 5 May, strikers barricaded roads leading to the Asbestos mine, intercepted a car carrying four plain-clothed officers and, undeterred by warning shots, attacked the men with fists and boots, leaving them unconscious in the ditch. By the end of the day, twelve officers had received similarly rough treatment and three of their cars had been wrecked, burned, or stolen.[45] The next day, 6 May 1949, a justice of the peace read the riot act from the steps of the parish church and the police launched a merciless wave of retaliatory raids and arrests.

Amidst the violence, public support for the cause of the miners was growing, fanned by sympathetic newspaper reports, such as those of Gérard Pelletier in *Le Devoir*. Prominent members of the Catholic clergy also sided with the miners, expressing outrage at the government's hard-line attitude and launching a fundraising campaign that yielded more than $500,000 for the miners and their families.[46] Among them was Monseigneur Joseph Charbonneau, whose epic battle with Duplessis over the Asbestos strike culminated in his resignation as archbishop of Montreal and exile to Victoria, BC, in February 1950. When the miners eventually returned to work, it was on terms negotiated by another bishop, Monseigneur Maurice Roy of Quebec City. The settlement yielded minimal gains for the workers and certainly no cleanup of the environmental-health situation that would continue causing asbestosis and silicosis, and raising the risk of lung cancer in the region for many more decades.[47]

Politically, the asbestos strike crystallized opposition to the Duplessis regime as would no other event, before or since. It did so by underlining many of the failings identified by his critics: complicity with big business, political arrogance, and disdain for the plight of ordinary, working-class Quebecers. In the 1950s, with the strike and *Refus global* fresh in their memory, two groups of intellectuals and activists emerged to contest the conservatism nationalism of the Duplessis regime. On the one hand, a new current of reform-minded liberalism was emerging, particularly around the journal *Cité libre*. On the other, a modern critique of traditionalist nationalism, dubbed *neo*-nationalism, was growing from within the movement itself.

Influenced by the Catholic Left in France and especially by personalist intellectuals like Emmanuel Mounier,[48] the new liberalism envisaged a secular society and an active role for the state in the promotion of social justice and the elimination of economic inequalities. These ideas pervaded the seminar rooms of the Faculté des Sciences Sociales at Laval University, where a new generation of French-Canadian elites learned scientific approaches to sociology, economics, and political science under the guidance of its founder and dean, Father Georges-Henri Lévesque. They are most often associated with the journal *Cité libre*, founded by Pierre Elliott Trudeau and Gérard Pelletier in 1950 in the wake of the asbestos strike. *Cité libre* attacked virtually every aspect of the Duplessis regime. It promoted a strong, secular state in a province where the government celebrated Catholicism and relied on priests and nuns for the delivery of educational, health, and social services. It supported the right of workers to organize, to bargain collectively, and to strike if necessary, in a province where the government consistently, and sometimes with great force, backed corporate interests against those of organized workers. In a province where the collective interests and identity of French Canadians had coalesced around the idea of provincial autonomy, moreover, *Cité libre* cut against the grain by rejecting nationalism of any stripe and promoting the idea of a strong, pluralist, *federal* state in which Quebec would retain just those powers bestowed on it by the BNA Act and which were needed to promote social justice and individual freedoms within the province's borders.[49]

Flowing out of earlier, more progressive currents such as the ALN and the Bloc populaire, the neo-nationalism of the 1950s drew from several sources. It was promoted by a new generation of social scientists at the Université de Montréal, especially the economists at the École des Hautes Études Commerciales and Lionel Groulx's successors in the history department: Michel Brunet, Maurice Séguin, and Guy Frégault. It was nurtured by the work of the Tremblay Commission, whose extensive report and associated studies used modern, social-science methods to delve into the inequities of the federal system. And it was personified by André Laurendeau, who left the legislative assembly in 1948 and worked to renew French-Canadian nationalism as editor of *L'Action nationale* and as assistant editor of *Le Devoir* through most of the 1950s.

As economic, social, and political critics, the neo-nationalists had much in common with reform-minded liberals. They rejected the Duplessis regime with its ties to big business, its lax ethical standards, and its traditional conception of a French-Canadian nation bound by language, faith, and the land. They urged Quebecers to embrace the urban, industrial society of the mid-twentieth century. They supported trade unionism, promoted a secular, interventionist state, and argued for greater government presence in education, health, and social services. At the heart of their analysis, however, remained a French-Canadian nation, which although less thoroughly identified with its religious and agricultural components, was still defined by its common history, language, and culture. So while *Cité libre* and the Laval-based social scientists argued for a strong federal government to promote social justice and facilitate the exercise of *individual* liberty, the neo-nationalists held that French Canadians *collectively* had been disadvantaged within Confederation and that only a strong Quebec state charged with defending their rights and promoting their interests could correct the situation.[50]

Although they offered different solutions, Duplessis's liberal and neo-nationalist critics shared an analysis of the problems plaguing postwar Quebec. The province's economy and social structure were increasingly modern, by any definition of that term. But its political and social institutions were based on an all-too-traditional reading of the society's needs and priorities. The result was a situation they called *déphasage*, meaning that francophone Quebecers were out of step, lagging behind, and failing to claim an equal share in the new standard of living offered by postwar prosperity and progress. What was needed now was not so much *la survivance*, as defined and celebrated by nationalists earlier in the century, as *le ratrappage*—or catching up. This new analysis was based on the revelations of postwar social science and especially on studies conducted by intellectuals working at Laval, at Université de Montréal, and under the auspices of several government commissions. Francophone Quebecers, it emerged, were dramatically under-represented within the business elite and in other high-income professions. On average, they had lower incomes, poorer health, and more difficulty finding decent housing than most other Canadians, with particularly steep deficits when compared to Ontario and to English-speaking Quebec (although certainly not with Atlantic or Aboriginal Canadians).

Many critics traced the problem to deficiencies in the province's educational system. As late as 1958, and despite the introduction of mandatory schooling under Godbout, only 13 percent of francophones completed high school; the level for Protestants was almost three times higher.[51] Teachers in the French-Catholic system continued to be poorly trained; only a small fraction (much smaller than in the Protestant system) had university degrees. Amidst the profusion of technical, craft, and domestic-arts schools, there was no overarching vision for secondary education, so the path to the universities—generally through the private *collèges classiques*—remained obscure and little travelled. As late as 1960, barely 3 percent of francophones in their early twenties were full-time university students, compared to 11 percent of English speakers.[52] And with Duplessis's refusal to accept federal grants for higher education, the province's university system—although it had expanded in 1954 with the addition of the Université de Sherbrooke—remained inadequate and vastly underfunded.

The Union Nationale government's failure to modernize the education system became a lightning rod for opposition in the 1950s. Well over half of the briefs presented to the Tremblay Commission pointed out problems with the school system.[53] Serious cracks were appearing in the traditional structure, which left planning and coordination in the hands of denominationally based Public Instruction Committees. With postwar demographic expansion, the Catholic committee and its school commissions were having more and more difficulty recruiting the teaching nuns, brothers, and priests that had allowed the system to operate so cheaply. By 1960, when teaching brother Jean-Paul Desbiens published his anonymous essay under the title *Les Insolences du Frère Untel* ("The Impertinences of Brother Anonymous"), the writing was already on the wall. Quebecers should not tolerate the impoverished state of their culture and especially their language, and education was the key. Desbiens was a harsh critic of the French-Canadian dialect, which had lately been dubbed *joual*, a phonetic rendering of *cheval*, or horse. In an engaging and irreverent text that enjoyed huge popularity, Desbiens attributed this impoverished language and culture to a repressive, dogmatic, and fragmented school system that had no vision for the future.[54]

Catholic hospitals and social-service agencies were run along similar lines. The welfare state had made some headway federally, as we have seen, over Quebec's constitutional objections. Notwithstanding the new unemployment, family allowance, and hospitalization initiatives, health and social welfare remained provincial responsibilities, and, under the Union Nationale, the province remained wedded to the traditional system whereby its participation was essentially financial. Services were delivered by a two-pronged denominational network of private Protestant and Catholic agencies, the latter operated mainly by women's religious congregations such as the Grey Nuns, the Sisters of Providence, and the Soeurs de la miséricorde (Sisters of Mercy).

Made public long after the fact, the scandal of "Duplessis orphans" reveals the pressures under which this system was operating in the postwar years, which saw a growing crisis in the province's network of crèches and orphanages. Montreal's Société d'adoption et de protection de l'enfance (Adoption and Child Protection Society) promoted legal adoption as the best solution to the growing problem of institutional overcrowding and acted as a clearing house for thousands of adoptions until its absorption by a provincial agency in 1972.[55] Thousands of less fortunate children, however, remained institutionalized, moving from crèches to orphanages and, in some cases, into establishments such as Mont-Providence school in Rivière-des-Prairies, which Duplessis's government redesignated as a psychiatric institution in order to take advantage of health-care funding available from Ottawa. Now labelled psychiatric patients, some of these children suffered physical, psychological, and even sexual abuse in such institutions. Their grievances were made public in 1992, when a committee of survivors launched a class-action suit against the provincial government and the Catholic Church, eventually prompting an official apology from Quebec City and payment of a modest degree of financial compensation.

The Duplessis regime was criticized, finally, for its poor track record on political ethics. Indeed, in public memory, the idea of a "great darkness" evokes nothing so much as a time when the premier's authoritarianism revealed a disregard for modern, liberal conceptions of civil rights and when patronage and political corruption rose to new heights. Duplessis's well publicized entanglement with the millenarian religious sect, the Jehovah's Witnesses, is a case in point. Between 1944 and 1946, restaurateur Frank Roncarelli came forward to post over $80,000 in bail for some 390 Witnesses arrested in Montreal for distributing pamphlets critical of the Catholic Church. (Their campaign to proselytize the province's Catholics had been declared seditious and illegal during the war.) With the premier's consent and without any legitimate justification, the chairman of the Quebec Liquor Commission revoked Roncarelli's liquor license on 4 December 1946, effectively closing down his business and sparking a highly publicized legal battle that would remain before the courts until 1959. In the end, Roncarelli was vindicated and Maurice Duplessis himself was held to have committed a civil offence and ordered to pay $46,000 in personal damages.[56]

The premier's abuse of his powers in the Roncarelli case was part and parcel of a political culture known as *Duplessisme*, which was characterized by widespread patronage, electoral shenanigans, influence peddling, and the like. Historian Suzanne Clavette, in a recent reassessment, has described him as neither a dictator, as his harshest critics would have it, nor the *bon père de famille* described by his admirers. He was rather, in her terms, a "petty provincial despot": a partisan authoritarian whose stock in trade was favouritism. Duplessis ruled his party with an iron fist, she reminds us, served as his own Attorney General; personally commanded the police force and appointed all provincial judges; awarded government contracts without calls for tender and on the understanding that 10 percent be returned to the Union Nationale campaign fund; provided bursaries to educate the children of his political supporters;

and rewarded his closest allies with special license plates, which by arrangement with the police allowed them to ignore speed limits and other rules of the road.[57] So by the mid-1950s, and notwithstanding his persistent popularity, Duplessis was just as open to charges of political corruption as the Taschereau Liberals had been twenty years earlier. Those charges were articulated in no uncertain terms by two Catholic priests, Gérard Dion and Louis O'Neill, in 1956. Their manifesto on political immorality in the province, called *Lendemain d'élections,* raised hard questions about that summer's election campaign, sold 100,000 copies when published as a pamphlet, and was extensively excerpted and discussed in the province's newspapers.[58] Both men were progressive Catholic educators and their public denunciation of the lax ethical standards of the province's politicians serves to illustrate two important trends: the growing impatience of intellectuals, social activists, and to some extent the general public with the traditional way of conducting politics, and the widening rift between the conservative, authoritarian Union Nationale government and a diverse and increasingly progressive Catholic Church, one in which the dogmatic traditionalists, by the late 1950s, were fewer and farther between than at any previous time.

So were the 1930s, 1940s, and 1950s really a period of profound darkness? From the vantage point of the 1960s when, as we shall see, a wave of economic, social, cultural, and political reform swept the province, the waters of the preceding decades must have seemed brackish indeed. And yet, particularly during Duplessis's second and longer turn in the premier's chair, evidence of Quebec's new identity as a modern, urban, industrial society could be found anywhere one cared to look. Agriculture mechanized rapidly in the 1940s and 1950s, as horses and oxen were replaced by tractors and combines, causing productivity and farm size to increase and the rural population to dwindle. Union membership in 1957 was approximately five times its 1932 level.[59] Quebec authors, painters, and musicians were creating innovative works that actively questioned traditional assumptions and values, such as the moral superiority of rural

Calypso singer Lord Caresser performing at Rockhead's Paradise, 28 April 1951. In Montreal, people of African descent had by the 1940s and 1950s developed a strong local identity, especially in the Little Burgundy neighbourhood along St. Antoine Street. Most were working-class English speakers of Caribbean or African-American origin. Jazz, blues, and gospel music were strong elements of their culture and provided a living to some, including Oscar Peterson (1925–2007), who emerged from Little Burgundy to become one of the great jazz pianists of all time. Another key figure was Rufus Rockhead (d. 1981 at age 93), an immigrant from Jamaica who, when this photo was taken in April 1951, had been operating his iconic nightclub, Rockhead's Paradise, on St. Antoine Street for twenty years. The image depicts the downstairs bar at Rockhead's, with Trinidadian calypso singer Lord Caresser (Rufus Calendar) serenading a crowd of patrons. During its long history, the show bar upstairs featured the best of the local jazz musicians, plus touring acts of the calibre of Billie Holliday, Sarah Vaughan, and Cab Calloway. *Library and Archives Canada*

life. Meanwhile, Radio-Canada broadcast its first television programs in 1952 and the proportion of Quebec homes equipped with a TV rose at an astonishing rate thereafter, from just under 10 percent in 1953 to almost 90 percent in 1960.[60]

As the fabric of society changed in these and many other important respects, signs of impatience with the traditionalist, authoritarian political regime were expressed at different times and in different ways. We have seen some of them in this chapter, including in the pages of *Cité libre* and *Le Devoir*, and in political and social manifestos published respectively by a group of rebellious artists in 1948 and by a pair of progressive priests in 1956. A different but not unrelated kind of impatience was expressed on St. Patrick's Day in 1955, as hockey fans spilled out of the Montreal

Forum and into the surrounding streets furious at league president Clarence Campbell's decision to suspend their hero, Maurice "Rocket" Richard, for his role in a bloody fight in Boston days earlier. Richard was arguably the best hockey player in the world, playing to a largely French-Canadian public, but on a team and in a league owned and controlled by wealthy anglophones. His story has often been presented, occasionally with some nuance, as the perfect allegory for that of the ordinary, French-speaking, working-class Quebecer. Many fans believed that the Rocket's punishment was disproportionate to his role in the fracas; he had received a stick to the head from Boston player Hal Laycoe, retaliated in kind with several wild slashes of his own, and then punched an official who had intervened.

St. Catherine Street at night, Montreal, Quebec, 1955. Not all aspects of Quebec society and culture in the decades prior to 1960 fit comfortably with the well-worn idea of a "Great Darkness." The bright lights of the restaurants, bars, cafés, and cinemas along St. Catherine Street in Montreal, pictured here in 1955, seem to suggest a much less sombre existence, at least for some. During American prohibition, Montreal had gained a reputation as an open city with a vibrant nightlife, featuring all manner of bars, nightclubs, and cabarets and easy access to illicit pleasures such as gambling and commercialized sex. Despite the moral purity agenda of many Catholic organizations and the best efforts of reform-minded municipal politicians, the city retained its reputation as a party town in the postwar period. *Canada Science and Technology Museum*

It is impossible to say whether a Toronto Maple Leaf of Anglo-Celtic extraction would have been treated as harshly by the league president for a similar offence. But the sentiment on St. Catherine Street was that the Prairie-born Campbell, an Oxford-trained lawyer and former military officer living in Montreal, cracked down on Richard because he was French speaking and thereby deprived the Rocket of a scoring title and the Montreal Canadiens of a championship. The story, however, did not end with the ignominious Richard Riot of March 1955. The anger and frustration expressed on St. Patrick's Day turned over the ensuing five years into pride, jubilation, and a new kind of confidence in what French Canadians could achieve when the team, led by Richard, ran off a never-to-be-equalled string of five consecutive Stanley Cup championships.[61]

When Maurice Duplessis died suddenly in 1959, few could deny that the province had reached the end of an era. He had been an arch-conservative, authoritarian leader who put his indelible stamp on the place and the people he governed for the better part of a quarter century. But no individual could have held back the tide of modernizing forces that had been transforming the province since the Second World War. With Duplessis's defiant finger no longer plugging the dike, time was short indeed for "traditional" Quebec. Strong new waves of social and cultural change and of political and institutional reform would breach all remaining barriers to modernization in the 1960s.

ELEVEN

"LE DÉBUT D'UN TEMPS NOUVEAU"

The Quiet Revolution: there is no more widely circulated phrase in Quebec's historical lexicon. But neither is there a clear consensus on what the indelible metaphor really means. Historian Lucia Ferretti offers a strict definition of the Quiet Revolution as a brief moment between 1959 and 1968, during which, "on the strength of a broad social consensus . . . the Quebec state pursued the dual objectives of an accelerated modernization on the Welfare State model and, very clearly, of the national promotion of francophone *Québécois*."[1] But in their influential *Short History of Quebec*, Brian Young and John Dickinson evoke a longer and more broadly defined revolution, one that spanned the sixties and the seventies, that "period of rapid change in Quebec as institutions were swept away, transforming state, economy, family, and society."[2]

Which was it? A set of reforms instituted by a visionary government in the space of a few years? A wave of changes that swept all areas of life in the province over the course of two decades? Or was it perhaps the coming of age of the modern Québécois nation with a growing sense of identity and purpose and new demands for political autonomy? Answer "all of the above" and you will begin to get an idea of the impact of this idea on the way recent generations of Quebecers think, speak, and write about their collective past.[3]

The consensus evoked by Ferretti began to emerge in 1959 with the sudden death of Maurice Duplessis at the age of 69. Duplessis's immediate successors, Paul Sauvé (who also died suddenly) and former labour minister Antonio Barrette, showed signs of greater openness to reform. They accepted federal tax credits in lieu of direct funding for university education, for example. But the revolution that Quebecers remember began with the election of former federal cabinet minister Jean Lesage the following June. Lesage had won the Liberal leadership in 1958 and, for the 1960 election, surrounded himself with a diverse group of forward-thinking professionals dubbed the *Équipe de tonerre* (thunder team), including the prominent jurist and Rhodes Scholar Paul Gérin-Lajoie and the charismatic television journalist from the Gaspé region, René Lévesque. The Lesage Liberals promised voters a fresh start after sixteen straight years of *Duplessisme*, using the slogan *C'est le temps que ça change* (It's Time for a Change). Apparently the electorate agreed, for on 22 June 1960, they handed the Liberals a clear victory, if not quite a landslide: 51 percent of the popular vote and a seven-seat majority in the legislative assembly.

Higher standards of political ethics and the establishment of a modern, transparent political culture were high priorities for the Lesage team. Long disadvantaged by the electoral map, the Liberals redrew it in an attempt to give more equitable representation to the quickly growing cities, towns, and suburbs. They also lowered the voting age in provincial elections from twenty-one to eighteen and instituted new regulations in the area of campaign spending, aiming to reduce the size and impact of secret contributions.[4] Institutional reforms in the areas of education, health, and social welfare were another top priority. In 1961, Gérin-Lajoie, as minister for youth, announced an increase in the age for mandatory school attendance from fourteen to fifteen and a plan to provide free textbooks to all schoolchildren.[5] And a commission of inquiry into the state of the education system was soon appointed, headed by Father Alphonse-Marie Parent, the vice-rector of Laval University. Hospitals and social welfare institutions were still privately run and denominational when Lesage took power and the situation was further complicated by the recent history of federal initiatives in these areas. In 1957, for instance, Ottawa had established a hospital insurance scheme in which the Duplessis government then refused to participate. The Lesage government acted quickly to reverse the provincial position, signing on to the scheme and introducing Quebec's hospital insurance program. But other matters would take more time and study. So in December 1961 the Lesage government launched yet another public inquiry, the Comité d'étude sur l'assistance publique, to be chaired by Judge Émile Boucher.

Maintenant ou jamais: Maîtres chez nous. In office since June 1960, the Quebec Liberal Party and Premier Jean Lesage sought a renewed mandate in September 1962. The election was essentially a plebiscite on the nationalization of the hydroelectric industry, the major economic reform proposed by the government and championed by the Minister of Natural Resources, René Lévesque. The iconic slogan "Maîtres chez nous"—"Masters in our own house"—evoked this proposed shift from private to public ownership in the energy sector; the powerful fist clenched around bolts of electricity in this poster is an interesting, if less well remembered, visual clue to this original meaning. But "Maîtres chez nous" came to be understood much more broadly as a call to modern francophone Quebecers to assume full control of their resources, industries, and institutions . . . and, by extension, of their political destiny. *Parti Libéral du Québec*

"Intensely reformist" as regards the province's social institutions, the Lesage Liberals were also nationalists who believed that Quebecers should take control of their own resources and development policies. In the early 1960s, they actively promoted the venerable idea that the province's vast hydroelectric resources should be harnessed and developed in the collective interest of all Quebecers. A key figure in this campaign was René Lévesque, in his new role as minister of natural resources. The Liberals presented this project as part of Quebec's struggle for decolonization, indeed as the key that would open the door to economic liberation. "A people such as ours must use all the tools of economic liberation it may possess," they claimed in a 1962 manifesto. "In the first place, we must assert ourselves in fields such as finance, industry, and commerce [and . . .] apply ourselves, without delay or hesitation, to the exalting task of Quebec's economic liberation. . . . For the first time in their history, the people of Quebec have an opportunity to become masters in their own house."[6]

Nationalizing the remaining private electric "trusts" was a big step and one that was certain to alienate some powerful business interests. So the Lesage government put the proposal before the public in a general election, held barely two years into its initial mandate. The election was scheduled for November 1962 and the Liberals built their campaign around the iconic slogan *Maîtres Chez Nous* (Masters in Our Own House). Three days before the vote came a sign of the times: the first televised election debate in Quebec history, pitting Lesage against Daniel Johnson of the Union Nationale. The leaders spoke for almost two hours on four themes, including the Liberal plan to nationalize the hydroelectric industry. Johnson tried to establish some distance between his party and that of Maurice Duplessis, describing the Union Nationale as youthful and energetic but also battle-tested. Lesage's language was more colourful, and the discursive distance he created between his government and those of the 1950s was far greater, tarring Johnson in the process with the brush of *Duplessisme*. "You have a choice," the premier intoned, "between freedom and a return to the chains of an infernal machine which has disappeared and which must not be reborn, and also between freedom and the cudgels (*matraques*) of the old provincial police, the old one."[7]

Lesage made a strong impression in the debate and easily won his bid for re-election, carrying sixty-three of ninety-five seats in the legislature and 56 percent of the popular vote. Six weeks later, the government announced its expropriation of the remaining private power corporations in the province and the integration of their assets into the provincial power utility, as well as the terms of the compensation offers it would make to shareholders of the dozen or so firms involved. These acquisitions become official 1 May 1963, making Hydro-Québec, a publicly owned provincial corporation, one of the largest enterprises active in Quebec and a major player in the development of the energy sector. *Maîtres chez nous* indeed!

Expropriation of the hydroelectric trusts was one of the pillars of the Lesage years and of any "strict" definition of the Quiet Revolution. Education reform was another. The Parent Commission held public hearings in 1961 and 1962 and published the first volume of its massive report in April 1963, followed by two others in 1964 and 1966. This extensive inquiry confirmed what many critics had been saying for years. The problems within Quebec's system of schools, colleges, and universities were legion. Population growth, urbanization, and postwar prosperity had created unprecedented demand for educational services at all levels. But the existing infrastructures were woefully inadequate. Huge investments were needed in buildings, libraries, laboratories, and teacher training. More than this, the educational network was a patchwork governed by traditional interests rather than an integrated system with a clear, central, *modern* ethos or philosophy of education. Only the state had the power and the resources to craft and implement such a global vision and to coordinate services at all levels. The Parent Commission therefore recommended the creation of a provincial Ministry of Education, headed by a member of Cabinet, whose mission would be to promote and coordinate education from pre-school to graduate school, both in the public and private sectors.

Legislation based on the Parent Commission's report was passed into law on 19 March 1964. Although it retained the principle of denominational schools, Bill 60 dismantled the old Public Instruction infrastructure and created both a provincial Ministry of Education, with Gérin-Lajoie as founding minister, and a new advisory body called the Conseil supérieur de l'Éducation, in which both Catholic and Protestant religious leaders continued to have a voice. As Gérin-Lajoie expressed it: "The Ministry of Education will be the basic instrument of what I call [Quebec's] new vocation of progress and creation."[8]

So that it might be an effective instrument, one of the minister's first priorities would be to redraw the administrative boundaries of Quebec's school commissions. In September 1964, he introduced "Operation 55," a campaign designed to establish fifty-five school boards in a territory where in the past there had been about 1,500.[9] Also on the agenda were major reforms to the province's system of higher education, although these would have to wait until after 1966, when Daniel Johnson's Union Nationale government replaced the Lesage Liberals. A key innovation was the creation in 1967 of a post-secondary institution unique in North America: the tuition-free general and vocational colleges known as CÉGEPs (Collège d'enseignement général et professionnel). The law creating these new colleges was introduced by the Johnson government in January and passed into law on 29 June 1967; the first CÉGEPs opened their doors to students in the fall of that year. A year later, the government established the Université du Québec system, with its first three branches located in Montreal, Trois-Rivières, and Chicoutimi and with new campuses to be added later in Hull, Rimouski, and Rouyn. Quebec thus became the first Canadian province to establish the kind of hub-and-spokes model for public universities which had been successful in the United States and which encouraged many more young people, particularly French speakers, to attend university because it allowed them to do so closer to home.[10]

Meanwhile, Quebecers undertook a similarly thorough rethinking of their social service network. The Boucher Committee's report, delivered in June 1963, clarified a number of issues regarding the future of public assistance programs in the province. It articulated sixty-nine recommendations, emphasizing the need for the provincial government to "intensify the application of a global economic and social policy" and to "accept, in both theory and practice, a more creative and dynamic role in the area of social security and, in particular, of homecare services."[11] In addition to the primacy accorded to the state, the Boucher report emphasized the importance of professionally trained experts—doctors, nurses, psychologists, and especially social workers—in the delivery of modern social welfare services. This approach would replace the traditional system in which the bulk of the services were delivered in institutional settings by minimally trained Catholic nuns.[12] The state should deliver its own, professional social welfare services, rather than simply funding private, religiously segregated initiatives as in the past.

Such a vast undertaking, however, would take time and, as with education, would outlive the Lesage government. Indeed, the principal outcome of the Boucher Committee's work was a new Social Assistance Law that was passed on 12 December 1969 by a Union Nationale government and that established a number of important principles, such as the fundamental right of all persons in need, regardless of the reason for their poverty, to state-sponsored social assistance.[13]

These were not, of course, all of the institutional reforms that Quebecers associated with the Quiet Revolution. There were many more, and they often came in bunches, as in 1964 when the Lesage government opted out of the Canada Pension Plan to create its own provincial Régime des Rentes, reformed the Civil Code so as to eliminate the centuries-old legal incapacity of married women, and adopted a modernized labour code. The Lesage government was also active in mobilizing French-Canadian capital in such a way as to foster both homegrown business development and social mobility for francophones. Among these initiatives were the Société générale de financement (1962), which provided financial support to small and medium businesses; a state-run steel foundry known as SIDBEC (Sidérurgie québécoise, 1965) designed to support heavy industry and reduce its reliance on imported steel; and especially the Caisse de depôt et de placement du Québec (1965), charged with managing the substantial assets of the province's new pension plan and a major player in Quebec's financial markets ever since.[14]

The much-heralded Ministry of Education, moreover, was just one of a spate of new ministries, departments, and agencies established during the Lesage years, when the modernized provincial state grew in size and complexity.[15] The expanded bureaucracy was staffed by a record number of civil servants, most of them university trained and driven by modern policies inspired by the most recent social-scientific knowledge.[16] The presence in Cabinet after 1963 of the former director of the McGill University business school, Eric Kierans, meant that the government had access to the latest ideas around resource development, counter-cyclical spending, investment in social programs, and so on. Other economic and social experts worked behind the scenes in advisory roles, including the distinguished economist Jacques Parizeau, a consultant to the Lesage government who went on to play a key role in the sovereignty movement.

Quebec celebrities Renée Claude, Gilles Vigneault, and Stéphane Venne at Expo '67. Singer Renée Claude's biggest hit, "Le début d'un temps nouveau," written by Stéphane Venne, was released in 1970. Claude and Venne are both pictured here three years earlier at a reception held during Expo '67. They are standing on either side of Gilles Vigneault, the poet, songwriter, and singer whose contributions to Québécois folk and popular music included such odes to collective identity as "Gens du pays" and "Mon pays." Needless to say, the "country" (*pays*) evoked in both titles was Quebec, not Canada. *Library and Archives Canada*

All of this expert advice, whether generated in Cabinet, by consultants and civil servants, or within specially appointed commissions of inquiry, helped the Lesage government pursue its primary goal: *le ratrappage*—or "catching up" to other jurisdictions with regard not simply to income levels and standards of living (although this was part of it) but also with respect to the role of the democratic state in providing the services, structures, and information to facilitate the development of modern, liberal societies.

For many, however, the idea of a Quiet Revolution has meant more than the brief, intense period of institutional reform inaugurated by the Lesage government in the early 1960s. The metaphor also refers to that turbulent, exciting period extending through the 1960s and the 1970s when the baby boomers came of age and when a broad set of social and cultural changes remade Quebec in a more modern, progressive mould.[17] "The times they are a' changin'," in Bob Dylan's phrase, a sentiment echoed in Quebec by singer Renée Claude, whose "Le début d'un temps nouveau" (1970), with words and music by Stéphane Venne, became a kind of anthem. *"C'est le début d'un temps nouveau,"* sang Claude. *"La terre est à l'année zero; la moitié des gens n'ont pas trente ans; les femmes font l'amour librement; les hommes ne travaillent presque plus; le bonheur est la seule vertu."*[18]

Religion was both a fulcrum and a yardstick for this unprecedented shift. Sweeping institutional reforms certainly meant a loss of power and prestige for the Catholic Church. But the changes went much further, into the area of religious beliefs, practices, and identities. For during the Quiet Revolution, Quebec's Catholics turned their backs on their faith with an enthusiasm rivalled only by that with which they had embraced it in the nineteenth century. The indicators are startling. By 1981, there were about half as many priests in the province as there had been in 1961, even though the population had increased by over 20 percent.[19] Quebec's Catholics were less and less inclined to attend Sunday Mass or to observe the other rituals and obligations associated with the faith. This was despite a major overhaul of the liturgy introduced in 1965, on the heels of the Second Vatican Council. The reforms were designed to make Catholic religious practice more relevant, appealing, and modern. Priests now faced the congregation during Mass, which was celebrated in French (or English) rather than Latin. Parishioners could attend services on Saturday evening if Sunday morning was inconvenient, and the Church tried to appeal to the youth of the 1960s by offering special Masses in which hymns were replaced with folk or rock music. Still, Catholics stayed away in droves.[20] Between 1961 and 1971, regular Sunday attendance was cut in half in the diocese of Montreal and fell even more dramatically (from 67 percent to 27 percent) in the largely rural and suburban Saint-Jean diocese on the south shore. Men were more likely to catch the secularization bug than women, and the young were vastly more susceptible than their elders, with only 12–15 percent of young adults (aged twenty to thirty-four) attending Mass on a regular basis by 1971.[21]

Family, gender, and sexuality were areas in which the Church displayed an entrenched resistance to change, which alienated a younger generation of Quebecers and helped drive them away from the religion of their ancestors. Like other North Americans, Quebecers in the 1960s

"Non à la pilule," La Presse, final edition, Monday, 29 July 1968. Pope Paul VI stunned Catholics around the world in July 1968 by taking a firm stance against most forms of contraception, including the Pill. With the encyclical *Humanae Vitae,* the pontiff chose to reinforce the Church's traditional view of sexuality. Sex was to be confined to the marital bed and any attempt to interfere with God's design by impeding the primary function of sexual intercourse, i.e., procreation, was a sin. This conservative moral and theological position proved to be seriously out of step with the times, ignoring global population pressure and growing demands for gender equity within marriage. In Quebec and elsewhere, many Catholic women chose to ignore the Papal decree, taking their distance from the Church's teachings and reinforcing the secularization trend already underway. *La Presse*

participated in a "sexual revolution," which challenged the traditional moral codes restricting sexual activity to the marital bed and, in the Catholic variant, to the specific purpose of procreation. By the time Pope Paul VI issued his famous 1968 encyclical condemning all forms of "artificial" birth control, including the new contraceptive pill, Quebec's women had already begun their dramatic transition towards smaller families, with the help of this and other new reproductive technologies. Although birth rates had been edging downwards since early in the century, the precipitous drop in the 1960s and 1970s was among the most dramatic social trends of the period. The average Quebec woman in 1958 would have given birth to four children, a figure that fell sharply to just over two children in 1968, and then still further to 1.7 children per Québécoise in 1978.[22] In few other areas did the Church's inability to change with the times appear so starkly.

By the end of the 1970s, moreover, Quebecers were 30 to 35 percent less likely to get married than they had been in 1960. The modern trend towards consensual unions had emerged and would continue apace in the ensuing decades.[23] Those Quebecers who chose marriage found the institution radically changed by the 1964 revision of the Civil Code, which eliminated the legal incapacity of married women. (The law, incidentally, was introduced by Claire Kirkland-Casgrain, the first woman ever elected to the provincial legislature.) Marriage was further transformed by the new federal divorce law that came into effect in July of 1968. Quebecers in their thousands took advantage of the liberalized law, which expanded the grounds on which divorce could be obtained and vastly reduced the difficulty and expense involved in the process.[24]

Quebecers living through the 1960s and 1970s experienced these social and cultural shifts in different ways. For the many young Catholics who turned their backs on the Church, there was surely a sense of liberation, of awakening to new possibilities, of stepping into the light. Others, older perhaps and more attached to tradition, found much to worry about in the sudden abandonment of the old ways and the instability it engendered, and not just within marriages.[25] For some, the abandonment of Catholicism was readily conflated with a profound crisis of the French-Canadian or Québécois identity. "This [secular] world view based on earthly realities, individual freedom of choice, and the abundance of material goods destroyed the symbolic space within which the French-Canadian nation had found its coherence and its meaning," writes historian Jean Hamelin.[26]

Whether seen as a breath of fresh air or a dangerous contagion, the growing refusal of Quebec's Catholics to accept the moral authority of the Church was not unrelated to the energetic social movements of the period, especially those involving workers, women, students, and Aboriginal people. In turning away from religion, Catholics were seeking liberation from a hierarchical, authoritarian system based on old ideas such as faith, tradition, and order. In lamenting the fragmentation of Quebec society, traditionalists often cited the conflict generated by protest groups as they took to the streets to challenge older conceptions of social order. And if the refrain "C'est le début d'un temps nouveau" rang true during the 1960s and 1970s, it was largely because social movements in general became increasingly militant and politicized, just as they did in the United States during the civil rights and antiwar struggles of the same period.[27]

Quebec's labour movement, for instance, grew in scale as its critique of capitalism and its appeals to workers for social and political action intensified. There were roughly 400,000 unionized workers in the province in 1961 and that number more than doubled in the ensuing twenty years, reaching 880,000 (about 35 percent of wage earners) by 1981.[28] The backdrop for this was a shifting economic climate as the postwar prosperity that persisted through the 1960s gave way, beginning in about 1973, to a period of slower growth, higher unemployment, and inflation. Quebec's labour force, at the same time, was profoundly transformed by structural changes in the economy. These included the relative decline of traditional blue-collar jobs in the manufacturing and resource sectors, and the corresponding growth of white- and pink-collar employment in government, health, educational, and other service sectors.

Entering the 1960s, the province had two main labour federations. The older was the Confédération des travailleurs catholiques du Canada (CTCC), which although it had begun admitting non-Catholics in the 1940s, was still a French-Canadian Catholic organization in name and in philosophy. For its part, the Fédération des Travailleurs du Québec (FTQ) was formed in 1957 when two competing federations amalgamated. The FTQ was characterized by its association with international craft unionism and its ties to the Canadian Labour Congress (CLC), formed in 1956 in the wake of the AFL-CIO merger in the United States. In the course of the 1960s and 1970s, both organizations changed in dramatic, unprecedented ways, and a third major federation took the stage.

The CTCC set the tone at its 1960 convention by abandoning its former religious identity, removing references to Catholic social doctrine from its charter, and changing its name to the Confédération des syndicats nationaux (CSN).[29] In the 1960s and 1970s, it played a major role in organizing public and para-public sector employees, while moving sharply to the left ideologically. The CSN also began to link the national and labour questions, adopting a strongly articulated socialist critique and framing Quebec's national oppression as a by-product of capitalist exploitation.[30] The FTQ, meanwhile, remained the most important organization numerically throughout this period, representing over half of all organized workers in 1976 and more than tripling its membership between 1961 and 1981.[31] This success owed much to the resources the federation commanded as part of a network of international unions that included the AFL-CIO in the United States and the CLC in Canada. The leadership may well have presented this internationalism as a source of strength,[32] but as debates over language intensified and as the sovereignty movement gained momentum, the FTQ's strong ties to its American and Canadian federations came to be seen as a liability in francophone Quebec. Under Louis Laberge's leadership—he narrowly won the presidency in 1964 but then remained in the post for almost twenty-seven years—the FTQ won greater autonomy from the CLC and promoted a political agenda that was both social-democratic in orientation and increasingly friendly to the sovereignty movement.

The emergence of a strong federation of teachers' unions, the Centrale de l'enseignement du Québec (CEQ), also reflects trends that can be observed elsewhere in the province's labour movement. The CEQ began in 1945 as a federation of Catholic teachers' unions but later expanded to embrace many other groups of workers, especially in the public sector. Like the CSN, it shed its Catholic identity in the 1960s, becoming the Corporation des Enseignants du Québec in 1967 and the Centrale de l'enseignement du Québec in 1974. It also became increasingly militant on workplace issues, especially the right to strike in the public sector. By the mid-1970s, the CEQ was radical enough ideologically to promote a kind of pedagogy of class struggle; one of the documents it published in 1974 was entitled *École et lutte de classes au Québec* (School and Class Struggle in Quebec). It also participated fully in the mobilization of Quebec's labour movement around the national question, sparked in particular by the Saint-Léonard schools debate and the October Crisis (see below).

Quebec's labour leaders certainly contributed to the political debates and reforms of the 1960s. The CSN and the FTQ, for example, strongly supported the creation of a Ministry of Education in a brief submitted jointly to the Parent Commission in 1962. FTQ representatives participated in forty-three commissions and other consultative bodies in 1967 alone.[33] The labour federations also worked tirelessly to organize the growing numbers of public servants needed by the modernizing state. They lobbied the Lesage government to adopt the new labour code in 1964. The legislation recognized the right to strike for workers employed by hospitals, school boards, and municipalities. Teachers and civil servants were included the following year. Public-sector employees exercised this right frequently in the ensuing years, with Montreal's Catholic teachers and transit workers hitting the picket lines in 1967, to be followed by liquor commission employees the next year. When Montreal's firefighters and police officers staged an illegal sixteen-hour strike on 7 October 1969, however, the results were ugly. Taxi drivers used the occasion to demonstrate against the long-standing airport monopoly of a private-car service (Murray Hill Limousines) and saw their protest spread into generalized rioting and looting, especially along St. Catherine Street. A provincial police officer was killed, and 108 people were arrested in what CBC journalists described as "Montreal's night of terror."[34]

Like the labour unions, women's organizations in Quebec became stronger, more militant, and more visible, especially in the 1970s, when a new more radical feminist movement emerged to engage the struggle for gender equality. Since the belated success of the campaign for provincial suffrage, Quebec women had remained active in their support of various causes. Women had been deeply affected by the social and economic changes of the 1940s and 1950s and especially active in consumer associations and the Catholic families' movement.[35] A wide range of associations spoke and acted on behalf of specific groups, from rural women to university graduates and from Aboriginal to Jewish women.[36] But these had tended to be narrowly based and to mirror the province's class, religious, and linguistic divisions. They lacked a unifying ideology, a common struggle, and an effective central organization.

In the 1960s, Quebec women began to challenge gender inequities more vigorously than ever before. They did so in the bedroom by using contraception to take greater control of their reproductive lives. They did so in the workplace, as labour-force participation rates increased significantly, reaching at least 37 percent for married women in 1971.[37] They did so in the province's modernized education system by completing secondary school, attending CÉGEP and university, and entering male-dominated professions in unprecedented numbers.[38] They did so by pressuring governments in Quebec City and Ottawa to modernize legislation concerning a married woman's civil status and her access to divorce. And they did so by organizing for change on a broader scale. Formed in 1966, the Fédération des Femmes du Québec grew out of a 1965 event commemorating the 25th anniversary of provincial suffrage. It became the new umbrella organization for women's associations of all kinds, with a secular, non-denominational charter in tune with the changing times. And it helped pressure the Pearson government in Ottawa to empanel, in February 1967, a Royal Commission on the Status of Women in Canada, to be chaired by Toronto journalist Florence Bird.

Meanwhile in the United States, well-educated, activist women who had gained experience in the civil rights and antiwar movements were turning their attention to the global issue of sex-based oppression. The results were an international exercise in "consciousness-raising" and a wave of political mobilization around the idea of women's liberation. This more radical approach to gender politics arrived in Quebec in 1969, a year that had already seen 141 strikes and the "night of terror" just described, to which Montreal's municipal authorities responded with a rather extraordinary anti-demonstration bylaw. In November 1969 a group of 200 women—mainly activists in various labour and nationalist organizations—chose to defy that bylaw and stage a unique night-time protest in which they marched in chains through the streets of the metropolis. Arrested and jailed for the night, these women gave voice to a new, more militant feminism than that of the FFQ, one that was specific and autonomous and that treated women's experience as distinct from men's, thus requiring specific action on that basis.[39] In the ensuing weeks, they formed a radical feminist group, the Front de libération des femmes du Québec (FLFQ), which in 1970 and 1971—a period when revolutionary nationalism in the province was at its height—urged Quebec women to stand up and fight against both national and sexual oppression with their slogan *Québécoises deboutte!*[40]

Early in the new decade, moreover, the work of the Bird Commission was completed and, on 28 September 1970—about a week before the start of the October Crisis (see below)—its 540-page report was released.

The report tracked the structural sexism that permeated virtually every realm of activity in Canada and formulated 167 recommendations for substantive change.[41] Québécoises, as we have seen, had been shedding their time-worn place amidst Canada's more traditional women—as measured by birth rates, religious observance, labour-force participation, access to the professions, and so on—and joining the ranks of its most modern. It is not surprising, then, that they acted swiftly to support and implement the commission's recommendations. On reproductive freedom, for example, the report proposed the decriminalization of abortion in Canada. When Dr. Henry Morgentaler appeared in court to defend his choice to offer safe abortions to Quebec women—he had opened a clinic in 1969, only to be arrested by Montreal police—women's groups rallied in his support. The commission also recommended the creation of permanent government agencies to protect and promote women's equality. With the backing of the FFQ, the provincial government responded by establishing the Conseil du statut de la femme in 1973. Women's representation within the provincial government increased after 1976, when the Parti Québécois (see below) began to bring prominent women into Cabinet, beginning with television personality Lise Payette. Payette became minister responsible for the status of women and, in 1978, the PQ government adopted a policy paper entitled *Pour les Québécoises: Égalité et Indépendance* as the framework for its policies on gender equity in the coming years.[42]

The growing activism of Aboriginal communities in Quebec in this period is also important, although it does not enter into most discussions of the Quiet Revolution. First Nations groups were among the most disadvantaged in the 1960s, in Quebec as in other parts of Canada. Reliance on social assistance programs was high, per-capita income levels were less than half those of non-Aboriginal Canadians ($600 compared to $1,400 in 1966), and educational attainments were poor, with only 6 percent of students completing high school.[43] First Nations people had been infantilized by federal policy, which although it offered them some material advantages, denied them full citizenship. Women had won the right to vote in Quebec provincial elections in 1940, for example, but the province's Aboriginal people were unable to do so before 1969. First Nations women, moreover, were doubly disadvantaged because, until the

Indian Act was modified in 1985, they forfeited their Indian status and with it their right to live on Native reserves as soon as they married a non-Aboriginal man. As the federal government studied the situation, awareness of the injustices suffered by First Nations people in North America was increasing, aided by the emergence of the American Indian Movement (or "Red Power") south of the border and by the success of the Indians of Canada Pavillion at Expo '67, which surprised and educated many with its story of "poverty, unfulfilled treaties, forced religion and the unhappy experiences of children in residential schools."[44] Aboriginal people began to organize politically and, in 1968, the National Indian Brotherhood was born and was soon acting and speaking on behalf of Native groups across Canada—as it would do until 1982 when it was superseded by the Assembly of First Nations.[45]

An area of particular concern for Aboriginal groups was education, especially the threat posed by mainstream schools to the survival of Native languages and their role in perpetuating negative stereotypes. Quebec's history curriculum and textbooks, for example, still presented the Iroquois in New France in the most unflattering terms, as godless savages bent on torture and massacre. In response, the Mohawk people on the Kahnawake Reserve south of Montreal established the Kahnawake Survival School in 1977. Run by Mohawk educators independently from local school boards, the school taught children the ancestral language, emphasized tribal traditions and culture, while preparing them for material survival in a changing labour market.[46] First Nations groups were also concerned with the growing contradiction between traditional Aboriginal land rights and modern economic development initiatives that treated rural and northern environments as potential sources of timber, minerals, and especially hydroelectric energy. It was on this front that the major battle of the 1970s was waged.

It began in April 1971 when Robert Bourassa's Liberal government announced plans for a huge hydroelectric development project in the James Bay region of northern Quebec. The project would involve a major reconfiguration of thousands of square kilometres of traditional hunting and trapping territories and the flooding of vast areas of forest on which the region's Cree and Inuit populations had long-standing claims. Bourassa's announcement came without any prior consultation with these

Aboriginal groups. Contracts were tendered and, in the spring of 1972, the massive construction site on the La Grande River was opened. In response, the Inuit and Cree organized a concerted judicial and media campaign to block the James Bay project. In October 1972, the Grand Council of the Cree and the Northern Quebec Inuit Association filed for an injunction to have the construction work suspended. When Superior Court Judge Albert Malouf granted the injunction, it was widely regarded as a major victory for Aboriginal rights in the province, even though the decision was overturned on appeal a week later. Extensive media coverage of these events, most of it sympathetic to the Native cause, brought both sides to the realization that a negotiated agreement was the only way forward.

Ultimately, the outcome was the James Bay and Northern Quebec Agreement of 1975, which allowed the project to proceed but also created a new wildlife management structure, environmental protection measures, and a system of income supports for Aboriginal hunters. Cree and Inuit leaders obtained over $230 million in direct financial compensation, to be paid over twenty-one years. They would retain full control over the territory (over 5,000 square kilometres) closest to their communities and exclusive hunting and fishing rights in a further territory of some 60,000 square kilometres, while ceding title to a third area—by far the largest—to the province.[47] Like Quebec's women, then, Aboriginal communities in the province had not necessarily been empowered by the social and political reforms of the 1960s. But both groups would stand up and be counted in the 1970s.

So, too, in this new era when *"la moitié des gens n'ont pas trente ans,"* would the province's youth. François Ricard has written about a "lyric generation" of French Canadians born in the early postwar years (1947–52) and who came of age during the late 1960s, contributing new creative energy, new ideas, and a new spirit of social and political activism to virtually every field of endeavour.[48] Whether or not they were "lyric," young Quebecers in the 1960s and 1970s were certainly worldlier and better educated than any previous generation. More of them benefited from longer exposure to the newly reformed school system and high school completion became widely shared objective, if not quite a social norm. Post-secondary education expanded apace, so that in 1970, the province's universities enrolled over 80,000 students, fully four times the

Student demonstration in Montreal, October 1968. Theology students from the Université de Montréal were among the thousands who marched in solidarity with striking students in Quebec's new CÉGEP system on 21 October 1968. Major protests swept the province's post-secondary institutions in the 1968–69 academic year, including the CÉGEP strike in October, the occupation of Sir George Williams University's Computer Centre in January and February, and the McGill Français demonstration in late March. © *Bettman/Corbis*

1962 level, with a further 100,000 attending the new CÉGEPs.[49] At the same time, the burgeoning campuses fostered an activist student culture that supported liberation movements of all kinds, denounced injustice and oppression wherever they appeared, and embraced a utopian vision in which *their* generation, uncorrupted by power or privilege, could set society on the right track. The campuses of Montreal and Quebec City, it turns out, were not so very different from those of Berkeley and Paris in the late 1960s and early 1970s.

Militant demands for student power were heard loudly in the fall of 1968, beginning with a student occupation of the CÉGEP Lionel-Groulx in Saint-Thérèse, north of Montreal. The former classical college had a well-established reputation for student activism. Its student union channelled a prevailing mood of distrust concerning the ability of the province's revamped system of post-secondary education to respond to growing demand. Students had already won representation on various administrative bodies and committees. But they were frustrated with improvised and overcrowded facilities, high rates of failure on exams, low rates of acceptance to universities, chronic student indebtedness, and the absence of a second French-language university in Montreal; the Université du Québec à Montréal (UQAM) was founded a year later, in 1969. So on 8 October 1968, students went into action, voting to occupy their school rather than continue negotiations with administrators. In the ensuing days, the student protest caught on like wildfire. A week after the occupation in Sainte-Thérèse, students in fully two-thirds of the province's CÉGEPs were on strike, as were political science students at Université de Montréal and art students at the École des Beaux Arts. A week after that, on 21 October, students from across the province participated in a mass march through the streets of the metropolis. CÉGEP students, as McGill student journalist Robert Chodos wrote in 1969, "were being trained for jobs that didn't exist in the colonial Quebec economy; and those who planned to go to university—many more than the government had expected—were concerned that French-speaking university places were unlikely to exist either."[50]

If the French-language universities were not expanding quickly enough, perhaps the solution was to guarantee places for francophones at McGill University. The McGill Français movement took that position and culminated in another massive march through the streets of Montreal, this one during the evening of 28 March 1969. Close to 10,000 students from across the province marched to McGill's Roddick Gates, denouncing the English-language university as a bastion of colonialism, demanding its conversion to French, and carrying banners reading "McGill Français" and "McGill aux Québécois."[51] Anti-colonial ideas and rhetoric were characteristic of the student movement at this time (images of Ché Guevara were on display . . .) but its association with Quebec nationalism (. . . so too were posters of the revolutionary *indépendantiste* Pierre Vallières) was original.

Two months before the McGill Français demonstration, events across town at Sir George Williams University had turned on quite a different debate about colonialism, while taking student protest in the province to a new level. Students staged a two-week occupation of the university's Computer Centre, located in the upper reaches of the Henry F. Hall Building, to protest the university's handling of accusations of

The Daniel-Johnson Dam on the Manicouagan River, about 200 kilometres north of Baie-Comeau. This massive hydroelectric dam, formerly known as Manic-5, was built over a ten-year period using over two million cubic metres of concrete. Premier Daniel Johnson Sr. died here on 26 September 1968, the night before he and fellow politicians Jean Lesage and René Lévesque were to inaugurate the new structure. One year later to the day, a special ceremony was held at Manic-5, at which the dam was dedicated to Daniel Johnson. The rapid development of the province's enormous energy potential by a publicly owned utility, Hydro-Québec, was one of the signature achievements of the modern Quebec state in the 1960s and 1970s. *Québec, Ministre des ressources naturelles et de la faune*

racism against Perry Anderson, an assistant professor in the biology department. Anderson was accused of giving unfair treatment (in the form of unjustified failing grades) to a group of Black students from the city's West Indian community. On 29 January, at least 200 students, including Anderson's six accusers, occupied the Computer Centre in an attempt to pressure the university to deal more effectively with the charges. Negotiations continued during ten days of peaceful protest. But on 11 February, with about 100 students still occupying the premises, a police riot squad was called in to force them out. In the chaos of the confrontation, the student activists struck out against the technology they had been living with, tossing thousands of computer punch cards out of the ninth-floor windows, attacking the computers with axes and, ultimately, setting the facility on fire. In the end, ninety-seven protesters were arrested and charged with causing over $2 million worth of damage to university property.[52]

Place Ville-Marie, photographed in March 2011. Montreal's iconic modernist skyscraper, Place Ville-Marie, was designed by New York architect Ioeh Ming Pei and built on Dorchester Street (later René-Lévesque Boulevard) between 1959 and 1962. The authors of one of the best guide books to Montreal architecture describe it as follows: "The 42-storey tower is cruciform, and thus allows good penetration of natural light throughout the building, despite the large area covered by each floor. The shape is rather appropriate for the largest Catholic city north of Mexico, founded originally as a mission for the conversion of Indian allies." François Rémillard and Brian Merrett, *Montreal Architecture: A Guide to Styles and Buildings* (Montreal: Meridian Press, 1990). *Photograph by Peter Gossage.*

The 1960s and 1970s, then, were a time of protest and of social upheaval in Quebec. Most of that unrest was grounded in various, often contradictory analyses of the inequities of the past. But it also drew on progressive, sometimes utopian visions of a better society in the future. Quebecers had done much more than modernize their systems of governance, education, and social welfare. They had constructed the largest hydroelectric dam of its kind in the world, the impressive Daniel-Johnson dam and Manic-5 generating station. In Montreal, they had built a jewel of a city, a true metropolis with an international profile, an increasingly impressive skyline, and a wide range of urban services, including a fine new concert hall, Place des Arts, inaugurated in 1963, and the gleaming new subway system, the *Métro*, which opened in October

1966. Particularly during the municipal regime of Jean Drapeau, the city was able to attract major international events such as Expo '67, the spectacularly successful World's Fair held in the summer of that year, and a decade later, the financially troubled 1976 summer Olympics. The city's new major league baseball team began playing in the summer of 1969 as the Montreal Expos—the name an awkward (but bilingual) homage to the 1967 World's Fair. And its beloved professional hockey team, the Canadiens, seemed almost invincible, twice winning strings of four consecutive Stanley Cups, led by French Canadian heroes with names like Béliveau, Cournoyer, Savard, and Lafleur.

For many, however, the biggest mega-project of all was the "Dream of Nation" in Susan Mann's apt phrase: the dream of national independence for a sovereign Quebec. Generally speaking, Quebec's nationalist movement in the sixties and seventies was neither revolutionary nor especially quiet. Notwithstanding the brutal tactics and Marxist rhetoric of the Front de libération du Québec (FLQ), most nationalists believed that greater autonomy for Quebec could only be achieved through peaceful, democratic means. At the same time, Quebec nationalists drew strength from their society's collective accomplishments, embraced their newly forged identity as Québécois and Québécoises rather than French Canadians, and sought greater autonomy for their province, up to and including independence, through public debate and the political process.

Early in the 1960s, several organizations emerged to promote the idea that the only way forward for Quebec was political independence. One strand of that movement was organized as the Rassemblement pour l'indépendance nationale (RIN) in 1960. A founding member of the new party, the scientist and federal civil servant Marcel Chaput, published an influential book in 1961, *Pourquoi je suis separatist*, explaining why he was a "separatist" (he had been one since 1937) and urging others to convert to the cause.[53] Another strand, which was more conservative in outlook, was organized by Dr. René Jutras as Le ralliement national (RN) in 1964.[54] Meanwhile, shocked Quebecers witnessed the first volley in an eight-year wave of political violence in the name of independence, when on 21 April 1963, an FLQ bomb exploded in a shed behind a Canadian Forces recruitment centre in Montreal, killing a maintenance worker, William Victor O'Neill.

Why did certain people start actively and openly working for Quebec independence in the early 1960s? And why did the sovereignty movement gain so much strength later in the decade and especially in the 1970s? These are difficult but important questions. Part of the answer, surely, is that new evidence was emerging in support of what nationalists had been saying for decades: that Confederation was a bad deal for French Canadians. Expert studies using the latest social-science methods showed significant gaps in income, education, and opportunity between French- and English-speaking Canadians. Both the provincial Tremblay Commission of the late 1950s and the federal Royal Commission on Bilingualism and Biculturalism (launched in 1963) contributed to this analysis. Statistics generated for the latter showed that in 1961 the average annual income of a male worker of British origin in Canada was 25 percent higher than that of his French-Canadian counterpart. The same comparison within Quebec yielded an even more startling income gap, with men of British origin earning fully 52 percent more than French Canadian breadwinners.[55] *Indépendantistes* like Chaput read these kinds of figures as an indictment of the federal system, which in its hundred-year history had allowed one "founding nation" to flourish and prosper much more fully than the other.

At the same time, French Canadians were feeling a growing sense of pride in their distinctive character and their ability to fend for themselves. *Maîtres chez nous* translated into a growing belief in the transformative power of the modern state, and specifically the provincial government in Quebec City. This made the idea of a single level of government run essentially by French Canadians seem more feasible and more attractive than ever before. Isolated linguistically on the media-rich North American continent, Quebecers also developed their own, distinctive popular culture with its own celebrities, its own hit TV series, and its own set of shared assumptions: a *culture* that was modern and North American in nature, but in which messages were transmitted in French. That those who shared this distinct cultural identity should reimagine themselves as a Québécois nation fully deserving of its own, independent political institutions seems unsurprising from this perspective.[56] And some nationalists, especially the more youthful and radical among them, were inspired by post-colonial liberation struggles underway in Africa, South

America, Ireland, and other places, where colonized peoples were fighting for the freedom to act on a global stage as independent nation-states.

The 1960s also saw the spread of the neo-nationalist thinking that had emerged during the Duplessis era. Whether or not they joined the independence movement (and many did not), most nationalists during the Quiet Revolution embraced modern economic, social, and political ideas. They believed in a secular society and a democratic, interventionist state, while retaining a core belief in the collective destiny of the French-Canadian people. Historians, interestingly, played a significant role here. Most influential were those at the Université de Montréal who argued that the eighteenth-century Conquest had diverted Quebec from its "normal" course of development by supplanting its natural leaders with a British ruling class, supported by a complacent and profoundly conservative Catholic Church. But for this interruption, in this view, Quebec's "normal development" would surely have included an eventual transition, by revolutionary or other means, from French colony to independent nation-state.[57]

Other key ideas for the nationalists were grounded in more recent history. Among these was the "Compact Theory" of Confederation, according to which the 1867 arrangement was not so much an agreement among the various provinces as it was a pact between two *peoples*: the French Canadians who had been settled in the St. Lawrence Valley since the 1600s and those of British origin who had begun arriving in the 1760s. By this logic, French Canadians should retain certain rights and a certain status within Canada, failing which they might reasonably be expected to withdraw. Quebec, as the sole province in the federation with a French-speaking majority, could claim to speak for one of the country's two founding peoples. It followed that Quebec was not *"une province comme les autres"* and that it ought to seek some form of special status within a revised federation. This was the position taken in the 1960s by Claude Ryan, the brilliant but austere former Catholic Action militant who was director and lead editorialist at *Le Devoir* from 1963 to 1978, and by Daniel Johnson in his role as Union Nationale leader and premier from 1966 until his death in 1968. Its most tangible result was the recognition of Quebec's "international capacity" as a member of la Francophonie due to the pressure exerted by France at conferences held in the former French West African colonies, Gabon and Niger, between 1968 and 1970.[58]

Quebecers had also witnessed the growing power of the federal state in the years since the Second World War and many concluded that Ottawa's vision for the country was a highly centralized one with little room for provincial autonomy. This impression was reinforced in the 1960s as Liberal governments in Ottawa, under pressure from a strong CCF–NDP caucus on their left, expanded their slate of universal social programs. Despite real benefits to workers and families, nationalists continued to criticize these federal programs as examples of federal interference in Quebec's affairs. Sensitivity to these kinds of issues, meanwhile, was increasing because of the shifting demographic balance, both within Quebec and across Canada. As they had during the exodus of the later nineteenth century, Quebec's nationalists began to worry about the precarious position of the French language in Canada, pointing to rapidly falling birth rates among French Canadians, high rates of assimilation into English-language use in the other provinces, and a new wave of international immigrants, few of whom were from francophone nations and most of whom seemed to gravitate towards the English language.

For all of these reasons, the nationalist critique of Confederation grew in stridency and in popular appeal during the mid-1960s, as the Canadian federal arrangement approached its centenary. Liberal governments in Ottawa responded to the challenge with the aforementioned "B and B" Commission, which led to official languages legislation (enacted in 1969), and in particular by recruiting members of Quebec's liberal intelligentsia into their ranks. During the federal election campaign of 1965, Lester Pearson's Liberals attracted "Three Wise Men" as star candidates from Quebec. These were labour leader Jean Marchand, journalist Gérard Pelletier, and law professor Pierre Elliott Trudeau, all of them sceptical of Quebec nationalism and strongly associated in the public mind with ethics, social justice, Cité libre, and the asbestos strike. They were also Cabinet material and, when the votes were counted, Pearson had won his second successive minority government and all three were given important seats at the Cabinet table, including Trudeau as minister of justice.

The following year, 1966, the Union Nationale returned to power in Quebec under the leadership of Daniel Johnson. Johnson benefited from

Quebec Pavillion and the Minirail at Expo '67. The glass-sided Quebec pavilion was supposed to evoke the relationship of "Man" to nature, but the three headings were equally anthropocentric: Man's challenge, showing Quebec as the explorers and pioneers found it; Man's struggle with his environment, showing the progress from frontiersman to citizen whose domain is a vast workshop; and the forward drive of a people, showing the vigour of Quebec's advance as both industrial and cultural centre. *Library and Archives Canada*

his party's popularity in rural areas (still over-represented despite the reformed electoral map) and from his appeal to the growing nationalist sentiment, framed in a 1965 book as "independence if necessary but not necessarily independence."[59] With a "soft-nationalist" party in power in Quebec City, a trio of prominent Liberals representing Quebec within the federal Cabinet, and, on occasion, an FLQ bomb exploding in the streets of Montreal, the national question came to dominate the political agenda as never before. The years 1967 and 1968 were among the most dramatic. In Montreal on 24 July 1967, during his official visit to Expo '67, French president Charles De Gaulle fanned the separatist flames, sparked a major diplomatic incident, and astounded just about everyone in attendance when he declared from a City Hall balcony: "*Vive Montréal! Vive le Québec! Vive le Québec libre!!*" Later the same year, the hugely popular Lévesque quit the provincial Liberal Party over its refusal even to debate the constitutional option he had come to espouse and articulate: full sovereignty for Quebec, combined with a commercial and monetary union with the rest of Canada. Lévesque rallied like-minded nationalists from within and beyond Lesage's Liberal Party into a new, sovereignist political formation, the Mouvement souveraineté-association. A year later, in October 1968, he succeeded in uniting most of the democratic, sovereignist forces in a new party, the Parti Québécois, devoted to the achievement of sovereignty-association by peaceful, democratic means.

The political landscape, meanwhile, was shifting in Ottawa as well. Lester Pearson retired late in 1967 and the following spring, Pierre Trudeau was chosen as the new Liberal leader. In the ensuing election campaign, Trudeau certainly helped his cause when he stood up (on national television) to an ugly mob protesting his presence at the Saint-Jean Baptiste parade. The very next day, 25 June 1968, he swept into power on the strength of his apparent courage in the face of "separatist" agitation, his newly acquired rock star status—he was youthful, sophisticated, telegenic, and supremely articulate in both languages— and his reputation as someone who knew Quebec well and could keep its troubling aspirations in check. This was the "Trudeaumania" election and the Liberal majority was impressive. With 155 seats, against 77 for the Conservatives and 22 for the NDP, the Liberals formed the first majority government in Ottawa since 1958.

Politically, Quebec in the late sixties and throughout the seventies featured a clash between two ideologies, represented by these two leaders: Trudeau's federalism, framed around such worldly values as social justice, individual liberty, and multiculturalism, versus Lévesque's nationalism, focused on the democratic right of peoples, and in particular of the Québécois people, to collective self-determination.[60] It is interesting indeed that these battle lines were drawn in 1968, an extremely significant year in the politics of North America. Trudeau and Lévesque, the Canadian and the Québécois, were members of a progressive generation that believed in social justice, the modern state, and the power of the democratic process. Others who held similar values did not fare so well in 1968, particularly south of the border where both Senator Robert F. Kennedy and Dr. Martin Luther King Jr. fell victim to assassins' bullets. In 1968, Trudeau was elected prime minister of Canada and Lévesque founded the party that would unite the independence movement and set the terms of a political and constitutional debate that would preoccupy Quebec, and Canada, for the ensuing forty years . . . and counting.

Nineteen-sixty-eight was also the year in which Pierre Vallières published the original French edition of his memoir, *White Niggers of America*, which became a key text for the Front de libération du Québec.[61] The FLQ was comprised of a dozen or so small, armed cells committed to both Quebec independence and to revolutionary socialism; they were certainly not prepared to wait for the results of a "bourgeois" democratic process. These young men (and they were mostly men) used hidden explosive devices to target symbols of federal power, the British connection, and the affluence of Quebec's English-speaking minority. These included the Canadian Armed Forces, the postal service, the City of Westmount, the Montreal Stock Exchange, and McGill University. Over 200 bombs were planted between 1963 and 1970, often in the red letter boxes of the Canadian Postal Service—an innocuous but accessible symbol of federal power—killing several people and injuring dozens. The terrorist attacks were designed to attract international media attention and to provoke fear and political instability. It was the same brand of political violence associated with post-colonial liberation movements in the "Third World" and it was quite successful in attracting attention and generating fear, although not so much in other ways.[62]

The FLQ's campaign of violence culminated in October 1970 with a pair of high-profile kidnappings, one of which ended in a brutal murder. The crisis began on 5 October, when British Trade Commissioner James Cross was taken hostage from his Montreal home by an FLQ cell. The kidnappers made a series of demands, communicated through the media, including the release of convicted FLQ terrorists (styled political prisoners) and the public broadcast of a rambling manifesto. No prisoners were released, but the manifesto was read on Radio-Canada; and the Quebec government, on 10 October, offered the kidnappers free passage to a foreign country in exchange for the release of Cross. That same day, however, another FLQ cell abducted a second public figure. Aged forty-nine, Pierre Laporte had been a distinguished journalist and was then minister of labour and immigration in the province's new Liberal government, elected only six months earlier and led by the young economist Robert Bourassa.

Press conference during the October Crisis. Lawyer Robert Lemieux (seated) spoke on behalf of the FLQ in its negotiations with government authorities during the crisis of October 1970. He is pictured here during a tense press conference held in Montreal on the evening of Tuesday 13 October, alongside CSN leader Michel Chartrand, who had risen to make an emphatic point. The discussion focused on the refusal of federal and provincial authorities to comply with FLQ demands, particularly the release from prison of 23 convicted terrorists, in exchange for the safe return of hostages James Cross and Pierre Laporte. Two days later, on Thursday 15 October, both men spoke at a rally held at the Paul Sauvé Arena, at which, according to Lysiane Gagnon in *La Presse*, "some 3,000 people overtly demonstrated their support for the FLQ, shouting the name of the movement and vigorously applauding [members] Pierre Vallières [and] Charles Gagnon," as well as Chartrand and Lemieux (*La Presse*, 16 October 1970, A2). Both men were arrested under the terms of the War Measures Act, invoked that Friday, 16 October, by the federal government. © *Bettman/Corbis*

A week later, on 16 October, with the support of Bourassa and Mayor Jean Drapeau, the federal government took decisive but controversial action. Trudeau's government sent the Canadian Armed Forces into the streets of Montreal and invoked federal emergency legislation, the War Measures Act, citing the existence of a state of "apprehended insurrection." Never before used in peace time, the legislation imposed a regime of martial law under which the FLQ was officially outlawed and some civil liberties were suspended, including freedom from arrest without due process of law. Authorities used these expanded powers to round up over 450 individuals, including poets Gaston Miron and Gérard Godin, singer Pauline Julien, family-planning advocate Dr. Serge Mongeau, and the intrepid journalist and man-about-town Nick Auf der Maur (a most unlikely terrorist).[63] Most of those arrested without charge were sovereignists but few of them had anything to do with the revolutionary elements on the far left of the movement.

Shortly after Trudeau invoked the War Measures Act, the crisis sank to a sickening new depth. At 12:30 a.m. on 18 October, the lifeless body of Pierre Laporte was found in the trunk of a car near the Saint-Hubert airport on the south shore; he had been strangled with the chain he wore around his neck. Bourassa went on television and radio that afternoon to eulogize his colleague and condemn the killers. "Pierre Laporte," he said,

> was the victim of hatred, of a criminal hatred the likes of which Quebecers and Canadians have not seen before. He gave his life in the defence of fundamental freedoms, having spent an entire week of cruel anguish awaiting this tragic fate. I say to these individuals who murdered him that they are forever unfit to be Québécois or to be French Canadians.[64]

With the province reeling from the assassination of Laporte, counterterrorism efforts were intensified. In early December, authorities located James Cross and negotiated his release, in exchange for which his captors were granted safe passage to Cuba. As to Laporte's killers, they were soon arrested and indicted on criminal charges. Two of them, Paul Rose and Francis Simard, were convicted of murder and sentenced to life in prison, while others were convicted of lesser offences, including kidnapping and accessory to murder.

The political fallout from the October Crisis was extensive, but two aspects stand out. The first was Trudeau's invocation of the War Measures Act, which polarized Canadians and Québécois at the time and has continued to do so since. Many English Canadians admired his refusal to negotiate with the FLQ and his willingness to use every means available to bring the separatists/terrorists to their knees. "Just watch me," is among his most quoted quips, uttered in response to a journalist who asked how far he would dare go to defuse the crisis.[65] Quebec nationalists have interpreted this intransigence much differently, suggesting that it did nothing to prevent the death of Laporte (perhaps even precipitating it, according to some), ran roughshod over basic human rights, brought federal troops into the streets of Montreal, and led to the unlawful arrest of hundreds of innocent people. That Trudeau, a francophone Montrealer, should have left for Ottawa in 1965 only to return in 1970 as the leader of the forces of federal oppression has been a source of consternation for many who believe he took advantage of the situation in order to repress his political enemies.

The second long-term consequence of the October Crisis was that political violence in the name of Quebec independence was permanently discredited. Democratic sovereignists like René Lévesque, whose Parti Québécois had won seven seats in the 1970 election, shared in the outrage provoked by the FLQ's recourse to kidnappings, extortion, and murder: tactics that brought global media attention of an extremely negative kind to the cause of Quebec independence. Lévesque's reaction to the crisis was as calm and measured as one could hope in the circumstances. He denounced the terrorist action in the strongest terms but also vigorously opposed the hard line taken by the Trudeau and Bourassa governments. October 1970, then, showed Quebecers the kind of struggle for independence they emphatically did not want. But it did not in any way tarnish the Parti Québécois or the idea of Quebec sovereignty in general. Indeed, in the wake of the October Crisis, the democratic sovereignty movement made huge strides in popular and electoral support.

Tracking that support is an interesting exercise, one that has kept Quebec pollsters, journalists, and political scientists busy since the 1960s. In 1966, as we have seen, the Liberal "*équipe de tonnerre*" was defeated by Daniel Johnson's Union Nationale, this despite attracting more votes than the victorious party.[66] This was the only general election ever contested by the RIN and the RN, and although they elected no MLAs, almost one Quebecer in ten (9 percent) voted for one of the two fledgling separatist parties. Four years later, it was Robert Bourassa's turn to defeat an incumbent premier, Jean-Jacques Bertrand, who had succeeded the late Daniel Johnson. Just as interesting was the performance of the new, sovereignist third party, the PQ, which polled 23 percent of the votes and elected seven members to the legislature, although Lévesque himself was defeated. Three years later, in 1973, the PQ increased its share of the popular vote to 30 percent and, despite sending only six members to the legislature, was able to form the official opposition. The October election gave the Bourassa Liberals almost 55 percent of the popular vote and all but 8 of the 110 seats in the National Assembly, as the legislature was now known, having been renamed in 1969 by the Bertrand government. Although the PQ had won one less seat than in 1970, its supporters could celebrate the fact—frankly impossible a mere decade earlier—that three

René Lévesque on provincial election night, 29 October 1973, at the Paul Sauvé Arena. The Parti Québécois was only five years old when, in 1973, it formed the official opposition in Quebec City for the first time. The sovereignist party was more popular than ever, attracting 30 percent of the popular vote, compared to 23 percent in 1970. But the celebration was bittersweet since despite having attracted almost one-third of the popular vote, the PQ would send only six members to the National Assembly, one fewer than in the previous election. Some began calling for electoral reform and perhaps a system of proportional representation in order to prevent these sorts of anomalies, which are a side effect of the first-past-the-post parliamentary system. *Library and Archives Canada*

in ten Quebecers had voted for a sovereignist party that now formed the official opposition.

Any jubilation felt by sovereignty supporters in October 1973, however, would pale in comparison to their reaction to the next general election, held on 15 November 1976. Well in advance of that election, the PQ had clarified its position on Quebec's eventual accession to sovereignty. An electoral victory on its own, they declared in 1974, would not trigger a declaration of independence. Rather, a Lévesque government would hold a referendum, with a favourable result triggering sovereignty negotiations with the federal government. This step-by-step approach made the PQ a viable electoral option for voters who may have been unhappy with the Liberal Party's record on the economy or its failure to quell the flaring linguistic debate but who were not prepared to endorse secession from Canada.

O.K. *Everybody Take a Valium!*, Terry Mosher (Aislin), 1976. The *Gazette*'s brilliant political cartoonist had René Lévesque calling for calm in the wake of his party's surprising electoral victory on 15 November 1976. *McCord Museum*

Despite the Liberals' difficulties and the upward trend in PQ fortunes, the result of the 1976 election surprised everyone. When all the votes were counted, René Lévesque's eight-year-old sovereignist party had won 41 percent of the popular vote and a clear majority (71 of 110 seats) in the National Assembly. "I never thought I could be so proud to be Québécois," declared an emotional Lévesque in his victory speech, capturing the sentiments of thousands of supporters who poured into the streets for the euphoric celebration. "*On n'est pas un petit peuple,*" he continued, in a passage that defies translation, "*on est peut-être quelque chose comme un grand peuple!*"[67] Of course, the euphoria displayed by sovereignists was matched by the angst and confusion felt by those, especially in the anglophone minority, who bitterly opposed the PQ project as portending the breakup of Canada. More people, after all, had voted against Parti Québécois candidates than had supported them. But the federalist vote was split between Bourassa's Liberal's (34 percent) and a briefly resurgent Union Nationale (18 percent), which under the leadership of Rodrigue Biron, managed to win eleven seats, in part by attracting a significant number of federalist voters disgruntled with the Liberal approach to language legislation. Language legislation, indeed, would be the first order of business for the Parti Québécois government once in power. Bill 1, the Charter of the French Language, was framed by Camille Laurin, minister of cultural development, then withdrawn, revised, and recast as Bill 101, which passed into law on 26 August 1977.

Heated debates over language policy and legislation had, by this time, assumed a central place in provincial politics. The discussion began almost a decade earlier, with a 1968–69 controversy surrounding the children of Italian immigrants in suburban Saint-Léonard, northeast of Montreal. The crux of the matter was that the local Catholic school commission had decided to require children whose mother tongue was neither English nor French—Quebecers would soon begin referring to them as "allophones"—to attend classes in French only. The measure was designed to reverse a long-standing and robust trend that had seen a majority of immigrant parents in the Montreal region send their children to English schools.[68] Local parents, many of them Italian immigrants, were not amused. They organized a parents' association that vigorously opposed and, on occasion, physically confronted the school commissioners, gaining the support in the process of the English-language media. Immigrant parents had long based their preference for English on its reputation as the language of business and a pre-requisite for material success anywhere in North America. But their arguments here were based on rights, not interests, and in particular, on the idea that the fundamental principle as regards children's education in a liberal, democratic society should be freedom of choice.[69]

The conflict over Saint-Léonard's schools touched a raw nerve in Quebec society and it spun into a protracted and divisive debate over linguistic rights and the status of the French language more generally. Ultimately, Jean-Jacques Bertrand's government made two distinct responses. First, it named a commission of inquiry headed by linguist Jean-Denis Gendron to examine a wide range of issues surrounding majority and minority language rights in the province. The commission sat until 1973, when it produced a comprehensive report whose three volumes dealt with the language of work, linguistic rights, and ethnic groups respectively. But the Saint-Léonard situation became so tense in the summer and fall of 1969 that the government decided to legislate without waiting for Gendron's recommendations. The result was Bill

63, which made French classes available to all immigrants and required all children attending school in English to acquire a basic knowledge of French. The legislation did not restrict access to English schools, despite growing support within the francophone population for such a measure. Instead, Bill 63 supported the fundamental position espoused by the Italian community of Saint-Léonard. All parents, regardless of ethnic or linguistic origin, were to be guaranteed freedom of choice as regards the language, French or English, in which their children would be taught.

To say that Bill 63 did not offer sufficient protection to the French language to satisfy the growing nationalist sentiment in the province would be an understatement. In the April 1970 election, popular support for the Union Nationale crumbled as many disappointed nationalists defected either to the upstart Parti Québécois or to Camil Samson's rural-based, populist, right-of-centre Ralliement créditiste. Bourassa's Liberals knew they needed to pass new language legislation but could afford to wait until after the Gendron Commission had delivered its report. The result was Bill 22 (July 1974), which proclaimed French to be the sole official language of Quebec (notwithstanding official bilingualism at the federal level), promoted the use of French in the business world, and created a new agency to oversee the law and its application, the Régie de la langue française (French Language Board). On the sensitive matter of schools, Bill 22 went a significant step further than Bertrand's 1969 legislation. Although freedom of choice in the language of instruction remained a stated principle, a measure of coercion was introduced for the first time. Access to English schools would be restricted to children who, when tested, could demonstrate a sufficient knowledge of English.

The new, comprehensive language law was pitched to Quebecers as a reasonable compromise between the *collective* rights of francophones to the protection and promotion of their language and identity and the *individual* rights of parents, business people, and others to choose their language of instruction or commerce in an officially bilingual country.[70] But it drew attacks from both sides, not least in the form of some 160 written submissions to the parliamentary committee studying the bill. For nationalists and some labour groups, the protections it offered to the French language did not go far enough. Anglophones and immigrant groups, on the other hand, were angered by the measure, which limited freedom of choice in education and commerce and raised the rather pitiful spectre of five-year-old children being subjected to testing by provincial language bureaucrats in order to attend their local schools.

So when the Liberals ran for re-election in 1976, many anglophone and allophone voters were so outraged with Bill 22 that they abandoned their traditional allegiance to the Liberal Party. This helped a handful of Union Nationale candidates win seats but, mainly, it weakened the Liberals, who were contending at the same time with the defection of "soft nationalists" to the Parti Québécois. The rest, as they say, is history. As we have seen, René Lévesque won the 1976 election. And in 1977, his government passed Bill 101, the French Language Charter, a much more comprehensive and restrictive language law than anything that had come before.

Indeed, the law's designation as a "charter" reflected the weight assigned to it by its authors, who viewed the French language as a central dimension of the modern Québécois identity, one that ought to be vigorously protected and promoted. To increase the visibility of French in the province, all commercial billboards and signs were to be displayed in the official language only. To promote the use of French in the workplace, managers in the private and public sectors were to address their employees in that language. French was to be the only language used in official correspondence within and between government agencies. All provincial ministries, departments, agencies, and even professional associations were to be known by their French names only. Laws passed by the National Assembly were to be promulgated in French alone, although they might (and did) continue to be made available in English translation. As to schools, the Lévesque government was prepared to go where Bourassa had not in promoting French-language education by tightly restricting access to English schools. Freedom of choice as an operating principle was abandoned and children were required to attend French schools except in three specific circumstances: if they or their siblings were already students in the English system; if their parents were only posted to Quebec temporarily; or if their parents had themselves been educated in Quebec's English-language school system.[71]

Bill 101 loomed over the late 1970s in Quebec like no other piece of legislation, before or since. For many anglophones, it amounted to an insult—a rejection. The provincial government was showing its true colours. It was prepared to run roughshod over individual rights and liberties for the sake of a unilingual Québécois identity and culture. Small wonder, from this perspective, if tens of thousands of English-speaking Quebecers voted with their feet, preferring to take their chances in Toronto, Calgary, or Vancouver than to deal with the new restrictions and with the government bureaucrats—widely derided as "language police"—whose job it was to enforce them. Small wonder as well if large American or English-Canadian corporations like the Sun Life Insurance Company decided to pull up stakes and move their operations out of Quebec rather than deal with the province's language bureaucracy and its two-tiered taxation structure.[72]

For many others, however, particularly those growing numbers of francophones who now identified themselves as Québécois, the French Language Charter was the culmination of a process of self-affirmation and identity formation that had begun with the start of the Quiet Revolution in 1960. It was the basis for a fresh start and for new understanding of how things would operate in the schools, shops, offices, and streets of modern Quebec in the late twentieth century. It was a national coming of age: proof that the old era of French-Canadian deference to anglophone capital and influence was well and truly over, and that the *Maîtres chez nous* rhetoric was well on its way to becoming a concrete reality. And it was a first step towards the promised land of national sovereignty, a foreshadowing, for better or for worse, of what an independent Quebec might look like.

TWELVE

SOVEREIGNTY IN QUESTION

On 20 May 1980, three years into its mandate, the Parti Québécois government led by René Lévesque asked Quebecers to decide their collective future. The vote was conducted under rules set out in a new Referendum Act, passed in 1978. Two formal campaign organizations were established and strict limits on financial contributions were imposed. The carefully crafted question asked voters to state not whether they wanted Quebec to become an independent country but rather whether they authorized the provincial government to negotiate a sovereignty-association arrangement with Ottawa. It also promised them the opportunity to vote again later on the substance of any such negotiated agreement. The question also referred indirectly to a policy paper published by the government in November of 1979 under the title *Québec-Canada: A New Deal.*[1] During the campaign that followed, its content became well known to most: a new arrangement in which Quebec, within the framework of an economic and monetary union, would enjoy the full powers of a sovereign country. The bottom line, then, was that a "Yes" vote would indicate support for the idea that Quebec was a nation whose elected representatives could and should interact and negotiate on a nation-to-nation basis with the Canadian government in Ottawa.

Quebec's political class quickly divided into a "Yes" camp, led by Premier René Lévesque, and a "No" camp, led by Liberal opposition leader Claude Ryan; Robert Bourassa had resigned in the wake of his 1976 defeat and been replaced by the former *Le Devoir* editor. The population divided, too, not just along predictable ethnic and linguistic lines but also among age groups and within neighbourhoods and families. There were strong arguments made by people of good faith in both camps. René Lévesque was as eloquent and passionate

Referendum day, May 1980. A smiling René Lévesque casts his "Yes" vote in the 1980 sovereignty referendum amidst a crowd of journalists and photographers. Lévesque's appeal for a mandate to negotiate the terms of "sovereignty-association" (meaning Quebec's secession from Confederation coupled with an ongoing economic partnership with Canada) was defeated by a margin of 60 percent to 40 percent. His emotional speech at the Paul Sauvé Arena that evening was among the most memorable in the political history of the province. © J.P. Laffont/Corbis

as ever, declaring that Quebecers had exceptional talent, knowledge, and resources; that their "normal" development as a people had been interrupted by the Conquest and Confederation; and that in the course of the Quiet Revolution they had proven themselves ready and able to assume the responsibilities and the burdens of nationhood. The bookish, meticulous Ryan could never rise to Lévesque's rhetorical heights. But he effectively communicated his own preference for a more cautious way forward, emphasizing recent improvements in the economic and political status of francophone Quebecers *within* Canada. In the end, Ryan's federalist forces won the day, with 60 percent voting "No" on referendum day. Sovereignists were bitterly disappointed but Lévesque was philosophical in defeat. Speaking with difficulty over an outpouring of applause and song—Gilles Vigneault's *Gens du pays* was by then an unofficial national anthem—Lévesque uttered perhaps his most quoted phrase: "*Mes chers amis, si je vous ai bien compris, vous êtes en train de dire: à la prochaine fois.*"[2]

Canadian Prime Minister Pierre Elliott Trudeau speaking at a "No" rally held at the Paul Sauvé Arena, 14 May 1980. In this speech, Trudeau promised constitutional reform in the event of a victory by the federalist forces in the sovereignty referendum held six days later. He was true to his word, but the kinds of reforms he initiated, and which were enshrined in the Constitution Act of 1982 over the objections of the Quebec government, did little to quell sovereignist sentiment in the province. *Library and Archives Canada*

Not yet concerned about the next time, the federalist camp could look back on two campaign events that had helped their cause after early polling had suggested a possible defeat. On 9 March, Lise Payette offended women on the "No" side by comparing them to a schoolbook character, Yvette, who embodied traditional female values such as deference, subservience, and domesticity. Federalists pounced on the gaffe and harnessed the trope to their cause, organizing Yvette meetings attended by thousands of women who resented Payette's implication: that to be a modern, progressive woman in 1980s Quebec meant to be a sovereignist. The other key moment was a major "No" rally held at the Paul Sauvé Arena on 14 May, just six days before the vote. The star speaker was Prime Minister Pierre Elliott Trudeau, who was back in power in Ottawa, having resigned and then returned to win the February 1980 federal election. Trudeau had taken a hard line throughout the campaign, stating that his government had no intention of negotiating sovereignty-association in the event of a "Yes" vote. He repeated the warning at the Paul Sauvé Arena. But he also took a more conciliatory tack, declaring that a "No" victory in the referendum would be interpreted by his government as a mandate for constitutional reform, not as complacent support for the status quo.[3] It was a promise with weighty consequences, as we shall see.

However they interpreted the result, Trudeau, Ryan, and most of English Canada were relieved after the votes were counted, just as Lévesque, Payette, Jacques Parizeau, and nationalists in every corner of Quebec were disappointed. Something had ended that day, not the dream of a sovereign Quebec—although he did not live to see it, Lévesque's reference to *la prochaine fois* was prophetic—but something real and tangible just the same. The 1980s were a time when the spirit of renewal, energy, and possibility that had characterized the Quiet Revolution began to fade, as new, harder attitudes and exigencies—many of them framed by economic recession, mounting public debt, and neo-conservative thinking—moved into the foreground. By May of 1980, "Le début d'un temps nouveau" was well and truly a thing of the past.

In the immediate aftermath of the 1980 referendum, Pierre Elliott Trudeau was anxious to deliver on his promise that a "No" vote would mean constitutional reform rather than the status quo. To the Canadian prime minister, however, renewed federalism did not and could not mean any kind of special status for Quebec. He was more interested in three things: first, "patriation" of the constitution, in other words creating a *Made in Canada* foundational document to replace the British North America Act of 1867; second, a workable amending formula allowing the revised constitution to be modified in Canada, not London, according to a specified process; third, a constitutionally enshrined Charter of Rights and Freedoms to guarantee fundamental human rights and liberties to Canadian citizens.

As Trudeau began to push this constitutional agenda forward, René Lévesque's Parti Québécois government won re-election in the general election on 13 April 1981, running on a solid legislative record and soft-pedalling sovereignty with the promise that no new referendum would be held during a second mandate. With the stinging defeat of 1980 such a recent memory, the PQ's strong showing in 1981 was a surprise to many. Lévesque's party won 49 percent of the popular vote and elected eighty members to the newly expanded 122-seat National Assembly, compared to 46 percent and 42 seats for Claude Ryan's Liberals. And although he did not resign until the fall of 1982, the Liberal defeat in 1981 also presaged the end of Ryan's term as leader and ultimately the return of Robert Bourassa to active politics. Bourassa, the skilled economist, had accepted various teaching assignments in Europe and the United States following his 1976 defeat. He would return to the leadership of the party in 1983 and lead the Liberals into their successful 1985 election campaign.

With Trudeau in power in Ottawa, Lévesque with a fresh mandate in Quebec City, and constitutional reform on the agenda, the 1981 election also set the stage for a new round of federal–provincial discussions and, ultimately, for a profound constitutional crisis. Since the 1960s, federal–provincial First Ministers Conferences had been held frequently and had become a regular feature of Canadian federalism. These conferences could focus on any and all pressing issues of the day; energy and the economy were frequent fare in the late 1970s and early 1980s, for example. But they most often dealt with jurisdictional, and therefore constitutional, issues. In 1971, at a conference held in Victoria, BC, the eleven first ministers (representing Ottawa and the ten provinces) had even agreed on a new accord that would have patriated the constitution, enshrined bilingualism and a bill of rights, and (over objections from the host province) adopted an amending formula granting veto power to the two largest provinces, Quebec and Ontario. The federal and Quebec leaders, Trudeau and Bourassa, were both familiar figures in the early phases of their careers. Bourassa agreed to the deal, known as the Victoria Charter, on behalf of Quebec, but he was unable to rally nationalists to the accord and ultimately retracted his support when Ottawa refused to modify it in such a way as to give the provinces more control over social policy.

Trudeau's post-referendum approach, then, was to host federal–provincial conferences in Ottawa in September 1980 and November 1981 at which he, Lévesque, and the nine other provincial premiers sat down to try to hammer out a new deal for Canada. During the second of these conferences, on 5 November 1981, the federal government reached an agreement with nine of the ten premiers, isolating Quebec, the province whose growing secessionist movement had sparked these discussions in the first place. Up to that point, Lévesque had been part of a group of eight dissident premiers opposed to Ottawa's proposals. But he was

left out of overnight negotiations held in the kitchen of the Chateau
Laurier hotel on the night of 4–5 November 1981, having famously
chosen to sleep across the river in Hull (now Gatineau), Quebec. The
Quebec premier described his exclusion from those discussions as a
betrayal—in his memoirs, he wrote about the "night of the long knives,"
using an unfortunate but tenacious image drawn from the history of
Nazi Germany.[4] The next day he left the meeting, refusing to endorse an
agreement that included a Charter of Rights and Freedoms (which the
eight dissident premiers had previously opposed) but did not contain
the provisions they had supported for opting out of federal programs
with compensation for equivalent provincial ones. The premier perhaps
assumed that the "Kitchen Accord" would go no further. In his view,
after all, Quebec enjoyed a traditional veto over major constitutional
changes, specifically those affecting its legislative powers. But Trudeau's
government preferred an imperfect consensus to the unilateral patriation
it had been threatening should no agreement prove possible. And when
the Lévesque government referred the matter to the Quebec Court of
Appeal, the decision came back in the negative: no Quebec veto power
existed in law, according to the judgment rendered by the Court in April
1982 and upheld by the Supreme Court of Canada that December.

By that time, the deed was done. The 1982 Constitution Act was
approved by nine provincial governments and the federal Parliament
and was proclaimed the supreme law of the land on 17 April 1982 at
an elaborate Ottawa ceremony featuring Elizabeth II in her role as
Queen of Canada. Trudeau and his provincial colleagues had succeeded
in providing Canadians with an up-to-date constitution, a complex, five-
tiered amending formula with no specific veto power for any province
(although on major issues all provinces have a veto since unanimous
consent is required), and a Charter of Rights and Freedoms that became
the cornerstone of Canadian jurisprudence in the ensuing decades. At
the same time, by overriding Quebec's traditional and much-cherished
privilege of a constitutional veto, and by patriating a constitution to which
the government that claimed to represent one of the country's founding
peoples was not a signatory, Trudeau's government unleashed a sequence
of events that, in 1995, came within a few thousand votes of leading to a
victory for the secessionist forces in a sovereignty referendum.

As a turning point in the history of Quebec nationalism, then, the 1982 patriation may be as significant as the Riel execution in 1885, the 1917 Conscription Crisis, or the election of Jean Lesage in 1960. For nationalists, it seemed to prove the bankruptcy of a federal regime that could so blatantly ignore the wishes of Quebec's elected government. Two years later, in the 1984 federal election, Quebecers displayed their outrage at the polls, rejecting the Liberals (now led by John Turner and in deep trouble over energy policy in western Canada) and helping native son Brian Mulroney lead the Conservatives to their first majority government since John Diefenbaker's in 1958. Mulroney was a fluently bilingual, Laval-trained corporate lawyer who came from humble roots in Baie-Comeau, in eastern Quebec. He was also a fiscal conservative in the mould of Margaret Thatcher and Ronald Reagan, a free-trade proponent, and a skilled and experienced industrial negotiator who pledged to launch a fresh round of constitutional discussions aimed at bringing Quebec back into the fold.

Interestingly, René Lévesque supported these initiatives and proposed to his caucus what became known as the *beau risque*. The gamble was to put sovereignty on the back burner and to work with the new Conservative government to try to accommodate Quebec's demands within the federal system. The proposal led to deep divisions within the PQ; to the resignation of important Cabinet ministers such as Denis Vaugeois and Camille Laurin, the chief author of the French Language Charter; and ultimately to Lévesque's decision to retire from political life in June 1985, to be replaced as leader by Pierre-Marc Johnson. Johnson, the son of the late Union Nationale premier Daniel Johnson, was an impressive intellectual with degrees in both law and medicine. But he was not an especially strong leader. And he was forced to defend his party's unpopular economic record while in government, including the increasingly hard line it had taken against the public-sector unions. So, with the sovereignty forces in disarray, at least for the moment, Robert Bourassa returned to power in Quebec City on 2 December 1985. This was probably the most remarkable comeback in the province's political history, even though Bourassa, who was never popular personally, failed to carry his own Bertrand riding. Nonetheless, his Liberals won ninety-nine seats in the National Assembly and 56 percent of the popular vote, reducing the PQ from eighty to twenty-three seats.

Leaders' debate on English radio, 1985. The governing Parti Québécois and the opposition Liberals both entered the 1985 campaign with new leaders. Pierre-Marc Johnson (right) had replaced Lévesque as PQ leader and premier, while Robert Bourassa (left) had reclaimed his party's leadership after a long hiatus in academia. They met for an English-language debate at the CJAD radio studios in Montreal, an exchange moderated by McGill University principal David Johnston, later Governor General of Canada. © *Robert Linney*

With the like-minded Mulroney and Bourassa in power in Ottawa and Quebec City, then, and with the bitter rivals Trudeau and Lévesque out of the picture, it seemed as if it might be possible finally to answer the perennial question for English Canadians, "What Does Quebec Want?" On 9 May 1986, Robert Bourassa and his intergovernmental affairs minister Gil Rémillard provided a rather precise answer to that question, presenting a series of five constitutional demands to Ottawa. Framed as the "minimum" conditions for Quebec's signature on a revised 1982 constitution, these demands were as follows: Ottawa must retreat from its activities in areas of provincial jurisdiction such as health and post-secondary education; Quebec must be formally recognized as a "distinct society" within Canada; Quebec's "traditional" veto on constitutional changes affecting its legislative powers must be restored and enshrined in the constitution; three of the nine judges on the Supreme Court of Canada must be from Quebec; and Quebec must be granted full control over its immigration policy.

The Meech Lake Monster, Terry Mosher (Aislin), 1988. With the Meech Lake Accord, signed in June 1987 at his official summer residence, Prime Minister Brian Mulroney attempted to resolve the growing political crisis by enshrining in the Canadian constitution a number of key Quebec demands, including its formal recognition as a "Distinct Society." But by re-opening the thorny constitutional debate, had Mulroney created a monster? *The Gazette*'s Terry Mosher (Aislin) seems to have thought so when he drew this cartoon in 1988. He was proven right in 1990 when the three-year deadline for ratification by all ten provincial governments expired, killing the deal and fueling support for sovereignty in Quebec. *McCord Museum*

With this wish list as a starting point and a great deal of offstage negotiation already underway, Mulroney convened his provincial counterparts in June 1987 to a First Ministers Conference at the prime minister's official summer residence on Meech Lake, in the Gatineau hills north of Ottawa. The resulting agreement, which responded in substance if not in precise detail to all five Quebec demands, became known as the Meech Lake Accord. It was a complex legal instrument that would have done a number of things. Most significantly, it would have enshrined in the constitution a particular status for Quebec—the status of a "distinct society." It would also have recognized linguistic minorities as a fundamental characteristic of Canada, given the provinces a role in Senate and Supreme Court nominations, instituted mandatory First Ministers Conferences, and guaranteed the provinces financial compensation if they chose to opt out of federal programs—a key Lévesque demand in 1981, as we have seen.

According to the 1982 constitution, which applies in Quebec despite the provincial government's refusal to sign, such a fundamental amendment required the unanimous approval, within three years, of the federal Parliament and of all ten provincial legislatures. Although the accord had powerful opponents, including former prime minister Trudeau and most Aboriginal leaders, who felt that it ignored their concerns, most of the provinces ratified it quite quickly. In Quebec, there was strong support for the agreement, which seemed to offer substantial advantages over the status quo as well as a framework through which the indignity of 1982 could be undone. There was still some distance to go, however, between the signature and the final ratification of the Meech Lake Accord, the deadline for which would arrive in the summer of 1990. As it happened, the conciliatory mood of June 1987 quickly passed and events conspired to fan the flames of nationalism in the province.

One such event was the sudden death of René Lévesque on 1 November 1987, struck down by a heart attack at the age of sixty-six. The ensuing days and weeks saw an incredible outpouring of sympathy and respect, both for the man and for his original vision of a sovereign Quebec. The unexpected and dramatic passing of its founder and first leader gave the modern sovereignty movement a hero—perhaps even a martyr—to rebuild around, and it certainly played a role in the resurgence of the PQ and of the independence movement in the coming months. Shortly after Lévesque's death, PQ leader Pierre-Marc Johnson—whose moderate constitutional position was in line with the *beau risque*, focusing on "national affirmation" rather than sovereignty—resigned. He was replaced in March 1988 by Jacques Parizeau, the uncompromising *indépendantiste* who had been Lévesque's finance minister.

Later that year, on 15 December 1988, the Supreme Court of Canada handed down a long-awaited decision that effectively dismantled the provisions of the French Language Charter (Bill 101) requiring all commercial signs to be in French only. The Bourassa government reacted

René Lévesque's state funeral in Quebec City, Thursday, 5 November 1987. At least 2,000 mourners gathered outside the Notre-Dame de Québec Cathedral and Basilica to pay their respects and bear witness to the former premier's final journey. Lévesque's widow, Corinne Côté-Lévesque, followed a Sûreté du Québec honour guard as they carried her husband's flag-draped casket down the steps of the cathedral. The assembled mourners greeted the passage of the fallen leader with spontaneous applause, refrains of Vigneault's "Gens du pays" personalized, as is the custom, with "Mon cher René" in place of the title lyric, and chants of *Merci! Merci! Merci!* © *Christopher J. Morris/Corbis*

swiftly, adopting a law (Bill 178) that maintained the requirement that exterior signs be in French only, while allowing bilingual signage indoors as long as French was predominant. To pass this law, the government famously invoked the "notwithstanding clause," which had been included in the 1982 constitution and which allowed legislatures to pass certain measures *notwithstanding* any infringement to human rights and freedoms, as defined by the Charter (including freedom of speech, the central issue in this instance), that they might entail. Bill 178 was yet another of those politically explosive compromises that seem to run through Quebec history. It was not nationalist enough for Parizeau's PQ, which surprised no one by railing against any attempt to weaken the French Language Charter. And it was too nationalist for members of Quebec's anglophone community, which was outraged that the provincial legislature could take such a cavalier approach to a serious ruling on fundamental rights and freedoms handed down by the highest court in the land. "Rights are rights are rights," declared the eloquent Minister of the Environment, Clifford Lincoln, as he quit the Bourassa Cabinet along with two other English-speaking Liberals. Others pursued the protest by launching the short-lived Unity and Equality Parties, committed to national unity and linguistic equality. The latter sent four Montreal-area MNAs to Quebec City in the next general election.

Fast-forward now from the divisive debate over Bill 178 to the long, hot summer of 1990. The barricades had been in place at Oka since March (see Chapter 13) when, on 22 June, the three-year deadline for ratification of the Meech Lake Accord expired. Since 1987, vigorous opposition had emerged from several quarters. There was anger, certainly, over the way the agreement had been reached: eleven white men in suits bargaining behind closed doors. (Only certain sessions of the First Ministers Conferences were televised, and Aboriginal and territorial leaders had not been represented.) There was concern about the special status that the distinct society clause would have accorded to Quebec. Would it override the Charter of Rights and Freedoms? Would it threaten universal social programs? And what about gender equality and Aboriginal rights?

Citing these objections and others, Liberal governments in New-foundland and New Brunswick had already revoked their Tory predecessors' ratification of the agreement. But the Mulroney government waited until early June, barely two weeks before the deadline, to hold an urgent new constitutional conference. By introducing a series of compromises and provisions for further constitutional revision—on Senate reform, gender equality, territorial representation, and minority language issues, for instance—these discussions resulted in a fresh agreement signed by all ten provincial premiers, including New Brunswick's Frank McKenna and Newfoundland's Clyde Wells, who was a constitutional expert and Trudeau protegé. Mulroney bragged famously that in holding these discussions at the last possible moment, he had "rolled the dice" and won a high-stakes gamble. But events proved otherwise. In the Manitoba legislature, where unanimous approval was required to circumvent a lengthy public consultation process, Aboriginal MLA Elijah Harper refused to give his assent, arguing that the agreement ignored First Nations concerns. Wells had planned to submit the revised agreement to a free vote in the Newfoundland legislature, where it very likely would have been defeated. But when Manitoba failed to ratify prior to the June deadline, the Meech Lake Accord was essentially dead, so the Newfoundland vote was cancelled.

Speaking in the National Assembly in the evening after the deadline had passed, Bourassa was defiant: "English Canada must understand very clearly," he said, "that whatever is said or done, Quebec is, today and always, a distinct society, free and capable of assuming its destiny and its development." Accordingly, future negotiations with Ottawa would be on a bilateral basis—quite a remarkable statement, actually, and a harbinger of the new reality: one in which Quebec would *act* more and more like a distinct society or associate state within the Canadian federation without actually being recognized as such by the constitution.[5]

After the rejection of the Meech Lake Accord, pro-sovereignty sentiment spread like wildfire in the province. Quebecers were outraged at the failure of a proposal that, after all, contained only a *minimal* set of constitutional demands. Indeed, the death of Meech had real and lasting political consequences, especially because it drove so many soft nationalists into the sovereignty camp. Prominent among these, to say the least, were a group of federal MPs, including Mulroney's law-school friend, former ambassador to France, and Cabinet colleague Lucien Bouchard. Bouchard had quit the Conservative Party that May, unable to support the Cabinet proposals that would alter and, in his view, dilute the agreement. On 25 July 1990, he and six other Quebec MPs (five former Tories and one former Liberal) announced their mutual solidarity and their intention to work within the federal parliament towards Quebec independence. These were the origins of the Bloc Québécois, a new, sovereignist federal party, which elected its first MP on 13 August 1990 when Gilles Duceppe won a by-election in Montreal's Laurier-Sainte-Marie riding. Under the leadership of Bouchard and later Duceppe, the party won a clear majority of Quebec ridings in each of the first six federal general elections in which it participated, prior to its stunning defeat in the May 2011 election. This remarkable string began in 1993, when the fledgling party won fifty-four of seventy-five Quebec seats and 49 percent of the popular vote in the province—if nothing else, a clear indication of the growing strength of the sovereignty option in the early 1990s.[6]

Le bloc québécois!, Serge Chapleau, 1992. Political cartoonist Chapleau commented on Lucien Bouchard's unique position as leader of a federal party committed to Quebec sovereignty. Chapleau's bloc is a Rubik's cube nicely redecorated to symbolize the puzzle of federal-provincial relations during the constitutional crisis of the 1990s. *McCord Museum*

The day after Meech died, on 23 June 1990, the federal Liberals named a new leader: Jean Chrétien, a key Trudeau Cabinet minister and one of the artisans of the "Kitchen Accord" of 1981. Chrétien's position on the constitution seemed vague but optimistic. "We could live with Quebec's five demands," he explained, "but we will offer new solutions in time for the next election."[7] Mulroney's federal Tories, of course, were still in power, but they had been weakened in Quebec by the defeat of Meech and in western Canada by the emergence of the populist, fiscally conservative Reform Party and its persuasive leader, Preston Manning. Quebec's constitutional status dominated federal and provincial politics for the next two years. As polls showed unprecedented support for sovereignty in the province, both the provincial and federal governments appointed special commissions to study the political and constitutional future of Quebec. Such were the terms of reference given to the provincial commission headed by federalist Michel Bélanger and sovereignist Jean Campeau, which delivered its report in March 1991 and recommended, among other things, that a second sovereignty referendum be held before the end of the following year. Bourassa's Liberal government pledged instead to hold a referendum on sovereignty only if no new proposals were forthcoming from Ottawa; any such proposals would also be subject to popular ratification via referendum.

Meanwhile, the Mulroney government was holding inquiries and consultations of its own in order to determine what kind of "new solutions" might offer a way out of the deepening constitutional crisis. With respected former prime minister Joe Clark now installed as the federal minister of constitutional affairs, the government managed successfully to negotiate yet another, more comprehensive constitutional agreement: the Charlottetown Accord, which was signed by federal, provincial, territorial, and Aboriginal leaders at Charlottetown on 28 August 1992. The accord would have recognized both Quebec's position as a distinct society and the principle of Aboriginal self-government; given the provinces greater control over natural resources and cultural policy; enshrined in the constitution the right to opt out of federal programs, with compensation; encouraged the interprovincial flow of goods, services, and labour; and introduced significant institutional reforms, particularly regarding the Supreme Court and the Senate.[8] Prominent critics included Pierre Trudeau, who called the agreement "a mess" in a speech delivered, oddly, at a Montreal Chinese restaurant called *La Maison du Egg Roll*; the PQ's Jacques Parizeau, for whom, not surprisingly, the additional powers it ceded to Quebec were insufficient; and Preston Manning, who stridently opposed the distinct society clause and argued that the Senate-reform measures did not go far enough. In November the deal was submitted to two simultaneous referendums: one in Quebec, administered by provincial authorities; and one in every other province and territory, administered by Elections Canada. The results could only be interpreted as another crushing defeat for Mulroney's campaign to bring Quebec back into the constitutional fold. Only four provinces and the Northwest Territories voted in favour of the proposal, which was defeated by a margin of 55 percent to 45 percent, with four western provinces voting decisively against the agreement. And in Quebec, where voter turnout was highest, the proposal was rejected by a clear margin, with 57 percent of participants voting "No" to Charlottetown.[9]

The defeat within two years of two separate agreements aimed at undoing the "betrayal" of 1982 meant, fundamentally, that the stage was set for a second referendum on Quebec sovereignty. But when Charlottetown was declared DOA in November 1992, not all the actors were yet in their places. Mulroney, although applauded in many quarters (but lambasted in others) for his work on the free trade agreements (see Chapter 13), had spent all his political capital trying to fix the constitution. He resigned the Tory leadership and his successor, British Columbia's Kim Campbell, led the party in 1993 to one of the most spectacular defeats in Canadian electoral history. The coalition that Mulroney had built between social and fiscal conservatives, many of them living west of Ontario, and Quebec's soft nationalists crumbled as two new political parties—Manning's Reform Party and Bouchard's Bloc Québécois—claimed those constituencies for themselves, each gaining upwards of fifty seats, with Lucien Bouchard named leader of the official opposition. Amazingly, the Tories, having swept the 1984 election and having been re-elected with 169 members in 1988, were reduced to just two MPs. For their part, the Chrétien Liberals ran a consistent, well-funded campaign structured around a detailed "Red Book" of electoral promises, mostly focused on the economy. When the votes were counted on 25 October 1993, Chrétien had survived some rather vicious Conservative attack ads and his party's poor performances in Quebec and the West to win a majority government.

The electoral cycle in Quebec also dictated that a new team would soon be chosen to lead the provincial government. Like Mulroney, Robert Bourassa was ready to step down, so the provincial Liberals turned to Daniel Johnson Jr., whose father and brother had both led Quebec governments. Johnson replaced Bourassa in January 1994 and served as premier until the September election. This vote saw the disappearance of one third party (the anglophone-rights Equality Party) and the emergence of another, L'Action démocratique du Québec (ADQ), led by the centre-right nationalist and former Liberal youth wing president Mario Dumont. Although the popular Dumont did manage to win his riding, the main result was that Quebec's political pendulum swung back from the Liberals to the PQ, now led by Parizeau and energized by two failed attempts to renew Canadian federalism. The Parti Québécois won thirty more seats than the Liberals (seventy-seven versus forty-seven) even though the popular vote was split rather evenly, with both major parties receiving just over 44 percent. This seemed to indicate a slight drop in support for sovereignty since the 1993 federal election, when the PQ allies in the Bloc had polled at almost 50 percent. But it was certainly strong enough for the new PQ government to carry through with its main electoral promise: to hold a fresh referendum on Quebec sovereignty early in the mandate.

So by September 1994 the stage was set, the actors were in their places, and the curtain could be raised on the drama of the 1995 referendum. On 6 December 1994, the Parti Québécois government presented a draft bill on the sovereignty of Quebec, copies of which (in a strategy reminiscent of 1980) were made available to every household in the province.[10] The preamble to this document was intentionally left blank, to be filled in later through a collective process of reflection and self-definition. The path to sovereignty was to be somewhat different from the step-by-step process proposed in 1980. The first order of business, justified in the preamble and stated directly in Article 1, was to declare flatly and solemnly that "Quebec is a sovereign country." With that out of the way, the law would authorize the government of Quebec "to conclude, with the Government of Canada, an agreement the purpose of which is to maintain an economic association between Quebec and Canada."[11] The document then went on to deal briefly with a series of substantive matters such as the drafting of a constitution, the definition of Quebec's national territory, currency (Canadian), treaties, alliances, the continuity of law, and the apportionment of property and debt. The bill was intended to be a foundational document for the new, sovereign Quebec, and would come into force only in the event that a majority of Quebec electors declared their explicit support for its provisions in a referendum. And there was to be a one-year interval between such a (winning) referendum and actual independence.

The ensuing months, needless to say, were a period of intense debate over the prospect of independence. With an electorate that seemed to be almost evenly split on the question, it was also a time of sustained efforts by both camps to sway voters in one direction or the other. The Parizeau government tried to build a consensus around its option and, perhaps, a sense of inevitability—or even destiny. It did so in part through consultations with experts, interest groups, and ordinary Quebecers. From 6 February until 19 April, for example, the Commission nationale sur l'avenir du Québec—chaired by former Conservative

Sovereignty supporters during the 1995 referendum campaign. The symbolism of the posters and placards used by the "Yes" side in this campaign was revealing. Rather than the "black hole" of uncertainty to which federalist leaders so often referred, these brightly coloured images evoked hope and positive energy. A "Yes" vote, they proclaimed, would mean yes to the Canadian dollar, yes to NAFTA, yes to the environment, yes to jobs and the economy, and yes to a new era of social and political peace. Sovereignist campaigners also displayed portraits of the movement's two most charismatic leaders, René Lévesque and Lucien Bouchard, as well as the ubiquitous fleur-de-lys flag, here emblazoned with a hand-painted "*Oui*."
© *Jacques Grenier, Le Devoir*

Minister Monique Vézina—heard, read, and studied upwards of 6,000 submissions, concluding that a declaration of sovereignty followed by an offer of economic partnership with Canada was the nearest thing available to a consensus option for Quebec's political future.[12] Giving added weight to the sovereignty project was an agreement to work together on its behalf, reached on 12 June among the leaders of the three nationalist parties—Parizeau of the PQ, Bouchard of the Bloc, and, surprisingly to some, ADQ leader and former provincial Liberal Mario Dumont.

By early September, as the government prepared to drop the writs for an October referendum, it was ready to reveal the content of the long-awaited preamble to the proposed sovereignty legislation. The text, co-written by a team that included the novelist and playwright Marie Laberge and the poet Gilles Vigneault, was rich in agrarian metaphors and crafted to inspire patriotism: "The time has come for us, tomorrow's ancestors, to make ready for our descendants, harvests that are worthy of the labours of the past," it said. It also contained many of the key concepts found in the nationalist conception of Quebec history: ideas like strength, struggle, courage, and destiny, as well poetic allusions to the harsh climate and the ability of the people to survive despite great hardships. ("We know the winter in our souls . . . its blustery days, its solitude, its false eternity and its apparent deaths.") And it included a harsh indictment of Canadian federalism, evoking an illusory 1867 "promise of equality" between French and English Canada, a Canadian state that had "contravened the federative pact, by invading in a thousand ways areas in which we are autonomous," a detrimental 1982 constitutional accord that "hoodwinked" the province's elected leaders, and a Canada that instead of celebrating "the alliance between its two founding peoples, has instead consistently trivialized it and decreed the spurious principle of equality between the provinces."[13]

The unveiling of the poetic preamble at the Grand Théatre de Québec, intended surely as a solemn moment of national affirmation, was instead disrupted by flag-waving federalist protesters, many of them apparently elderly and some of them wearing military decorations.[14] Although the incident is often forgotten, nothing could illustrate more clearly the lack of a true consensus in the province, either over the way its collective history should be framed (an increasingly hot topic in the ensuing years) or over the best path forward for the Quebec people.

With polls continuing to show a clear advantage for the federalist side, the Referendum decree was adopted in the National Assembly on 1 October 1995, marking the official start to the campaign—which would culminate in a vote on 30 October. The question was shorter than in 1980, but it also contained references to recent events and documents, knowledge of which was assumed. "Do you agree," asked the government, "that Quebec should become sovereign after having made a formal offer to Canada for a new economic and political partnership within the scope of the bill respecting the future of Quebec and the agreement signed on June 12, 1995?" At the start of the campaign, the "No" side had a small but consistent lead in the polls and seemed to be headed for a relatively easy victory. But on 7 October, the "Yes" campaign played its trump card, pulling the cagey and curmudgeonly Jacques Parizeau into the wings and introducing Lucien Bouchard as the new leader of the sovereignty campaign and principal negotiator with Canada in the event of a "Yes" vote.

Bouchard was passionate, direct, and articulate, and his personal popularity had been growing since his defection from the Tory camp

Jacques Parizeau Hooked by Lucien Bouchard, Terry Mosher (Aislin), 1995. The fortunes of the nationalist camp in the lead-up to the 1995 referendum improved substantially after 7 October, when it was announced that Lucien Bouchard would replace Jacques Parizeau as leader of the "Yes" campaign and as Quebec's principal negotiator with Canadian officials in the event of a positive result for the pro-sovereignty forces. In an editorial cartoon published in *The Gazette* soon afterwards, Aislin's comment was characteristically irreverent. *McCord Museum*

in 1990. In December 1994, the entire province had watched as he fought for his life against necrotizing fasciitis ("flesh-eating disease"), ultimately winning the battle but losing a leg to amputation. Jean Charest, a fellow member of the Mulroney Cabinet in the 1980s and now federal Conservative leader, knew him well and understood the impact his leadership could have. "I knew right away that the campaign had changed," he told reporters ten years later.[15] And indeed, the "Yes" numbers kept rising, despite two potentially damaging gaffes made by Bouchard on the weekend of 14–15 October. First, he deliberately ignored the complexities of the situation by stating publicly that there would be "something magical about a Yes vote. With a wave of our magic wand, we will stir up a feeling of solidarity among Quebecers." And second, he framed a common nationalist complaint about falling birth rates in the most unfortunate possible terms, describing Quebec as "one of the white races that has the fewest children."[16] No matter. Quebecers liked Bouchard and were willing to forgive his mistakes. And support for the "Yes" side continued to climb.

Meanwhile, the "No" camp, led by Daniel Johnson but with key contributions by Chrétien and Charest, hammered away at the themes of uncertainty, instability, and economic danger. In forceful campaign speeches and interviews, Charest frequently used the frightening image

Unity Rally in Montreal, 27 October 1995. Thousands of participants came from across Canada to stage a mass demonstration in favour of Canadian unity and to plead with Quebecers to vote against sovereignty in the referendum. Sovereignists derided the event as a "love-in" and complained that the money spent by organizers on free or deeply discounted air and train fares should have been counted against the "No" side's campaign spending limits. Quebec's chief electoral officer later agreed and proceeded to lay charges on that basis; they were eventually dropped. Did the massive appeal by other Canadians sway enough Quebecers to make the difference in the sovereignty vote, held three days later? Jacques Parizeau apparently thought so, as his explosive remarks on referendum night suggest. *Photograph by Peter Gossage*

of a "black hole" to describe the situation Quebecers would face should they vote for sovereignty. Although the "Yes" camp belittled these "scare tactics," it was true that after voting in favour of sovereignty, Quebec would need to negotiate new arrangements with the Canadian government on a wide range of issues, from citizenship and territory to currency and trade, assets and debts. The federalists warned that it could be a messy divorce (another metaphor in wide circulation) despite the solemn and reassuring language of the PQ's sovereignty bill. At the same time, federalists tried to counter the "Yes" camp's focus on the humiliations of federalism by proudly waving the Canadian flag, celebrating Canada's bilingual and multicultural heritage, and arguing for a conception of Québécois identity that was consistent with a broader and inclusive Canadian nationality and citizenship. The culmination of these efforts came on Friday 27 October when tens of thousands of people (estimates range from 40,000 to 100,000 people) converged on Montreal's Dominion Square to wave the Maple Leaf and listen to speeches by Chrétien, Johnson, Charest, and others. Many participants at the massive "Unity Rally" had come from other parts of Canada. Most saw it as a chance to help keep their country together and felt that they were participating in something important, no matter how the vote turned out the following Monday. Some had their air, train, or bus fares subsidized by federal tax dollars, a fact that was later interpreted by the chief electoral officer of Quebec as a contravention of Quebec's 1978 referendum law and its provisions on campaign spending.

When the first votes started coming in on referendum night, federalists began to panic and sovereignists to celebrate. Early returns suggested that the "Yes" option might win, perhaps even by a substantial margin. But astute political analysts like the *Journal de Montréal's* Michel C. Auger knew better. The federalist support was strongest on the Island of Montreal and in western Quebec, he explained to a TV audience, and these populous regions would be among the last to report. So in all likelihood, the "No" side would make up the difference and finish the evening with a narrow victory. Auger was right. When all 4.7 million votes had been counted (this was fully 93.5 percent of those eligible) the Parti Québécois's second sovereignty referendum had been defeated by a margin of only 54,000 votes—about the number of people it takes to fill the Olympic Stadium.

Although no longer the leader of the "Yes" camp, Jacques Parizeau was still the PQ premier of Quebec. Next to the narrow result, his bitter comments in defeat were the most striking and memorable episode of an emotional referendum night. On the one hand, he said, the "Yes" side had won a victory of sorts: 60 percent among "*us*," the francophones of Quebec. "We were so close to a country. Well, it's been delayed a little . . . not for long, not for long," he declared. "It's true; it's true that we've been defeated, but basically by what? By *money and ethnic votes*, essentially." Next time, by capturing 63 percent or 64 percent of francophone votes, he predicted, the sovereignty project would pass and Quebecers would have their country.[17] Parizeau resigned in disgrace the next day. His tirade had undone years of work intended to resituate Quebec nationalism as a modern, pluralist, inclusive, civic project based on certain shared values, rather than a traditional, quasi-tribal battle for political supremacy, pitting an ethnic *us* against an ethnic *them*.

THIRTEEN

CONTEMPORARY QUEBEC

By the second decade of the twenty-first century, the sovereignty debates of the 1980s and 1990s had begun to fade into memory. Students entering high school in 2010 had no recollection of these struggles, although they might have learned about them from their parents, in school, on television, or perhaps from a book like this one. Political life in the province had moved on to consider other questions. Still, about 40 percent of the population continued to support sovereignty. And opposing positions on Quebec's identity—as a sovereign nation in waiting, as a Canadian province, or as something in between—continued to lend structure and substance, for good or ill, to electoral politics at all levels.

Since the 1980s, the two main political parties in the province had evolved into relatively stable coalitions built around opposing constitutional options, respectively sovereignist and federalist. In fact, the Parti Québécois and the Quebec Liberal Party shared power remarkably evenly between 1976 and 2012, with each party in office for eighteen years.[1] Third parties made inroads on only three occasions. In the 1989 general election, running on a platform of linguistic rights for anglophones and opposition to Bill 178, the Equality Party won four seats on the Island of Montreal (see Chapter 12). Founded in 1994 after the failure of the Meech Lake Accord, the centre-right autonomist party Action démocratique du Québec (ADQ) elected a single candidate in the general election of that year: its youthful, charismatic leader Mario Dumont. The socially and fiscally conservative ADQ had significant appeal outside metropolitan Montreal, to the point where the party was able form the official opposition in 2007, although these gains were all but wiped out the next year (see below). At the same time, at the other end of the political spectrum, a new sovereignist option, Québec Solidaire, emerged to the left of the Parti Québécois, promoting environmental issues, gender equality, and social justice and managing to elect one member, Dr. Amir Khadir, during the 2008 general election.[2]

Quebec at the turn of the twenty-first century, then, had a distinct political culture that, in a curious and novel way, reproduced the polarities experienced by earlier generations. The traditional battle lines—whether *Rouge* versus *Bleu* or Liberal versus Nationalist—had now given way, in fact and in the public vernacular, to *fédéraliste* versus *souverainiste*. But contemporary Quebec was also a modern, complex society, living with all the pressures and possibilities of the contemporary world and adapting in its way to new economic, social, technological, environmental, and cultural challenges. So we begin this final chapter with a discussion of Quebec's economy, society, and culture at the turn of the new millennium. Then, in the final pages, we return to politics in order to trace the contours of a political landscape that was permanently transformed by the identity crisis of the 1980s and 1990s, certainly, but by contemporary, twenty-first-century issues as well.

In the last quarter of the twentieth century, Quebec's workplaces and marketplaces were reshaped by the same global economic forces affecting other industrialized societies. Economic growth was much weaker than during the postwar boom, a trend that brought double-digit unemployment to the province for a number of years.[3]

As manufacturing shifted to developing countries, the loss of industrial jobs touched many communities profoundly. Until the mid-1970s, for instance, Huntingdon was a thriving textile town with an important woollen mill and several smaller operations. In the ensuing thirty years, the local economy suffered a long decline culminating in the bankruptcy of its two largest employers, Huntingdon Mills and Cleyn and Tinker, in 2004 and 2005. The town's widely publicized problems with teen vandalism were typical of many communities that had lost their industrial vocation and identity. The situation was just as difficult for struggling single-industry towns located further afield in the resource-rich periphery. In 1954, the Iron Ore Company of Canada had begun mining operations in Shefferville, some 600 kilometres north of the port city of Sept-Îles. The iron mine reached the peak of its output in the 1970s. But the tide soon turned and in 1985 the company ceased production for good. Thrown out of work, most of the 4,000 or so non-Aboriginal residents simply left, returning the site to the local Innu and Naskapi people, who began to promote it as a tourism and hunting destination.[4]

In this challenging climate, Quebec's governments used various strategies to stimulate economic growth and job creation. In the Parti Québécois's second term, for example, there was a distinct move away from state intervention and towards policies designed to foster growth in the home-grown private sector. Despite its fiscal retrenchment, then, the Lévesque government still managed to stimulate French-Canadian business expansion by allowing taxpayers to deduct investments in small Quebec-based companies, thereby generating $5 billion in investment capital by 1987. As a result, the number of companies on the Montreal Stock Exchange tripled within a three-year period, and francophone enterprises financed a number of major takeovers. These measures reinforced the trend that saw francophone capital, expertise, and entrepreneurship moving out of the public sector and into private enterprise. Widely described as Quebec Inc., the pattern is reflected in the career of Michel Bélanger, a senior civil servant in Quebec City who became president of the Montreal Stock Exchange and the first president of the Banque Nationale when it was formed in 1979.

Concurrently with deindustrialization and with Quebec's new emphasis on the private sector, the increasingly globalized economy of the late twentieth century meant the establishment of large trading zones like the European Union (1993). The issue gained immediacy in the mid-1980s when the Canadian and American governments began bilateral negotiations for the creation of a free-trade zone, eliminating most tariffs and other barriers to trade between the two countries. An agreement was reached in 1987 between the Mulroney government and Ronald Reagan's Republican administration. Opposition to free trade was strong in English Canada, particularly during the 1988 federal election campaign when Liberals and New Democrats both opposed the agreement, arguing that it threatened Canada's economic sovereignty, cultural industries, and social programs. Most Quebecers were unmoved by these objections. They saw free trade rather as a boon to the province's flagging export industries and were not especially worried about Canadian economic or cultural sovereignty. So Mulroney won re-election in 1988 with continuing support from Quebec. The Free Trade

Agreement came into effect in 1989, to be superseded five years later by the North American Free Trade Agreement (NAFTA), which expanded the free-trade zone to include Mexico.

Quebec's new generation of private-sector entrepreneurs were favourable to these kinds of arrangements, using them to expand their international business in everything from newsprint to jet aircraft. But there were currents of opposition as well. In April 2001, when leaders of thirty-four countries met in Quebec City to consider the idea of an expanded free-trade zone that would include North, South, and Central America, thousands of people demonstrated in the streets of *la vieille capitale*, drawing widespread media attention especially after the protest turned violent and riot police resorted to tear gas.[5]

As the twentieth century reached its end, globalization and de-industrialization were often described as aspects of a "new economy" for which rapid technological change was a driving force. In the 1980s, today's world of high-tech digital communications was still well in the future. Reporters covering the first sovereignty referendum, for instance, would have written their stories on desktop computers with perhaps 254K of RAM, having only just graduated from typewriters. Over the next thirty years, Quebecers felt the impact of the digital revolution, both as consumers of the latest gadgets and as participants in the new high-technology industries. As traditional labour-intensive industries declined, other businesses thrived by developing high-tech solutions to old problems. Indeed, some of Quebec's most successful private ventures in these years were in high-technology sectors. Bombardier Aerospace, for instance, dates from 1986, when Bombardier Inc.—long established as a manufacturer of snowmobiles and railway cars—acquired the financially troubled Canadair operations from the federal government. This launched an aviation division that grew through acquisitions (including the famous Learjet corporation in 1990) to become the world's third-largest civil aircraft manufacturer.[6] Another example is the North American design studio for the French video-game giant Ubisoft, which opened in 1997 in Montreal's Mile-End district. Ubisoft Montreal had a workforce of some 1,600 in February 2007, when it announced new investments that would allow it to expand to 3,000 employees by 2013, making it the largest video-game design studio in the world.[7]

Bombardier Challenger models 605 and 300. Joseph-Armand Bombardier began producing snowmobiles in Valcourt, Quebec, in 1942. During the 1970s and 1980s, the company built up its reputation as a leader in subway transit and railway equipment. Then a series of acquisitions in the aerospace industry made Bombardier a global leader in aviation, producing business, commercial, and regional jets. *Bombardier, Inc.*

These high-tech success stories, however, were told against a backdrop of economic fragility. By the 1980s, the unprecedented prosperity of *les trente glorieuses* had given way to slower growth and more unstable economic times. One important result was a crisis in public finances. With tax revenues falling and with expensive health, education, and social assistance programs to maintain, governments all over the West began to preach and practise the neo-conservative, supply-side economics known in Britain as Thatcherism and in the United States as Reaganomics. At the same time, a "new world order" was emerging in global politics. The demolition of the Berlin Wall in 1989 symbolized the end of the Communist era in the former Soviet Bloc and the transition to free-market economies and democratically elected governments in Russia, Poland, the reunified Germany, and the rest of Eastern Europe. The next year, 1990, signalled the end of the racist Apartheid regime in South Africa. In the meantime, beginning perhaps with the Iran hostage crisis of 1980, Islamic fundamentalism emerged as a potent geopolitical

Good News, Sir, Your Operation Is Scheduled for Tomorrow, Serge Chapleau, 1996. Political cartoonist Chapleau used dark humour to comment on the painfully long and potentially life-threatening wait times for surgery in the mid-1990s. The chronically underfunded public health system has been a major political issue in recent decades. *McCord Museum*

force, with its most radical elements using terrorist tactics to foster a climate of global anxiety and instability.

Like all North Americans, Quebecers felt the political, social, and personal impact of these global shifts. If ill or injured they might well get stuck in an overcrowded emergency room or suffer excruciating wait times for surgery in a context where governments were anxious to balance the books and prepared to slash ballooning health-care costs in order to do so. They also experienced "the new world order" in direct and sometimes tragic ways. Quebecers, on the whole, were surprisingly supportive of Canada's ten-year combat mission against Taliban insurgents in Afghanistan. But they also paid a terribly high price for it. Of the thirty-two Canadian soldiers killed in action in 2009, for example, thirteen were based at Canadian Forces Base Valcartier near Quebec City, and one at the Bagotville airbase in the Saguenay region.[8]

Meanwhile, Quebec retained the distinctive sociological profile it had acquired during the Quiet Revolution. No longer a bastion of conservative Catholic family values, the province remained a singularly liberal and open society, particularly with regard to sexuality, marriage, and reproduction. Birth rates remained extremely low, as modern Quebec women continued to exercise their reproductive freedom, often combining careers with motherhood and relying on extensive, state-subsidized daycare services.[9] Falling birth rates were a source of worry for governments since they meant an aging population and correspondingly greater strains on the health care and social service networks. As Lucien Bouchard demonstrated during the 1995 referendum campaign (see Chapter 12), they also sent up alarm bells for nationalists concerned about a decline in the demographic strength of the majority group—those of French-Canadian origin.

Equally distinctive was the Quebec approach to marriage, which saw more people choose never to marry and more couples decide to forego matrimony and live together in consensual unions. In this context, the stigma once associated with "illegitimate" childbearing evaporated to the point where a clear majority of children (almost two-thirds in 2009) were born to unmarried parents.[10] Matrimony had become distinctly optional for modern Quebec families, and to a much greater extent than in other Canadian provinces.[11] Divorce rates, too, were higher than elsewhere in Canada. In 2003, the odds of a Quebec couple splitting before their thirtieth anniversary were virtually fifty-fifty, compared to less than two-in-five across Canada, and under one-in-five in Newfoundland and Labrador.[12] All of this meant a profusion of non-traditional families, including those headed by unmarried couples, single-parent families (the situation in 2001 for one in five children living at home), and blended families of various configurations. Gay and lesbian Quebecers, meanwhile, made great strides in their struggle for equal rights and an end to discrimination. Quebec took the lead in establishing legal recognition for committed gay and lesbian relationships when, in 2002, it passed legislation instituting civil unions for same-sex couples in advance of any other province and two years before the federal government declared same-sex marriage legal in 2004.

For Quebec women, the feminist activism of the 1970s certainly reaped substantial benefits in the ensuing decades. In addition to more sexual and reproductive freedom, women gained greater access to all levels

Street scene in Montreal's Gay Village. The Village is one of the largest in the world, stretching eastward for about two kilometres along St. Catherine Street from St. Hubert to Papineau Streets. In 2009, blogger Pierre Chantelois evoked both the history of homophobia in Montreal and the emergence of the Village as a trendy residential area famous for its restaurants and nightlife, and with considerable appeal as a tourist destination for the international LGBTQ community. "This urban area," he wrote, "after a long history of repression, is now held up as an example and promoted internationally by the very people who used to decry its existence a few short years ago. . . . It now seems possible that the two communities, heterosexual and homosexual, can live in peace in Montreal." See Pierre Chantelois, "Le village gai de Montréal devient piétonnier pour l'été," posted 7 June 2009, retrieved 16 February 2012 from the website *Les Beautés de Montréal*, http://lesbeautesdemontreal.com/2009/06/07/le-village-gai-de-montreal-devient-pietonnier-pour-lete. *Photograph by Olivier Vallerand*

of education, to meaningful jobs, to the professions, and to leadership positions in almost every area of activity. Provincial politics was just one such area, but an interesting and important one. The first Cabinet formed by René Lévesque in 1976 contained twenty-three men and only one woman, Lise Payette, whose portfolio was highly gendered (Status of Women and Consumer Affairs). Many more women were recruited into Cabinet positions in the ensuing decades; the proportion in the 1990s hovered around one-quarter to one-third. But a few years into the new century, two successive Liberal governments claimed the gender high road by naming equal numbers of men and women to Cabinet and by placing women in the most visible and sensitive positions, such

Liberal politicians Yolande James and Jean Charest. The photograph shows Charest escorting James to the National Assembly seat she won in a September 2004 by-election. After her re-election as MNA for Nelligan in 2007, she was named Minister of Immigration and Cultural Communities in Jean Charest's Liberal minority government; she held her seat in the 2008 election and became Minister of Families in a 2010 cabinet shuffle. Born to immigrant parents in Montreal in 1977, James holds degrees in both civil and common law from the Université de Montréal and Queen's University, respectively. As a powerful, articulate, well-educated woman of colour, she is a thoroughly modern *Québécoise* and, for many, a symbol of the province's commitment to gender equity and cultural diversity. Ironically, this photograph also features another more traditional symbol: the crucifix that continues to hang in the National Assembly despite the resolutely secular character of Quebec civil society and the recommendation of the Bouchard-Taylor Commission that it be removed. *CP PHOTO/Jacques Boissinot*

as finance, education, culture, and justice.[13] Although not framed as a response to this initiative, the Parti Québécois' nomination of former Cabinet minister Pauline Marois as its leader in June 2007 might certainly be read in this light.

Full gender equality, however, was still a dream rather than an everyday reality. Crude and more subtle forms of sexism persisted, whether in the home or the workplace, in popular culture, on the Internet, or in advertising, where highly sexualized images of submissive women were regularly used to sell beer, cars, and so on. There was still an active sex trade in urban centres and women working as prostitutes and strippers were among the most vulnerable members of society. Violence against women remained a major problem; there were far too many grisly news reports about women like Cinthia Toussaint, the twenty-three-year-old Montreal woman whose body was found in a manhole in May 2010, apparently the victim of an enraged ex-boyfriend.

The greatest outrage of all was committed on 6 December 1989 when Marc Lépine carried an assault rifle into the École Polytechnique, the Université de Montréal's prestigious engineering school. Lépine coldly singled out young women and brutally murdered fourteen of them before turning the weapon on himself. The event recalled a previous rampage in 1984, when a psychotic Canadian soldier, Denis Lortie, opened fire in the National Assembly building, killing three people before the legislature's sergeant-at-arms, René Jalbert, talked him into a quiet surrender. And it foreshadowed two subsequent school shootings in Montreal: Valery Fabrikant's at Concordia University in 1992, in which five professors were gunned down by a colleague who had been denied tenure; and Kimveer Gill's at Dawson College in 2006, in which a young student, Anastasia De Sousa, lost her life and dozens more were seriously injured. Marc Lépine's 1989 attack was in this brutal mould. But it was also unique in that it was explicitly framed as an act of misogyny: Lépine killed only women and, in a suicide note cum manifesto, blamed women in general and feminists specifically for his failures in life, especially his failed attempts to become an engineer. In the long run, the horrific attack at the École Polytechnique raised the profile of violence against women as a social and political issue. It also fuelled a campaign to reform federal firearms legislation, which bore fruit in 1995 when the Chrétien government created the Canadian Firearms Registry, requiring the registration of millions of shotguns and rifles owned by Canadians.[14]

Strong support for gun control is consistent with what many Quebecers think of as their "social-democratic" approach to the role of the state. This was certainly how the Bloc Québécois positioned itself during its heyday, from 1993 to 2011. And it helps make sense of the astounding NDP gains in the May 2011 election, where they went from one Quebec MP to fifty-nine. As political philosopher Charles Taylor has argued, social democracy has become, for many Quebecers, a defining characteristic of their society, as has a variety of liberalism that emphasizes collective over individual rights.[15]

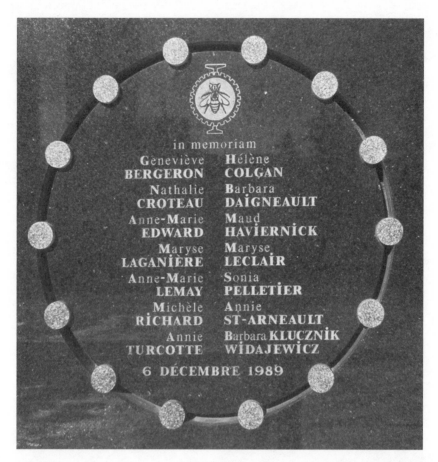

in memoriam

Geneviève   Hélène
BERGERON   COLGAN

Nathalie   Barbara
CROTEAU   DAÏGNEAULT

Anne-Marie   Maud
EDWARD   HAVIERNICK

Maryse   Maryse
LAGANIÈRE   LECLAIR

Anne-Marie   Sonia
LEMAY   PELLETIER

Michèle   Annie
RICHARD   ST-ARNEAULT

Annie   Barbara KLUCZNIK
TURCOTTE   WIDAJEWICZ

6 DÉCEMBRE 1989

Memorial plaque honouring the fourteen women killed at the École Polytechnique on 6 December 1989. This sober tribute in stone is embedded in the west exterior wall of the École Polytechnique's main building, where the shootings took place. It is one of the hundreds of commemorative objects, events, and spaces that have been dedicated to the memory of these women and to the prevention of violence against women in the decades since the tragedy. In 1991, for example, the Parliament of Canada designated 6 December as the National Day of Remembrance and Action on Violence Against Women. And to mark the tenth anniversary of the massacre, the City of Montreal commissioned artist Rose-Marie Goulet to design a new memorial in granite and steel, entitled *Nef pour quatorze reines* (Nave for Fourteen Queens) and installed in a public space near the Université de Montréal campus, which had been renamed Place du 6-décembre-1989. *Wikimedia Commons*

Quebecers shared some of these values, along with their cold climate and a passion for hockey, with Scandinavian countries such as Finland, roughly comparable to Quebec in terms of population and GDP.[16] For reasons that are not immediately clear, the two societies also shared a more troubling distinction: they both had relatively high suicide rates.

In 2007, Finland had the highest rate in Scandinavia and one of the highest in Western Europe, while Quebec had the highest incidence of suicide in Canada.[17] As in other Western countries, a substantial majority of suicide victims in the province (80 percent in 2007) were male, and suicide remained the leading cause of death for men aged 20–40.[18] Experts studying these trends must certainly take into account the pace and amplitude of the social, cultural, and economic change experienced at the turn of the twenty-first century, with particular attention to the ongoing challenge of replacing traditional values and institutions with new ones capable of providing nurture, stability, and a sense of purpose and identity to young people, especially boys and young men.

Social problems such as suicide, substance abuse, and domestic violence were particularly acute within Quebec's Aboriginal communities. The picture of social and economic conditions that emerged from the federal Royal Commission on Aboriginal Peoples (1991–96) was bleak indeed. The massive report showed that Indian and Inuit people in the mid-1990s were more likely to be unemployed, to rely on social assistance, to live in substandard housing, and to die in infancy than the average Canadian. Quebec's eleven First Nations certainly shared in these trends, with household income levels in line with those of the province's poorest towns and neighbourhoods.[19] At the same time, Quebec's Native communities continued the struggle begun in the 1960s and 1970s for greater control over ancestral lands and resources and, increasingly, for a measure of political autonomy.

There were significant victories along the way, as in 1978 when the landmark James Bay and Northern Quebec Agreement (see Chapter 11) was extended to cover Innu territories in northeastern Quebec, and in 1984 when the Cree-Naskapi Act superseded the federal Indian Act in the territory it covered and implemented a degree of self-government. More recently, in 2002, the Quebec government signed a new agreement with the Cree of Northern Quebec called *La Paix des Braves*, which resolved a long legal battle over implementation of the James Bay and Northern Quebec Agreement, and established a fifty-year arrangement for sharing both jurisdiction and the financial benefits of further hydroelectric development in the region. *La Paix des Braves* was also important symbolically, in the words of Bernard Landry, the Parti Québécois premier who signed it on behalf of the province, because "it opened a new era of collaboration and a real nation-to-nation relationship between the Cree and Quebec."[20]

Such a climate of collaboration and mutual respect would have been difficult to imagine a mere twelve years earlier. In the summer of 1990, plans to expand a golf course onto a small tract of forest near Oka sparked an armed standoff and a major political crisis over Aboriginal rights. The Mohawk people of nearby Kanesatake had for generations laid claim to the pine grove in question; their ancestors had planted the trees in the late nineteenth century and the area included a sacred burial ground. But efforts to assert Aboriginal title over it had been frustrated at every turn, most recently in 1986 when the federal Department of Indian Affairs and Northern Development rejected the Kanesatake people's specific land claim after almost a decade of negotiations. When the town of Oka announced its development plan for the pine grove, the Mohawks took direct action to block the project by barricading the access road on 11 March. Members of the militant "Warrior" faction were among them and were soon patrolling the barrier in full guerrilla mode, wearing masks and battle fatigues and carrying rifles and other weapons. On 11 July, the confrontation escalated in dramatic fashion when the provincial police force, the Sûreté du Québec (SQ), stormed the barricade.[21] The result was disastrous: a deadly gun battle in which an SQ officer, Marcel Lemay, was shot and killed; complete failure to resolve the armed standoff; and the expansion of the crisis to the south-shore Kahnawake reserve. There, in solidarity with the group at Oka, Mohawk warriors blocked the highways crossing their land, including the Mercier Bridge, the main link to Montreal for tens of thousands of suburban commuters.

The standoff at the barricades lasted eleven weeks. In early August, the Quebec government called in the Canadian Armed Forces to reinforce the beleaguered provincial police. The crisis was eventually resolved in late September through negotiation and pressure tactics and without further bloodshed. But the costs were high. Marcel Lemay, a thirty-one-year-old family man, had been killed. Racial tensions had reached the boiling point, particularly between francophones in south-shore communities like Chateauguay and the Mohawks of nearby Kahnawake. Even the simmering linguistic debate had been affected, as some francophones

The Oka crisis. *Le Devoir*, 12 July 1990. On 11 July 1990, 100 Sûreté du Québec officers in riot gear stormed the barricades at Oka. SQ constable Marcel Lemay was killed in the ensuing gun battle. This photograph, depicting a triumphant Mohawk Warrior atop a wrecked police vehicle, was published the following day on the front page of *Le Devoir*. Might the provocative image have contributed to a hardening of francophone public opinion against the Mohawk position in this dispute? *CP PHOTO/Tom Hanson*

complained of pro-Mohawk bias in the English-language media while some anglophones painted the Québécois majority as fundamentally intolerant of racial difference.[22] In the end, some forty-two Mohawks were arrested and brought to trial for their role in the violent confrontation. Only two, Ronald Cross and Roger Lazone, were convicted on any of the charges they faced.[23] As to the idea of expanding the golf course, it was scuttled by the town of Oka and rendered moot when the federal government purchased the pine grove to be administered under the terms of the Indian Act. Ten years after the crisis, in 2000, the Kanesatake Mohawks reached agreements with the federal government granting them a degree of control over some 960 hectares of territory. The accords were hailed by some as a step towards self-government but were resented by others in the Mohawk community as evidence of further federal paternalism. "As far as they were concerned," writes Aboriginal historian Olive Patricia Dickason, "the land had always been theirs."[24]

The Oka crisis highlights one aspect of the perennial tension between tradition and modernity, in this case between the traditional land claims of Quebec's First Nations and the development agenda of modern capitalism at the turn of the new millennium. Environmental issues were a central part of this increasingly complex discussion. At Oka, after all, the Mohawks were fighting to preserve a pine forest slated for suburban, leisure development.[25] Awareness of the ecological impact of development projects framed with reference to "modernity" and "progress" was rising in this period, and all such projects were now routinely assessed in terms of their environmental impact and sustainability. Established in 1978 by the first Parti Québécois government, the Bureau d'audiences publiques sur l'environment (BAPE) conducted public hearings into almost 300 projects between 1978 and 2011, including many relating to highways, landfills, dams, and more recently wind farms and shale gas development.[26]

Quebecers certainly value the natural environment. But there was a dissonance here for those still attached to the *Maîtres chez nous* economic model, which featured a high degree of state involvement and emphasized the large-scale exploitation of the province's vast forest, mineral, and energy resources. The flagship of that development strategy since the Quiet Revolution had been, without question, the government-owned electrical utility, Hydro-Québec. The massive public corporation focused on increasing its already impressive capacity to generate hydroelectric power—a form of energy that, while it had a major impact on northern ecosystems and on Aboriginal communities, did not rely on burning fossil fuels or contribute to the same extent to greenhouse gas emissions.[27]

Quebecers learned some important lessons about development, technology, and the environment when, in early January 1998, they were forced to deal with a winter storm like no other. The great ice storm struck southern Quebec between 4 and 10 January, when up to 100 millimetres of freezing rain and ice pellets fell in the hardest-hit regions (in the Montérégie, southeast of Montreal), coating trees, cars, homes, and power lines with a thick layer of ice. Falling tree limbs and the sheer weight of ice brought down thousands of kilometres of electrical and telephone lines, crushing in the process many of the great steel hydroelectric pylons that, for many, symbolized energy and modernity in the province. The resulting power failures, combined with falling temperatures in the ensuing days, created a serious crisis and put those without alternative heat sources—a large proportion of Quebecers heat their homes with electricity—at risk of hypothermia. The province declared a state of emergency on 6 January, Canadian Forces personnel were deployed again—this time to assist with the recovery effort— and crews worked day and night to repair the massive damage to the hydroelectric grid. Almost one million Hydro-Québec customers were without service at the depth of the crisis.[28] Schools were closed and some of their buildings converted into temporary shelters that provided beds and hot meals to thousands.

The ice storm and its aftermath demonstrated the generosity of spirit of the Quebec people, as volunteers rushed to staff emergency shelters and as those who had a woodstove or a fireplace welcomed others into their homes for days and weeks at a time. But the ultimate lessons were about the extent of the province's dependency on electrical energy, about the fragility of modern life in a cold climate, and about the vulnerability of even the most durable technologies, like Quebec's much-vaunted hydroelectric system, in the face of environmental catastrophe.

If, as essayist François Ricard argues, a "lyric generation" came of age during the Quiet Revolution, then certainly that tradition of creative expression was carried on and expanded by Québécois artists, poets, musicians, and writers in the ensuing thirty years or so. Already a prolific author and playwright in the 1960s and 1970s, Michel Tremblay staged his theatrical masterpiece, *Albertine en cinq temps*, in 1984, to be followed by dozens of powerful personal plays, novels, stories, and screenplays. Although the much younger Céline Dion can be a polarizing figure, her rags-to-riches story, along with her impressive technique as a pop vocalist, made her a much-loved icon of Quebec popular culture beginning in the 1980s. For every international diva, moreover, there were thousands of singers, songwriters, musicians, and composers contributing to a Quebec music scene that had never been more vital. Witness the popularity of singer-songwriters like Richard Desjardins, the Rouyn native who combined a successful musical career with documentary filmmaking while at the same time emerging as an important environmental and political activist. Witness also the success of the Montreal International Jazz Festival, which was conceived by

The January 1998 ice storm. Three million Quebec consumers lost electrical power during the 1998 ice storm, for periods ranging from a few hours to as long as a month. More than 3,000 kilometres of the province's massive distribution system were affected, including 16,000 hydroelectric poles, 4,000 transformers, and 150 steel pylons supporting high-voltage power lines. Although built to withstand 45 millimetres of ice, which was over three times the Canadian standard, many of these towers buckled under the weight of the ice—as much as 75 millimetres of it—that accumulated between 4 and 10 January 1998. Dairy farming (heavily reliant on electric milking machines), maple sugar production, and forestry were among the most severely affected economic sectors. Hydro-Québec later concluded that power outages might have been avoided by burying these high-voltage lines, but the cost of such a program was found to be prohibitive (on the order of $11 billion). And so the collapsed steel pylons were replaced with more steel pylons. See Kerry Mara et al., "Glazed Over: Canada Copes with the Ice Storm of 1998," *Environment* 41:1 (1999), 9–10. *Le Journal*

impresarios Alain Simard and André Ménard and launched in 1980, and which became one of the most important events of its kind in the world. As in theatre and music, so too have Quebecers excelled in other performing arts—including comedy, which has had its own hugely successful Montreal-based festival since producer Gilbert Rozon founded *Juste pour rire* (Just for Laughs) in 1983.

Quebec cinema was also a major success story, building on the tradition established in the 1970s with films like Claude Jutra's iconic *Mon Oncle Antoine* (1971) and including director Denys Arcand's string of triumphs since the 1980s. In 1986, Arcand's *Le Déclin de l'Empire Américan* won the International Critics Award at the Cannes Festival and was nominated

Montreal band Arcade Fire at the 2011 Grammys. Front man and lead singer Win Butler spoke on behalf of the other members of Arcade Fire after winning the Grammy Award for album of the year. "I just want to say thank you, merci, to Montreal, Quebec, for taking us and giving us a home and place to be in a band," said Butler. Contemporary Quebec has fostered creative talent on an impressive scale, the best of it garnering international audiences and recognition. As world-renowned musicians who got their start in bilingual, culturally diverse Montreal, the members of Arcade Fire are following in the footsteps of Oscar Peterson, Leonard Cohen, Kate and Anna McGarrigle, and many others. *AP Photo/Matt Sayles*

for an Academy Award in the Best Foreign Language Film category, an honour he later won (in 2003) for *Les Invasions Barbares*. Pioneers like Jutra and Arcand certainly inspired other filmmakers, to the point where French-language productions from Quebec came to dominate Canada's Genie Awards for cinema. At the 2006 award ceremony, for example, Jean-Marc Vallée's film *C.R.A.Z.Y.* was honoured with the Best Picture, Best Actor, and Best Director awards (among others), and was also recognized as the top-grossing Canadian film in terms of box-office receipts.

Whether in music, film, television, radio, or literature, moreover, the home-grown, French-language "star system" nurtured by television in the 1950s and 1960s persisted and thrived in the ensuing decades. Media attention and celebrity status were granted not just to those few who made it big on the international stage—like Céline Dion; Guy Laliberté, founder of the hugely successful *Cirque du Soleil*; and the internationally acclaimed theatrical director, producer, and actor Robert Lepage. In fact, there were many more *vedettes* (stars) who stayed and made their careers in the province and particularly in Montreal, which has become as dynamic a centre of francophone culture and creativity as one is likely to find anywhere on the planet.

The province's political landscape, meanwhile, changed in significant ways in the years following the second sovereignty referendum in 1995. Soon after the vote, Lucien Bouchard left Ottawa to replace Jacques Parizeau as PQ leader and provincial premier. Bouchard promised no new referendums on sovereignty until "winning conditions" were achieved; this was code, of course, for polling numbers predicting a victory for the "Yes" side. The focus of his government, instead, was to be on reining in government spending while attempting to maintain levels of service in key areas such as health, education, and social services.

With the referendum result having been so close, many Quebecers speculated in the late 1990s about what might have happened had it gone the other way. What, by extension, might be the consequences of a successful sovereignty vote in the future? Although all parties in the National Assembly insisted on the territorial integrity of Quebec, the issue of partition reared its head in 1996–97. Dozens of municipalities, many of them on Montreal's West Island, passed resolutions stating their intention to remain in Canada should Quebec decide to separate. Quebec's First Nations had taken a similar position on referendum day in 1995. Despite the history of paternalism by federal authorities, over 96 percent of the voting members of the Cree nation voted to stay in Canada should Quebec decide to secede.[29] These post-referendum years also saw the completion of the process, begun in the 1960s, of secularizing the province's system of public education. Although it required a constitutional amendment to accomplish, Bouchard's government acted in 1997 to eliminate the denominational (Catholic and Protestant) School Commissions, which had remained after the reforms of 1964, replacing them with a system of linguistic school boards that fit better with the cultural and linguistic realities of the 1990s.[30]

In 1998, Quebecers were asked to return to the polls, this time for a provincial election, not a referendum. Bouchard had been premier for almost two years but had never run in a general election as the PQ chief. The opposition leader, Daniel Johnson Jr., was seen as no match for the popular sovereignist. So Jean Charest, the federal Tory leader from Sherbrooke who had made an excellent showing in the 1995 "No" campaign, was recruited to lead the provincial Liberals into a November election. Charest did well in the election, polling slightly above the PQ in the popular vote but coming second where it counts—in the distribution of seats, which was almost identical to 1994. He stayed on as leader of the opposition while his former colleague Bouchard ramped up the fiscal-restraint measures, working to cut government spending, reduce annual deficits to zero, and start paying down the provincial debt.

Meanwhile, Chrétien's Liberal government in Ottawa, with leadership from Intergovernmental Affairs Minister Stéphane Dion, was preparing legislation to clarify the role and responsibility of the federal government in the event of an eventual "Yes" vote on sovereignty. Dion submitted three questions about such a scenario in a formal Reference to the Supreme Court in 1996. The Court's judgment, rendered two years later, declared that, in the event of a clear majority vote on a clear sovereignty question, the Canadian government would be legally bound to negotiate the secession of the province and any subsequent ties between Ottawa and Quebec City. The ensuing Clarity Act, drafted by Dion and passed by the Chrétien government in 2000, seemed to question the broad consensus in Quebec that defined a clear majority as 50 percent plus one. It angered provincial authorities by giving the House of Commons the power to determine whether or not a clear majority had expressed itself in any referendum, to decide whether a proposed referendum question was considered clear before the public vote, and to override any referendum decision deemed to violate the Clarity Act. So the Quebec government, in return, passed its own law emphasizing the province's right to self-determination under international law.

Neither piece of legislation would matter unless the sovereignists got their wish for a third referendum. As it happened, this was not to be, at least not in the short term. Lucien Bouchard was still the sovereignty movement's most eloquent and persuasive advocate, even though his cost-cutting agenda had begun to erode his popularity. So his unexpected retirement in March 2001 dealt a significant blow to the PQ's chances of staging a referendum in the near future. Bouchard's successor, Bernard Landry, was an experienced parliamentarian and administrator. But his dry style and technocratic image limited his ability to attract new converts to the cause. Landry was also saddled with his government's commitment to an extensive series of municipal mergers. The controversial measure took effect on 1 January 2002. By its terms, and without any local consultations, over 200 suburban municipalities were swallowed up by their larger neighbours. Montreal, for example, expanded to cover the entire island, if only briefly. Jean Charest saw an opportunity and understood that the most irate opponents of the PQ's forced amalgamations were in Montreal-area municipalities like Pointe-Claire and Westmount, where he could build on electoral strength. So the Liberals promised legislation that would allow the disgruntled communities to hold local referendums and, with a positive result, regain their autonomy. They also fired volley after volley at the government's management of the chronically underfunded health-care system, which featured long wait times, aging infrastructure, and a shortage of family doctors, particularly in rural areas. So when the votes were counted on 14 April 2003, the Liberals were back in power, having won 46 percent of the popular vote and 76 of the 125 National Assembly seats.

This was just a few months after infighting within the federal Liberal Party had led Jean Chrétien to announce his intention to resign. In December 2003, he was replaced as leader and prime minister by his chief rival, Quebecer Paul Martin, who, as minister of finance, had been a key player in Ottawa's successful campaign for fiscal restraint. But in February 2004, a scandal broke around the federal Liberals that hobbled Martin while seeming to provide further ammunition to the sovereignty forces. During the constitutional crisis of the mid-1990s, the Chrétien government had operated a sponsorship and advertising program, the purpose of which was to raise the profile of the Canadian "brand" in the Quebec political market. On 10 February, the federal Auditor General, Sheila Fraser, reported that up to $100 million of the $250 million sponsorship program had been awarded to Liberal-friendly advertising firms and Crown corporations in exchange for little or no work. Martin claimed that he had had no knowledge of the scandal prior to the Auditor General's report and ordered a Commission of Inquiry, to be headed by Justice John H. Gomery of Montreal. Martin also fired former minister of public works Alfonso Gagliano from his post as ambassador to Denmark. Quebecers followed the televised proceedings of the Gomery Commission with a special interest, both because the botched campaign had been designed for their consumption and because so many of those implicated in the scandal were Quebecers.

While it outraged most Quebecers, the sponsorship scandal did not provide as much traction for the sovereignty cause as the nationalists had hoped. It did, however, contribute to an important realignment in federal politics. By this time, the remnants of the once-proud Progressive Conservative party had reunited with the Western populists who had splintered off in the early 1990s. In the 28 June 2004 election, the freshly unified Conservative Party of Canada, led by Stephen Harper, posed a more credible threat to the Liberals than they had faced since 1993. Seriously weakened by the scandal and now led by Martin, who was disliked by those loyal to Chrétien and who could appear indecisive, the federal Liberals managed to win only a minority government. Under the leadership of Gilles Duceppe, the Bloc Québécois carried over 40 percent of the vote and matched their 1993 record by winning fifty-four of the seventy-five federal seats from Quebec.

When the Martin government returned the country to the polls less than two years later in January 2006, the result was another tight election with no party winning a majority of seats. But this time, the Liberals were reduced to 103 of the 308 seats in parliament and to only 30 percent of the popular vote. It was Stephen Harper who, having won 124 seats, would form a Conservative minority government—a government that went on to win a stronger minority in 2008 and then a clear majority in the May 2011 election. The first non-Quebecer since Lester Pearson in the 1960s to serve more than a few months as prime minister of Canada, Harper became more and more comfortable speaking French and seemed to display reasonably good political instincts where Quebec was concerned. In November 2006, for example, the House of Commons overwhelmingly passed a government motion recognizing that "the Québécois form a nation within a united Canada." This was certainly not the constitutionally enshrined "distinct society" status that had been on the negotiating table from 1987 through 1992. But it was meaningful to many Quebecers and widely applauded in the province.

As we have seen, the question of Quebec's identity as a nation has been a central and compelling one throughout the history of the province. Jacques Parizeau's speech on referendum night (see Chapter 12) revealed his conception of an ethnic and linguistic nation, an exclusive *us* to which he spoke and claimed to belong. Parizeau's Québécois nation shared both a common language and the French-Canadian heritage, including the modern, secularized legacies of the Quiet Revolution as well as the older traditions inherited from an intensely Catholic past. But where did that leave the English-speaking minority? And where, especially, did it leave the immigrant groups on which Quebec had come to rely, both to fill important niches in the labour market and to compensate for low birth rates and the relentless aging of the population?

In the late twentieth century, sources of immigration to Quebec had broadened to include countries whose religious and cultural practices were vastly different from the Christian heritage that, despite the secularization of the Quiet Revolution, was still a key reference point in the province. New patterns of ethnic, religious, and cultural diversity fuelled continuing debates about access to English schools and, more recently, polemics about the "reasonable accommodation" of minority groups and customs. There was evidence, moreover, that the integration of immigrants of African, Latin American, Middle Eastern, and Southeast Asian origin was not going particularly well. Trudeau's conception of multiculturalism, a cherished principle elsewhere in Canada, was considered a poor fit for the province, given the insecurity of its linguistic majority. But the provincial government's alternative model of ethnic pluralism, dubbed interculturalism, was lagging behind in its effort to improve material conditions for these non-European immigrants, who consistently earned less and were more likely to be unemployed than other Quebecers.[31]

The low point in this discussion was reached in January 2007 when the municipality of Hérouxville, located about fifty kilometres north of Trois-Rivières, adopted a set of "*normes de la vie*" (norms of life) directed at non-Christian immigrants—few of whom, by the way, had ever set foot in the small, homogeneous, francophone community. Nevertheless, municipal councillors felt the need to describe to potential immigrants the expected standards of behaviour in Quebec. Christmas trees, lights, and carols, they explained, had no particular religious significance and

Designing new accommodations for religious difference. The hijab became a contentious issue within the Quebec amateur soccer world when, during a tournament in Laval in February of 2007, an eleven-year-old Muslim girl named Asmahan (Azzy) Mansour was removed from a game because she was wearing a hijab. The referee cited FIFA's Law 4, which stipulates that a player may not wear anything that can pose a danger to herself or another player. The Quebec Soccer Federation subsequently upheld the ruling and banned the hijab from all soccer games in Quebec. Trained at the Université de Montréal, industrial designer Elham Seyed Javad proposed a practical solution: a sports hijab featuring a snugly fitting hood attached to a shirt worn under the team jersey, with no loose or untucked fabric that might constitute a hazard. The issue of head scarves and girls' soccer was one of many that focused attention on accommodation practices for members of religious minorities in 2007 and 2008. *Photograph by Peter McCabe*

were part of the community's traditions and norms. But other religious symbols, such as ritual weapons (the Sikh kirpan) and the head and face coverings (hijab, niqab) worn by many Islamic women would not be tolerated. Public schools were now secular and did not provide space or time for prayer by religious minorities. Quebec was an open and tolerant society and reasonable efforts to accommodate ethnic and religious difference should be made. But many of the accommodations made in recent years, they felt, had been "frankly unreasonable," such as the case in which police officials had been instructed to make sure Orthodox Jewish men were dealt with by policemen, not policewomen. Women in this society, moreover, were equal to men and should not be stoned to death or burned alive; nor was female "circumcision" to be tolerated.[32]

The degree of xenophobia and ignorance displayed in this document attracted international media attention, most of it focusing on the incredible admonition to immigrant men not to stone or burn their wives and daughters. Premier Charest responded in February by appointing the Consultation Commission on Accommodation Practices Related to Cultural Differences, to be headed by two respected academics: the renowned political philosopher Charles Taylor and the prolific historical sociologist Gérard Bouchard, incidentally the brother of the former premier. Their report was delivered in 2008 and concluded that there was no profound crisis over cultural difference. Media coverage of various reported cases of "unreasonable accommodation," they argued, was the source of countless exaggerations and distortions and, therefore, of much of the anxiety.[33] A calmer, more thoughtful, and less reactive approach was the way forward. "[I]ntegration through pluralism, equality and reciprocity," they wrote, "is by far the most commendable, reasonable course." At the same time, they argued, everyone involved must appreciate the unique position of French-speaking Quebecers regarding the entire issue of cultural integration. Quebecers of French-Canadian heritage, it would seem, were still learning to behave as a confident, self-assured majority, capable of accommodating the differences and aspirations of smaller, less powerful groups within the collectivity.

As Bouchard and Taylor were beginning to tour the province, holding hearings and developing their positions on interculturalism, open secularism, and harmonization practices, the Liberal government faced the electorate to seek a third consecutive mandate. Charest called the election for 26 March 2007, hoping to profit politically from a federal budget that he expected to favour the province and to demonstrate his ability to work with the Harper government. The debate over reasonable accommodation had polarized the electorate to some extent, with the rural, ethnically homogeneous areas more inclined to sympathize with the Hérouxville town council. Some elements of that cause were adopted by the ADQ's Mario Dumont, who argued that Quebec needed to be explicit about its norms, values, and identity and should adopt a formal constitution to clarify those matters. Under its new leader André Boisclair (Bernard Landry had resigned in June 2005), the Parti Québécois pledged to hold a public consultation on sovereignty early in the mandate. But there was little public appetite for a third referendum on independence. And some of the sovereignist vote, in any case, was being drained off by the fledgling Québec solidaire party, while more conservative nationalists found the ADQ to be an interesting option. So when the votes were counted, the Liberals and the PQ had both lost ground, while the ADQ made spectacular gains, winning 41 of 125 seats in the legislature and forming the official opposition for the first time in its brief history. The biggest losers were André Boisclair and the sovereignist PQ, who lost nine seats and fell below 30 percent in popular support, prompting Boisclair's resignation and the nomination of Pauline Marois to succeed him.

Parti Québécois leader Pauline Marois makes a point in the National Assembly, March 2011. *Le Soleil*, 30 March 2011. Marois was the first woman to lead a major political party in the province. She replaced André Boisclair after the latter's stinging defeat in the 2007 provincial election. *CP PHOTO/Jacques Boissinot*

For his part, Jean Charest was now the head of a minority government, only the second such administration in the province's history. It was rather a short-lived government, however, as Charest decided to return to the polls in December 2008 to seek the majority that had eluded him the previous year. In this he was successful as the Liberal position in the National Assembly rose from a minority (48) to a bare majority: 66 of the 125 seats. But the big stories on the morning after the vote seemed to be the excellent showing of the PQ, which had once again drawn over 40 percent of the votes, enough to form the official opposition, and the crumbling of the ADQ, which fell back to seven seats and saw its dynamic young leader announce his resignation and, later, his decision to leave active politics and become a TV talk-show host.

Without the benefit of a crystal ball or a time machine, it would be foolish indeed to conclude this book with any kind of prediction about Quebec's political and constitutional destiny. It is possible, however, to outline two competing perspectives, focusing on the recent history of the sovereignty movement and on the question that many readers may wish us to address in closing: whether or not a successful referendum seems likely at any point in the future.

The first perspective is as follows: the sovereignty option remains attractive to a significant minority of Quebecers, as the polling numbers show. But its proponents have now lost two straight referendums. They are prone to internal dissension and have had chronic difficulties around unity and leadership. In all likelihood, the sovereignty forces will never generate more support than the 49.4 percent they managed in 1995, with a strong leader and in the wake of a string of dramatic rejections by the rest of Canada. Many in the Quebec electorate, moreover, are tired of the divisive constitutional debate and ready for new faces and new ideas. Few now feel the burning resentment against economic colonialism that fired the generation of the Quiet Revolution. All in all, then, nationalists would do well to give up on their dream of an independent Quebec and focus on other things.

While this is a comforting view for some, a converse perspective can also be argued: that the long-term trend in support for sovereignty is strongly upwards. In 1966, parties promoting independence were marginal, attracting less than 9 percent of the popular vote and electing no members. But their successor organization, the Parti Québécois, has formed majority governments in four provincial elections since then. Between 1993 and 2011, sovereignists consistently held a majority of the Quebec seats in the federal Parliament (although this was no longer the case after the NDP sweep in 2011). The share of "Yes" votes in the two plebiscites on sovereignty is also sharply upwards, from 40 percent in 1980 to over 49 percent—including some 60 percent of francophones—in 1995. Economically, the province is no longer as dependent on the rest of Canada as it once was, and there is greater faith in Quebec's ability to go it alone, particularly under the terms of NAFTA. Given these patterns, then, it seems likely that at some point in the future, a majority of Quebecers will support sovereignty, the "Yes" side will win a referendum, and the federal government will have no choice but to negotiate.

So which is it? Could a new, dynamic leader, a fresh approach, or perhaps some new gaffe or outrage by the federal government sufficiently galvanize the sovereignty movement to take them over the top, into the promised land of 50 percent plus one? Or was the 49.4 percent obtained in 1995, with an electorate stoked by post-Meech outrage and a charismatic leader in Lucien Bouchard, the best the sovereignty forces are likely to do any time soon? Knowing the answers to these questions remains as difficult today as it was in 1995. And so it remains impossible to say with any certainty what kind of political space Quebec may become in the future.

We can say a number of things, however, about what Quebec *is* in the present . . . about what it has become in the course of its history. Quebec is a beacon of French-language culture in North America. It is a nation within a nation, and was so recognized, symbolically at least, by the federal Parliament in 2006. It is a subordinate political partner in the federal system, but one that has special status in fact if not in law by virtue of a range of powers that other provinces do not exercise, in key areas such as taxation and immigration. It is a curious and fascinating political space in which "mainstream politics" have since the 1980s been distilled into a running contest between sovereignist and federalist coalitions, with third parties occasionally adding some variety. It is also, finally, a society which continues to search for its collective identity, a search well illustrated by the work of the recent Bouchard-Taylor Commission, and one which faces a number of significant challenges. Among these is the difficulty of convincing its substantial and dynamic English-Canadian and immigrant communities to feel included in a new, pluralist Quebec identity, with a commitment to French as the common public language as one of its core values.

It remains possible that future historians will tell the story of Quebec's social, cultural, and political life at the turn of the twenty-first century as a key chapter in the long march towards independence. But it is virtually certain that in their narratives, like ours, the struggle over national identity and political sovereignty will have to share space with different kinds of questions, such as those surrounding globalization, technology, gender, sexuality, minorities, and the environment. Sorting out the tensions and dissonances between various approaches to these issues— traditional, modern, or postmodern—will remain a key challenge for historians and citizens in the new century, whether or not we see some clear resolution of the national question.

NOTES

INTRODUCTION: TRADITION AND MODERNITY

1. See, for example, Éric Bédard, with the collaboration of Myriam D'Arcy, *Enseignement et recherché universitaires au Québec: L'histoire nationale negligée* ([Montreal]: Coalition pour l'histoire and Fondation Lionel-Groulx, 2011).

2. Social and gender historian Denyse Baillargeon made this point eloquently in a rejoinder to Éric Bédard. See Baillargeon, "Histoire: Le soi-disant déclin de l'histoire nationale au Québec," *Le Devoir*, 14 October 2011, A9.

3. See Ronald Rudin, *Making History in Twentieth-Century Quebec* (Toronto: University of Toronto Press, 1997).

4. Gérard Bouchard, *Entre l'Ancien et le Nouveau Monde: Le Québec comme population neuve et culture fondatrice* (Ottawa: Les Presses de l'Université d'Ottawa, 1996), 9.

5. Damien-Claude Bélanger, *Prejudice and Pride: Canadian Intellectuals Confront the United States, 1891–1945* (Toronto: University of Toronto Press, 2011), 6.

6. Jocelyn Letourneau, *Le Québec, les Québécois: Un parcours historique* (Quebec: Éditions Fides, 2004), 6.

7. Lianne McTavish and Jingjing Zheng, "Rats in Alberta: Looking at Pest-Control Posters from the 1950s," *Canadian Historical Review* 92, no. 3 (2011): 545; Patricia E. Roy and John Herd Thompson, *British Columbia: Land of Promises* (Don Mills, ON: Oxford University Press, 2005), 2–6.

8. In 1981, the Institut québécois de recherché sur la culture (IQRC) began publishing detailed histories of twenty-one regions and the two metropolises within Quebec. For the volume on the largest part of the Eastern Townships, see Jean-Pierre Kesteman, Peter Southam, and Diane Saint-Pierre, *Histoire des Cantons de l'Est* (Sainte-Foy, QC: Les Presses de l'Université Laval, 1998).

9. For a recent examination of how Anglo-Quebecers continue to be viewed as antagonists in the province's national development, see Paul Zanazanian, "Towards Developing an 'Anglo-Québécois' Information Resource Book for School History Teachers in Quebec: Thoughts from a Qualitative Study," *Journal of Eastern Townships Studies* 36 (2011): 69–95.

10. On the increasing domination of Montreal within the province, see Letourneau, *Le Québec, les Québécois*, 102–104.

11. Jocelyn Létourneau, "The Debate on History Education in Quebec," in *New Possibilities for the Past: Shaping History Education in Canada*, ed. Penney Clark (Vancouver: UBC Press, 2011), 93.

1 THE FUR TRADE COLONY

1. Guy Laperrière, *Les Cantons de l'Est* (Sainte-Foy, QC: Les Presses de l'Université Laval, 2009), 15–18.

2. William R. Morrison, *The North: The Yukon and Northwest Territories* (Toronto: Oxford University Press, 1998), 28–35; Serge Courville, ed., *Atlas historique du Québec: Population et territoire* (Sainte-Foy, QC: Les Presses de l'Université Laval, 1996), 5–9, 13; R. Cole Harris, ed., *Historical Atlas of Canada*, vol. 1, *From the Beginnings to 1800* (Toronto: University of Toronto Press, n.d.), 1–6.

3. Raynald Parent, "L'effritement de la civilisation Amérindienne," in *Histoire du Québec*, ed. Jean Hamelin (Montreal: France-Amérique, 1976), 34–39. On the Abenakis, see Colin G. Calloway, *The Western Abenakis of Vermont, 1600–1800: War, Migration, and the Survival of an Indian People* (Norman: University of Oklahoma Press, 1990).

4. Parent, "L'effritement," 30, 33, 41–44; John Dickinson and Brian Young, *A Short History of Quebec*, 3rd. ed. (Montreal: McGill-Queen's University Press, 2003), 6–7; Richard White, *The Middle Ground: Indians, Empires and Republics in the Great Lakes Region, 1650–1815* (Cambridge: Cambridge University Press, 1991), 37–39.

5. See D.K. Richter, "War and Culture: The Iroquois Experience," *William and Mary Quarterly* 40 (1983): 529–59; Dickinson and Young, *Short History*, 8–10; and Parent, "L'effritement," 30–31.

6. Parent, "L'effritement," 46–47, 56–57, 115; Denys Delâge, *Bitter Feast: Amerindians and Europeans in Northeastern North America, 1600–64*, trans. Jane Brierley (Vancouver: UBC Press, 1993), chap. 2.

7. Parent, "L'effritement," 48–49.

8. See, for example, Carole Devens, "Separate Confrontations: Gender as a Factor in Indian Adaptation to European Culture in New France," *American Quarterly* 38 (1986): 461–80.

9. Delâge, *Bitter Feast*, 56–57; White, *The Middle Ground*, chap. 3.

10. Marcel Trudel, *Introduction to New France* (Toronto: Holt, Rinehart and Winston, 1968), 6–7; Jacques Mathieu, "L'Héritage d'Adam," in Hamelin, ed., *Histoire du Québec*, 65–67.

11. Brett Rushforth, "The Establishment of a French Empire in North America," in Stéphan Gervais, Christopher Kirby, and Jarrett Rudy, eds., *Quebec Questions: Quebec Studies for the Twenty-First Century* (Don Mills, ON: Oxford University Press, 2011), 5.

12. Christian Morissonneau, "Champlain's Dream," in *Champlain: The Birth of French America*, ed. Raymonde Litalien and Denis Vaugeois, trans. by Käthe Roth (Montreal: Les éditions du Septentrion and McGill-Queen's University Press, 2004), 258.

13. See Ramsay Cook, "Donnacona Discovers Europe: Rereading Jacques Cartier's Voyages," in *The Voyages of Jacques Cartier* (Toronto: University of Toronto Press, 1993), xxix–xxxi.

14. O.P. Dickason, "The Sixteenth-Century French Version of Empire: The Other Side of Self-Determination," in *Decentering the Renaissance: Canada and Europe in Multidisciplinary Perspective, 1500–1700*, ed. Germaine Warkentin and Carolyn Podruchny (Toronto: University of Toronto Press, 2001), 88.

15. Rushforth, "The Establishment of a French Empire," 5.

16. Peter Pope, "The Practice of Portage in the Early Modern North Atlantic: Introduction to an Issue in Maritime Historical Anthropology," *Journal of the Canadian Historical Association*, n.s. 6 (1995): 20–21.

17. Bernard Allaire, "The European Fur Trade and the Context of Champlain's Arrival," in *Champlain*, ed. Litalien and Vaugeois, 50–58.

18. Mathieu, "L'Héritage," 85–86.

19. Éric Thierry, "A Creation of Champlain's: The Order of Good Cheer," in *Champlain*, ed. Litalien and Vaugeois, 135–83.

20. Laurier Turgeon, "The French in New England before Champlain," in *Champlain*, ed. Litalien and Vaugeois, 98.

21. Alain Beaulieu, "The Birth of the Franco-American Alliance," in *Champlain*, ed. Litalien and Vaugeois, 153–60.

22. Allan Greer, "La Nouvelle-France dans le contexte d'histoire des Amériques," in *Mémoires de Nouvelle-France: De France en Nouvelle-France*, ed. Philippe Joutard and Thomas Wien (Rennes: Presses Universitaires de Rennes, 2005), 159–60.

23. Allan Greer, *The People of New France* (Toronto: University of Toronto Press, 1997), 5.

24. Conrad Heidenreich, "The Beginning of French Exploration Out of the St. Lawrence Valley:

Motives, Methods, and Changing Attitudes towards Native People," in *Decentering the Renaissance*, ed. Warkentin and Podruchny, 241–43.

25. R. Douglas Francis, Richard Jones, and Donald B. Smith, *Origins: Canadian History to Confederation*, 5th ed. (Scarborough, ON: Nelson, 2004), 48.

26. Jacques Mathieu, "Les programmes de colonisation," in *Histoire*, ed. Hamelin, 98–99; Morissonneau, "Champlain's Dream," 264–65. The quote is from Rushforth, "The Establishment of a French Empire," 8.

27. Dominique Deslandres, "Champlain and Religion," in *Champlain*, ed. Litalien and Vaugeois, 191–204.

28. Heidenreich, "Beginning of French Exploration," 244–45; Francis et al., *Origins*, 52.

29. Delâge, *Bitter Feast*, 291–97.

30. See the chapter on Marie de l'Incarnation in Natalie Zemon Davis, *Women on the Margins: Three Seventeenth-Century Lives* (Cambridge, MA: Harvard University Press, 1995).

31. K.M. Morrison, "Montagnais Missionization in Early New France: The Syncretic Imperative," *American Indian Culture and Research Journal* 10, no. 3 (1986): 1–23.

32. Carole Blackburn, *Harvest of Souls: The Jesuit Missions and Colonialism in North America, 1632–1650* (Montreal: McGill-Queen's University Press, 2000), 22–25.

33. See J. Steckley, "The Warrior and the Lineage: Jesuit Use of Iroquoian Images to Communicate Christianity," *Ethnohistory* 39 (1992): 478–509.

34. See Peter N. Moogk, *La Nouvelle France: The Making of French Canada—A Cultural History* (East Lansing, MI: Michigan State University Press, 2000), 47; and Blackburn, *Harvest of Souls*, chap. 3.

35. Heidenreich, "Beginning of French Exploration," 245–46.

36. See Allan Greer, "Colonial Saints: Gender, Race, and Hagiography in New France," *William and Mary Quarterly* 57, no. 2 (2000): 323–48.

37. Parent, "Leffritement," 50; Matthieu, "Les programmes," 100.

38. Thomas Wien, "Vie et transformation du coureur de bois," in *Mémoires de Nouvelle-France*, ed. Joutard and Wien, 181.

39. White, *The Middle Ground*, 57–58, 68, 75.

40. John A. Dickinson, "La guerre iroquoise et la mortalité en Nouvelle-France, 1608–1666," *Revue d'histoire de l'Amérique française* 36 (1982): 31–54; Louise Dechêne, *Le Peuple, l'État et la Guerre au Canada sous le Régime français* (Montreal: Boréal, 2008), 94–105. On the Dollard myth, see Patrice Groulx, *Pièges de la mémoire: Dollard des Ormeaux, les Amérindiens et nous* (Hull, QC: Vents d'Ouest, 1998).

41. Matthieu, "Les programmes," 103, 121, 123–24.

42. Gilles Havard, "Virilité et 'ensauvagement': Le corps de coureur de bois (XVIIe et XVIIIe s.)," *Clio: Histoire, femmes et société* 27 (2008): 57–74; Arnaud Balvay, "Tattooing and Its Role in French–Native American Relations in the Eighteenth Century," *French Colonial History* 9 (2008): 1–14.

2 THE SETTLEMENT COLONY

1. Peter N. Moogk, *La Nouvelle France: The Making of French Canada—A Cultural History* (East Lansing, MI: University of Michigan Press, 2000), 107.

2. Pierre Goubert, *The Ancien Régime French Society, 1600–1750* (New York: Harper and Row, 1969), 102, 130, 134.

3. Brett Rushforth, "The Establishment of a French Empire in North America," in *Quebec Questions: Quebec Studies for the Twenty-First Century*, ed. Stéphan Gervais, Christopher Kirby, and Jarrett Rudy (Don Mills, ON: Oxford University Press, 2011), 10.

4. Moogk, *La Nouvelle France*, 105.

5. Thomas Wein, "Sur quelques migrations transatlantiques," in *Mémoires de Nouvelle-France: De France en Nouvelle-France*, eds. Philippe Joutard and Thomas Wien (Rennes: Presses Universitaires de Rennes, 2005), 300.

6. Moogk, *La Nouvelle France*, 106.

7. Moogk also includes 900 slaves, though there were closer to 4,200. Moogk, *La Nouvelle France*, 113.

8. Allan Greer, *The People of New France* (Toronto: University of Toronto Press, 1997), 20–25; Denys Delâge, *Bitter Feast: Amerindians and Europeans in Northeastern North America, 1600– 64*, trans. Jane Brierley (Vancouver: UBC Press, 1993), 246–58; Robert C.H. Sweeny, "What Difference Does a Mode Make? A Comparison of Two Seventeenth-Century Colonies: Canada and Newfoundland," *William and Mary Quarterly*, 3d series, 63, no. 2 (2006), 288.

9. See Louise Dechêne, *Le Peuple, l'État et la Guerre au Canada sous le Régime français* (Montreal: Boréal, 2008), 219–21.

10. Jacques Mathieu, "Province de France (1663–1700)," in *Histoire du Québec*, ed. Jean Hamelin (Montreal: France-Amérique, 1976), 132–33.

11. Ibid., 136–37.

12. Dechêne, *Le Peuple, l'État et la Guerre*, 29, 223.

13. S.D. Standen, "Politics, Patronage and the Imperial Interest: Charles de Beauharnais's Disputes with Gilles Hocquart," *Canadian Historical Review* 60 (1979): 22.

14. Mathieu, "Province de France," 136–39.

15. Ibid., 131; Moogk, *La Nouvelle France*, 73; Dechêne, *Le Peuple, l'État et la Guerre*, 222.

16. Dechêne, *Le Peuple, l'État et la Guerre*, 224–25.

17. Dechêne states that there were initially few resident seigneurs to assume the position of militia captain, and that they avoided it as it became more onerous in the eighteenth century. Dechêne, *Le Peuple, l'État et la Guerre*, 235, 240–43, 247–55.

18. See Moogk, *La Nouvelle France*, chap. 3.

19. See K.A. Stanbridge, "England, France and their North American Colonies: An Analysis of Absolutist State Power in Europe and in the New World," *Journal of Historical Sociology* 10, no. 1 (1997): 27–55, esp. 37.

20. Terence Crowley, "'Thunder Gusts': Popular Disturbances in Early French Canada," in Canadian Historical Association, *Historical Papers/Communications historique* 14, no. 1 (1979): 11–32; Dechêne, *Le Peuple, l'État et la Guerre*, 268–71.

21. Louise Dechêne, *La Partage des Subsistances au Canada sous le Régime Français* (Montreal: Boréal, 1994); Dechêne, *Le Peuple, l'État et la Guerre*, 19, 30, chap. 7.

22. Mathieu, "Province de France," 163.

23. Ibid., 160; Moogk, *La Nouvelle France*, 84.

24. See W.J. Eccles, "The Social, Economic, and Political Significance of the Military Establishment in New France," in *Essays on New France* (Toronto: Oxford University Press, 1987); Dechêne, *Le Peuple, l'État et la Guerre*, 139–45. Dechêne notes (149–52) that the nobility lost interest in commanding the militia units when the officer corps of the professional army became Canadianized, with the result that the militia simply became a reserve of conscripts.

25. Sweeny, "What Difference Does a Mode Make?" 284.

26. Jean-Pierre Hardy, *Chercher fortune en Nouvelle-France* (Montreal: Libre Expression, 2007), 103, 111.

27. Rotures were approximately 150 metres wide and 1,600 metres deep. John Dickinson and Brian Young, *A Short History of Quebec*, 3rd ed. (Montreal: McGill-Queen's University Press, 2003), 32.

28. See Louise Dechêne, *Habitants and Merchants in Seventeenth-Century Montreal*, trans. Liana Vardi (Montreal: McGill-Queen's University Press, 1992), chap. 7; and Allan Greer, *Peasant,*

Lord, and Merchant: Rural Society in Three Quebec Parishes, 1740–1840 (Toronto: University of Toronto Press, 1985), chaps. 4 and 5.

29. Greer, *People of New France*, 31–33.

30. Alain Laberge, "L'immigrant migrant ou les chemins de l'enracinement au Canada sous le régime français," in *Mémoires de Nouvelle-France*, ed. Joutard and Wien, 167–78.

31. For details, see Moogk, *La Nouvelle France*, 224–27; and Dickinson and Young, *Short History*, 86–87.

32. Hardy, *Chercher fortune*, 17–18, 78–83.

33. Allan Greer, "La Nouvelle-France dans le contexte d'histoire des Amériques," in *Mémoires de Nouvelle-France*, ed. Joutard and Wien, 158–59.

34. Hardy, *Chercher fortune*, 85–88, 192.

35. See D. Miquelon, "Canada's Place in the French Imperial Economy: An Eighteenth-Century Overview," *French Historical Studies* 15 (1988): 432–43.

36. Hardy, *Chercher fortune*, 164–72; Roger Magnuson, *Education in New France* (Montreal: McGill-Queen's University Press, 1992), 86, 90.

37. Hardy, *Chercher fortune*, 185.

38. See R.C. Harris, "The Extension of France into Rural Canada," in *European Settlement and Development in North America*, ed. James Gibson (Toronto: University of Toronto Press, 1978), 27–45.

39. Louis Lavallée, *La Prairie en Nouvelle-France, 1647–1760: Étude d'histoire sociale* (Montreal: McGill-Queen's University Press, 1992), chap. 5; Colin M. Coates, *The Metamorphoses of Landscape and Community in Early Quebec* (Montreal: McGill-Queen's University Press, 2000), chap. 6; Hardy, *Chercher fortune*, 104–105; Dechêne, *Le Peuple, l'État et la Guerre*, 309–14, 326–27, 333–34.

40. Mathieu, "Province de France," 152.

41. Moogk, *La Nouvelle France*, 195–209.

42. Peter Moogk, "Apprenticeship Indentures: A Key to Artisan Life in New France," in Canadian Historical Association, *Historical Papers/Communications historique*, 6, no. 1 (1971): 66–70.

43. Hardy, *Chercher fortune*, 31–32.

44. Simon Schama, *Rough Crossings: Britain, the Slaves and the American Revolution* (Toronto: Viking Canada, 2005), 68; Evelyn Powell Jennings, "State Enslavement in Colonial Havana, 1763–1790," in *Slavery Without Sugar: Diversity in Caribbean Economy and Society Since the 17th Century*, ed. Verene A. Shepherd (Tampa: University of Florida Press, 2002), 160, 165.

45. See Marcel Trudel, with Micheline D'Allaire, *Deux siècles d'esclavage au Québec* (Montreal: Hurtubise HMH, 2004); see also the review of this book by Gilles Havard in *Revue d'Histoire de l'Amérique française* 59 (2005): 180–82; Hardy, *Chercher fortune*, 33; and Brett Rushforth, "'A Little Flesh We Offer You': The Origins of Indian Slavery in New France," *William and Mary Quarterly* 60 (2003): 777–808.

46. See Greer, *People of New France*, 85–88; Delâge, *Bitter Feast*, 312–16; and Denyse Beaugrand-Champagne, *Le Procès de Marie-Josèphe-Angélique* (Outremont: Libre Expression, 2004).

47. See Guillaume Aubert, "'The Blood of France': Race and Purity of Blood in the French Atlantic World," *William and Mary Quarterly*, 3d series, 61, no. 3 (2004): 439–78; and Saliha Belmessous, "Assimilation and Racialism in Seventeenth and Eighteenth-Century French Colonial Policy," *American Historical Review* 110, no. 2 (2005): 322–49.

48. Dickinson and Young, *Short History*, 68.

49. Greer, *People of New France*, 18–19, 40–41, 63, 79–84.

50. Greer, "La Nouvelle-France," 163.

51. See K.M. Morrison, "Baptism and Alliance: The Symbolic Mediations of Religious Syncretism," *Ethnohistory* 37 (1990): 429–33; and Karen Anderson, *Chain Her by One Foot: The Subjugation of Women in Seventeenth-century New France* (London: Routledge, 1991).

52. Nancy Shoemaker, "Kateri Tekakwitha's Tortuous Path to Sainthood," in *Negotiations of Change: Historical Perspectives on Native American Women*, ed. Nancy Shoemaker (New York: Routledge, 1995), 60–66; David Blanchard, ". . . To the Other Side of the Sky: Catholicism at Kahnawake, 1667–1700," *Anthropoligica* 24 (1982): 97. For a detailed study on Tekakwitha's life and beatification, see Allen Greer, *Mohawk Saint: Catherine Tekakwitha and the Jesuits* (Oxford: Oxford University Press, 2005). Cornelius Jaenan suggests that "religious dimorphism," the simultaneous adhesion to the tenets of Catholicism and the traditional native belief system, was more common than syncretism. See his "Amerindian Responses to French Missionary Intrusion, 1611–1760: A Categorization," in *Religion/Culture: Comparative Canadian Studies*, ed. William Westfall et al. (Ottawa: Association for Canadian Studies, 1985), 185, 192–93. James Axtell claims, on the other hand, that Native converts were as Christian as their European counterparts. See his "Were Indian Conversions Bona Fide?" in *After Columbus: Essays in the Ethnohistory of Colonial North America* (New York: Oxford University Press, 1988).

53. See Jan Grabowski, "Searching for the Common Ground: Natives and French in Montreal, 1700–1730," *Proceedings of the French Colonial Historical Society* 18 (1993): 59–73; and "French Criminal Justice and Indians in Montreal, 1610–1760," *Ethnohistory* 43, no. 3 (1996): 405–29.

54. Dale Miquelon, *New France, 1701–1744: "A Supplement to Europe"* (Toronto: McLelland and Stewart, 1987), 156; Thomas Wien, "Vie et transformation du coureurs de bois," in *Mémoires de Nouvelle-France*, ed. Joutard and Wien, 182.

55. Jan Noel, "'Nagging Wife' Revisited: Women and the Fur Trade in New France," *French Colonial History* 7 (2006): 45–60.

56. André Lachance and Sylvie Savoie, "Violence, Marriage, and Family Honour: Aspects of the Legal Regulation of Marriage in New France," in Tina Loo and Lorna McLean, eds, *Historical Perspectives on Law and Society in Canada* (Toronto: Copp Clark Longman, 1994), 147–49.

57. Greer, *People of New France*, 69–70; Dickinson and Young, *Short History*, 100–101.

58. Hardy, *Chercher fortune*, 154.

59. Dickinson and Young, *Short History*, 43–44.

60. See Terrence A. Crowley, "Women, Religion, and Freedom in New France," in *Women and Freedom in Early America*, ed. L.D. Eldridge (New York: New York University Press, 1997); Jan Noel, "Caste and Clientage in an Eighteenth-Century Quebec Convent," *Canadian Historical Review* 82 (2001): 465–90; and Leslie Choquette, "'Ces Amazones du Grand Dieu': Women and Mission in Seventeenth-Century Canada," *French Historical Studies* 17, no. 3 (1992): 627–55.

61. Alan Gowans, *Church Architecture in New France* (Toronto: University of Toronto Press, 1955), 66–67; Moogk, *La Nouvelle France*, 210; Marcel Trudel, *Introduction to New France* (Toronto: Holt, Rinehart and Winston, 1968), 245–47.

62. Ollivier Hubert, "Ritual Performance and Parish Sociability: French-Canadian Families at Mass from the Seventeenth to the Nineteenth Century," in *Households of Faith: Family, Gender and Community in Canada, 1760–1969*, ed. Nancy Christie (Montreal: McGill-Queen's University Press, 2002), 41–43; Dechêne, *Le Peuple, l'État et la Guerre*, 449–51.

63. Moogk, *La Nouvelle France*, chap. 9.

64. See Cornelius Jaenan, *The Role of the Church in New France* (Toronto: McGraw-Hill Ryerson, 1976), chap. 6; Greer, *People of New France*, 35–36; Hubert, "Ritual Performance," 40, 60–63; Hardy, *Chercher fortune*, 186–99; and Marie-Aimée Cliche, "Unwed Mothers, Families and Society during the French Régime," in *Canadian Family History: Selected Readings*, ed. Bettina Bradbury (Toronto: Copp Clark Pitman, 1992), 33–65.

3 THE MILITARY COLONY

1. Louise Dechêne, *Le Peuple, l'État et la Guerre au Canada sous le Régime français* (Montreal: Boréal, 2008), 109–19.

2. Ibid., 195–96. On the origins of the militia stereotype, see her chapter 1.

3. John Dickinson and Brian Young, *A Short History of Quebec* (Montreal: McGill-Queen's University Press, 2003), 72–74; Dale Miquelon, *New France, 1701–1744: "A Supplement to Europe"* (Toronto: McClelland and Stewart, 1987), 154–58.

4. Jacques Mathieu, "Province de France (1663–1700)," in *Histoire du Québec*, ed. Jean Hamelin (Montreal: France-Amérique, 1976), 176.

5. For details, see Dechêne, *Le Peuple, l'État et la Guerre*, 155–63.

6. See Colin G. Calloway, *The Western Abenakis of Vermont, 1600–1800: War, Migration, and the Survival of an Indian People* (Norman: University of Oklahoma Press, 1990); and Dechêne, *Le Peuple, l'État et la Guerre*, 167–87.

7. Cornelius Jaenan, *Friend and Foe: Aspects of French-Indian Cultural Contact in the Sixteenth and Seventeenth Centuries* (Toronto: McClelland and Stewart, 1976), 288–89.

8. For details, see Gilles Havard, *The Great Peace of Montreal of 1701: French–Native Diplomacy in the Seventeenth Century* (Montreal: McGill-Queen's University Press, 2001).

9. See Dale Miquelon, "Les Pontchartrain se penchent sur leurs cartes de l'Amérique: Les cartes et l'impérialisme, 1690–1712," *Revue d'histoire de l'Amérique française*, 59 (2005): 153–71, which rejects Eccles's thesis that France pursued an aggressive imperialist policy in the West after 1701.

10. W.J. Eccles, "The Social, Economic, and Political Significance of the Military Establishment in New France," in *Essays on New France* (Toronto: Oxford University Press, 1987), 110.

11. Miquelon, *New France*, 160–64; S.D. Standen, "'Personnes sans caractère': Private Merchants, Post Commanders, and the Regulation of the Western Fur Trade, 1720–1745," in *De France en Nouvelle France*, ed. Hubert Watelet (Ottawa: Les Presses de l'Université d'Ottawa, 1994), 265–95.

12. Richard White, *The Middle Ground: Indians, Empires, and Republics in the Great Lakes Region, 1650–1815* (Cambridge: Cambridge University Press, 1991), 120–27.

13. See Dechêne, *Le Peuple, l'État et la Guerre*, chap. 8.

14. Dickinson and Young, *Short History*, 44, 47; Dechêne, *Le Peuple, l'État et la Guerre*, 351.

15. Dechêne plays down the importance traditionally given to the corruption of Intendant Bigot and the rivalry between Governor Vaudreuil and General Montcalm, stressing instead the logistical problems. See *Le Peuple, l'État et la Guerre*, chap. 10.

16. Erica M. Charters, "Disease, Wilderness Warfare, and Imperial Relations: The Battle for Quebec, 1759–1760," *War in History* 16, no. 1 (2009): 10–15.

17. See N.Z. Nicolai, "A Different Kind of Courage: The French Military and the Canadian Irregular Soldier during the Seven Years' War," *Canadian Historical Review* 70 (1989): 53–75; Dechêne, *Le Peuple, l'État et la Guerre*, 379–81, 445–48.

18. See P.M. MacLeod, "Microbes and Muskets: Small Pox and the Participation of the Amerindian Allies of New France in the Seven Years' War," *Ethnohistory* 39, 1 (1992): 42–57.

19. Dickinson and Young, *Short History*, 49.

20. R. Douglas Francis, Richard Jones, and Donald B. Smith, *Origins: Canadian History to Confederation*, 5th ed. (Scarborough, ON: Nelson, 2004), 178–89; Gordon M. Day, *The Identity of the St. Francis Indians* (Ottawa: National Museums of Canada, 1981), 60–65; Calloway, *Western*, 244–46.

21. Cornelius Jaenan, "French Sovereignty and Native Nationhood during the French Regime," in *Sweet Promises: A Reader on Indian-White Relations in Canada*, ed. J.R. Miller (Toronto: University of Toronto Press, 1991), 19–44.

22. See Dechêne, *Le Peuple, l'État et la Guerre*, 387–93.

23. Christophe Horguelin, "Le XVIIIe siècle des Canadiens: Discours publique et identité," *Mémoires de Nouvelle-France: De France en Nouvelle-France*, ed. in Philippe Joutard and Thomas Wien (Rennes: Presses Universitaires de Rennes, 2005), 210–15, 218–19; Dechêne, *Le Peuple, l'État et la Guerre*, 438–45, 457–49.

24. Dickinson and Young, *Short History*, 42–43, 54.

25. For a brief description of the criminal justice system in New France, see Jean-Pierre Hardy, *Chercher fortune en Nouvelle-France* (Montreal: Libre Expression, 2007), 131–41.

26. Quoted in Dale Miquelon, ed., *Society and Conquest: The Debate on the Bourgeoisie and Social Change in French Canada, 1700–1850* (Toronto: Copp Clark, 1977), 36.

27. Fyson provides a succinct but comprehensive overview of the question in "The Canadiens and the Conquest of Quebec: Interpretations, Realities, Ambiguities," in *Quebec Questions: Quebec Studies for the Twenty-First Century*, ed. Stéphan Gervais, Christopher Kirby, and Jarrett Rudy (Don Mills, ON: Oxford University Press, 2011), 18–31.

28. Jean Hamelin, "What Middle Class?" in *Society and Conquest*, ed. Miquelon, 217–19.

29. Eccles, "The Social, Economic, and Political Significance," 114–17.

30. See José Igartua, "A Change in Climate: The Conquest and the *Marchands* of Montreal," in Canadian Historical Association, *Historical Papers/Communications historiques* 9, no. 1 (1974): 115–34.

4 POLITICAL CONFLICT AND REBELLION

1. Gilles Paquet and Jean-Pierre Wallot, *Lower Canada at the Turn of the Nineteenth Century: Restructuring and Modernization* (Ottawa: Canadian Historical Association, Booklet No. 45, 1988), 6.

2. See Fernand Ouellet, *Lower Canada, 1791–1840: Social Change and Nationalism* (Toronto: McClelland and Stewart, 1980), chap. 5. In 1791, 80 percent of the 165,000 people in Lower Canada were members of farm families. The seven children born to the average family was a birth rate similar to other parts of Canada and the United States. John Dickinson and Brian Young, *A Short History of Quebec*, 3rd ed. (Kingston: McGill-Queen's University Press, 2003), 110–12.

3. See Serge Courville, "Villages and Agriculture in the Seigneuries of Lower Canada: Conditions of a Comprehensive Study of Rural Quebec in the First Half of the Nineteenth-Century," *Canadian Papers in Rural History* 5 (1986): 121–49.

4. See Paquet and Wallot, *Lower Canada*, 6, 19; Christian Dessureault and John A. Dickinson, "Farm Implements and Husbandry in Colonial Quebec, 1740–1840," in *New England/New France 1600–1850*, ed. Peter Benes (Boston: Boston University Press, 1992), 110–21; and David-Thierry Ruddel, "Clothing, Society, and Consumer Trends in the Montreal Area, 1792–1835," in *New England/New France*, ed. Benes, 122–34.

5. Robert C.H. Sweeny, "What Difference Does a Mode Make? A Comparison of Two Seventeenth-Century Colonies: Canada and Newfoundland," *William and Mary Quarterly*, 3rd series, 63, no. 2 (2006): 291. For a useful analysis of the agricultural crisis debate, see Robert Armstrong, *Structure and Change: An Economic History of Quebec* ([Canada]: Gage, 1984), chap. 6.

6. Geoffrey Bilson, *A Darkened House: Cholera in Nineteenth-Century Canada* (Toronto: University of Toronto Press, 1980), 179.

7. Dickinson and Young, *A Short History*, 112–14, 131; Michael Cross, "The Shiners' War," *Canadian Historical Review* 54 (1973): 1–26.

8. See J.I. Little, *Ethno-Cultural Transition and Regional Identity in the Eastern Townships of Quebec* (Ottawa: Canadian Historical Association, Canada's Ethnic Group Series, Booklet No. 13, 1989).

9. See Dickinson and Young, *A Short History*, 72.

10. Paquet and Wallot, *Lower Canada*, 12; J.I. Little, "British Toryism 'Amidst a Horde of Disaffected and Disloyal Squatters': The Rise and Fall of William Bowman Felton and Family in the Eastern Townships," *Journal of Eastern Townships Studies* 1 (1992): 13–42. Donald Fyson points out, however, that French Canadians were the majority of the justices of the peace, and their seigneurial elite held high offices. "The Canadiens and the Conquest of Quebec: Interpretations,

Realities, Ambiguities," in *Quebec Questions: Quebec Studies for the Twenty-First Century*, ed. Stéphan Gervais, Christopher Kirby, and Jarrett Rudy (Don Mills, ON: Oxford University Press, 2011), 28.

11. Lucien Lemieux, *Histoire du catholicisme québécois. Les XVIIIe et XIXe siècles*. Tome 1, *Les années difficiles (1760–1839)* (Montréal: Boréal, 1989), 101–109.

12. Michel Ducharme, *Le Concept de liberté au Canada à l'époque des révolutions Atlantiques, 1776–1838* (Montreal: McGill-Queen's University Press, 2010), 85–86, 211–12.

13. Little, *Ethno-Cultural Transition*, 9.

14. J.I. Little, *Loyalties in Conflict: A Canadian Borderland in War and Rebellion, 1812–1840* (Toronto: University of Toronto Press, 2008), 57–67.

15. Allan Greer, *The Patriots and the People: The Rebellion of 1837 in Rural Lower Canada* (Toronto: University of Toronto Press, 1993), chaps. 3 and 8.

16. See Jean-Paul Bernard, *The Rebellions of 1837 and 1838 in Lower Canada* (Ottawa: Canadian Historical Association, Booklet No. 55, 1996); and Elinor Kyte Senior, *Redcoats and Patriots: The Rebellions in Lower Canada, 1837–38* (Ottawa: Canada's Wings, 1985).

17. Dickinson and Young, *A Short History*, 165–66; Little, *Loyalties in Conflict*, 83–90.

18. See John J. Duffy and H. Nicholas Muller, *Anxious Democracy: Aspects of the 1830s* (Westport, CT: Grenwood Press, 1982).

19. Fernand Ouellet, *Lower Canada, 1791–1840: Social Change and Nationalism* (Toronto: McClelland and Stewart, 1980), 322. On one of these trials, see Murray Greenwood, "The Chartrand Murder Trial: Rebellion and Repression in Lower Canada, 1837–1839," *Criminal Justice History* 5 (1984): 129–59.

5 THE LIBERAL STATE

1. See Donald Fyson, *Magistrates, Police and People: Everyday Criminal Justice in Quebec and Lower Canada, 1764–1837* (Toronto: University of Toronto Press, 2006), 6–11.

2. On the question of Durham's "racism," see Michel Ducharme, "L'État selon Lord Durham: Liberté et nationalité dans l'Empire brittanique," *Cahiers d'Histoire* 18, no. 2 (1998): 49–57.

3. Jacques Monet, "Sir Charles Bagot," *Dictionary of Canadian Biography Online*, retrieved 9 January 2012 from http://www.biographi.ca/009004-119.01-e.php?id_nbr=3224.

4. See William G. Ormsby, *The Emergence of the Federal Concept in Canada, 1839–1845* (Toronto: University of Toronto Press, 1969); and Jacques Monet, *The Last Cannon Shot: A Study of French-Canadian Nationalism, 1837–1850* (Toronto: University of Toronto Press, 1969).

5. On the erosion of women's property and political rights in Canada East, see The Clio Collective, *Quebec Women: A History*, trans. Roger Gannon and Rosalind Gill (Toronto: Women's Press, 1987), 122–26; and John Dickinson and Brian Young, *A Short History of Quebec* (Montreal: McGill-Queen's University Press, 2003), 189–90.

6. See Brian Young, *George-Etienne Cartier: Montreal Bourgeois* (Montreal: McGill-Queen's University Press, 1981).

7. See David T. Ruddell, *Québec City, 1765–1832* ([Ottawa]: National Museums of Canada, n.d.), chap. 4. In his recent revisionist study, which focuses only on their criminal justice role, Fyson (*Magistrates, Police, and People*) places more emphasis on the local community ties of the magistrates.

8. See J.I. Little, "'The fostering care of Government': Lord Dalhousie's 1821 Survey of the Eastern Townships," *Histoire sociale/Social History* 43 (2010): 193–212.

9. See Stephen Kenny, "'Cahots' and Catcalls: An Episode of Popular Resistance in Lower Canada at the Outset of the Union," *Canadian Historical Review* 65 (1984): 184–208.

10. J.I. Little, *State and Society in Transition: The Politics of Institutional Reform in the Eastern Townships, 1838–1852* (Montreal: McGill-Queen's University Press, 1997), chaps. 4 and 5.

11. See J.I. Little, "Colonization and Municipal Reform in Canada East," *Histoire sociale/Social History* 14 (1981): 92–121.

12. See Wendie Nelson, "'Rage against the Dying of the Light': Interpreting the Guerre des Éteignoirs," *Canadian Historical Review* 81 (2000): 551–81.

13. See Andrée Dufour, *Tous à l'école: État, communautés rurales et scolarisation au Québec de 1826 à 1859* (Montreal: Hurtubise HMH, 1996); and Little, *State and Society in Transition*, chaps. 6 and 7.

14. Dickinson and Young, *Short History*, 155–56. See also Bruce Curtis, "Representation and State Formation in the Canadas, 1790–1850," *Studies in Political Economy* 28 (1989): 59–87.

15. See, for example, J.I. Little, "'Labouring in a Great Cause': Marcus Child as Pioneer School Inspector in Lower Canada's Eastern Townships, 1852–59," *Historical Studies in Education* 10 (1998): 85–115.

16. Quoted in Jan Noel, *Canada Dry: Temperance Crusades Before Confederation* (Toronto: University of Toronto Press, 1995), 65.

17. J.I. Little, "A Moral Engine of Such Incalculable Power: The Temperance Movement in the Eastern Townships, 1830–52," *Journal of Eastern Townships Studies* 11 (1997): 5–38.

18. See Noel, *Canada Dry*.

19. Jean-Marie Fecteau, *La liberté du pauvre. Sur la regulation du crime et de la pauvreté au XIXe siècle Québécois* (Montreal: VLB Éditeur, 2004), 132–35.

20. André Cellard, *Histore de la folie au Québec de 1600 à 1850* (Montreal: Boréal, 1991).

21. Fecteau, *La liberté du pauvre*, 123–27, 136–37, 150.

22. Ibid., 147, 161, 174.

6 THE NATIONALIST REACTION

1. Paul-André Linteau, René Durocher, and Jean-Claude Robert, *Quebec: A History, 1867–1929* (Toronto: James Lorimer, 1983), 200.

2. John Dickinson and Brian Young, *A Short History of Quebec* (Montreal: McGill-Queen's University Press, 2003), 181.

3. Jacques Monet, "French-Canadian Nationalism and the Challenge of Ultramontanism," in Canadian Historical Association, *Historical Papers/Communications historiques* (1966): 41–55; Nive Voisine, *Histoire de l'église Catholique au Québec, 1608–1970* (Montreal: Fides, 1971), 46–49.

4. Quoted in Mason Wade, *The French Canadians 1760–1967*, vol. 1 (Toronto: Macmillan, 1968), 346.

5. Ibid.

6. See Arthur Silver, *The French-Canadian Idea of Confederation, 1864–1900* (Toronto: University of Toronto Press, 1997).

7. See Brian Young, *Promoters and Politicians: The North-Shore Railways in the History of Quebec, 1854–85* (Toronto: University of Toronto Press, 1978); and J.I. Little, *Nationalism, Capitalism, and Colonization in Nineteenth-Century Quebec: The Upper St. Francis District* (Montreal: McGill-Queen's University Press, 1989), chap. 7.

8. J.I. Little, *Ethno-Cultural Transition and Regional Identity in the Eastern Townships of Quebec* (Ottawa: Canadian Historical Association, Canada's Ethnic Group Series, Booklet No. 13, 1989), 15–27.

9. Dickinson and Young, *Short History*, 142, 151.

10. Linteau, Durocher, and Robert, *Quebec: A History*, 28–29.

11. See René Hardy and Normand Séguin, *Forêt et société en Mauricie* (Montreal: Boréal Express/ Musée National de l'Homme, 1984), 23–39; and Camil Girard and Normand Perron, *Histoire du Saguenay-Lac-Saint-Jean* (Quebec: Institut Québécois de Recherche sur la Culture, 1989), 157–84, 198–202.

12. See the discussion in Little, *Nationalism, Capitalism, and Colonization*, chaps. 1 and 5.

13. Translated by Claude Bélanger in "Documents sur le Programme catholique de 1871/ Documents on the Catholic Programme of 1871," *Quebec History*, retrieved 9 January 2012 from http://faculty.marianopolis.edu/c.belanger/quebechistory/docs/catholic/text-e.htm.

14. See Roberto Perin, *Rome in Canada: The Vatican and Canadian Affairs in the Late Victorian Age* (Toronto: University of Toronto Press, 1990).

15. See H. Blair Neatby, *Laurier and a Liberal Quebec: A Study in Political Management* (Toronto: McClelland and Stewart, 1973), 93.

16. See Carl Berger, *The Sense of Power: Studies in the Ideas of Canadian Imperialism, 1867–1914* (Toronto: University of Toronto Press, 1970).

17. See A.I. Silver, "Some Quebec Attitudes in an Age of Imperialism and Ideological Conflict," *Canadian Historical Review* 57 (1976): 40–61.

18. René Hardy, *Les Zouaves: Une stratégie du clergé québécois au XIXe siècle* (Montreal: Boréal Express, 1980).

19. See Carman Miller, *Painting the Map Red: Canada and the South African War, 1899–1902* (Montreal: McGill-Queen's University Press, 1993).

20. Quoted in Neatby, *Laurier and a Liberal Quebec*, 115–16.

7 AN INDUSTRIAL REVOLUTION

1. Serge Courville, *Quebec: A Historical Geography*, trans. Richard Howard (Vancouver: UBC Press, 2008), 142–43.

2. See, for example, the following studies: Fernand Ouellet, *Histoire économique et sociale du Québec, 1760–1850* (Montreal: Fides, 1971); Michel Brunet, *Les Canadiens après la conquête* (Montreal: Fides, 1969); A. Faucher and M. Lamontagne, "History of Industrial Development," in *Essais sur le Québec contemporain/Essays on Contemporary Québec*, ed. Jean-Claude Falardeau (Quebec City: Presses de l'Université Laval, 1953), 23–44; and John McCallum, *Unequal Beginnings: Agriculture and Economic Development in Quebec and Ontario until 1870* (Toronto: University of Toronto Press, 1980). For a wide range of interpretations, see René Durocher and Paul-André Linteau, eds., *Le "Retard" du Québec et l'infériorité économique des Canadiens français* (Trois-Rivières: Éditions Boréal Express, 1971).

3. Figures in this paragraph are from Jean Hamelin and Yves Roby, *Histoire économique du Québec, 1851–1896* (Montreal: Fides, 1971), 262. The industrialization process in Montreal is well described by Bettina Bradbury, *Working Families: Age, Gender, and Daily Survival in Industrializing Montreal* (Toronto: McClelland and Stewart, 1993), chap. 1, 22–48. For broader studies, see especially Paul-André Linteau, René Durocher, and Jean-Claude Robert, *Quebec: A History, 1867–1929* (Toronto: James Lorimer and Company, 1983), chap. 7, 116–38; and John Dickinson and Brian Young, *A Short History of Quebec*, 3rd ed. (Montreal: McGill-Queen's University Press, 2003), especially chap. 4, 106–53. Industrial capitalism transformed smaller communities as well; see Peter Gossage, *Families in Transition: Industry and Population in Nineteenth-Century Saint-Hyacinthe* (Montreal: McGill-Queen's University Press, 1999), especially chap. 2, 36–78.

4. Dickinson and Young, *A Short History of Quebec*, 169.

5. Robert E. Babe, *Telecommunications in Canada: Technology, Industry and Government* (Toronto: University of Toronto Press, 1990), 38.

6. A useful historical overview can be found at Parks Canada, Lachine Canal National Historic Site, consulted 10 August 2010, http://www.pc.gc.ca/eng/lhn-nhs/qc/canallachine/index.aspx. See also Bradbury, *Working Families*, 26, and especially Gerald Tulchinsky, *The River Barons: Montreal Businessmen and the Growth of Industry and Transportation, 1837–53* (Toronto: University of Toronto Press, 1977), 220–28.

7. Dickinson and Young, *A Short History of Quebec*, 127.

8. Hamelin and Roby, *Histoire économique du Québec*, table 3, 267.

9. Ibid., 263.

10. The increase between 1851 and 1871 was spectacular, from barely $100,000 to over $14 million. Ibid., table 3, 267.

11. Joanne Burgess, "L'Industrie de la chaussure à Montréal, 1840–1870: De l'artisanat a la fabrique," *Revue d'histoire de l'Amérique française* 31, no. 2 (1977): 187–210.

12. These numbers, for 1872, were provided by a well-paced contemporary, William Patterson, and cited in Hamelin and Roby, *Histoire économique du Québec*, 269.

13. Ibid.

14. Gossage, *Families in Transition*, 46–47.

15. Chad Gaffield et al., *History of the Outaouais* (Quebec City: Institut québécois de recherche sur la culture, 1997), 174.

16. Hamelin and Roby, *Histoire économique du Québec*, table 2, 264.

17. For an Eastern Townships example from the early twentieth century, see Ellsworth Lorimer and Peter Gossage, "A Craftsman Remembers: Recollections of the Dominion Snath Company, Waterville, 1920–1939," *Journal of Eastern Townships Studies* 7 (1995): 71–88.

18. Hamelin and Roby, *Histoire économique du Québec*, table 3, 267. A careful study of the garment industry in a slightly earlier period is Mary Ann Poutanen, "For the Benefit of the Master: The Montreal Needle Trades during the Transition, 1820–1842" (MA thesis, McGill University, 1986).

19. Hamelin and Roby, *Histoire économique du Québec*, 270.

20. See Peter Bischoff, "Des Forges du Saint-Maurice aux fonderies de Montréal: Mobilité géographique, solidarité communautaire et action syndicale des mouleurs, 1829–1881," *Revue d'histoire de l'Amérique française* 43, no. 1 (1989): 3–29.

21. Hamelin and Roby, *Histoire économique du Québec*, 88–91. For a detailed account of the violent August 1879 clash between rival groups of Irish and French-Canadian longshoremen, see Peter C. Bischoff, *Les Débardeurs au port de Québec. Tableau des luttes syndicales, 1831–1902* (Montreal: Éditions Hurtubise, 2009), 266–76.

22. Details in this paragraph are from Jean-Pierre Kesteman et al., *Histoire des Cantons de l'Est* (Sainte-Foy, QC: Institut québécois de recherche sur la culture, 1998), 154, 365, 367, and 766, n. 58.

23. Compared to just $1.3 million in 1871; Hamelin and Roby, *Histoire économique du Québec*, 267.

24. A.B. McCullough, *Primary Textile Industry in Canada: A History and Heritage* (Ottawa: Supply and Service Canada, 1992), 185–86; Jacques Ferland, "Syndicalisme 'parcellaire' et syndicalisme 'collectif': Une Interprétation socio-technique des conflits ouvriers dans deux industries québécoises, 1880-1914," *Labour/Le Travail* 19 (1987), 83–84.

25. Jacques Rouillard, *Le syndicalisme québécois: Deux siècles d'histoire* (Montreal: Boréal, 2004), 17.

26. Ibid., 23. See also H. Clare Pentland, "The Lachine Strike of 1843," *Canadian Historical Review* 29, no. 3 (1949): 255–77, and Dan Horner, "Solemn Processions and Terrifying Violence: Spectacle, Authority, and Citizenship during the Lachine Canal Strike of 1843," *Urban History Review* 38, no. 2 (2010): 36–47.

27. See Bischoff, "Des Forges du Saint-Maurice aux fonderies de Montréal," 24–28.

28. Rouillard, *Le syndicalisme québécois*, 22, and Denise Latrémouille, "La courte carrière de Médéric Lanctôt en Outaouais," retrieved 18 June 2011 from http://www.histoirequebec.qc.ca/publicat/vol11num1/v11n1_5ml.htm.

29. From a level of twenty-two in 1880. Rouillard, *Le syndicalisme québécois*, table 1, 29.

30. Ibid., 31.

31. Ibid., 24–25.

32. Ibid., 26–27. See also Linteau, Durocher, and Robert, *Quebec: A History*, 180.

33. Linteau, Durocher, and Robert, *Quebec: A History*, 166.

34. Ibid., 166–68. On the French-language commercial press and its economic liberalism, see Fernande Roy, *Progrès, harmonie, liberté: Le libéralisme des milieux d'affaires francophones de Montréal au tournant du siècle* (Montreal: Boréal, 1988).

35. Christian Dessureault, "L'évolution de la productivité agricole dans la plaine de Montréal, 1852–1871: Grandes et petites exploitations dans un système familiale d'agriculture," *Histoire sociale/Social History* 38 (2005): 235–65.

36. Normand Perron, "Genèse des activités laitières," in Normand Séguin, ed., *Agriculture et colonisation au Québec* (Montreal: Boréal Express, 1980), 123. Mario Gendron et al., *Histoire du Piémont des Appalaches: La Montérégie* (Sainte-Foy, QC: Les Éditions de l'IQRC, 1999), 162–64.

37. Gérard Bouchard, *Quelques arpents d'Amérique. Population, économie, famille au Saguenay, 1838–1971* (Montreal: Boréal, 1996).

38. These figures for the installed energy capacity of hydraulic sites in Quebec are from Claude Bellavance, *Shawinigan Water and Power, 1898–1963: Formation et decline d'un groupe industriel au Québec* (Montreal: Boréal, 1994), appendix 1.2, 393.

39. Ibid., 72. The quoted material is the authors' translation.

40. Hamelin and Roby, *Histoire économique du Québec*, 265–67.

41. The figures were $14 million in 1910 and $130 million in 1929. Linteau, Durocher, and Robert, *Quebec: A History*, 311–33.

42. Kesteman et al., *Histoire des Cantons de l'Est*, 320–21.

43. Ibid., 325.

44. Linteau, Durocher, and Robert, *Quebec: A History*, 319.

45. Bryan Palmer et al., "Working-Class History," in *The Canadian Encyclopaedia*, retrieved 15 June 2011 from http://www.thecanadianencyclopedia.com/index.cfm?Params=A1ARTA0008710&PgNm=TCE.

46. Linteau, Durocher, and Robert, *Quebec: A History*, 414–45.

8 CITIES AND TOWNS

1. See Paul-André Linteau, *Histoire de Montréal depuis la Confédération* (Montreal: Boréal, 2000), 40–41, 314. Certain information in the next three paragraphs was also drawn from Linteau's study: for population figures, see pp. 44–45; for annexations, see p. 79; and for public architecture, see p. 90.

2. Jean Claude Marsan, *Montreal in Evolution: Historical Analysis of the Development of Montreal's Architecture and Urban Environment* (Montreal: McGill-Queen's University Press, 1981), 245.

3. Jean Hamelin and Yves Roby, *Histoire économique du Québec, 1851–1896* (Montreal: Fides, 1971), 362. The quoted material is the authors' translation.

4. Linteau, *Histoire de Montréal*, 148.

5. Peter Gossage, *Families in Transition: Industry and Population in Nineteenth-Century Saint-Hyacinthe* (Montreal: McGill-Queen's University Press, 1999), 27–28.

6. Hamelin and Roby, *Histoire économique du Québec*, 128; John A. Dickinson and Brian Young, *A Short History of Quebec*, 3rd ed. (Montreal: McGill-Queens University Press, 2002), 207; Christian Pouyez et al., *Les Saguenayens: Introduction à l'histoire des populations du Saguenay, XVIe–XXe siècles* (Sillery: Presses de l'Université du Québec, 1983), 95–124.

7. J.I. Little, "Like a Fragment of the Old World: The Historical Regression of Quebec City in Travel Narratives and Tourist Guidebooks, 1799–1913," *Urban History Review*, forthcoming.

8. Chad Gaffield et al., *History of the Outaouais* (Quebec City: Institut québécois de recherche sur la culture, 1997), 261–66; Odette Vincent-Domey, *Filles et familles en milieu ouvrier: Hull, Québec, à la fin du 19e siècle* (Montreal: Regroupement des chercheurs-chercheures en histoire des travailleurs et travailleuses du Québec, 1991).

9. Gossage, *Families in Transition*, 22.

10. See Christopher Armstrong and H.V. Nelles, *Monopoly's Moment: The Organization and Regulation of Canadian Utilities, 1830–1930* (Philadelphia: Temple University Press, 1986).

11. The preceding discussion of Montreal's water utility draws on Linteau, *Histoire de Montréal*, 131.

12. See Denyse Baillargeon, *Babies for the Nation: The Medicalization of Motherhood in Quebec, 1910–1970* (Waterloo: Wilfrid Laurier University Press, 2009).

13. Linteau, *Histoire de Montréal*, 224; Michèle Dagenais, *Montréal et l'eau: Une histoire environnementale* (Montreal: Boréal, 2011), 123.

14. Peter Gossage, "Louis Côté," *Dictionary of Canadian Biography Online*, retrieved 6 May 2011 from http://www.biographi.ca/009004-119.01-e.php?&id_nbr=7312&interval=20&&PHPSESS ID=tdkj9tq72dke236boroe7ad3o3.

15. They had been banned in the oldest streets of Montreal (those situated within the former perimeter of the fortifications) since the eighteenth century. Jean-Claude Robert, *Atlas historique de Montréal* (Montreal: Art Global/Libre Expression, 1994), 113.

16. See Gossage, *Families in Transition*, illustration 12, taken from *Canadian Illustrated News*, 16 September 1876, facing p. 11.

17. Chad Gaffield et al., *History of the Outaouais*, 390–91.

18. Linteau, *Histoire de Montréal*, 134.

19. Ibid., 270. See also "De l'avoine à l'électricité," *Centre d'histoire de Montréal*, retrieved 6 May 2011 from http://ville.montreal.qc.ca/portal/page?_pageid=2497,3090490&_dad=portal&_ schema=PORTAL.

20. Paul-André Linteau, *The Promoters' City: Building the Industrial Town of Maisonneuve, 1883–1918* (Toronto: James Lorimer, 1985), 88–89.

21. Linteau, Durocher, and Robert, *Quebec: A History*, 362–63; René Verrette, *Idéologies de développement régional: Le cas de la Mauricie, 1850–1950* (Sainte-Foy, QC: Les Presses de l'Université Laval, 1999), 357; Gaffield et al., *History of the Outaouais*, 256; Jean-Pierre Kesteman, Peter Southam, and Diane Saint-Pierre, *Histoire des Cantons de l'Est* (Sainte-Foy, QC: Institut québécois de recherche sur la culture, 1998), 384.

22. See T.D. Regehr, "Ames, Sir Herbert Brown," *The Canadian Encyclopedia*, retrieved 6 May 2011 from http://www.thecanadianencyclopedia.com/index.cfm?PgNm=TCE&Params=A1ARTA00 00179.

23. Gilles Lauzon, *Habitat ouvrier et révolution industrielle: Le cas du Village St-Augustin* (Montreal: Regroupement des chercheurs-chercheures en histoire des travailleurs et travailleuses du Québec, 1989); Gilles Lauzon, "Cohabitation et déménagements en milieu ouvrier montréalais: Essai de réinterprétation à partir du cas du village Saint-Augustin (1871–1881)," *Revue d'histoire de l'Amérique française* 46, no. 1 (1992): 115–42; Tracey Madigan, "Get a Move On," *CBC News Online*, 28 June 2005, retrieved 5 May 2011 from http://www.cbc.ca/montreal/features/ movingday/.

24. Bettina Bradbury, *Working Families: Age, Gender, and Daily Survival in Industrializing Montreal* (Toronto: McClelland and Stewart, 1993).

25. Denyse Baillargeon, *Making Do: Women, Family and Home in Montréal during the Great Depression* (Waterloo, ON: Wilfrid Laurier University Press, 1999).

26. Tania Martin, "Housing the Grey Nuns: Power, Religion and Women in Fin-de-siècle Montréal" (M. Arch. thesis, McGill University, 1995).

27. Peter Gossage, "Les enfants abandonnés à Montréal au 19e siècle: La crèche d'Youville des Soeurs Grises, 1820–1871," *Revue d'histoire de l'Amérique française* 40, no. 4 (1987): 537–59.

28. Linteau, *Histoire de Montréal*, 108.

29. Janice Harvey, "Dealing with 'The Destitute and the Wretched': The Protestant House of Industry and Refuge in Nineteenth-Century Montreal," *Journal of the Canadian Historical Association,* n.s., 12 (2001): 73–94; "Our History," *Old Brewery Mission,* retrieved 5 May 2011 from http://www.oldbrewerymission.ca/obm_history.htm.

30. Martin Tétreault, "Les maladies de la misère: Aspects de la santé publique à Montréal, 1880–1914," *Revue d'histoire de l'Amérique française* 36, no. 4 (1983): table 2, 512.

31. Joseph Gauvreau, "La Goutte de lait," *L'École sociale populaire* 29 (1914), cited in Terry Copp, *The Anatomy of Poverty: The Condition of the Working Class in Montreal, 1897–1929* (Toronto: McClelland and Stewart, 1974), 26.

32. Copp, *The Anatomy of Poverty,* 17.

33. Patricia Thornton and Sherry Olson, "A Deadly Discrimination among Montreal Infants, 1860–1900," *Continuity and Change* 16, no. 1 (2001): 95–135. See also J.I. Little, *Crofters and Habitants: Settler Society, Economy, and Culture in a Quebec Township, 1848–1881* (Montreal: McGill-Queen's University Press, 1991), 84–89.

34. Annmarie Adams, Kevin Schwartzman, and David Theodore, "Collapse and Expand: Tuberculosis Therapy in Montreal, 1909, 1933, 1954," *Technology and Culture* 49, no. 4 (2008): 915.

35. Ibid., 913.

36. Linteau, Durocher, and Robert, *Quebec: A History,* 24.

37. Linteau, *Histoire de Montréal,* 53–54; James H. Marsh, "Plague: The 'Red Death' Strikes Montreal," *The Canadian Encyclopedia,* retrieved 6 May 2011 from http://www.thecanadianencyclopedia.com/index.cfm?PgNm=ArchivedFeatures&Params=A2103. See also Michael Bliss, *Plague: A Story of Smallpox in Montreal* (Toronto: HarperCollins Publishers, 1991).

38. "Adoption de mesures exceptionnelles pour contrer l'épidémie de grippe espagnole au Québec," *Bilan du siècle,* retrieved 6 May 2011 from http://bilan.usherbrooke.ca/bilan/pages/evenements/275.html. For an interesting perspective on the Spanish Flu epidemic in Montreal, see Magda Fahrni, "'Elles sont partout...': Les femmes et la ville en temps d'épidémie, Montréal, 1918–1929," *Revue d'histoire de l'Amérique française* 58, no. 1 (2004): 67–85.

39. Adams, Schwartzman, and Theodore, "Collapse and Expand," 909; Linteau, *Histoire de Montréal,* 221–22; Valerie Minnett, "Disease and Domesticity on Display: The Montreal Tuberculosis Exhibition, 1908," *Canadian Bulletin of Medical History* 23, no. 2 (2006): 381–400.

40. By 1915, there were twenty-three such dispensaries located in as many Catholic parishes in Montreal, in addition to five dispensaries catering to the city's anglophone population. Baillargeon, *Babies for the Nation,* 113.

41. Ibid., table 5, 27.

42. Richard L. Cruess, MD, "Brief History of Medicine at McGill," *McGill Faculty of Medicine,* retrieved 6 May 2011 from http://www.medicine.mcgill.ca/medicine/about/history/.

43. "Mark Twain in Montreal," *The New York Times* (10 December 1881), retrieved 6 May 2011 from http://www.twainquotes.com/18811210.html.

44. Gossage, *Families in Transition,* table 3.7, 93.

45. The proportions of religious teaching personnel in the Catholic system were 11 percent in 1853 and 48 percent in 1887. Dickinson and Young, *Short History of Quebec,* 174.

46. Roger Magnuson, "Collèges classiques," *The Canadian Encyclopedia,* retrieved 6 May 2011 from http://www.thecanadianencyclopedia.com/index.cfm?PgNm=TCE&Params=A1ARTA0001757. See also the recent work on this topic by Christine Hudon, Louise Bienvenue, and Ollivier Hubert, which emphasizes the role of the *collège classique* in forging middle-class masculine identities in the province. See for example Louise Bienvenue and Christine Hudon, "'Pour devenir homme, tu transgresseras...': Quelques enjeux de la socialisation masculine dans les collèges classiques québécois (1880–1939)," *Canadian Historical Review* 86, no. 3 (2005): 485–511.

47. The school was located in the town of Roberval. See Laurie Goulet, "Communautés religieuses féminines et éducation au Saguenay-Lac-Saint-Jean," *Encyclobec*, retrieved 6 May 2011 from http://www.encyclobec.ca/main.php?docid=381.

48. Dickinson and Young, *Short History of Quebec*, 261; Micheline Dumont and Nadia Fahmy-Eid, *Les couventines: L'éducation des filles au Québec dans les congrégations religieuses enseignantes, 1840–1960* (Montreal: Boréal Express, 1986), 21; Ruby Heap, "Urbanisation et éducation: La centralisation scolaire à Montréal au début de XXe siècle," in Canadian Historical Association, *Historical Papers/Communications historiques* 20, no.1 (1985): 132–55.

49. Note that the source for this estimate is the radical liberal newspaper *Le Pays*, which was banned in 1913 by Montreal Archbishop Paul Bruchési for its anti-clerical views. Cited in Linteau, Durocher, and Robert, *Quebec: A History*, 209.

50. Linteau, *Histoire de Montréal*, 238.

51. Library and Archives Canada, "Montreal Amateur Athletic Association" fonds (textual records), retrieved 6 May 2011 from http://collectionscanada.gc.ca/pam_archives/index. php?fuseaction=genitem.displayItem&lang=eng&rec_nbr=100095&rec_nbr_list=100095,37 27876,112886,2855556,3722509,3662246,105190,1819309,4051961,3657195. On athletics in nineteenth-century Montreal and especially activities like snowshoeing and lacrosse borrowed from First Nations people, see Gillian Poulter, *Becoming Native in a Foreign Land: Sport, Visual Culture, and Identity in Montreal, 1840–85* (Vancouver: UBC Press, 2009).

52. Michael McKinley, *Hockey: A People's History* (Toronto: CBC/McLelland and Stewart, 2006), 19, 24–25.

53. Ibid., 86–89; Julie Perrone, "The King Has Two Bodies: Howie Morenz and the Fabrication of Memory," *Sport History Review* 41, no. 2 (2010): 95–110.

54. Craig Heron, *Booze: A Distilled History* (Toronto: Between the Lines, 2003), 154–55.

55. There were 394 members from Montreal and 154 from Saint-Pierre-Apôtre parish at the turn of the twentieth century. Lucia Ferretti, *Entre voisins: La société paroissiale en milieu urbain: Saint-Pierre-Apôtre de Montréal, 1848–1930* (Montreal: Boréal, 1992), table 8, 165.

9 NATIONALS AND LIBERALS

1. See Fernande Roy, *Progrès, Harmonie, Liberté: Le libéralisme des milieux d'affaires francophones à Montréal au tournant du siècle* (Montréal: Boréal, 1988).

2. Lucia Ferretti, *Entre voisins: La société paroissiale en milieu urbain: Saint-Pierre-Apôtre de Montréal, 1848–1930* (Montréal: Boréal, 1992).

3. Paul-André Linteau, René Durocher, and Jean-Claude Robert, *Quebec: A History, 1867–1929* (Toronto: James Lorimer, 1983), 486–87.

4. Joseph Schull, *Ontario Since 1867* (Toronto: McClelland and Stewart, 1978): 165. The 1911 census showed that these figures were only slightly exaggerated. Some 202,442 persons of French origin were enumerated, representing about 8 percent of the provincial population of 2.5 million. Canada, *Fifth Census of Canada* 1911, vol. 2 (Ottawa: King's Printer, 1913), table 2, 368–69.

5. Chad Gaffield, *Language, Schooling, and Cultural Conflict: The Origins of the French-language Controversy in Ontario* (Montreal: McGill-Queen's University Press, 1987), 34.

6. As a language of instruction, French was to be allowed in the first two elementary years only. In 1913, the directive was modified so as to permit the teaching of French, as part of the curriculum, for a maximum of one hour per day.

7. Danielle Gauvreau, Diane Gervais, and Peter Gossage, *La Fécondité des Québécoises 1870–1970: D'une exception à l'autre* (Montreal: Boréal, 2007) chap. 2, especially 49–70.

8. See Chapter 8 and Peter Gossage and Danielle Gauvreau, "Canadian Fertility in 1901: A Bird's Eye View," in Peter Baskerville and Eric Sager, eds., *Household Counts: Canadian Families*

and Households in 1901 (Toronto, University of Toronto Press, 2007): 59-109. For a detailed description of demography and family structure in one industrial town, see Peter Gossage, *Families in Transition: Industry and Population in Nineteenth-Century Saint-Hyacinthe* (Montreal and Kingston: McGill-Queen's University Press, 1999).

9. Chad Gaffield, "Language, Education, and Family." Unpulished paper presented to the Third Carleton Conference on the History of the Family, Ottawa (Carleton University), 1997.

10. Anonymous, "Recensement," *La Patrie*, 26 July 1910. The 1901 census had reported that the average number of persons per Quebec household (5.36) was only 7 percent higher than the overall Canadian average, a finding that the author of this editorial found impossible to believe. Of course, his explanation—systematic under-enumeration of French Canadians—does not necessarily follow from these figures.

11. Gauvreau, Gervais, and Gossage, *La Fécondité des Québécoises*, 17–44.

12. See also Peter Gossage, "La Revanche des berceaux," in *Oxford Companion to Canadian History*, ed. Gerald Hallowell (Toronto: Oxford University Press, 2004), 543.

13. Desmond Morton, "World War I," in *The Canadian Encyclopaedia*, retrieved 9 May 2011 from http://www.thecanadianencyclopedia.com/index.cfm?PgNm=TCE&Params=A1ARTA000 8716.

14. Quoted in Robert Craig Brown, "Sir Robert Laird Borden," *Dictionary of Canadian Biography Online*, retrieved 9 May 2011 from http://www.biographi.ca/009004-119.01-e.php?&id_nbr=7 998&interval=15&&PHPSESSID=v5ks536kj8u5hj6mei4loilou0.

15. Ibid.

16. CBC Digital Archives, "Royal 22nd Regiment: Canada's Fighting 'Van Doos,'" retrieved 9 May 2011 from http://archives.cbc.ca/war_conflict/first_world_war/topics/579/; and "History," *Van Doos*, retrieved 9 May 2011 from http://www.vandoos.com/history.html.

17. Brown, "Sir Robert Laird Borden."

18. Quoted in Elizabeth Armstrong, *The Crisis of Quebec, 1914–18* (1937; reprint, New York: AMS Press 1967), 220, n. 31.

19. Ibid., 228.

20. A detailed discussion of the Easter Riots can be found in Martin F. Auger, "On the Brink of Civil War: The Canadian Government and the Suppression of the 1918 Quebec Easter Riots," *Canadian Historical Review* 89, no. 4 (2008): 503–40.

21. Groulx's career as a historian is discussed in Ronald Rudin, *Making History in Twentieth-Century Quebec* (Toronto: University Press, 1997), especially chap. 2, 48–92.

22. See Fernande Roy, *Histoire des idéologies au Québec aux XIXe et XXe siècles* (Montreal: Boréal, 1993), 79–82. *L'Action française* was published from 1917 to 1928.

23. A nice summary of this is in Linteau, Durocher, and Robert, *Quebec: A History*, 532–35.

24. That vision has been aptly described as "a strategy of retrenchment, based on the conservation of traditional values and structures." Ibid., 528.

25. Ibid., 534.

26. Les Semaines sociales de l'École sociale populaire, *La Famille* (Montreal: École sociale populaire, 1923), 287. The quoted material is the authors' translation.

27. Lucie Piché, *Femmes et changement sociale au Québec: L'apport de la Jeunesse ouvrière catholique féminine, 1931–1966* (Montreal: Boréal, 2003).

28. Susan Mann, *The Dream of Nation: A Social and Intellectual History of Quebec*, 2nd ed. (Montreal: McGill-Queen's University Press, 2002), 231.

29. See Ross Gordon, "The Historiographical Debate on the Charges of Anti-Semitism Made Against Lionel Groulx" (MA thesis, University of Ottawa, 1996). Montreal had by far the largest Jewish community in the province, but small numbers settled in the other towns and cities as well. For an interesting glimpse of Jewish life in Sherbrooke, see Michael Benazon, "Ostropol on

the St. Francis: The Jewish Community of Sherbrooke, Quebec—A 120-Year Presence," *Journal of Eastern Townships Studies* 12 (1998): 21–50.

30. John Dickinson and Brian Young, *A Short History of Quebec*, 3rd ed. (Montreal: McGill-Queen's University Press, 2003), 248.

31. Linteau, Durocher, and Robert, *Quebec: A History*, 464.

32. A recent biography of Bouchard is Frank Guttman, *The Devil from Saint-Hyacinthe: Senator Télesphore-Damien Bouchard* (Bloomington, IA: Indiana University Press, 2007).

33. Quoted in Patrice Dutil, "Godfroy Langlois," *Dictionary of Canadian Biography Online*, retrieved 31 August 2010 from http://www.biographi.ca/009004-119.01-e.php?&id_nbr=8233&&PHPSE SSID=l1qi848niebvofm2sp7gjp0e96.

34. Yvan Lamonde, *Histoire sociale des idées au Québec*, vol. 1 (Saint-Laurent: Fides, 2000), 438–39.

35. Dutil, "Godefroy Langlois."

36. This paragraph is largely drawn from The Clio Collective, *Quebec Women: A History*, trans. Roger Gannon and Rosalind Gill (Toronto: The Women's Press, 1987), 252–61.

37. Although she was writing as Julien St-Michel, she left no doubt in this passage, addressed to the province's men, as to her gender or her sentiments: "Prenez vite vos dispositions," she wrote, "c'est notre ultimatum, payez-nous comme la plus inexpérimenté de vos sténographes, comme un chauffeur d'automobile sans license, telle une commis de magasin à la campagne, ou bien nous interrompons notre service, nous changeons de 'job,' nous louerons des chambres, nous organiserons des tag-day et des kermesses, nous tirerons les cartes, nous ferons les modèles aux expositions de mode, c'est à prendre ou à laisser." Julien Saint-Michel, *The Labor World/Le Monde ouvrier*, 10 July 1919, in Micheline Dumont and Louise Toupin, *La Pensée féministe au Québec: Anthologie 1900–1985* (Montreal: Éditions du remue-ménage, 2003), 211.

38. See Ronald Rudin, *Banking en français: The French Banks of Quebec, 1835–1925* (Toronto: University of Toronto Press, 1985); Paul-André Linteau, *The Promoters' City: Building the Industrial Town of Maisonneuve, 1883–1918* (Toronto: James Lorimer, 1985); and especially Fernande Roy, *Progrès, harmonie, liberté: Le libéralisme des milieux d'affaires francophones de Montréal au tournant du siècle* (Montreal: Boréal, 1988).

39. Linteau, Durocher, and Robert, *Quebec: A History*, 467.

40. Roy, *Histoire des idéologies au Québec*, 59–60. The quoted material is the authors' translation. The original quotation, in French, is as follows: "Ces hommes d'affaires, on l'a vu, s'accommodent d'une forme de nationalisme où l'individualisme passe avant les valeurs communautaires. S'enfermer dans la province de Québec, refuser l'ouverture sur le monde, c'est tourner le dos au progrès et favoriser le retard économique des Canadiens français."

41. Election results for 1897–1931 can be found in Linteau, Durocher, and Robert, *Quebec: A History*, table 52, 502.

42. Ibid., 500.

43. Réal Bélanger, "Sir Wilfrid Laurier," *Dictionary of Canadian Biography Online*, retrieved 31 August 2010 from http://www.biographi.ca/009004-119.01-e.php?&id_nbr=7514&&PHPSESS ID=l1qi848niebvofm2sp7gjp0e96.

44. Linteau, Durocher, and Robert, *Quebec: A History*, 487.

45. Dickinson and Young, *Short History of Quebec*, 258.

46. Bernard L. Vigod, *Quebec before Duplessis: The Political Career of Louis-Alexandre Taschereau* (Montreal: McGill-Queen's University Press, 1986), 32.

47. He wrote: "L'opinion demande qu'on cesse de concéder les coupes de bois et les chutes d'eau aux conditions actuelles; que les coupes et les forces motrices naturelles concédées à l'avenir, le soient à charge de la coupe réglée, d'une culture et d'une exploitation qui assureront le maintien intégral de l'étendue territoriale en forêt et de la valeur économique en essences; que toute concession forestière ou hydraulique consentie par les pouvoirs publics, le soit pour un temps fixe

et limité, par bail emphythéotique qui deviendra nul de plein droit dès que le locateur négligera d'en accomplir les conditions." Errol Bouchette, *L'Indépendance économique du Canada français, nouvelle édition, précédée d'une étude de Rodrigue Tremblay* (1906; reprint, Montreal: La Presse, 1977): 205; retrieved 11 May 2011 from http://classiques.uqac.ca/classiques/bouchette_errol/independance_econo_cf/independance_eco_Can_fr.pdf.

48. Vigod, *Quebec before Duplessis*, 130–31; Richard Jones, "Gouin, Sir Lomer," in the *Dictionary of Canadian Biography Online*, retrieved 20 June 2011 from http://www.biographi.ca/009004-119.01-e.php?BioId=42298.

49. Linteau, Durocher, and Robert, *Quebec: A History*, 478.

50. This is not a direct quote but rather Vigod's summary, in *Quebec before Duplessis*, 84.

51. Vigod, *Quebec before Duplessis*, 85–87.

52. See Chantale Quesney, "De la charité au Bonheur familial: Une histoire de la Société d'adoption et de la protection de l'enfance à Montréal" (PhD diss., Université du Québec à Montréal, 2010), chap. 1, and Denyse Baillargeon, "Orphans in Quebec: On the Margins of Which Family?" in *Mapping the Margins: The Family and Social Discipline in Canada, 1700–1975*, ed. Nancy Christie and Michael Gauvreau (Montreal: McGill-Queen's University Press, 2004), 305–26.

53. Peter Gossage, "*La marâtre*: Marie-Anne Houde and the Myth of the Wicked Stepmother in Quebec," *Canadian Historical Review* 76, no. 4 (1995): 563–97.

54. Paul Laverdure, "Sunday in Quebec, 1907–1937," Canadian Catholic History Association *Historical Studies* 62 (1996), 47–61. See also Vigod, *Quebec before Duplessis*, 138; Dickinson and Young, *Short History of Quebec*, 263.

55. Laverdure, "Sunday in Quebec," 53.

10 A GREAT DARKNESS?

1. Paul-André Linteau, René Durocher, Jean-Claude Robert, and François Ricard, *Quebec since 1930*, trans. Robert Chodos and Ellen Garmaise (Toronto: James Lorimer, 1991), table 1, 9.

2. See Bettina Bradbury, *Working Families: Age, Gender, and Daily Survival in Industrializing Montreal* (Toronto: McClelland and Stewart, 1993); Denyse Baillargeon, *Making Do: Women, Family and Home in Montreal during the Great Depression*, trans. Yvonne Klein (Waterloo, ON: Wilfrid Laurier University Press, 1999).

3. Baillageron reports a Canadian jobless rate of 27 to 33 percent, adding that Quebec was one of the provinces "most affected by unemployment." Baillargeon, *Making Do*, 5.

4. They were submitted in 1931 and 1932. See Bernard Vigod, *Quebec before Duplessis: The Political Career of Louis-Alexandre Taschereau* (Montreal: McGill-Queen's University Press, 1986), 153, 199.

5. Susan Mann, *The Dream of Nation: A Social and Intellectual History of Quebec*, 2nd ed. (Montreal: McGill-Queen's University Press, 2002), 37.

6. In 1933, some 60,000 individuals applied for direct relief in Montreal alone. Since most were household heads with, on average, four or five dependents, this figure represents about 250,000 people, fully 30 percent of the city's population. These figures and much of the preceding discussion are drawn from Linteau et al., *Quebec since 1930*, 49–58.

7. See Andrée Lévesque, *Virage à gauche interdit: Les Communistes, les socialistes et leurs ennemis au Québec, 1929–1939* (Montreal: Boréal Express, 1984); Sean Mills, "When Democratic Socialists Discovered Democracy: The League for Social Reconstruction Confronts the Quebec Problem," *Canadian Historical Review* 86, no. 1 (2005): 53–81.

8. The precise figure is 9 percent of the non-agricultural workforce, down from 17 percent in 1921; Linteau et al., *Quebec since 1930*, 43.

9. Mann, *The Dream of Nation*, 240. See also Serge Courville, "Taking the Land," in *Quebec: A Historical Geography*, trans. Richard Howard (Vancouver: UBC Press, 2008), chap. 8, 153–89.

10. See especially Vigod, *Quebec before Duplessis*, 205–209.

11. Ibid., 191–93.

12. Herbert Quinn, *The Union Nationale: Quebec Nationalism from Duplessis to Lévesque*, 2nd enlarged ed. (Toronto: University of Toronto Press, 1979), 63–65; Vigod, *Quebec before Duplessis*, 171.

13. Quinn, *The Union Nationale*, 57.

14. *Le Devoir*, 8 November 1935, quoted in Herbert Quinn, *The Union Nationale*, 53; the quoted material is the authors' translation.

15. Summarized in Quinn, *The Union Nationale*, 58–60.

16. Jacques Rouillard, *Le syndicalisme québécois: Deux siècles d'histoire* (Montreal: Boréal, 2004), 75, 87–88.

17. John Dickinson and Brian Young, *A Short History of Quebec*, 3rd ed. (Montreal: McGill Queen's University Press, 2003), 293. Rural voters were especially valuable given the outdated electoral map, by which they still elected 63 percent of MLAs despite accounting for only 37 percent of the population. Ibid., citing Herbert Quinn, *The Union Nationale*, 69.

18. Lucien Cannon, *Rapport de la Commission royale sur la Sûreté Provinciale et la Police des liqueurs dans le district de Montréal* (Montreal: District judiciaire de Montréal, 1944), 18; J.P. Brodeur, *La délinquance de l'ordre* (Montreal: Hurtubise HMH, 1984), 107; Magaly Brodeur, *Vice et corruption à Montréal, 1892–1970* (Quebec City: Presses de l'Université du Québec, 2011), 43–45.

19. Rouillard, *Le syndicalisme québécois*, 68. The Padlock Act remained on the books for twenty years, until it was ruled unconstitutional by the Supreme Court of Canada in 1957.

20. For reactions from the democratic Left, and particularly from Montreal members of the League for Social Reconstruction, see Mills, "When Democratic Socialists Discovered Democracy."

21. The promise was stated in the House of Commons in March 1939, and reiterated in the September days following Germany's invasion of Poland: "Let me say that as long as this government may be in power, no such measure will be enacted." House of Commons Debates, 30 March 1939, cited in J.L. Granatstein and J.M. Hitsman, *Broken Promises: A History of Conscription in Canada* (Toronto: University of Toronto Press, 1977), 127; see p.133 for the text of King's 8 September statement.

22. Claude Bélanger's brief biography of Adélard Godbout was useful here. See Claude Bélanger, "Adélard Godbout," *Quebec History: Biographies of Prominent Quebec Historical Figures*, retrieved 15 May 2011 from http://faculty.marianopolis.edu/c.belanger/quebechistory/bios/godbout.htm. See also Dominique Marshall, *The Social Origins of the Welfare State: Québec Families, Compulsory Education, and Family Allowances, 1940–1955*, trans. Nicola Doone Danby (Waterloo, ON: Wilfrid Laurier University Press, 2006).

23. Villeneuve's episcopal letter was widely published, including in the Montreal daily *La Patrie*, on Sunday 3 March 1940, 43. See also Laurent Laplante, "Les femmes et le droit de vote: L'épiscopat rend les armes," *Cap-aux-Diamants* 21 (1990): 23–25, and Nive Voisine, ed., *Histoire du catholicisme québécois*, vol. 3, tome 1: *Le XXe siècle, 1898–1940* (Montreal: Boréal Express, 1984).

24. Joseph LaVergne, "Les femmes ont gagné le droit de suffrage," *La Patrie*, 26 April 1940, 6. Women in wartorn France, Belgium, and Italy, by the way, would still have to wait several years for the right to vote: 1944 for France and 1946 for Belgium and Italy. Swiss women could not vote until 1971. Dickinson and Young, *A Short History of Quebec*, 286–87, and The Clio Collective, *Quebec Women: A History*, trans. Roger Gannon and Rosalind Gill (Toronto: Women's Press, 1987), 321.

25. The law was passed on 3 February 1944; see Rouillard, *Le syndicalisme québécois*, 98–100.

26. Marshall, *Social Origins of the Welfare State*, ix.

27. Isabelle Gournay, ed., *Ernest Cormier and the Université de Montréal* (Montreal: Canadian Centre for Architecture, 1990); see also Jean-Claude Marsan, *Montreal in Evolution: Historical*

Analysis of the Development of Montreal's Architecture and Urban Environment (Montreal: McGill-Queen's University Press, 1990).

28. To summarize in terms borrowed from historian Bernard Vigod, Godbout's government "enacted reforms of its own and accepted both a constitutional amendment and precedent-setting federal legislation in the realm of social security." Vigod, *Quebec before Duplessis*, 253.

29. J.L. Granatstein and J.M. Hitsman, *Broken Promises*, chaps. 5 and 6, was especially useful in the preparation of this section.

30. Ibid., 145.

31. Ibid., 159.

32. Ibid., 171; the figure of 85 percent for francophones is from Linteau et al., *Quebec since 1930*, 104; the 64 percent figure is from Desmond Morton, *A Short History of Canada* (Toronto: McClelland and Stewart, 2001), 198.

33. Granatstein and Hitsman, *Broken Promises*, 234.

34. Linteau et al., *Quebec since 1930*, 107.

35. The Clio Collective, *Quebec Women*, chap. 12, 277–300; Ruth Roach Pierson, *Canadian Women and the Second World War* (Ottawa: Canadian Historical Association, Booklet No. 37, 1983).

36. See Lucie Piché, *Femmes et changement social au Québec: L'apport de la Jeunesse ouvrière catholique féminine, 1931–1966* (Quebec City: Presses de l'Université Laval, 2003); Louise Bienvenue, *Quand la jeunesse entre en scène* (Montreal: Boréal, 2003); and Michael Gauvreau, *The Catholic Origins of Quebec's Quiet Revolution, 1931–1970* (Montreal: McGill-Queen's University Press, 2005).

37. Denise Lemieux and Michelle Comeau, *Le mouvement familial au Québec, 1960–1990: Une politique et des services pour les familles* (Sainte-Foy, QC: Presses de l'Université du Québec, 2002).

38. Francophone Quebecers often use the term to refer to any small, suburban, single-family dwelling, independent of architectural style or design.

39. There is a useful article about the adoption of the flag on the *Bilan du siècle* website; see "Adoption par l'Assemblée législative du fleurdelisé comme drapeau officiel du Québec," *Bilan du siècle*, retrieved 26 November 2010 from http://www.bilan.usherb.ca/bilan/pages/evenements/890.html.

40. Linteau et al., *Quebec since 1930*, 282.

41. See Claude Bélanger, "Tremblay Report and Provincial Autonomy in the Duplessis Era (1956)," *Marianopolis College Quebec History*, retrieved 18 May 2011 from http://faculty.marianopolis.edu/c.belanger/quebechistory/readings/tremblay.htm. The discussion also draws on Linteau et al., *Quebec since 1930*, chap. 27, 276–83.

42. The seminal work on Duplessis's "liberalism" is Gilles Bourque, Jules Duchastel, and Jacques Beauchemin, *La société libérale duplessiste* (Montreal: Les Presses de l'Université de Montréal, 1994). There is a succinct and useful summary in Roy, *Histoire des idéologies au Québec*, 95–98.

43. Translated excerpt from the "Refus Global Manifesto," *The Canadian Encyclopedia*, retrieved 5 September 2010 from http://www.thecanadianencyclopedia.com/index.cfm?PgNm=TCE&Params=A1SEC873549.

44. Rouillard, *Le syndicalisme québécois*, 132. The demand for union involvement in personnel decisions reflected the persistence of corporatist ideas within the CTCC and was a particular red flag for the company manager.

45. Fraser Isbester, "Asbestos 1949," in *On Strike: Six Key Labour Struggles in Canada, 1919–1949*, ed. Irving Abella (Toronto: James Lorimer, 1974), 181.

46. Rouillard, *Le syndicalisme québécois*, 133–34.

47. Jessica van Horssen, "Body Politics in Asbestos, Quebec," paper presented at the Annual Meeting of the Canadian Historical Association, Carlton University, Ottawa, 24–27 May 2009.

48. Postwar, Catholic personalism has been defined by historian Michael Gauvreau as not so much a doctrine as "a point of departure which, while insisting upon the spiritual dimensions of human existence, allowed Christians to easily incorporate elements of the post-war fashions in Marxist social analysis and existentialist psychology." Gauvreau, *The Catholic Origins*, 44.

49. Louis Balthazar, *Bilan du nationalisme au Québec* (Saint-Laurent: Éditions de l'Hexagone, 1990), 112; Roy, *Histoire des idéologies au Québec*, 101–102; Linteau et al., *Quebec since 1930*, 254–57.

50. Balthazar, *Bilan du nationalisme au Québec*, 116–20; Roy, *Histoire des idéologies au Québec*, 98–99.

51. The figure is 36 percent; Linteau et al., *Quebec since 1930*, 247.

52. Ibid., 248.

53. The figure is 140 out of 240; reported in ibid., 247.

54. Michèle Lacombe, "Les Insolences du Frère Untel," *The Canadian Encyclopaedia*, retrieved 5 September 2010 from http://www.thecanadianencyclopedia.com/index.cfm?PgNm=TCE&Params=A1ARTA0004015.

55. A thoughtful and rigorous history of the SAPE is Chantale Quesney, "De la charité au Bonheur familial: Une histoire de la Société d'adoption et de la protection de l'enfance à Montréal" (PhD diss., Université du Québec à Montréal, 2010).

56. See Michel Sarra-Bournet, *L'affaire Roncarelli: Duplessis contre les Témoins de Jéhovah* (Quebec: Institut Québécois de Recherche sur le Culture, 1986), esp. 60–62.

57. Suzanne Clavette, "Maurice Duplessis et son époque. Que maintenir, que réévaluer?" in *Duplessis: Son milieu, son époque*, ed. Xavier Gélinas and Lucia Ferretti (Quebec: Septentrion, 2010), 413–14.

58. Ibid., 402.

59. The raw figures are 72,159 for 1931, and 352,023 for 1957. These are estimates published in Gérald Bernier and Robert Boily, with Daniel Salée, *Le Québec en chiffres de 1850 à nos jours* ([Montreal]: ACFAS, 1986), 302–303. Note, however, that union membership in Ontario, where the number of unions throughout the period was about double, grew by a factor of seven in the same interval. See also Dickinson and Young, *A Short History of Quebec*, 287.

60. Linteau et al., *Quebec since 1930*, 287. The exact figures are 9.7 percent and 88.8 percent; the latter figure, for 1960, is well above the overall Canadian ratio of 80.6 percent.

61. A useful and extremely detailed account is provided in David Di Felice, "'The Richard Riot': A Socio-Historical Examination of Sport, Culture, and the Construction of Symbolic Identities" (MA thesis, Queen's University, 1999). For an accessible treatment of Richard's cultural legacy, see Benoit Melançon, *The Rocket: A Cultural History of Maurice Richard*, trans. Fred A. Reed (Vancouver: Greystone Books, 2009).

11 "LE DÉBUT D'UN TEMPS NOUVEAU"

1. Lucia Ferretti, "La Révolution tranquille," *L'Action nationale*, December 1999, retrieved 8 June 2011 from http://www.action-nationale.qc.ca/index.php?option=com_content&task=view&id=315&Itemid=36&searchresult=1. The quoted material is the authors' condensed translation. The original French text is as follows: ". . . le bref moment pendant lequel, fort d'un large consensus social l'État québécois, son personnage principal, a été à la fois intensément réformiste et intensément nationaliste. Entre 1959 et 1968 en effet, c'est-à-dire du gouvernement de Paul Sauvé à celui de Daniel Johnson avec un sommet sous Lesage, l'État québécois a poursuivi en même temps un objectif de modernisation accélérée sur le modèle de l'État-providence et un objectif très net de promotion nationale des Québécois francophones."

2. John Dickinson and Brian J. Young, *A Short History of Quebec*, 3rd ed. (Montreal: McGill-Queen's University Press, 2003), 305.

3. See Jocelyn Létourneau and Sabrina Moisan, "Young People's Assimilation of a Collective Historical Memory: A Case Study of Quebeckers of French-Canadian Heritage," in *Theorizing Historical Consciousness*, ed. Peter Sexias (Toronto: University of Toronto Press, 2004), 109–28.

4. René Durocher, "The Quiet Revolution," *The Canadian Encyclopedia*, retrieved 18 June 2011 from http://www.thecanadianencyclopedia.com/index.cfm?PgNm=TCE&Params=A1ARTA000 6619. Despite the changes to the electoral map, urban voters were still significantly underrepresented. See Alan Siaroff, "Electoral Bias in Quebec Since 1936," *Canadian Political Science Review* 4, no. 1 (2010): 62–75.

5. William J. Smith and Helen M. Donahue, *The Historical Roots of Quebec Education* (Montreal: McGill University Office of Research on Educational Policy, 1999), 27, 39.

6. Liberal manifesto issued during the 1962 election campaign, quoted in Jean-Louis Roy, *Les programmes électoraux du Québec*, tome 2, *1931–1966* (Montreal: Leméac, 1971), 394–95; The quoted material is the authors' translation. The original French text is as follows: "Un peuple comme le nôtre, doit se servir des instruments de libération économique dont il peut disposer. D'abord, nous devons nous affirmer dans des domaines comme ceux des finances, de l'industrie et du commerce . . . Le moment est venu de nous attaquer à fond, sans délai et sans hésitation, à l'oeuvre exaltante de la *libération économique du Québec* . . . Pour la première fois dans son histoire, le peuple du Québec peut devenir maître chez lui! L'époque du colonialisme économique est révolue. Nous marchons vers la libération!"

7. "Vous avez le choix entre la liberté et le retour aux chaînes d'une machine infernale qui est disparue et qu'il ne faut pas faire renaître, et aussi entre la liberté et les matraques de la vieille police provinciale, l'ancienne." Quoted in "Tenue d'un débat télévisé entre Jean Lesage et Daniel Johnson," *Bilan du siècle*, retrieved 2 June 2011 from http://www.bilan.usherb.ca/bilan/pages/ evenements/20825.html; the quoted material is the authors' translation. See also the excerpt from this debate which has been posted to the Radio-Canada website at http://archives.radio-canada.ca/emissions/392/.

8. "Le ministère de l'Éducation sera l'instrument de base de ce que j'appelle la nouvelle vocation de progrès et de création." Quoted in "Entrée en vigueur de la Loi 60 créant un ministère et un Conseil supérieur de l'Education," *Bilan du siècle*, retrieved 3 June 2011 from http://www.bilan. usherb.ca/bilan/pages/evenements/1642.html.

9. Paul-André Linteau, René Durocher, Jean-Claude Robert, and François Ricard, *Quebec since 1930*, trans. Robert Chodos and Ellen Garmaise (Toronto: James Lorimer, 1991), 485–86. The initiative wound up establishing 64 consolidated school boards: 55 Catholic and 9 Protestant. See Smith and Donahue, *The Historical Roots of Quebec Education*, 44; Robert Gagnon, *Histoire de la Commission des écoles catholiques de Montréal* (Montreal: Boréal, 1996), 245–46.

10. Linteau et al., *Quebec since 1930*, 488–90.

11. Quoted in "Création d'un Comité d'étude sur l'assistance publique," *Bilan du siècle*, retrieved on 3 June 2011 from http://www.bilan.usherb.ca/bilan/pages/evenements/1411.html; the quoted material is the authors' translation. The original French text is as follows: "[Que] le gouvernement du Québec devrait, dans les limites de ses attributions, intensifier l'application d'une politique économique et sociale d'ensemble. . . . Le gouvernement du Québec devrait se reconnaître en théorie et en pratique un rôle de plus en plus dynamique et créateur en matière de sécurité sociale et notamment en matière d'assistance à domicile."

12. In fairness, it should also be said that the religious personnel within the Catholic social service sector were increasingly well trained—often at Université de Montréal's School of Social Work—and well aware of modern approaches to social intervention such as casework, groupwork, and the like. For a case study in the child services sector, see Chantale Quesney, "De la charité au Bonheur familial: Une histoire de la Société d'adoption et de la protection de l'enfance à Montréal" (PhD diss., Université du Québec à Montréal, 2010).

13. It also incorporated new definitions of "family head" and "dependant" that were cast in such a way as to ensure that single mothers in particular could get access to relatively generous cash supplements to their household budgets. See Ferdinand Makola, "Les Mères monoparentales et l'aide sociale au Québec de 1960 à 1990. De l'assistance à l'incitation au travail" (MA thesis, Université de Sherbrooke, 2002).

14. Kenneth McRoberts, *Quebec: Social Change and Political Crisis*, 3rd ed. (Toronto: McClelland and Stewart, 1988), 132–34.

15. McRoberts lists "six new ministries, nine consultative councils, three regulatory bodies, eight public enterprises, and one administrative tribunal," all created between 1960 and 1966. Ibid., 136.

16. McRoberts is very precise: the number was 41,847; ibid.

17. See especially François Ricard's important essay on Quebec's baby boomers, published in English translation as *The Lyric Generation: The Life and Times of the Baby Boomers*, trans. Donald Winkler (Toronto: Stoddart, 1994).

18. "It's the beginning of a new era; the earth is at year one; half the population is under thirty; women make love freely; men hardly have to work anymore; happiness is the only virtue." Stéphane Venne, *Le début d'un temps nouveau* (1970). Lyrics retrieved 14 June 2011 from http://www.frmusique.ru/texts/c/claude_renee/debutduntempsnouveau.htm. See this site for the full lyrics.

19. There were 4,285 priests in 1961 for a population of 5.26 million, compared to 8,400 for 6.44 million in 1981. The trend for nuns was almost as dramatic; for religious brothers it was even more so, with membership in these communities declining by a full 75 percent between 1961 and 1978. See McRoberts, *Quebec: Social Change and Political Crisis*, 138–39.

20. Historian Jean Hamelin describes Quebec's Catholics in the 1960s as "Christians without antibodies" who contracted indifference, agnosticism, or atheism the way Aboriginal people in the seventeenth century caught smallpox. Jean Hamelin, *Histoire du catholicisme québécois, Le XXe siècle*, Tome 2, *De 1940 à nos jours* (Saint-Laurent: Boréal Express, 1984), 356.

21. Ibid., 277.

22. Tableau statistique, "Taux de fécondité selon le groupe d'âge de la mère, indice synthétique de fécondité et âge moyen à la maternité, Québec, 1951–2010," *Institut de la statistique du Québec*, retrieved 3 June 2011 from http://www.stat.gouv.qc.ca/donstat/societe/demographie/naisn_deces/naissance/402.htm. See also Danielle Gauvreau, Diane Gervais, and Peter Gossage, *La Fécondité des Québécoises, 1870–1970: D'une exception à l'autre* (Montreal: Boréal, 2007).

23. Note that the generic term "common-law marriages" should not be applied in Quebec, which has its own civil code and civil-law tradition and is emphatically not a common-law jurisdiction. Vocabulary aside, statistics show that the practice has expanded almost exponentially since the 1960s, as Quebecers turned away from formal marriage. The synthetic marriage rate for previously unmarried Quebec *men* was 948 per thousand in 1960, meaning that 19 in 20 eventually married. This rate had declined to 611 per thousand in 1980 and, by 2008, had fallen still more dramatically to 311 per thousand—meaning that only about 6 of 20 eventually married. Equivalent rates for *women* were 900 (1960), 622 (1980), and 310 (2008). Tableaux statistique, "Taux de nuptialité des célibataires selon le groupe d'âge, indice synthétique de nuptialité et âge moyen au premier mariage, par sexe, Québec, 1951–2010," *Institut de la Statistique du Québec*, retrieved 11 June 2010 from http://www.stat.gouv.qc.ca/donstat/societe/demographie/etat_matrm_marg/503.htm.

24. Almost 3,000 divorces were obtained by Quebecers in 1969, the first full year of the new regime, already a vast increase over the levels of the early 1960s, and a figure which would grow steadily through the 1970s. By 1981, the annual figure had reached some 19,000 divorces, or about 43 for every 100 marriages. Tableaux statistique, "Nombre de divorces et indice synthétique de

divortialité, Québec, 1969–2008," *Institut de la Statistique du Québec*, retrieved 11 June 2010 from http://www.stat.gouv.qc.ca/donstat/societe/demographie/etat_matrm_marg/6p4.htm.

25. The Catholic hierarchy appointed a commission headed by the sociologist Fernand Dumont to study the flagging participation of lay Catholics in the Church's mission and the future of the Catholic Action movement. The commission's 1971 report identified a religious crisis in the province, of which the most obvious indices were "the declining practice of worship, the abandonment of the priesthood, the indifference of youth, and the fragmentation of the Christian community." See Hamelin, *Histoire du catholicisme québécois, Le XXe siècle*, Tome 2, 353.

26. And he continues: "Having lost their symbolic place of belonging, French-speaking Quebecers were faced with a collective identity crisis. [. . . After 1965, the] euphoria of the Quiet Revolution gave way to disappointment. The initial reviews all point to failure: failure of the poets to build an imagined country; failure of the intellectuals to sketch a concrete representation of Quebec as a social community." Ibid., 273. The quoted material is the authors' translation.

27. Sean Mills has recently explored these themes in depth for 1960s Montreal; Sean Mills, *The Empire Within: Postcolonial Thought and Political Activism in Sixties Montreal* (Montreal: McGill-Queen's University Press, 2010). See also Bryan D. Palmer, *Canada's 1960s: The Ironies of Identity in a Rebellious Decade* (Toronto: University of Toronto Press, 2009).

28. Jacques Rouillard, *Le syndicalisme québécois: Deux siècles d'histoire* (Montreal: Boréal, 2004), table 5.1, 289.

29. It was long known to anglophones as the Confederation of National Trade Unions (CNTU), but that English name is no longer used.

30. Rouillard, *Le syndicalisme québécois*, 243. The new radicalism was too much for one group of about 30,000 union members, mainly in the manufacturing sector, who opposed the increasingly political character of the CSN's activities and split off to form the Confédération des syndicates démocratiques (CSD) in 1972.

31. Ibid., 302. The CSN's share was 20 percent.

32. Workers, after all, needed "to oppose international capitalism with a trade union movement which, as far as possible, can deal on even terms with these *enterprises tenataculaires*." Quoted in ibid., 306; the quoted material is the authors' translation.

33. Ibid., 292.

34. "Montreal's Night of Terror," *CBC Digital Archives*, retrieved 6 June 2011 from http://archives.cbc.ca/war_conflict/civil_unrest/clips/12238/.

35. See especially Magda Fahrni, *Household Politics: Montreal Families and Postwar Reconstruction* (Toronto: University of Toronto Press, 2005), and Marie-Paule Malouin, *Le Mouvement familial au Québec: Les Débuts, 1937–1965* (Montreal: Boréal, 1998).

36. The Clio Collective, *Quebec Women: A History*, trans. Roger Gannon and Rosalind Gill (Toronto: The Women's Press, 1987), 338–40.

37. Compared to 22 percent in 1961. Collectif Clio, *L'histoire des femmes au Québec depuis quatre siècles*, rev. ed. (Montreal: Le Jour, 1992), 472.

38. Fewer than one in twenty Quebec lawyers in 1961 were women, for example, but that ratio increased sharply, to almost one-fifth by 1981 and to over one-third by 1991. Annmarie Adams and Petra Tancred, *Designing Women: Gender and the Architectural Profession* (Toronto: University of Toronto Press, 2000), 132. These authors document similar trends for dentists, doctors, architects, and, to a lesser extent, engineers.

39. The Clio Collective, *Quebec Women: A History*, 355, 357.

40. See Mills, *The Empire Within*, 119–37. Also very useful is Stéphanie Lanthier, "L'impossible réciprocité des rapports politiques et idéologiques entre le nationalisme radical et le féminisme radical au Québec, 1961–1972" (MA thesis, Université de Sherbrooke), 1998.

41. The Clio Collective, *Quebec Women: A History*, 341–44.
42. For a much different interpretation of the relationship between contemporary gender politics and the PQ's sovereignty project, see Jeffrey Vacante, "Liberal Nationalism and the Challenge of Masculinity Studies in Quebec," *Left History* 11, no. 2 (2006): 96–117.
43. Appointed to study the social, economic, and educational situation of Native people, anthropologist Harry B. Hawthorn reported these figures in 1966. See Olive P. Dickason with David T. McNab, *Canada's First Nations*, 4th ed. (Don Mills: Oxford University Press Canada, 2009), 369–70.
44. "Expodition: Expo 67's Indians of Canada Pavillion," CBC Radio, broadcast 4 August 1967, *CBC Digital Archives*, retrieved 16 June 2010 from http://archives.cbc.ca/society/native_issues/clips/14916/. See also Myra Rutherdale and Jim Miller, "'It's Our Country': First Nations' Participation in the Indian Pavilion at Expo '67," *Journal of the Canadian Historical Association* 17, no. 2 (2006): 148–73.
45. Dickason and McNab, *Canada's First Nations*, 300.
46. See Dickinson and Young, *A Short History of Quebec*, 340.
47. The James Bay Cree and Inuit populations would have control over local government structures, including education, health, and policing services. They would also be able to negotiate significant modifications to the mega-project, including limits on water levels and even relocation of the first of the proposed dams. Dickason and McNab, *Canada's First Nations*, 392. See also John A. Price with Brian Craik, "James Bay and Northern Quebec Agreement," *The Canadian Encyclopaedia*, retrieved 6 June 2011 from http://www.thecanadianencyclopedia.com/index.cfm?PgNm=TCE&Params=A1ARTA0004098.
48. Ricard, *The Lyric Generation*.
49. Jean-Philippe Warren, *Une douce anarchie. Les années 68 au Québec* (Montreal: Boréal, 2008), 27.
50. Robert Chodos, "A Short History of Student Activism at McGill," in *McGill Student Handbook, 1969*, ed. R. Chodos, A. Feingold, and T. Sorell (Montreal: Students' Society of McGill University, 1969), 91–92. Much of this paragraph is from Warren, *Une douce anarchie*, 102–108.
51. See the discussion and photograph in Warren, *Une douce anarchie*, 199.
52. Located in downtown Montreal, Sir George Williams University merged with Loyola College in 1974 to form Concordia University. On the 1969 student action, see Dorothy Eber, *The Computer Centre Party* (Toronto: Tundra Books, 1969), and Mills, *The Empire Within*, 104–108.
53. Marcel Chaput, *Pourquoi je suis séparatiste* (Montreal: Éditions du Jour, 1961).
54. See René Jutras, *Québec libre* (Montreal: Éditions Actualité, 1964).
55. Jean-Paul Couturier, Wendy Johnston, and Réjean Ouellette, *Un passé composé: Le Canada de 1850 à nos jours* (Moncton: Éditions d'Acadie, 1996), table 17.1, 323.
56. See Susan Mann, *The Dream of Nation: A Social and Intellectual History of Quebec* (Montreal: McGill-Queen's University Press, 2002), 282–96. Benedict Anderson's ideas about the role of print media in the development of national consciousness and nationalist movements have a strong resonance here, especially insofar as they can be extrapolated out to encompass the electronic media of the twentieth century. See Anderson, *Imagined Communities: Reflections on the Origins and Spread of Nationalism*, rev. ed. (London: Verso, 1991).
57. Ronald Rudin, *Making History in Twentieth-Century Quebec* (Toronto: University of Toronto Press, 1997), 93–128.
58. See David Meren, "De Versailles à Niamey. Le patrimoine constitutionnel canado-britannique du Québec et sa participation au sein de la Francophonie, 1968–1970," *Globe* 13, no. 1 (2010): 99–124.
59. Daniel Johnson, *Égalité ou independence* (Montreal: Éditions de l'Homme, 1965). The term "soft-nationalist" would emerge later to distinguish moderate nationalists, those still open to

constitutional reform within Canada, from committed proponents of political independence for Quebec.

60. For an engaging development of this thesis, see the iconic, three-part documentary film on Trudeau and Lévesque directed by Donald Brittain for the CBC and the National Film Board of Canada: *The Champions*, Part 1, *Unlikely Warriors* (1978); Part 2, *Trappings of Power* (1978); Part 3, *The Final Battle* (1986). The series can be viewed online at http://www.nfb.ca/explore-by/director/Donald-Brittain/?&dir_range=All&lang=en; site last consulted 7 June 2011.

61. The original French edition was published in 1968 as *Nègres blancs d'Amérique* ([Montreal]: Éditions Parti pris, [1968]). The subtitle *Autobiographie précoce d'un "terroriste" québécois* was added to subsequent editions. In English, see Pierre Vallières, *White Niggers of America: The Precocious Autobiography of a Quebec "Terrorist,"* trans. Joan Pinkham (Toronto: McClelland and Stewart, 1971).

62. There has been a lot of interesting work on the FLQ and the October Crisis recently. For important studies in English, see especially Mills, *The Empire Within*, 163–86; Éric Bédard, "The Intellectual Origins of the October Crisis," in *Creating Postwar Canada: Community, Diversity, and Dissent, 1945–75*, eds. Magda Fahrni and Robert Rutherdale (Vancouver: UBC Press, 2008), 45–60; Michael Gauvreau, "Winning Back the Intellectuals: Inside Canada's 'First War on Terror,' 1968–1970," *Journal of the Canadian Historical Association* 20, no. 1 (2009): 161–90; and Palmer, *Canada's 1960s*, chap. 9, 311–65.

63. William Tetley, *The October Crisis, 1970: An Insider's View* (Montreal: McGill-Queen's University Press, 2007), 97.

64. "Pierre Laporte a été la victime de la haine, d'une haine criminelle que n'avaient pas encore connue les Québécois et les Canadiens. Il a payé de sa vie à défendre ces libertés fondamentales, et cela après avoir attendu durant toute une semaine dans une angoisse cruelle ce dénouement tragique. Je dis à ces individus qui l'ont assassiné qu'ils sont à tout jamais indignes d'être des Québécois et d'être des Canadiens français." Robert Bourassa, "Le dénouement tragique d'une semaine d'angoisse," *Le Devoir*, Monday, 19 October 1970, 1. The quoted material is the authors' translation.

65. See for example John English, *Just Watch Me: The Life of Pierre Elliott Trudeau: 1968–2000* (Toronto: Knopf Canada, 2009), which takes this quote as its title.

66. The Liberals won 47.2 percent of the votes but only 50 seats, compared to 40.9 percent and 56 seats for the Union Nationale.

67. "Novembre 1976: l'indépendance au pouvoir," *Radio-Canada*, retrieved 9 January 2012 from http://archives.radio-canada.ca/c_est_arrive_le/11/15/.

68. From 47 percent in 1930, the proportion rose to 65 percent at the end of the Second World War to 75 percent in 1963. Robert Gagnon, "L'École anglaise: Le choix des immigrants," *Le Devoir*, 3 May 1999, retrieved 9 June 2010 from http://archives.vigile.net/ecole/gagnonmythe2.html.

69. Christope Chikli, "La Crise de Saint-Léonard dans la presse montréalaise entre 1968 et 1969" (MA thesis, Universié de Sherbrooke, 2006).

70. Political philosopher Charles Taylor has a very useful discussion of individual versus collective rights in Canadian and Quebec conceptions of liberalism. See Taylor, "Shared and Divergent Values," in *Reconciling the Solitudes: Essays on Canadian Federalism and Nationalism* (Montreal McGill-Queen's University Press, 1993), 155–86.

71. Claude Bélanger's summaries of the language laws adopted between 1969 and 1977, posted to his Quebec history website at Marianopolis College, have been very useful in preparing this section; retrieved 26 September 2010 from http://faculty.marianopolis.edu/c.belanger/quebechistory/readings/langlaws.htm.

72. Sun Life, Canada's largest insurance company at the time, announced it was moving its head office from Montreal to Toronto on 6 January 1978, citing political instability in the wake of

the PQ election and Bill 101. Finance Minister Jacques Parizeau responded angrily to the news, which directly affected some 800 white-collar employees, calling Sun Life the "worst corporate citizen in the province [and] one of the worst exploiters of the Quebec economy." See "Fighting Words: Bill 101," *CBC Digital Archives*, retrieved 10 June 2010 from http://archives.cbc.ca/politics/provincial_territorial_politics/topics/1297-7466/.

12 SOVEREIGNTY IN QUESTION

1. The subtitle of that policy paper was just as telling: *The Québec Government Proposal for a New Partnership between Equals: Sovereignty-Association.* The wording of the 1980 referendum question was as follows: "The Government of Quebec has made public its proposal to negotiate a new agreement with the rest of Canada, based on the equality of nations; this agreement would enable Quebec to acquire the exclusive power to make its laws, levy its taxes and establish relations abroad—in other words, sovereignty—and at the same time to maintain with Canada an economic association including a common currency; any change in political status resulting from these negotiations will be effected with approval by the people through another referendum; on these terms, do you give the Government of Quebec the mandate to negotiate the proposed agreement between Quebec and Canada?"

2. Our rough translation: "My dear friends, if I've understood you correctly, you're in the midst of telling me: until next time." Turnout for the referendum was high, with 85.6 percent of registered voters casting a ballot. "Référendum 1980: L'avenir du Québec en question," Radio-Canada, retrieved 9 January 2012 from http://archives.radio-canada.ca/politique/provincial_territorial/dossiers/1294/.

3. "I know that I can make a most solemn commitment that following a 'No' vote," he declared, "we will immediately take action to renew the constitution and we will not stop until we have done that." Transcript in translation available online as "Speech at the Paul Sauvé Arena, Montreal, Quebec, May 14, 1980," retrieved 9 June 2011 from http://www.collectionscanada.gc.ca/2/4/h4-4083-e.html.

4. René Lévesque, *Mémoirs* (Toronto: McClelland and Stewart, 1986), 333.

5. "Rejet final de l'accord du lac Meech," *Bilan du siècle*, 22 June 1990, retrieved 9 October 2010 from http://bilan.usherbrooke.ca/bilan/pages/evenements/3504.html. The quoted material is the authors' translation. Original French for the quotation is as follows: "Le Canada anglais doit comprendre de façon très claire que, quoi qu'on dise et quoi qu'on fasse, le Québec est, aujourd'hui et pour toujours, une société distincte, libre et capable d'assurer son destin et son développement."

6. Quebec has had 75 federal seats throughout this period. The BQ won 54 in 1993, 44 in 1997, 38 in 2000, 54 in 2004, 51 in 2006, and 49 in 2008. It was crushed, however, by the NDP in the May 2011 election, winning only 4 seats, compared to 59 for Jack Layton's New Democrats.

7. "Élection de Jean Chrétien au poste de chef du Parti libéral du Canada," *Bilan du siècle*, 23 June 1990, retrieved 9 June 2011 from http://www.bilan.usherb.ca/bilan/pages/evenements/20862.html. The quoted material is the authors' translation. The original French is as follows: "Nous pouvons vivre avec les cinq conditions demandées par Québec . . . mais nous offrirons de nouvelles solutions pour les prochaines élections."

8. See James Bickerton, *Canadian Politics* (Toronto: University of Toronto Press, 2009), 14.

9. These figures are from "October 26, 1992 Referendum," *Directeur general des elections du Québec*, retrieved 9 June 2011 from http://www.dgeq.gouv.qc.ca/english/provincial/media/referendums.php?n=3.

10. "Dépot de l'avant-projet de loi sur la souveraineté du Québec," *Bilan du siècle*, 6 December 1994, retrieved 9 October 2010 from http://bilan.usherbrooke.ca/bilan/pages/evenements/3668.html.

11. "Draft Bill on the Sovereignty of Quebec," retrieved 23 July 2010 from http://www.solon.org/misc/referendum-bill.html.

12. "Publication du rapport de la Commission nationale sur l'avenir du Québec," *Bilan du siècle*, 19 April 1995, retrieved 9 October 2010 from http://bilan.usherbrooke.ca/bilan/pages/evenements/3698.html.

13. Bill 1, An Act Respecting the Future of Quebec (The Sovereignty Bill, Introduced 1995), Preamble, retrieved 23 July 2010 from http://www.sfu.ca aheard/bill1.html.

14. "Manifestation fédéraliste lors d'une cérémonie souverainiste à Québec," *Bilan du siècle*, 6 September 1995, retrieved 9 October 2010 from http://bilan.usherbrooke.ca/bilan/pages/evenements/21153.html.

15. "1995 Quebec Referendum a Period of High Drama," *CTV.ca*, 30 October 2005, retrieved 23 July 2010 from http://www.cp24.com/servlet/an/plocal/CTVNews/20051030/1995_referendum_051030?hub=CalgaryHome.

16. These statements were widely reported at the time. See for example Philippe Authier, "Bloc leader compares Yes vote to 'a wave of a wand,'" *The Gazette*, 16 October 1995, A6; and Elizabeth Thompson, "Bouchard draws fire on birthrate comments," *The Gazette*, 17 October 1995, A1.

17. The CBC Digital Archives has conserved a video recording of the entire speech. See "Separation Anxiety: The 1995 Quebec Referendum," retrieved 9 June 2011 from http://archives.cbc.ca/politics/federal_politics/topics/1891-12470/.

13 CONTEMPORARY QUEBEC

1. The PQ formed the government from 1976 to 1985 and from 1994 to 2003; the Liberals, from 1985 to 1994 and from 2003 until this book went to press in 2012.

2. At this writing, however, the surprising success of the NDP in the 2011 federal election, recent high-profile defections from the PQ caucus, the extreme unpopularity of Jean Charest's Liberal government, and the appearance of another centre-right party—the Coalition pour l'Avenir du Québec, led by former PQ Cabinet minister François Legault—suggest that some kind of re-alignment may be in store in the near future.

3. In 1993, for example, the jobless rate reached 13.2 percent. Institut de la Statistique du Québec, "Principaux Indicateurs Économiques—Québec," retrieved 18 June 2010 from http://www.stat.gouv.qc.ca/princ_indic.

4. Steven High's work on deindustrialization puts these trends into their North American perspective. See Steven High, *Industrial Sunset: The Making of North America's Rust Belt, 1969–1984* (Toronto: University of Toronto Press, 2003); Steven High and David W. Lewis, *Corporate Wasteland: The Landscape and Memory of Deindustrialization* (Toronto: Between the Lines, 2007). For a detailed Quebec study, see Jessica J. Mills, "What's the Point? The Meaning of Place, Memory, and Community in Point Saint Charles, Quebec" (MA thesis, Concordia University, 2011).

5. John Dickinson and Brian Young, *A Short History of Quebec*, 3rd ed. (Montreal: McGill-Queen's University Press, 2002), 373.

6. Bombardier Aerospace specializes in business, commercial, and amphibious airplanes, and employs almost 30,000 people worldwide. "About Us," *Bombardier Inc.*, retrieved 19 June 2010 from http://www.bombardier.com/en/corporate/about-us.

7. Ubisoft's titles are among most popular in the world, including the *Prince of Persia* and *Tom Clancy* series as well as *Assassin's Creed* (2007). As with Bombardier, they benefited from public support in an environment where governments were committed to job creation in high-tech industries. The expansion announced in 2007 was predicated on a new $19 million investment from a Liberal government in Quebec City, which had provided significant funding from the beginning, particularly for games developed locally and released with an immediately

available French version. See Michael French, "Ubisoft Montreal to become World's Biggest Studio," *Develop*, 9 February 2007, retrieved 19 June 2010 from http://www.develop-online.net/news/25657/3839m-to-help-add-1000-jobs-at-Ubisoft-Montreal.

8. CTV News, "Canadian Casualties in Afghanistan," *CTV.ca*, retrieved 22 June 2010 from http://www.ctv.ca/war/.

9. Birth rates hovered around 1.4 births per Québécoise in the mid-1980s before recovering slightly to reach the 1.7 mark in recent years (2007–11).

10. From 14 percent by 1980, the proportion reached 40 percent in 1991, topped 50 percent for the first time in 1995, and stood at 64 percent—almost two-thirds of all children—in 2009. Tableau statistique, "Naissances selon l'état matrimonial des parents, Québec, 1951–2010," *Institut de la statistique du Québec*, retrieved 23 June 2010 from http://www.stat.gouv.qc.ca/donstat/societe/demographie/naisn_deces/naissance/410.htm.

11. In 2001, only about 8 percent of Canadian children aged 0–14 lived in households headed by an unmarried a couple; in Quebec, the ratio was over three times higher at 29 percent. Anne-Marie Ambert, *Cohabitation and Marriage: How Are They Related?* (Ottawa: Vanier Institute of the Family Contemporary Family Trends Series, 2005), retrieved 22 June 2010 from http://www.vifamily.ca/sites/default/files/cohabitation_and_marriage.pdf.

12. See Anne-Marie Ambert, *Divorce: Facts, Causes, and Consequences*, 3rd ed. (Ottawa: Vanier Institute of the Family Contemporary Family Trends Series, 2009), retrieved 23 June 2010 from http://www.vifamily.ca/sites/default/files/divorce_facts_causes_consequences.pdf.

13. In addition to Premier Jean Charest, there were nine women and nine men in the Cabinet named after the 2007 election; and thirteen ministers of each gender after the 2008 election. Figures from the Assemblée nationale du Québec, "Nombre de ministres dans les cabinets et la représentation féminine depuis 1962," retrieved 24 June 2010 from http://www.assnat.qc.ca/fr/patrimoine/ministrescabinets.html.

14. The long-gun registry has been described as "a monument erected to our daughters" by Suzanne Laplante Edward, who became a gun-control activist after her daughter, Anne-Marie Edward, was killed at the École Polytechnique. "Quebec Disappointed with Gun Registry Vote," *CBC News*, 5 November 2009, retrieved 24 June 2010 from http://www.cbc.ca/canada/montreal/story/2009/11/05/qc-gun-registry-vote-reax.html. At this writing, the registry is slated to be destroyed by the Conservative majority government in Ottawa, with the Quebec government demanding that the part of the registry covering its territory be retained and handed over for provincial management.

15. Charles Taylor, "Shared and Divergent Values," in *Reconciling the Solitudes: Essays on Canadian Federalism and Nationalism* (Montreal: McGill-Queen's University Press, 1993), 155–86.

16. Statistics Finland gives a 2009 population of 5,351,427 (retrieved 9 October 2010 from http://www.stat.fi/tup/suoluk/suoluk_vaesto_en.html) and a 2009 GDP of EUR 171 billion ($240 billion CAD) (retrieved 9 October 2010 from http://www.stat.fi/til/vtp/index_en.html). Statistics Canada gives a 2009 figure of 7,782,561 for the population of Quebec (retrieved 9 October 2010 from http://www.statcan.gc.ca/daily-quotidien/090326/t090326a2-eng.htm) and a 2008 GDP figure of $302 billion CAD (retrieved 9 October 2010 from http://www40.statcan.ca/l01/cst01/econ15-eng.htm).

17. In 2007, some 1,091 Quebecers took their own lives, a rate of 14 suicides per 100,000 people, compared to a Canadian rate of about 11 per 100,000 in 2006. Finland's suicide rate was almost 19 deaths per 100,000 in 2007. World Health Organization, "Suicide Prevention and Special Programmes: Country Reports," retrieved 12 July 2010 from http://www.who.int/mental_health/prevention/suicide/country_reports/en/index.html. The rate of suicides in Quebec had reached 22 per 100,000 in 1999 and, like Finland's, declined measurably in first decade of the new century; see reference in note 18.

18. "Quebec Suicide Rate Slides," *CBC News*, 2 February 2009, retrieved 12 July 2010 from http://www.cbc.ca/canada/montreal/story/2009/02/02/mtl-suicide-rates-0202.html.

19. Alain Beaulieu, *Les Autochtones du Québec* (Montreal: Éditions Fides, 1997), 99–100.

20. "La paix des braves est signé," *Radio-Canada Nouvelles*, 8 February 2002, retrieved 13 July 2010 from http://www.radio-canada.ca/nouvelles/Politique/nouvelles/200202/07/003-cris-entente-rb.asp.

21. This may have been an effort to avert the violent internal conflict that had led to pitched battles and two deaths in another Mohawk community, Akwesasne, three months earlier. See Doug George-Kanentiio, "As I Saw It: The Real Oka Story," *The Gazette*, 13 July 2010, A15.

22. The financial cost to the federal and provincial treasuries was also significant: over $200 million, including $83 million to deploy the army, according to one authority. See Olive Dickason and David T. McNab, *Canada's First Nations: A History of Founding Peoples from the Earliest Times*, 4th ed. (Toronto: Oxford University Press, 2008), 322.

23. Ibid.

24. Ibid., 324.

25. Michel Girard, "The Oka Crisis from an Environmental History Perspective, 1870–1990," in *Consuming Canada*, ed. Chad Gaffield and Pam Gaffield (Mississauga: Copp Clark, 1995), 298–315.

26. The full list of BAPE reports is available online from *BAPE*, "Tous les rapports du BAPE," retrieved 13 June 2011 from http://www.bape.gouv.qc.ca/sections/rapports/tous/index.htm. At that time, the number of reports submitted since 1978 was 278.

27. Even Hydro-Québec doesn't claim that hydroelectricity is completely carbon neutral, just that it cuts greenhouse gas emissions significantly. "Greenhouse Gas Emissions and Hydroelectric Reservoirs," *Hydro-Québec*, retrieved 10 June 2011 from http://www.hydroquebec.com/sustainable-development/documentation/ges.html. Decaying trees in the areas flooded by hydroelectric dams release significant amounts of carbon dioxide and are, of course, no longer capable of producing oxygen.

28. "Début de la crise du verglas," *Bilan du siècle*, 5 January 1998, retrieved 10 June 2011 from http://www.bilan.usherb.ca/bilan/pages/evenements/3818.html.

29. Grand Council of the Crees, *Never Without Consent: James Bay Crees' Stand against Forcible Inclusion into an Independent Quebec* (Toronto: ECW Press, 1998), 12.

30. See David C. Young, "The Transition from Denominational to Linguistic School Boards in Quebec" (M.Ed. thesis, University of New Brunswick, 2000).

31. See Daniel Salée, "The Quebec State and the Management of Ethnocultural Diversity: Perspectives on an Ambiguous Record" in *The Art of the State-III: Belonging? Diversity, Recognition and Shared Citizenship in Canada*, ed. Keith Banting, Thomas Courchene, and Leslie Seidle (Montreal: Institute for Research on Public Policy, 2007), 105–42.

32. "Normes de la vie," *Hérouxville*, retrieved 26 July 2010 from http://municipalite.herouxville.qc.ca/normes.pdf. Note that this version of the document has been amended so as to remove the references to stoning.

33. The sensationalized events they cited included a sugaring-off party for Muslims that had served no pork products and featured a time-out for prayers (some girls who had been dancing in the space were mildly inconvenienced) and a Montreal fitness centre that had been pressured to install frosted windows in order to shield Chasidic boys in the area from the sight of women exercising in their gym clothes. Gérard Bouchard and Charles Taylor, *Building the Future: A Time for Reconciliation* (Quebec City: Commission de Consultation sur les pratiques d'accommodement reliées aux différences culturelles, 2008), 94–95.

INDEX

Page numbers in italics indicate illustrations and captions; ins. refers to illustrations and captions in the colour insert between pages 168–69.